EASTERN QUESTIONS IN THE
NINETEENTH CENTURY

By the same author:

*The Early Correspondence of Richard Wood, 1831–1841
Anglo-Ottoman Encounters in the Age of Revolution*

Eastern Questions in the Nineteenth Century

COLLECTED ESSAYS

VOLUME TWO

by

ALLAN CUNNINGHAM

Late Professor of History at Simon Fraser University

edited by

EDWARD INGRAM

FRANK CASS

First published 1993 in Great Britain by
FRANK CASS & CO. LTD.
Gainsborough House, Gainsborough Road,
London E11 1RS, England

and in the United States of America by
FRANK CASS
c/o International Specialized Book Services, Inc.,
5804 N.E. Hassalo Street,
Portland, Oregon 97213-3644

Copyright © 1993 Edward Ingram

British Library Cataloguing in Publication Data

Cunningham, Allan
Eastern Questions in the Nineteenth
Century: Collected Essays
I. Title   II. Ingram, Edward
956
ISBN 0-7146-3453-0

Library of Congress Cataloging-in-Publication Data

Cunningham, Allan, 1924–1988.
 Eastern questions in the nineteenth century: collected essays /
by Allan Cunningham; edited by Edward Ingram.
    p.   cm.
 Includes bibliographical references and index.
 ISBN 0-7146-3453-0
 1. Stratford de Redcliffe, Stratford Canning, Viscount,
1786–1880. 2. Great Britain—Foreign relations—19th century.
3. Turkey—History—Ottoman Empire, 1288–1918. 4. Great Britain—
Foreign relations—Turkey. 5. Eastern question. I. Ingram,
Edward.
DA536.S89C87   1993
949.61'015—dc20   92–17166
                                                              CIP

*All rights reserved. No part of this publication may be
reproduced in any form or by any means, electronic, mechanical,
photocopying, recording or otherwise, without the prior
permission of Frank Cass and Company Limited.*

Typeset by Vitaset, Paddock Wood, Kent
Printed in Great Britain by
Bookcraft (Bath) Ltd

To
*Christine
Clare
Peter
and
Alastair*

CONTENTS

Abbreviations		viii
Editor's Preface		xi
I	The Dragomans of the British Embassy at Constantinople	1
II	Stratford Canning, Mahmud II, and Muhammad Ali	23
III	The Sick Man and the British Physician	72
IV	Stratford Canning and the *Tanzimat*	108
V	The Preliminaries of the Crimean War	130
VI	The Wrong Horse? Anglo-Ottoman Relations before the First World War	226
Bibliography		249
Index		264

ABBREVIATIONS

Add. MSS	British Library, Additional Manuscripts
Adm.	Public Record Office, Admiralty Records
BD	*British Documents on the Origins of the War*
BSP	*British Sessional Papers*
CHBFP	*Cambridge History of British Foreign Policy*
FO	Public Record Office, Foreign Office Records

Sir Howard: What are those hills over there to the southeast?
Rankin: They are the outposts, so to speak, of the Atlas Mountains.
Lady Cicely: The Atlas Mountains! Where Shelley's witch lived! We'll make an excursion to them tomorrow, Howard.
Rankin: That's impossible, my leddy. The natives are verra dangerous.
Lady Cicely: Why? Has any explorer been shooting them?
Rankin: No. But every man of them believes he will go to Heaven if he kills an unbeliever.
Lady Cicely: Bless you, dear Mr Rankin, the people of England believe that they will go to heaven if they give all their property to the poor. But they don't do it. I'm not a bit afraid of that.

George Bernard Shaw,
Captain Brassbound's Conversion,
Act I

Preface

Allan Black Cunningham, who died suddenly and unexpectedly in the New Year of 1988 at the age of 63, was the first dean of arts and founding head of the department of history at Simon Fraser University. Educated at Durham University and Bedford College, London, where he was supervised by the redoubtable Dame Lillian Penson, in 1950 he joined the department of history in the University of the West Indies. He returned to England in 1955, to Royal Holloway College, London, moving in 1961 to St Antony's College, Oxford, as a senior research fellow. While there he edited the early correspondence of Richard Wood, in later life British consul-general at Damascus, for the Royal Historical Society. From Oxford he came to Canada. He belonged to the Royal Geographical Society as well as the Royal Historical Society and, during his twenties, led two expeditions to the Andes.

Professor Cunningham became better known in the United States than in Canada and was highly respected there. He spent 1971 at the Adlai Stevenson Institute at the University of Chicago, writing a book on higher education in North America and, in 1979, was awarded a Guggenheim Fellowship. His work was interrupted by sickness, partly the result of the tuberculosis he caught four years after moving to Canada. His enthusiasm for history never flagged, however. He was a magnificent lecturer to first-year classes, with an uncanny ability to arouse interest among his students. He is greatly missed.

Having had a lifelong interest in the Middle East, Cunningham, when he died, had been working for 25 years on a biography of Stratford Canning, surely one of the most famous diplomats of the nineteenth century – he has been accused of provoking the Crimean War – and on studies of the other British ambassadors at

Constantinople between the French Revolution and the First World War. His colleagues in the department, many of them hired by him in the university's early years, therefore decided that the most suitable memorial would be the publication of as much of this unfinished work as possible. I undertook to see what could be done and the president of the university, William Saywell, and the dean of arts, Robert C. Brown, generously offered to underwrite the cost.

Professor Cunningham's voluminous notes, written in ever tinier handwriting in ever tinier notebooks, include hundreds of unfinished drafts of chapters of books not written. These studies attest to Cunningham's frustration and disappointment. Biographers should admire or hate their subjects, but should beware of irritation and boredom. Cunningham clearly lost interest in Stratford Canning. He worked on him too long and found him wilting under the prolonged scrutiny. Nor could Cunningham finally decide how to handle him. He turned out not to be interesting enough for a biography; or not the sort of biography Cunningham had in mind. A psycho-historian might have done more with him. And his career, as a career, was not important enough. Cunningham was not interested in the United States and Switzerland, to which Stratford was posted in the years after the end of the Napoleonic Wars. The affairs of the Ottoman Empire, on the other hand, which did interest Cunningham passionately, could not be refracted through the prism of Stratford's five terms as British ambassador at Constantinople because, during many crucial developments, he was not there. Robert Adair negotiated the treaty of the Dardanelles in 1809; Viscount Strangford helped to prevent the Greek revolt from causing a Russo-Ottoman war; and Viscount Ponsonby handled the Muhammad Ali crises.

Stratford's moment came in the 1840s and early 1850s, the years of the *Tanzimat*, which he saw as a movement to reform the Ottoman Empire on European lines, and of the events leading to the outbreak of the Crimean War. But even here Cunningham was disappointed by Stratford. Cunningham instinctively, and correctly, played down the role of European diplomatists in the Ottoman Empire and played up the role of the Ottomans, giving them the responsibility for their own triumphs and disasters. He attributed neither the treaty of Bucharest, nor defeat at the hands of

Preface

Muhammad Ali, nor the outbreak of the Crimean War exclusively to European influence, whether beneficent or malign, and certainly not to British influence. Accordingly much of Cunningham's work was an attempt to pull Stratford off his pedestal as hero or ogre.

Cunningham's work on Stratford was incomplete (the chapter describing Stratford's activities during the Crimean War could not be found) and unresolved. The planned book was neither a biography nor the study of Stratford's career as British ambassador at Constantinople. Nor did it seem feasible to publish extracts of the work as a group of separate studies. Two books did appear feasible, however. This is the second, a collection of essays on the Ottoman Empire from the first Muhammad Ali Crisis of 1832–33 to the outbreak of the First World War. The first book collects Cunningham's work on the British discovery of the Eastern Question and series of encounters with the Ottomans from the Ochakov crisis of 1791 to the battle of Navarino in 1827.

Parts of Cunningham's work on Stratford Canning appear in both books. The first contains studies of Stratford's first mission to Constantinople, when he acted as a conduit for information between the Ottomans and the Russians during the negotiations leading to the treaty of Bucharest in 1812, and of his second, when he failed in 1826 to head off the need for the European intervention in the Greek war for independence that led to the destruction of the Turco-Egyptian fleet at the battle of Navarino. This book contains a similar study of Stratford's third mission to Constantinople in 1831 and publishes the famous memorandum in which he tried to persuade the foreign secretary, Viscount Palmerston, to intervene in Ottoman affairs in support of Sultan Mahmud II against the viceroy of Egypt, Muhammad Ali. This is followed by a short study of Stratford's conception of the Ottoman programme of reform known as the *Tanzimat*, and a long study of his role in the preliminaries of the Crimean War, in particular his responsibility for persuading the Ottomans in 1853 to reject the Vienna Note.

In addition to three studies of Stratford, the book contains studies of the British dragomans at Constantinople, on whom the British, who usually did not speak Turkish and rarely met Ottomans socially, relied for information and the conduct of their affairs; of the change in the British attitude to the Ottomans at the end of the nineteenth century; and of social and economic problems in the

Ottoman Empire in the decades leading up to the Crimean War. All of Cunningham's work casts interesting light on the aims and style of both British and Ottoman diplomacy in the Middle East from the late eighteenth to the early twentieth centuries and on social and economic conditions in the region. Often when he seems to be writing about the British, his attention is focused on the Ottomans.

Although I have made as few changes as possible to Cunningham's text, I have cut out chunks of the colourful detail he found irresistible. Travel books were his favourite reading. I have also brushed up his notes, for he was careless of technical details, and have supplied citations where necessary. Otherwise, the text is as Cunningham wrote it. I have not brought it up to date. The bibliography lists the works he evidently had read.

Acknowledgements are due to the Controller of Her Majesty's Stationery Office for the use of Crown-copyright material in the Public Record Office; to the Right Honourable the Earl of Elgin and Kincardine and the Right Honourable the Earl of Harewood for the use of family papers; and to the Trustees of the British Library and the Bodleian Library, and to St Anthony's College, Oxford, for the use of material from their collections. Earlier versions of Chapters I, and VI appeared in *St Antony's Papers*; of Chapter II in *Middle Eastern Studies*; and of Chapter IV in W.R. Polk and R.L. Chambers, eds., *Modernization in the Middle East*. I am grateful to the editors and publishers for permission to publish a revised version.

I am also grateful to Dr T. R. Ravindranathan of Pittsburg State University for help with sorting Professor Cunningham's papers, to Kevin McQuinn, and to Jodi D. Shupe and Terence J. Ollerhead of *The International History Review*, for help with research and editing and for preparing an immaculate typescript. They are the most pleasant associates imaginable.

Edward Ingram
Simon Fraser University
All Saints' Day 1991

CHAPTER I

The Dragomans of the British Embassy at Constantinople

The Levantine dragomans, or interpreters, who served the British embassy at Constantinople during the major part of the nineteenth century, were discussed and described in terms of opprobrium by so many people – travellers, ambassadors, Foreign Office clerks, historians – that their name became synonymous with unreliability, inefficiency, and disloyalty. David Urquhart called this sentiment of hostility 'dragomania' and we can put it in one kind of perspective by assigning it tentative dates. It may have received its original stimulus from the young and hypercritical Stratford Canning during his first (1810–12) mission to the Porte; it certainly gathered force with his second and third missions. A further impulse came with the advent of Viscount Palmerston as foreign secretary in 1830. Plans for reform were discussed, rather perfunctorily considering the outcry against the dragomans, from then until 1840, and a project for the introduction of Englishmen into the interpreter service was actually put in hand in 1841. One might well enquire why a function as indispensable to the tasks of the embassy at Constantinople as that of interpreter was left for so long in such supposedly unsatisfactory hands.

The word dragoman, from the Ottoman *tercüman*, is normally translated interpreter, but if the functions of the dragomans employed by the European embassies had not traditionally involved much more than attendance at interviews and the translation of diplomatic and commercial documents, they would not have become the controversial figures they were. In the great majority of cases, eighteenth- and nineteenth-century dragomans were Levantines, that is, the children of European but not necessarily purely European families long resident in the East. Whether Italian, Greek, Austrian, Russian, Vlach, or British, such men ordinarily lived in the same district of Constantinople, usually in the 'Frank quarter' of Pera or, more rarely, the Greek *Fener*. Only in the nineteenth century did a sharpening appreciation of the importance of embassy security lead the Foreign Office to examine these domestic arrangements.

From the beginnings of the British embassy in the days of Elizabeth I, families of Italian extraction predominated in its interpreter service, and the name of Pisani runs like a thread through more than two centuries of Levant Company and Foreign Office archives. The prominence of such families explains the percolation of words like *bagnio* and *seraglio* into common use among embassy officials and in the pages of the correspondence. These families, strange and rather tragic wanderers between two worlds, the one in which they lived and the other they served, knew the tongues of both. Probably any Pisani, generation after generation, could think in Greek, Turkish, and Italian, the languages most heard in the streets and on the wharves of the Golden Horn. Italian and Greek were common in the world of trade and commerce. Turkish itself and, of the European tongues, French were the means of diplomatic exchange. As to intercourse between ambassadors and dragomans, the British ministers were insisting on a competence in English, while still accepting men with a greater skill in French, by the third quarter of the eighteenth century.

Besides acting as intermediaries at interviews and translating the correspondence exchanged between the embassies and the Ottoman government, dragomans were negotiators in their own right, and frequently very skilled ones too. Marriages between Levantine and Ottoman families were rare, even perilous, but close friendships were common enough and in this way dragomans often came to be on amicable terms with high officials or ministers in the Ottoman bureaucracy. They could be expected to know a good deal about Ottoman institutions, politics, and diplomatic etiquette; what was of more obvious and immediate usefulness, they generally had means of knowing the balance of power in the divan at any given moment, the policies and opinions currently predominant there, and the men who stood highest in the Sultan's favour. In general terms, it might be said that the poorer type of dragoman in any embassy was a mere scavenger of gossip, whereas the best of them were valued and trusted servants. There is no shortage of tributes paid by British ministers to these versatile and nimble-witted men, in either the eighteenth or nineteenth centuries. Sir Robert Sutton, who stands at the threshold of the eighteenth, treated his 'Druggerman' as friend as well as agent, and this was the usual relationship. This particular dragoman enjoyed confidential communication with the office of the *reis effendi* and the grand vizier's deputy, and obtained military intelligence regarding the campaign on the Pruth against the Russians in 1711 from the Sultan's head chamberlain and other 'persons who certainly enter very far into the secrets of this government'.[1] In 1749 the services of the Pisani who was then dragoman to Sir James Porter were thought sufficiently meritorious for George II to confer on him the rather grand title of 'His Majesty's Translator of the Oriental Languages'.[2] This Pisani's son, Bartholomew, was the friend and confidant of a series of ambassadors including Sir Robert Ainslie (1780–94), the earl of Elgin (1799–1802), and Sir Robert Liston (1812–20).

Until the late eighteenth century, the incumbent of the British embassy at Constantinople was regarded by the Ottomans, quite reasonably, as the representative of his king before all else, but in reality the ambassador was the salaried servant of the Levant Company, which entrusted him with the supervision of British mercantile interests in the Ottoman Empire. In the course of time, British governments had come to show growing interest in the appointment until, by the eighteenth century, the company was simply ratifying the government's choice of candidate, while still paying his salary. Successive governments made contributions in various forms to the upkeep of the embassy, but it was not until 1804 that the ambassador severed most of his connections with the Levant Company. Up to 1804 he remained at the mercy of two sets of instructions, a position which became increasingly intolerable once the Foreign Office, itself newly established in 1782, found it necessary to watch the encroachment of Russia on the Ottoman Empire with greater concern than heretofore. The dramatic lessons in Near Eastern strategy and diplomacy administered by Napoleon finally made it imperative for the government to assume complete control of the embassy. Charles Arbuthnot, appointed British minister in 1804, was told to give his whole attention to political matters, and the Levant Company was advised to find itself a consul-general to supervise its commercial interests.[3]

As the position of ambassador had been anomalous for over a century, it is not surprising that the status and loyalties of the dragomans remained unresolved for some years more. Even after 1804, they were still appointed and paid by the Levant Company, although ambassadors were making growing demands upon the services of at least one of them, and at times of political stress sometimes employing two out of the four available. The pressure of diplomatic business on the embassy went on increasing as the official correspondence reveals; Ainslie's mainly commercial correspondence for a dozen pre-revolutionary years was smaller in amount than Elgin's political dispatches for the urgent years of 1800–2. Simultaneously, the dragomans found their work altering in character as well as amount, and the ambassadors could spare the dragomans correspondingly less for the work of the company. This produced friction between the embassy and the British merchants in Pera, who saw the embassy staff from the minister downwards as their paid servants. The dispute reached an acute stage as early as Elgin's embassy.

Lord Elgin, who went out to Constantinople as ambassador in 1799, found four dragomans and four *giovani di lingua*, or student interpreters, in the service of the Levant Company.[4] Anthony Dané, the first dragoman, was very old and soon retired, the first *giovane*, George Calavro, moving up to fourth dragoman. The man Elgin took as his political dragoman was almost inevitably Bartholomew Pisani, second dragoman before Dané retired, and a person of unequalled political experience and linguistic talent. Pisani had 30 years' company service behind him, had acted as embassy treasurer, embassy secretary, even chargé d'affaires and was also permanent *cancellier*, or archivist, to the company. Elgin's wish to make the most of Pisani's diplomatic experience in his dealings with senior Ottomans precipitated a long and acrimonious quarrel with Spencer Smith, the company's local agent. Smith had been appointed locum tenens by the Foreign Office until Elgin should arrive from England, and was piqued when it became necessary to surrender the ministerial title. Rediscovering an intense loyalty to the company, he organized the British merchants to protest to the Foreign Office against Elgin's annexation of Pisani although, in the first instance, Smith himself had suggested it.

Elgin, on his side, repeatedly told the foreign secretary that diplomatic work must have precedence over company interests, for a dragoman as for the ambassador. The casual, trading days were gone; the contest with the French Directory had now spread to the Near East, and the challenge needed to be met with every possible resource. Lord Grenville, president of the Levant Company as well as foreign secretary, was ideally placed to solve the issue and did so by recalling Smith, leaving the disposal of the dragomans, and the supervision of the company's interests, solely in the hands of Elgin.

Elgin was a kindly and considerate man, and with his accession to uncontested power he undertook the task, long overdue, of making more sensible arrangements for the dragomans' salaries. In recent years, inflationary tendencies had depressed the value of the Ottoman piastre. This created financial difficulties for recipients of fixed salaries in piastres, such as the ambassador himself and the consuls in the Levant, but the dragomans were the worst off because their income had been dwindling with the diminishing sale of embassy protections. These protections secured for a purchaser immunity from the Ottoman legal process and the enjoyment of British extraterritorial rights under the Capitulations, and were thus very attractive to Christian and Jewish merchants, refugees from Ottoman justice, and the like. Dragomans traditionally drew a commission from petitioners whose claims for protection were successfully introduced to the ambassador, and large sums were made in this way until Selim III's ministers felt constrained to protest against the excessive number of Ottoman subjects sheltering under the Capitulations. The European embassies were in no position to resist the pressure the Ottomans put upon them to curtail the practice, and the British dragomans' interest in a fixed salary seems to date from the early 1790s, when their commission from the sale of protections was shrinking from year to year. Elgin succeeded in introducing fixed and graded salaries, with no fees attaching to them, but they were far from generous and made no allowance for the upward spiral of commodity prices in Constantinople after 1794. To the end of his embassy, Elgin kept the financial predicament of his dragomans before Grenville's attention, though without further tangible result.[5]

In January 1807, the Russian and British ministers severed relations with the Ottoman government in protest against the ascendancy of the French minister, General Sébastiani, in the councils of the Porte. They both withdrew on British warships. The dragomans, as local residents and British-protected persons rather than British subjects, naturally stayed behind, and were in real danger when Admiral Duckworth appeared soon afterwards with warships and hostile intentions. They kept indoors while the Ottoman capital feverishly organized its defences, but Bartholomew Pisani was seized and imprisoned for two years, to be liberated in 1808 when Robert Adair came to repair relations. Pisani was sent down to the Dardanelles, where the treaty of 5 January 1809 was ultimately signed, and it was his command of languages and insight into the Ottoman mind, as revealed on this occasion, which gave Adair the high regard for the dragomans which he never lost. On reaching the Porte, Adair paid out 11,000 piastres to save the dragomans from 'immediate indigence', and asked the Foreign Office to treat the sum as a gift rather than as arrears of salary. He also forwarded a petition from all his 'Drogmans and Jeunes de langues' urgently requesting an adjustment of their salaries.[6]

Lacking an official residence, Adair passed his Eastern sojourn in a house rented from his political dragoman, Bartholomew Pisani, who was his most-used intermediary with the Ottomans during 1809.[7] By 1810 Pisani was ailing and it was necessary to bring Francis Chabert, nominally the third dragoman, into the diplomatic work. Chabert was a brilliant linguist, with the additional distinction that, during the fire which swept Pera in 1810, he attended at the endangered embassy while his own house burned to the ground.[8] Thus Adair began the habit, followed by all his successors, of choosing his political dragoman without regard for the Levant Company's order of seniority. There was no interference with the company's salary gradation, the 'political' interpreter simply receiving an extra £400 responsibility pay. Adair's confidant was the third dragoman; Viscount Ponsonby in the 1830s employed both the third and fourth as his. Generally speaking, Adair treated all his staff with consideration, supported their petitions to the Foreign Office zealously, and entertained them under his rented roof in the traditional eighteenth-century way. All his dragomans had access to the archives, and Chabert was taken completely into his confidence. Yet ironically, Adair had as his secretary a young man who was to change all this by keeping the staff at arm's length, distrusting dragomans as a point of principle, and seeking neither their friendship nor trust. This was Stratford Canning, who was only 23 when he succeeded Adair as head of the mission in 1810.

Stratford Canning's dislikes were comprehensive, and included the East ('a few months have passed away – my curiosity is satisfied – the novelty is gone'), the diplomatic career, the Ottomans, the salary, the European community, and the dragomans.[9] Stanley Lane-Poole says it was Canning who first envisaged the possibility of a 'regular school of student-interpreters composed of English gentlemen' and that 'he used every effort to improve the tone of the dragomans and raise them above suspicion'. But in a dispatch which Viscount Castlereagh sent to Canning's successor, Robert Liston, the foreign secretary explains that one Terrick Hamilton will be coming out from England as 'chief interpreter' when 'duly qualified', and this 'new institution', Castlereagh adds, was the arrangement of his predecessor, Marquis Wellesley.[10] Since Adair came home while Wellesley was still at the Foreign Office and Canning did not, and as Canning had no private correspondence with Wellesley, it seems likely that the 'new Institution' was inspired by Adair. Adair was irritated, as Elgin had been, by the demands made upon his time by the British merchants in Pera, and disliked the divided loyalties the dragomans necessarily felt. His allocation of the purely Levant Company work to Antonio Pisani and Calavro, and the employment of Bartholomew Pisani and Chabert for all political negotiations, was his own attempt to resolve the problem. Wellesley's intention to supply the ambassador with a Turkish-speaking lieutenant without disturbing the existing hierarchy of local dragomans, fits in with Adair's probable recommendations rather than with the known sentiments of Canning.[11] However, the latter's dislike of the dragomans from the start of his Eastern career, is insisted upon by his biographer, and was more than likely from what is known of his mistrustful, misanthropic character.[12] Where Adair spoke of 'the ancient and honourable' family of Pisani, Canning called the interpreters 'mongrels'. When he came home in 1812, there was not much regret at Pera. He had not, however, gone permanently. Seeing the Golden Horn first at the age of 21, he did not finally turn his back on it until he was 73.

Canning's successor in 1812 was Liston, under whom the dragomans were finally transferred to the complete jurisdiction of the ambassador. The Treasury was persuaded to introduce an improved salary scale and Liston was glad to be entrusted with its introduction, as he regarded himself as the originator, as far back as 1795 when he was a Levant Company servant, of the plan to abolish fees in favour of consolidated salaries. He blamed himself for the hardship the dragomans had experienced and discussed the problems of recruitment and remuneration with Castlereagh before leaving London. He had known Bartholomew Pisani for many years, and the others since they were *giovani*, and thought them 'men of ability who have served well, who have sometimes been entrusted with the management of delicate and difficult business, and who upon the whole have constant and full employment'. On reaching Constantinople, Liston found Bartholomew Pisani still drawing his former salary, although he had been first interpreter since 1800. Recent, inflationary years had led him into debt, and he was proposing to retire on a two-thirds pension and find more lucrative employment in the world of trade for his last working years. Liston was in consternation, telling Castlereagh that 'we cannot do without him'. Castlereagh eased these apprehensions by paying much, though not all, of the arrears Pisani claimed, and he also sent Chabert compensation for his losses in the 1810 fire. In ordering Liston to take over the dragomans, he told him to allocate one or more to look after commercial business, so it was now the Levant Company which was borrowing from the embassy. The company continued to pay the salaries, but according to the new scale laid down by the Foreign Office. The first dragoman's salary was quintupled (3,000 piastres to 15,000), others' salaries doubled, and the pittance of the *giovani* quadrupled. When the £400 for the confidential work of the 'political' dragoman is added, the interpreter service cost £3,000 a year.[13]

Between Stratford Canning's departure and the arrival of Viscount Strangford in 1821, Liston's somnolent interregnum and the quiescence of Eastern affairs stayed the growth of 'dragomania' at the Foreign Office; Terrick Hamilton went out but did not supplant Bartholomew Pisani, nor would Strangford take Hamilton into his confidence in the early stages of the Greek crisis.[14] Hamilton was not often used in the capacity of an interpreter either, and

Strangford preferred to evolve his opinions and and negotiate at the Porte with the assistance of his fifth dragoman, George Wood, regarding whom something must be said at this point.

Wood was that rare thing, a British-born dragoman. He does not appear in Elgin's list of dragomans for 1799, and seems to have been first employed when Elgin was in urgent need of interpreters to serve in Egypt. As British dragoman to the grand vizier, and then in the same capacity to the 'English in Egypt', Wood sufficiently impressed Elgin with the testimonials he brought back to be sent with an Ottoman mission to London shortly afterwards. He fell ill in England, missed the 'preferment' Lord Hawkesbury promised him, and returned to Constantinople, where he was relegated for a few years to purely commercial work and the litigation arising from the protection of British mercantile interests in the Ottoman courts. He re-entered the political sphere in 1821, rising suddenly at the expense of all his fellows. He is found conducting an intimate private correspondence with Strangford at the very time Hamilton was complaining to his friend, Robert Gordon, that the ambassador did not show him six dispatches a year.[15] Unlike Adair, Strangford evidently kept the key to *his* archives! When Strangford went to the congress of Verona, as second delegate to the duke of Wellington, he kept in touch with his Austrian colleague at Constantinople, Count Lutzov, and sent the *reis effendi* admonitions, through Wood, pleading for the Ottoman Empire to assist his advocacy of her cause by showing moderation in the suppression of the Greeks. Only Strangford's transfer to St Petersburg denied Wood a more lasting enjoyment of the position of 'political' dragoman.

Chabert became first dragoman on the retirement of Bartholomew Pisani in 1824, just a year before the winding-up of the Levant Company. About the same time, four new student-interpreters were sworn in. There was no premonition of the demise of the company until the very last months of its life and even then the earliest speculations regarding service under the Crown were characterized by curiosity rather than apprehension. The dragomans knew they were unpopular at home, and blamed Stratford Canning for it, but they were still confident of their indispensability.[16]

Stratford Canning returned to Constantinople in February 1826, and until the signing of the protocol of St Petersburg in May, tried very hard to bring the Ottomans to a realization of their danger, and to effect what, had it succeeded, would have amounted to an eleventh-hour accommodation between them and the Greeks. The Ottomans did not respond to Canning; they did react to the Russian ultimatum. Canning's chances of success were really infinitesimal, but he attributed his failure to the fact that his Austrian and Prussian colleagues, Baron Ottenfels and Count Miltitz, counterworked him at the Porte with the active help of his own chief interpreter, Chabert. A letter Canning received in later years said, 'You were uniformly betrayed. All your words were taken down by the Baron at C[habert]'s dictation. Your interviews with the R[eis] E[ffendi], in fact all the secrets confided by you, your opinion and views, were every evening registered, and the two villains saw each other and remained till late together.' The same letter asserted that Strangford, after his transfer to St Petersburg in 1824, kept up a correspondence with Miltitz which must have increased Canning's difficulties, and that it was from a copy of Crabbe's *Synonyms*, presented to him by Strangford, that Chabert devised the cypher for his shameful transactions with the Prussian minister. Canning 'decided rightly or wrongly that more injury would be done by disgracing the dragoman than by retaining and watching him', but he never trusted him again in diplomatic matters.[17]

Canning was replaced in 1829, only to return to the Ottoman Empire again in 1831 when, in order to negotiate with the Ottomans most advantageously on the question of the frontiers of the Greek state, he made a special arrangement for the conduct of confidential work. He selected three agents for his purposes, Dr MacGuffog, Stefanaki Vogorides, and David Urquhart. Each of this trio had important contacts; MacGuffog, the embassy physician, was also medical adviser to the Sultan; Vogorides, the mysterious, anglophile prince of Samos, had access to the Sultan and the favourites of the divan;[18] Urquhart, a frantic Russophobe whose views and publications did so much to advance the Ottoman cause in Great Britain, was on good terms with the grand vizier. Without being so good a Turkish speaker as he liked to give out, Urquhart hoped a career of dark intrigue, suited to his melodramatic temperament, was unfolding before him.[19] As for Chabert, Canning

> thought it best to have a frank explanation with him at once.

The Dragomans of the British Embassy 11

Delicacy was out of the question; my opinion of his character was no secret. I told him at our first meeting that it was unchanged . . . the sole test of his conduct, in my judgement, would be a success [in the frontier negotiations]; if my ship went down, his boat would infallibly share its fate. He bowed, and silently accepted the terms.[20]

Canning's ship did not founder; nor, as a result, did Chabert's boat. Nevertheless, Frederick Pisani, the third dragoman, replaced Chabert in the conduct of the embassy's public relations with the Ottoman ministers.

Viscount Ponsonby became ambassador to the Ottoman Empire in place of Canning in 1833, a year in which Russian supremacy in the councils of the Sultan seemed to have been secured by the sensational treaty of Unkiar Skelessi.[21] Ponsonby was less austere than Canning, and positively lax in matters of embassy routine and administration, but his amiable exterior concealed a strong will and great diplomatic resource. Chabert was given no opportunity to restore himself to favour, and the £400 he formerly enjoyed for the performance of the political work now went entirely to Frederick Pisani. The other dragomans were taken back into confidence and political employment by 1836, for Ponsonby used every means he could find to combat Russian influence, and expected all his staff, *giovani* included, to contribute to the struggle. When Urquhart came home at the end of 1834 to develop the anti-Russian thesis which obsessed him, his place among Ponsonby's closest confidants was filled by Richard Wood, who had just succeeded his late father as fifth dragoman. Wood soon attained a degree of intimacy with the ambassador unequalled in this period. He dined regularly with the Ponsonbys, who detested Pera and lived out at Tarabya on the Bosporus, shared the ambassador's stratagems and fears, and performed vital missions for him to Syria and Kurdistan.[22] In fact, Wood and his close friend, Etienne Pisani, helped Frederick Pisani to restore to the office of dragoman much of its former stature and importance. It was just about this time, however, when the Levantines were emerging from a period of disrepute, that the plan to Anglicize the interpreter service began to take shape at the Foreign Office.

The foreign secretary, Viscount Palmerston, discussed the question of reform with Canning before the latter went East again in 1831, and with Urquhart while he was in England. Palmerston was rightly dissatisfied with the expedients to which Canning had found it necessary to resort when he employed MacGuffog and Vogorides; and a situation in which the senior dragoman could not be trusted, while lesser-paid interpreters or complete outsiders who were not in official receipt of any salary at all performed the confidential work, clearly could not be allowed to go on. It was financially wasteful, prejudicial to diplomatic process, and productive of discord and jealousy among the Levantines.[23] In the first instance, Palmerston did not think it practicable to introduce a scheme for training British personnel, and believed that reform should consist of weeding out incompetents and replacing them with men already available in Pera. Thus his first comment on the subject, scrawled on a memorandum drawn up in 1831, says, 'Both Chabert and Pisani [i.e. Antonio, who had been second dragoman since 1800, and who was loyal without being very able] ought to be got rid of', to which is added the very relevant afterthought, 'Can more honest successors easily be found?'.[24] Palmerston himself thought the answer to his own question was in the negative, and favoured promoting George Wood to be 'political' dragoman. Wood's death in 1834 ended that idea, and Urquhart, arriving in England soon after, was able to canalize all further discussion towards the discovery of British replacements for the Levantines. Ponsonby, aloof and jealously protective of the reliable men like Richard Wood and Frederick Pisani, contributed nothing to the discussion from Constantinople, and after his quarrel with Urquhart in 1837 was more than ever disposed to work through men who were serving him well.

The débâcle of Unkiar Skelessi, the precariousness of the truce between the Sultan and Muhammad Ali, and the maturing plan to seek a revision of the existing Ottoman tariff, all lent point to the dragoman issue, which came to a head in 1838, soon after Urquhart went out to supervise the commercial negotiation with the Ottoman authorities. His parting shot had been typical: 'I feel perfectly certain of the failure of the proposal with regard to the tariff if the negotiations are undertaken through the machinery of the dragomans.'[25] Urquhartian sentiments are also apparent in the memorandum which opened up the whole question in January 1838. It was the work of one Murray, a clerk in the consular department of the Foreign Office. This was only appropriate as it was hoped to transfer at least one or two dragomans to harmless vice-consular posts while recruiting Turkish- or Arabic-speaking Englishmen for the more important stations such as Smyrna and Alexandria. The theme of consular reorganization had been chiefly developed by Colonel Patrick Campbell, consul-general in Egypt, and it was suggested that Campbell's ideas might be 'made the ground plan of an enlarged system for providing those efficient services of British subjects which are required' for the interpreter service too. Murray went on: 'An Ottoman minister is known to fear, because he cannot trust, any dragoman . . . and at the present time a British minister at Const[antino]ple cannot be said to have any certain means of ascertaining what are the real sentiments of an Ottoman minister.' The implication of this piece of Urquhartism was that Ottoman ministers went in fear of their confidential remarks to a British dragoman being repeated to other foreign ministers than the British. It would be different, however, if 'gentlemen of talent and education', linguistically qualified, went out as 'ostensible and important members of the embassy and of His Majesty's diplomatic service'.[26]

Unfortunately for this ideal, Turkish was not taught in any of the larger schools which prepared youths for the Indian service such as Haileybury and Addiscombe, and, upon enquiry by the Foreign Office, it was found that there was only one person in all London teaching Turkish. Murray, observing that 'the study of eastern languages . . . appears rarely to have been undertaken for pleasure', suggested that six or eight youths should be sent to learn Greek and Turkish in the lands where they were spoken. After three years of intensive study, they could come back and serve a year in the Foreign Office before taking up their Eastern appointments, whether as consuls, dragomans, or embassy attachés. Palmerston wondered whether men would be found who would undertake the language course without a guarantee of ultimate employment, and did not see how the men, if they went out, could be supervised in their studies. 'But I wish very much to get rid of the dragomans, the employment of and dependence upon whom is most injurious to our interests.' The disposition of 1831, to find local replacements, had changed by 1838.

Edmund Hammond, a clerk handling the Ottoman Empire at the Foreign Office, took up specifically the problem of personnel in a further memorandum, arguing that there should be no insuperable difficulty in finding the right candidates to take over as the existing dragomans dropped out of service through death or retirement.[27] Chabert was 'advanced in years', Antonio Pisani had served even longer, Calavro had done 42 years, and Frederick Pisani 41. 'The material point is to secure persons of approved fidelity for the transaction of the confidential business', and this meant 'British subjects upon whom entire trust and reliance may be placed, in lieu of foreigners, upon whom no reliance whatever can be placed'. Where did one find them? 'English education, and the spirit which pervades our public schools and universities, and the general tone of English society, instil into the mind of a young man those high feelings of honour and of principle which peculiarly distinguish the English character.' Hammond did not want the Levantines ousted at once, nor is it easy to see how they could have been. In fact, if the rather despised but plodding second dragoman had died in 1838 while Frederick Pisani was assisting at the commercial negotiations for the revised tariff, the ostensible as opposed to secret channels of communication with the Porte could hardly have been kept open. Wood was in Syria, Urquhart disgraced, Chabert unemployable, and Calavro dying. Only the *giovani* were left and of these Ponsonby was already employing Etienne Pisani full time. Hammond acknowledged only one real drawback to his proposals; future governments might alter, or revoke completely, any plan of action decided on by Palmerston – 'a system established by one government may in a few years be subverted by another . . . the caprices of an ambassador . . . might render a man, without any fault of his own, unfit for, or might exclude him from employment'. Still unconvinced that men would be found to take this occupational risk, Palmerston again shelved the problem, partly, one imagines, because the outbreak of war in the East in 1839, and the international complications proceeding from it, disinclined him to change his horses, however unsatisfactory, in mid-stream.

Action was only taken with the return of peace, and upon the basis of yet another memorandum, this one coming from Charles Alison, the second attaché at Constantinople. Alison, described by Stanley Lane-Poole as a 'Voltairean *laissez faire* personality' of 'subtle and penetrating' mind, was consulted on the advisability of sending out young men to learn Greek and Turkish, and he frankly placed more hope in the increasing knowledge of French among the Ottomans than in the possibility of the British producing respectable speakers of Turkish for themselves. He was, on the other hand, concerned at the number of Frenchmen, Austrians, and Russians finding employment in the Ottoman Empire on the strength of their competence in Turkish, and for this reason, if for none other, he believed the British government had no choice but to persevere with the linguistic training of its own nationals. He found five Frenchmen working in official capacities in the office of Reshid Pasha, the great advocate of westernization in the Ottoman Empire, and there were two more in his private household. Great Britain could not afford to be left behind or to rely for the local maintenance of her influence upon unofficial and unorthodox supporters like Vogorides. If the British government proposed to make an early decision for the recruitment of English dragomans, Alison wrote, he would guarantee to get them the best available tuition in Turkish and Greek. 'I will pledge myself to perform what I have stated, and to spare no pains, with fair stuff to deal with.'[28] The matter was quickly settled after this and Hammond, forgetting his usual parsimony, persuaded Palmerston to offer Alison an extra £100 per annum for supervising the progress of the candidates sent out. Overruling Hammond's suggestion that the first two candidates might be found at Rugby, Palmerston invited the vice-chancellors of Oxford and Cambridge each to supply a person of promise. After all the talk of British dragomans, one of the first two men selected was the son of the Italian professor of Italian at Cambridge. In 1845, two more students went out, one of whom was Percy Smythe, the gifted son of Stratford Canning's old *bête noire*, Lord Strangford. By 1849 these four men, trained to the satisfaction of Alison in the appropriate tongues, were on the paid staff of the embassy, and usually referred to as the oriental attachés. The name attaché was regarded as less obnoxious than dragoman and more suited to the dignity of young Englishmen.[29]

The reaction of the Chaberts and Pisanis to the modification of the old order is not known in any detail, and it is possible that Ponsonby, with his casual ways, encouraged at least some of them to hope that the axe would never fall. Ponsonby was highly satisfied with the contribution of Frederick Pisani to the successful outcome of the tariff negotiations, and in informing the Foreign Office of the signing of the commercial treaty of 1838 wrote, 'there is very much due to him for the skill and activity with which he exerted himself'. Ponsonby's attitude could not, of course, obscure the fact that his confidential diplomacy on political matters was still being conducted by Vogorides, except when Richard Wood was at Constantinople between missions, and it was precisely that confidential work which Palmerston wanted in British hands. It might have been allocated almost entirely to Wood, and Stratford Canning tried to tempt him back to it even after his appointment as consul at Damascus in 1841, but having once tasted freedom, Wood was unwilling to return to the city where he had been exposed to Urquhart's humiliations. He knew, in 1842, that Canning was ready to give him an attachéship if he wanted one; he preferred oblivion, and found it in greater measure than he really expected. Before that, and while his own future as a dragoman was still in doubt, Wood was as anxious as any of his fellows about their prospects, and he discussed his career in letters exchanged with his sailor friend, William Lyon, captain of a merchant vessel trading regularly in Levant waters. Lyon knew the East well and was a hostile critic of the Levantine dragomans, telling Wood, 'no one, not even Urquhart, has a worse opinion of our system of dragomans than I have'. He too thought 'it certainly would be well to pay several clever young men, and pay them well to learn the Turkish language', and 'as you are an Englishman in blood and feeling, and as Englishmen alone are to be declared capable of holding the situation of dragoman, you would rank among the first'. In fact he thought Wood's only serious competitor for the senior appointment was the person from whom he acquired his information of the trend of Foreign Office opinion, Urquhart, 'a strange fish, [who] has much talent, but little ballast'. It was a sound nautical judgement, and Lyon was not the only friend who thought Wood was foolish in allowing injured pride to hinder professional advancement.[30]

The degree of Wood's error in choosing a Syrian consulate before a return to the work of the embassy was only made apparent with the passage of time and the discovery that the Levantines were not as superfluous as the oriental attachés were expected to make them. Contrary to all predictions, the latter did not prove adequate to the tasks of personal negotiation and interpretation, and increasing paper work at the embassy was sufficient to tie them to their desks there and to leave little time or energy for anything else. It is quite startling to discover how many Levantines whose early demise or retirement was predicted in 1841 were still in active service when the Crimean War began, performing their traditional tasks to the exclusion of the oriental attachés who, by that time, were wholly engaged, along with the diplomatic attachés, in paper work. It had been thought that George Wood's generation of interpreters, steadily infiltrated by the succeeding one to which his son belonged, would have disappeared by the mid-1840s. Instead, the growth and spread of embassy duties made it necessary to promote the *giovani* before the older men died out, and in 1850 there were more Levantine dragomans in simultaneous service than ever before. Francis Chabert was still first dragoman, and receiving his salary as such, though devoting his labours exclusively to commercial affairs; Antonio Pisani, who had served Elgin, was still there as second; Frederick Pisani was third and 'political' dragoman; Robert Chabert and Etienne Pisani, appointed *giovani* with Richard Wood in 1823, became dragomans in 1841 when he was nominated to Damascus; Henry Simmons, a *giovane* with them, was promoted dragoman in 1849. Count Pisani, after 36 years' service, remained custodian of the archives although Hammond had deplored such an arrangement years before.[31]

Also contrary to expectation was the hostility Stratford Canning started to show towards the oriental attachés. 'It was new and unpleasant for him to have unknown youngsters thrust upon him by the Foreign Office, some of whom had no other recommendation than being the relatives of noblemen who were useful to the government', is his biographer's explanation,[32] in apparent disregard of the earlier claim that it was Canning who suggested the new *régime*, and the abundant evidence of Lane-Poole's own chapters which show that it was precisely with the 'relatives of noblemen' that Canning got along best. The biographer was as vague about the categories of attaché as he was concerning dragomans. Canning got on well enough with Percy Smythe, Lord Stanley of Alderley, Lord Napier and Ettrick, Lord Cowley and Lord Odo Russell; of these, only Smythe was an oriental attaché. The other three oriental attachés were not of noble family, and here the main complaint was against their health rather than their ancestry: 'they have not a sound constitution among them.' Perhaps the real cause of Canning's dissatisfaction with his diplomatic attachés was their refusal to become infected with his own zeal for Ottoman reforms.

When the Holy Places dispute flared up in 1850, Canning was discovering just how much of the burden of embassy work, both diplomatic and clerical, rested on the Levantine dragomans and himself. Pride in his own flawless health made him impatient of illness in others, and while he and the Levantines plodded on, negotiating, wrangling, pleading, and writing endlessly, he came to feel that the attachés, both oriental and diplomatic, did not pull their weight. 'Not one of them is equal to half the fatigue that I endure, and often after the departure of a messenger there is a general occultation of the minor luminaries.' The oriental attachés had, in effect, surrendered to the Levantines their traditional functions and had themselves become the auxiliaries of the diplomatic attachés. The duties of negotiation at the Porte fell squarely upon Frederick Pisani, Etienne Pisani, and Robert Chabert, and when Frederick finally declared himself too infirm for the daily journeys between Pera and the Porte, Stratford expressed 'concern at the loss of your more active services'.[33]

When the Crimean War actually broke out in 1854, it was only too apparent that the dragoman question had not been solved by the reform of 1841. Indeed the situation was deteriorating. Just prior to 1855, Francis Chabert, Antonio Pisani, and Robert Chabert died in swift succession, but because Palmerston had refused, over a period of years, to appoint any more Levantine *giovani*, there was now a dangerous shortage of reserves for the interpreter service. The oriental attachés, whose numbers had not increased beyond the original four, could not step into the breach, even temporarily. 'Mr. Wood is unfortunately deceased, Mr. Doria and Mr. Smythe are all but confirmed invalids, and Mr. Hughes, through Your Lordship's kindness, is about to find a more congenial sphere of exertions at Erzerum.' The foreign secretary, the earl of Clarendon, threw the problem back, enquiring plaintively if more British dragomans were really necessary in light of the vastly increased use of French by the Ottomans.[34] Stratford Canning needed no more encouragement and reverted frankly and with characteristic independence to the old habit of recruiting local men, Levantine or British, for the interpreterships. His first nominee was the son of a former Turkey merchant called Sarell, but by 1857 some very un-English names were creeping back into the register of dragomans – Stavrides, Revelaki, Alishan.[35] In 1860 another Englishman in the Levant, Alfred Sandison, became a dragoman, apparently by nomination also, and recruitment by civil service examination for the Ottoman Empire interpreterships only began in 1877. Then, as the examinations were conducted in London and British subjects alone could sit for them, the days of the Levantine dragoman were numbered.[36]

Stratford Canning left Constantinople finally in 1858. In his last years of service, he had become such a partisan of the Levantines that Hammond could write, apropos an increase of salary for them, 'I am perfectly prepared for his objecting to them [the new scales of payment] altogether, first because of his . . . inveterate dislike to the system of oriental attachés, and secondly because he will feel jealous at a suggestion for the benefit of the dragomans originating otherwise than from himself'. The Levantines did not die very willingly, nor very quickly, and several gave years of service after Canning's final departure. Frederick Pisani gave intermittent service to the year of his death, 1871. Henry Simmons died within a few weeks of him. Etienne Pisani, 'the faithful Etienne' as Stratford Canning called him, retired after the Franco-Prussian war, and died in 1882, stubbornly demonstrating how the climate which removed Palmerston's oriental attachés preserved the Levantine dragomans who were born to it.

NOTES

1. *The Despatches of Sir Robert Sutton*, ed. Akdes Nimet Kurat (London, 1957), p. 9.
2. Duke of Bedford to Porter, 12 Oct. 1749, in Liston to Cooke, private, 18 Sept. 1812, FO 78/79; A.C. Wood, 'The English Embassy in Constantinople', *English Historical Review*, xl (1925), 538.
3. A.C. Wood, *History of the Levant Company* (Oxford, 1935), p. 184.
4. The dragomans were Anthony Dané, Bartholomew Pisani, Antonio Pisani, Francis Chabert; the *giovani* were George Calavro, Frederick Pisani, Felix Navon, Constantin Aidé.
5. Copies of B. Pisani to Liston, undated, and Elgin to Pisani, 3 Jan. 1803, in Liston to Cooke, private, 18 Sept. 1812, FO 78/79; Adair to Canning, separate, 24 Sept. 1809, FO 78/64. The practice of selling *barats* or patents of protection

to Jewish and Armenian merchants to enable them to avoid Ottoman taxation was not stopped finally until the signing of the treaty of the Dardanelles in 1809. Liston believed some English ambassadors had made as much as £2–3,000 per annum from selling *barats*; see Liston to Grenville, 25 April 1795, FO 78/16.
6. Adair to Canning, 18 Nov. 1808, FO 78/60; 16 Jan. 1809, FO 78/63; 5 Jan. 1810, FO 78/68. The dragoman's petition is in the dispatch of 6 Jan. 1809. The exchange rate in 1809 was 18 piastres to the £; it had been 12½ in 1792.
7. The derelict state of the embassy building, and the consequences of several visitations by Ottoman officials after Arbuthnot's withdrawal, are described in Adair to Canning, 15 Sept. 1809, FO 78/64; repair work is discussed in Adair to Canning, 5 Jan. 1810, FO 78/68.
8. Adair to Wellesley, 22 April 1810, FO 78/68; Stratford Canning to Wellesley, 16 May 1810, FO 78/70; S. Lane-Poole, *Life of Stratford Canning* (London, 1888), i. 83.
9. See in particular Stratford's letters to Richard Wellesley, 9 Nov. 1809, and to his cousin George Canning, 8 Jan. 1810, in Lane-Poole, *Life*, i. 70, 77.
10. Lane-Poole, *Life*, i. 136 n.; Castlereagh to Liston, 27 March, Liston to Castlereagh, 11 July, 13 Dec. 1812, FO 78/79.
11. Adair to Canning, 9 April 1809, with two encls., FO 78/63.
12. Lane-Poole, *Life*, i. 68 n., 82, 96, 135.
13. Castlereagh to Liston, 27 March 1812, FO 78/79.
14. In fact, upon the appointment of Strangford, Hamilton was promoted to secretary of embassy, which explains his resentment of his chief's reserve.
15. Hamilton's plaintive letters to Gordon are in Add. MSS 43213.
16. Canning to George Lidell, 30 May 1825, FO 366/348; Wood, *Levant Company*, pp. 199 *et seq.*; according to a memorandum in FO to treasury, 21 May 1841, FO 78/467, the new *giovani* were Robert Chabert, Henry Simmons, Etienne Pisani, and Richard Wood, and the date of their appointment was 28 November 1823. Of Elgin's *giovani*, Calavro became a dragoman in 1800, and Frederick Pisani in 1814; Navon and Aidé had died or retired by 1823.
17. Lane-Poole, *Life*, i. 406–16.
18. Ibid., pp. 506–7.
19. G.H. Bolsover, 'David Urquhart and the Eastern Question 1833–37: A Study in Publicity and Diplomacy', *Journal of Modern History*, viii (1936), 444–67; C.K. Webster, 'Urquhart, Ponsonby and Palmerston', *English Historical Review*, lxii (1947), 327–51; his claim to have 'means of communication, and information wholly distinct from the regular diplomatic routine' is in Urquhart to Palmerston, 28 Feb. 1834, FO 78/249, and the virtual confession that he could not easily dispense with a dragoman is in a letter to Backhouse, 29 Sept. 1835, FO 78/266. Also see below, pp. 36–7.
20. Lane-Poole, *Life*, i. 509.
21. G.H. Bolsover, 'Lord Ponsonby and the Eastern Question, 1833–1839', *Slavonic Review*, xiii (1934), 99.
22. Wood's 'Memorandum on his Services' in Syria is in FO 78/961; a letter in the Wood Papers, Ponsonby to Wood, 4 Dec. 1834, shows that Wood held an appointment in an Ottoman department of state where confidential information was to be had. Ponsonby admits it is 'a wholly unusual proceeding'; Wood must 'allow the Pera world . . . to talk', and 'trust entirely to me to take care that you shall not suffer' at the Foreign Office.
23. Dragoman salaries at this time are specified in Mandeville to FO, 1 Oct. 1831,

FO 366/569. Francis Chabert, £1,100; Antonio Pisani, £500; Frederick Pisani, £300; George Calavro, £300; George Wood, £300; the *giovani* Etienne Pisani, Robert Chabert, and Henry Simmons were being paid £80 per annum, while Richard Wood was receiving £110. Chabert's salary was so high because it included the £400 given for 'political' work. Part of this £400 had to be surrendered to Frederick Pisani in 1832, and the rest of it later on. It was all going to Pisani by 1842, along with an extra £200 which Ponsonby added to Pisani's salary as from April 1837. Pisani's gross income of £900 in 1842 was almost three times the salary of an embassy attaché. See Aberdeen to Canning, 24 May 1842, FO 78/473.
24. Minute of Palmerston, 19 Oct. 1831, on Hammond's undated memo, FO 366/569.
25. For the negotiations, see C.K. Webster, *The Foreign Policy of Palmerston, 1831–41* (London, 1951), ii, ch. 7; the 'failure' predicted by Urquhart did not come to pass, but there were discrepancies between the Turkish and English versions of the commercial treaty of 1838 which produced difficulties later on. The Ottomans claimed the treaty allowed them a salt monopoly at Salonika, the British merchants that it admitted them to the wine trade in the Ottoman Empire. Pisani may be to blame for the discrepancies, but both Henry Bulwer, who conducted the negotiations on the British side, and Ponsonby were anxious to settle the business quickly. John Cartwright, the consul-general, assisted Bulwer in the negotiations, and even if he could not easily follow Pisani's discussions with the Ottomans, had enough Turkish to check the Turkish version against the English one. In any case, it was Ponsonby's responsibility to see that the two versions tallied. Pisani probably aimed at giving both sides what they wanted, hoping small and, to him, unimportant differences between the versions would not be noticed; see Stratford Canning to Aberdeen, 24 May 1842, FO 78/478.
26. Murray's 'Memorandum on the Dragoman System in the Levant', Jan. 1838, with Palmerston's minute of 6 Feb., FO 366/569.
27. Hammond's 'Memorandum respecting Dragomans', 14 Feb. 1838, and 'Further Memorandum', 25 April 1838, FO 366/569. Hammond believed any oriental language would be useful for a candidate submitting himself for an Ottoman Empire interpretership, possibly under the influence of William Fox-Strangeways' minute of 13 Feb. in which Turkish was described as 'a pedantic mixture of Tartar, Arabic and Persian'. Such vagueness was not unusual; Palmerston thought Arabic was the language of Persia.
28. Lane-Poole, *Life*, ii. 69; Alison to Hammond, undated, 1841, FO 366/569.
29. Hammond to Palmerston, 9 June 1841, in which Hammond wrote: 'I am not a Rugby man myself; but I hear a great deal of the manner in which the Rugby boys distinguish themselves in standing for Scholarships at Oxford'; Palmerston to vice-chancellors of Oxford and Cambridge, 21 Aug. 1841, FO 366/569. The men selected were Almeric Wood, William Doria (1841); Hon. Percy Smythe, T.F. Hughes (1845).
30. Canning to Wood, 17 April, Wood to Canning, 30 April 1842, Wood MSS. In replying, Wood wrote: 'The little consideration attached to the profession of dragoman, the constant and public attacks made upon the individuals themselves and the little respect they enjoyed in general not only made me anxious to quit it but the moral effect was such as to have induced Lord Ponsonby to employ me abroad in confidential missions'; William Lyon to Wood, 22 Feb., 19 Nov. 1836, 4 Sept. 1837, Wood MSS.

31. In his 'Memorandum' of 14 Feb. 1838, Hammond had written: 'If the system of dragomans is bad, the system which brings one of the body into the chancery and gives him habitual access to the archives of the embassy is much worse'; FO 366/569. Count Pisani, formerly Alexander Pisani, is sometimes listed as a *giovane*, but this is because his work in the chancery prevented his becoming a dragoman, long after he was linguistically qualified. He never became a dragoman, but enjoyed higher pay and status than the *giovani*. He went with Strangford to the congress of Verona in 1822, and was sent in 1833 to advise Ibrahim, the stepson of Muhammad Ali, not to come nearer to Constantinople than Konya.
32. Lane-Poole, *Life*, ii. 68.
33. Ibid., p. 136; Canning to Malmesbury, 29 May 1852, FO 366/569.
34. Canning to Clarendon, 3 June 1856, FO 78/1180; Clarendon to Canning, 13 Aug. 1856, FO 78/1165.
35. Canning to Clarendon, 4 May 1857, FO 366/569.
36. FO List (1878).

CHAPTER II

Stratford Canning, Mahmud II, and Muhammad Ali

In 1830, Lord Grey assembled the most aristocratic Cabinet of the century to inaugurate a more democratic age, and the Canningites did extremely well to insert four of their number into it. The Foreign Office was first offered to the marquis of Lansdowne and Lord Holland, but each refused and each, it seems, recommended Palmerston for it. It was Grey who brought in Viscount Melbourne, Charles Grant, and Viscount Goderich, and as the first obtained the Home Office, the second the Board of Control, and the third War and Colonies, Grey could hardly have done more for a parliamentary group whose founder he despised. It is also easy to see why Stratford Canning, who had no ministerial experience, was left out: Grey had numerous relatives of his own to accommodate. Nearly all of them suspected Palmerston as a Tory turncoat, and they disliked Stratford possibly more. Edward Ellice, Grey's brother-in-law, and Lord Durham, his son-in-law, could certainly be depended on to do Stratford every possible disservice. Furthermore, Grey himself needed men who would see him through the controversial days ahead, and Stratford was recognized as a very moderate reformer indeed.

Already there were glimmerings, noticed at dinner parties and reported back to headquarters by the clearing centre for political intelligence, Holland House, of that attachment to only the most carefully considered reform which was to turn Stratford into a supporter of Sir Robert Peel and Viscount Stanley in 1835. Stratford's known incompetence as a speaker clinched the matter: no Cabinet could carry a diplomat of many years' experience who would nevertheless be unable to defend his colleagues in the House, and Princess Lieven said Stratford's involuntary silence in Parliament enabled Russia to disregard him as long as he was in Britain. There is the extra point that in the gossip-ridden society of those times, Stratford's blameless private life was a silent condemnation of the more irregular ways of others and, where the Greys were concerned, his direct gaze and curling lower lip were never disciplined to conceal his contempt. If George Canning's worst enemy was his own tongue, Stratford's was his scornful eye.

With Cabinet office denied him, Stratford's next problem was his seniority. There was nothing within Palmerston's patronage equal to Stratford's talents, experience, and expectation. The parliamentary under-secretaryship went to Palmerston's close friend, Sir George Shee, and the permanent equivalent did not yet carry the prestige it later acquired from Edmund Hammond: to illustrate this, when Fox-Strangways, Palmerston's permanent under-secretary after 1835, was promoted to the diplomatic service in 1840, he was sent to Frankfurt. A return to the diplomatic service was all that remained, but at least Palmerston felt free to offer Stratford the highest post in it, and the best paid. Yet here, too, there was to be disappointment.

Lord Heytesbury, the British ambassador at St Petersburg, was very anxious to come home, and in April 1831, with Stratford's hopes of employment at home all but gone, Palmerston offered him the succession. Stratford accepted. Following the usual procedure, the foreign secretary then asked the Russian embassy to obtain the tsar's consent to the appointment. Whether the tsar himself was consulted at this stage or not, the reply came back from Count Nesselrode that Stratford was not acceptable, and Palmerston was begged to find someone else. This was an embarrassing and wholly unexpected development, and Palmerston got out of his difficulty temporarily by persuading Heytesbury to stay on and Stratford to go off on a special mission to the Ottoman Empire. But the appointment was only suspended, not withdrawn, and Stratford was actually gazetted for St Petersburg in October 1832, when he came back from Constantinople. Why the Russian government turned him down in 1831 is not easily explained, but it would appear that Nesselrode already knew, or the tsar actually said, that Stratford was *persona non grata* at the Russian court.

One thing is sure: Stratford was not rejected because he was detected at St Petersburg as a formidable antagonist of Russian designs in the Near East; on the contrary, a man who had been recalled by the Wellington Tories for his adherence to the policy of the treaty of London and the principle of collaboration with Russia, should have recommended himself to Nicholas I by such a record. Obviously, too, the Lievens were in no position to prevent the tsar accepting Stratford, even if they did describe him as difficult and disagreeable. Stratford found the Russian attitude 'a mystery', and so did Grey, who came round warmly to the appointment by 1832. Palmerston could only attribute it to instinctive dislike, and quoted, 'I do not like you, Doctor Fell'.[1] The mystery was never cleared up. The discovery that, in 1825, Stratford possibly offended the Grand Duke Nicholas by failing to pay him a farewell courtesy call, was rejected by Nesselrode and by the tsar himself as the original sin, without the benefit of further clarification, and when, after a long period in which Britain was only represented in Russia by a chargé d'affaires, a new ambassador went out in 1835, the choice was Sir Charles Bagot, who claimed to have once given Nicholas I 'such a rap on the knuckles as sovereigns are not in the habit of forgiving'. Bagot was accepted.[2] The irony is that Stratford's nomination to Russia was first broached in 1831 when his feelings were still in equipoise as between the claims of Russia upon the Ottoman Empire and the claims of the Ottoman Empire to survival. Within a year, as a result of his special mission of 1832 and after 20 years of uncertainty, Stratford reshaped his thinking on Near Eastern affairs in a fashion which made him at once Turcophile and increasingly Russophobe. He was not alone in his conversion. After the traumatic experience of watching the Russian advance to Adrianople in 1829, many British observers were forgetting the Greeks and discovering the Ottomans. The episode which completed Stratford's conversion was the Egyptian invasion of Syria: Ibrahim Pasha, herded out of Greece by negotiation and cajolery in 1828, was laying siege to the fortress of Acre by the spring of 1832, just as Stratford himself arrived at Constantinople, for his third stay.

Stratford went out muttering his customary complaints against the slings and arrows of the diplomatic profession, claiming that his honour was sacrificed to the whim of the tsar, but inwardly he was intrigued to see for himself the social changes which his Eastern correspondents claimed were transforming the Ottoman Empire almost daily before their eyes, and conscious too that behind him in Britain he had been witnessing the small beginnings of a genuine awakening and enlightenment with regard to the predicament of the

Ottoman Empire. The importance of this movement must not be exaggerated. British ministers and newspapers were far more preoccupied with Belgium, France, and Portugal in 1831 than with the more eastern regions of the Continent, and interest in Greece and Poland had slumped unquestionably, first because of the disintegration of the revolution and the rudderless condition of its affairs, and second, because of Russian suppression of the 1830 rising. There was much general speculation that the 1815 foundations were trembling, shaken by an ever-widening conflict between illiberal autocracy on the one side and revolution on the other.

Within the context of this argument between governments and peoples, Britain moved tentatively, her ministers claiming to deal with problems in a practical way, 'on their merits', yet undecided as to which among the great powers her working associates might be. The strongest and the weakest, Russia and Austria, were coming together again in a neo-Holy Alliance; Britain and France, the latter a state second only to Russia in real power, had yet to evolve a working partnership. The Whig leaders, true to the memory of Charles James Fox and any other principle a generation out of date, wanted some arrangement with France, but Louis-Philippe disappointed them at first, and got off the mark in foreign affairs with a meddling policy in Belgium and an annexationist one in North Africa. Like all his countrymen, Stratford saw Russia as the greatest individual force in Europe, and he now began to ask himself specifically what had hitherto only ruminated in his brain – upon what terms Britain might sustain the Ottoman Empire against Russia, and to what ends.

Behind him in Britain, the panic of 1829 was beginning to subside, more because domestic events were crowding out foreign affairs than because the new Whig ministry knew Tory fears of Russia to have been exaggerated. But 1829 had been a critical year, and its lessons were still being learnt, in St Petersburg and Constantinople as well as London and Vienna. Thus Sir Robert Gordon reminded his superiors from Constantinople that 'all hopes of defending Constantinople were abandoned by the Turks' themselves as the Russian army approached Adrianople. This loss of morale, so unusual in the Ottomans, was echoed in Tory cries of alarm. In July 1829, the duke of Wellington predicted: 'The Russian demands will be raised, and I can't say that the Porte has any means of resistance.' He vaguely added: 'We are certainly interested in preventing the extension of the

Russian power in Asia', but by October was referring meekly to 'schemes of ambition in Asia, which Russia may reasonably entertain'. The fall of Adrianople on 20 August obliged him to acknowledge that 'We can talk of nothing except in the tone and quality of a power that is degraded'. The earl of Aberdeen likewise viewed the march to Adrianople with a flutter of timid disapproval: Russia must know her actions 'cannot be regarded with indifference by this country', but a government which allowed a Russian army to get within 120 miles of Constantinople *was* indifferent, or totally impotent.[3]

It was Gordon who had fixed in his brother's mind a sharp image of the historic crisis at hand:

> Nothing but an immediate cessation of hostilities can possibly save this Empire from total destruction. The internal disorder is even more alarming than the danger with which it is threatened from without: disaffection and insubordination have reached the highest pitch. There no longer exists an embodied Turkish army; and the few scattered troops the Russians have fallen in with decline to offer any resistance.

Gordon himself impetuously offered to invite a British squadron through the Straits, but to 'preserve tranquillity' at the Porte, not to challenge the Russians. The Sultan refused the offer though it won for Gordon popularity which his government did not enjoy among Ottomans.[4]

As for the Russians, they found their victory too complete, and their opportunities greater than their nerve to seize them. The reality of late 1829 was wilder than any dream of Catherine the Great, for the Ottoman Empire was militarily broken, and totally vulnerable. No remotely comparable situation is to be found between 1774 and 1877. With an ancient and ingrained habit of spoliation by agreement behind them, the tsar and his ministers were afraid to go on alone and after much anxious deliberation they elected to maintain, because they were afraid to demolish, their debilitated neighbour. Unfortunately, they kept this momentous decision to themselves for far too long,[5] and anti-Russian neuroses in western Europe fattened on ignorance as well as misinformation.

Like Wellington, Aberdeen agreed that 'the existence of the Turkish Empire may be said at this moment to depend upon the absolute will and pleasure of the Emperor Nicholas. Whenever this feeble and precarious dominion shall cease, we ought not to occupy ourselves in vain efforts to restore its existence.' This was the moment for the British government to swing over sharply to the notion of a larger Greek state than it had hitherto wanted. Wellington spoke of re-creating a 'Greek Empire' and Aberdeen of establishing 'a solid power in Greece with which we may form a natural connection'. It is hard to credit that these were Aberdeen's sentiments less than a year after the Poros conference at which time he had been content that 'Greece' should be a principality in the Morea, without either Athens or independence. George IV approved, and Prince Polignac, now first minister to Charles X, went even further, producing in place of a plan merely to enlarge Greece another to liquidate the Ottoman Empire completely, a plan as detailed in its parcelling as any dream of Herzberg, the Prussian maniac of territorial mensuration. But the men who squandered the position regarding the Greek question left them by Canning in 1827 could hardly expect to shape the Ottoman question in 1829, and it was pointless now to blame others for their impotence in 1828, as Lord Ellenborough did when he declared, 'we have lost the Greek question by persisting in keeping Stratford Canning'.[6]

Even had the initiative still been theirs, the Tories could not have persisted with the idea of an enlarged Greece: it was foreign to their political training to enlarge a state created by force and revolution, and they were fundamentally no surer of controlling a larger than a smaller Greece. There was no 'natural connection' between Britain and the little Balkan state, though there had been one in Byron's time, and, knowing this, Wellington, Earl Bathurst, and Ellenborough soon curbed their foreign secretary's rash enthusiasm and opted for a small Greece. Wellington stated their final attitude, of withdrawal and disapproval: 'It would be absurd to think of bolstering up the Turkish Power in Europe. It is gone, in fact; and the tranquillity of the world along with it.' As to Greece, 'All I wish is to get out of the Greek affair without loss of honour, and without imminent risk for the safety of the Ionian Islands.'[7]

Aberdeen was obliged to write to his brother, 'I hope you have been preparing our Turkish friends for the independence of Greece. That is what we shall certainly establish. We have reduced the limits as much as we have been able.' The rather grand use of the first-person plural, and the implication that Britain still had a controlling role in the Greek business had some justification in the continuance in London of the old conference of the treaty powers, Britain, France, and Russia, but the Ottoman question was now, it seems, all but given up. This left Gordon in a highly embarrassing position at Constantinople and he quit his post at the first opportunity, saying that he would carry on to Britain if he found no letters at Malta ordering him back to his post![8] The change of ministry at the end of 1830 did not produce any spectacular reinvigoration of Eastern policies, and if the old-guard Tories had much to learn about the place of conservative principle in a dynamic world, the Whigs needed no less to let new interests temper old ideals. In the new ministry, there was a marked inclination to leave foreign affairs to Palmerston, the very man likely to see new interests most clearly. With his advent to office, there was an upward turn, a return from recent incoherence to Canningite purpose and a fresh appraisal of British interests in the Near and Middle East. It was long overdue. Calling Stratford to his house in Stanhope Street, the foreign secretary asked him to go East again on a special mission on behalf of Greece.[9]

The Whig proposals which Stratford carried to the East on his special mission in 1831 may now be mentioned, with a preliminary reminder of those they superseded. Up to the treaty of Adrianople, the Tories had taken their stand on a protocol of 22 March 1829, which made the Poros recommendations merely a basis for negotiation, and then only if the Greeks gave up all idea of obtaining Crete and Samos; surrendered any expectation of electing their own prince; and withdrew General Church and his guerrillas from Acarnania, on the northern side of the gulf of Corinth. In January, Britain had withdrawn her ships from the blockade of Crete, which was thereafter maintained only by the Russian squadron of Admiral Ricord. Then came the treaty of Adrianople in September, the result of which, in C.W. Crawley's words, was to 'increase Russian influence navally in the Black Sea, politically in the Principalities, and commercially in Turkey generally'.[10] Specifically, Russia adjusted her Danube frontier from the northern to the southern estuary of the great river, thus modifying the treaty of nearly 20 years before in which Stratford had taken a hand. Ottoman control of the Principalities was loosened almost completely by the compulsory evacuation of the Muslim population and the reduction of all

Ottoman strongpoints and garrisons, and Russian control was intensified by an arrangement which permitted her garrison to remain in Moldavia and Wallachia until the payment of an indemnity of 15 million ducats. The hospodars, once seven-year appointments, were now to govern for life, with Russian approval. Lastly, the Ottomans were bound, by a separate article, to accept the treaty of London and the March protocol, mentioned above. There followed a brief spasm in which the Tories favoured a greatly enlarged Greece, but by early 1830 they had returned some way towards their earlier preferences and had been able, in resumed conferences in London, to stipulate for a compromise: that is a less generous frontier – never clearly demarcated – from the estuary of the Aspropotamos on the west to Zeitoun (Lamia) in the east. This line, bordering the northern shore of the gulf of Corinth, excluded Acarnania, and Crete was withheld too, but full independence was accepted in principle, and the crown of Greece was officially offered to Prince Leopold of Saxe-Coburg, a safe and respectable German princeling related to the British, and most other, crowns.

While in opposition, the Whigs had argued for a more generous frontier for Greece, and for what Lord Holland called 'sufficient territory for national defence'. This argument correctly presumed that the Greeks would prefer to stand on their own feet than rely constantly on Russia, and foreshadows the Gladstonian argument about the breasts of free men by half a century. Within six weeks of coming to office at the end of 1830, Palmerston adopted the more generous Arta-Volo line again, as proposed by the ambassadors at the Poros conference, and although the Belgian crisis prevented the Greek conferences in London from resuming before September 1831, the change of British attitude was known during the intervening year both in Napoli and Constantinople, and Palmerston connived at Greek delays in evacuating Acarnania, even instructing the British Resident, Edward Dawkins, to assist the delays 'on any fair pretence'.[11] In that intervening period, Prince Leopold accepted – then resigned – the crown of Greece, frightened off according to the historian, George Finlay, by a scheming president who sacrificed his country to his own ambition, but daunted at least as much by the niggardly attitude of Britain and France, particularly the former, over the size of the new state as he was disconcerted by John Kapodistrias' candid advice that he must be ready to turn Greek Orthodox and fight for wider frontiers than those Europe seemed ready at the moment to provide. Had Leopold waited, Palmerston and Stratford would have given him such wider frontiers, but the crown of Belgium became available first, and he took it. The Greek president, soon to be assassinated, thereby helped to saddle the standing London conference with the difficulty of finding another king as well as enlarging the frontier. Good candidates were hard to find and, by elimination, the crown was offered in March 1832 to a 17-year-old Bavarian prince, Otto. Before that, on 26 September 1831, the conference sent Stratford to Constantinople to negotiate complete independence and the Arta-Volo frontier if he could. There was to be no bullying: if the Ottomans did not agree to this, or any other new frontier, Stratford was to come home. Before he set out, Stratford himself told Palmerston and Sir James Graham that they were giving him 'a fool's errand'.[12]

At least Stratford had a free hand. 'I can give you no further instruction as to the management of your negotiation,' Palmerston declared, 'which you will conduct in the way best calculated to succeed.'[13] In Paris, where he stopped briefly, his old friend, the Russian minister Pozzo di Borgo, and his old opponent, the comte de Sébastiani, now foreign minister, were similarly inclined to leave the negotiation with the Ottomans to him, telling him that the Russian and French residents in Greece would give their co-operation and the embassies at Constantinople their support.[14] Everyone, Stratford noticed in Paris, seemed sick of the Greek question, and only interested in Belgium and North Africa. When he reached Greece, he understood why. Even as he approached the shores of that country, he wrote sadly and apprehensively to his wife of what he expected to find:

It grieves me to the heart to say that I hear nothing good of the Greeks, as we approach their shores. No fresh crimes, that is all. But disunion, and party hatred, and political intrigue carried to the worst extremes. The Scripture expression – 'to the Greeks foolishness' – is forever running in my head, and I am at times half persuaded that they labour under a curse. Most certain is it that in spite of their heroic resistance to the Turks, their hairbreadth escape, and marvellous good fortune in establishing their independence, they do seem to want what is requisite to make a people and a government of them. And there are plenty of enemies of theirs and ours to note and to take advantage of their weakness. What, then, can I hope to do for them? Alas! I dare not trust myself with answering the question.[15]

Landing at Corinth, he rode to Napoli by horse, the scenery confirming much that Dawkins had reported in his dispatches home. Greece was an exhausted, desolated land. There was no national income beyond the gifts of Europe's philhellenes, the governments having without exception refused any more loans. The pro-Greek sentiments of ten years before had turned to scepticism and bitterness in many quarters, and international indifference had become a major Greek problem. Stratford told Palmerston that 'Greece' could well fall apart before he could obtain Ottoman recognition for it, and he was careful to cultivate the grand vizier, then controlling operations in Albania.[16] 'That part of the Morea which I crossed on my way thither,' wrote Stratford,

> was the very type of desolation. A few scattered flocks of sheep, here and there a ruined cottage or a herdsman's hovel, a stray horse or donkey, some little verdure in the valleys. . . . The Plain of Argos, as I descended in the evening from the hills, presented a field of greater promise, but the light was too faint for observation, and it had settled into a gloom before the arch of the towngate of Nauplia echoed to my horse's feet.[17]

In Napoli, he stayed with Dawkins, who had been at school with him, and from the resident he learned that a new national assembly had been convened only a day or two before his arrival, on 19 December at Argos, under a new president, Agostino Kapodistrias. He heard with special attention details of Russian activity in Greece which confirmed those growing suspicions, perceptible in the above letter to his wife.

John Kapodistrias, first president of Greece, had been assassinated a few weeks before on 9 October. At the time of his death, he had many enemies and few friends among the political and feudal leaders, real or aspiring, of Greece. The commercial and pirate magnates of Hydra and Spetsia were clamouring for compensation for their losses in the maritime war; the restless Maina people for the assets of local autonomy and due representation in national affairs, as well as justice for their incarcerated leader, Petrobey Mavromichalis. The constitutionalists like Mavrocordates, Trikoupis, and Zographos, who had enjoyed greater power in earlier days before the president lapsed into dictatorial habits and ruled through his subservient senate, fought the first battles for a free Greek press, but unavailingly. Responsible military leaders like Church had gone from the scene, and brave but irresponsible ones like Kolokotronis and Miaulis kept the country in turmoil, fighting Greeks as they had once fought Ottomans. The Acropolis, unheeded symbol of past greatness, was still held, much to their own surprise, by an Albanian garrison on the Sultan's behalf. In mid-August, Dawkins explained to Stratford, the trouble had all come to a head. The late president had ordered a blockade of Hydra, a great centre of disaffection. Miaulis countered by seizing the president's 'navy', two ships at Poros. The president's troops then attacked Poros, aided by the Russian admiral and resident, Ricord, who imposed a blockade, and in a rash moment of defiance Miaulis destroyed one of his captures, the *Hellas*, the best warship Greece possessed. Finally, on 9 October, the sons of Petrobey murdered their father's captor.[18]

Agostino Kapodistrias, who once succeeded Church in western Greece, now succeeded his own brother as president, not for long, but for long enough. Stratford never believed the first Greek president was a Russian puppet, but he was far less sure of Agostino, who commanded no one's loyalty. 'The new president is acknowledged on every side to be incompetent, and the residents are distracted, and each the focus of a group of Greeks.' The Argos assembly had split at once, and when Stratford reached Napoli, three groups vied for authority, one in Argos, one in Hydra, and one in Corinth. Stratford wrote to Palmerston,

> Greeks one and all lie, but there is no denying that John Capodistrias has pursued a bad system of government. The present government, which is only provisionally provisional, may possibly strengthen itself and survive, but if so, I am satisfied that it will owe its existence to Russian aid. Depend upon it, there is far too much of Russian influence here.[19]

The 'Russian influence' worrying Stratford was that exerted by Ricord in favour of the Kapodistrias dynasty. The former was blamed for having abetted the first president's arbitrary methods for keeping himself in power, and the second for a blockade of Poros in which the French and British naval captains had refused to join. Only the protests of the latter checked Ricord from going on to bombard Hydra. Stratford, anxious to 'conclude the last Act of the Greek drama', took an exaggerated view of these activities and concluded that Russia would rather keep Greece in turmoil than accede to a settlement finally brought about by other powers. Pozzo had seemed genuine enough, but he recalled that Matuszewic, the special Russian envoy sent to London on the Greek question, had so resisted Palmerston's wish for the Arta-Volo line that the foreign secretary had appealed over his head to St Petersburg. Agostino Kapodistrias also indicated where his loyalties lay in his opening address to the Argos assembly, where he spoke of 'the rights which Russia has earned the respect and gratitude of Greece'. Nesselrode had invited Agostino to maintain a direct correspondence with him, and Stratford's first impression of Constantinople was that a Russo-Ottoman treaty was in the air. Stratford's fears did not exceed those of other men. For the best part of a year, Dawkins had been pleading for a Greek king, and General Guilleminot, the French ambassador at Constantinople, was recalled in 1831 for telling Ottoman officials that France was about to declare war on Russia.[20]

What was to be done? The best way to counter Russian machinations, Stratford advised, was to set Greece on her feet, quickly and generously. In Paris, he had recommended giving the residents a credit of about £20,000 each to help the Greek government check pillage by its own soldiers and piracy by its own sailors. In Greece itself, things seemed more than ever in the melting pot – national solvency, choice of a king, the definition of frontiers. Agostino Kapodistrias presented his first budget to the Greek senate, and in it doubled his civil list and quadrupled the ecclesiastical estimates, asking £195,722 for the army, £50,640 for the navy, £15,585 for 'ecclesiastical affairs' and £6,023 for the justice department. At that moment, the new paper money of Greece carried a 45 per cent discount, and as Stratford observed to Palmerston, the country badly needed 'a ruler as rich as the reluctant Leopold'. An interview with the financial counsellor to the president showed that Greece had no prospect of buying out the *vakf*, the Muslim religious foundations and assets, far less the Turkish peasants. As to frontiers, pleading for the Arta-Volo line would have its problems since 'the map on which your protocols are founded, is little better, I fear, than the one which it has exploded'. The official Russian cartographer never visited the areas 'which he describes with such precision'.[21] The Ottomans, indoctrinated by Gordon, would dig in their toes over Samos, Crete, and Acarnania.

Stratford's chance to intervene usefully in Greek affairs soon came. The constitutionalists, Mavrocordates and Trikoupis, pleaded with him to take a hand, saying 'Providence had sent him at this critical moment',[22] but he waited first for a response from the president to the secessions from the national assembly. This came when the supposedly pro-Russian *klepht*, Kolokotronis, led out the new president's troops against Kolettis and the separate assembly of about 80 members at Corinth. For the benefit of Agostino, whom he met and disliked, Stratford drew up a memorandum on the grievances of the secessionists, which he thought made some impression. More important, he rallied the three residents to act together, and here his advice was undoubtedly successful. Through them he warned the incompetent foreign minister, Glarakis, that his mission to Constantinople 'can be of no use while civil war exists in this country'.[23] The residents also got a commission of Greeks set up to reconcile the three rival assemblies. In a lengthy report to Palmerston, written before he moved on, Stratford seconded Dawkins' plea for a king, or even a viceroy *ad interim*: in addition, he urged the London conference to ordain an amnesty for all discontented opponents of the president, and the authorization of prompt money credits to meet the immediate needs of the government and the destitute.[24] Palmerston replied that the London conference was 'delighted' with Stratford's doings, above all else for drawing the residents into harmony again. Soon afterwards, the discontented Greek deputies drove Agostino from Greece, and set up a new unified government. With the lightning conductor gone, the storm seemed worse than ever, and it endured until, and beyond, the proclamation in July 1832 of King Otto I, a Roman Catholic German with no time for constitutions or deputies, or even coronations.[25]

Stratford, meanwhile, moved on to Attica, over which the Sultan's grey flag still flew, to see the Parthenon. The ancient buildings of the Acropolis ravished his eye and filled his heart and, like other classical scenes, inspired his best writing.

> The temple of Theseus is the only marvel that has disappointed me. I have been a second time to reconcile myself with it, and I am sensible of

an improved effect; but there is a narrowness about it, and a lowness of the pediment, which I should not have expected. It is wonderfully preserved. The great temple of Minerva, on the summit of the citadel, is indeed a wonder; not so much for the ingenuity of its construction, as for the combination of massiveness and elegance, the beauty of the marble, and the exquisite finish of the reliefs.

He got cross with the recollection of Lord Elgin's handiwork, and thought the 'Scottish Earl might have better employed his time and money in fishing these [still buried reliefs] up, than in pulling down those reliefs which were still in their places'.[26] Yet Athens was no part of Aberdeen's Greece! Stratford went on his way, determined to win the Acropolis for Greece, the most priceless building in the world for a nation which, at that moment, had £4.15.7d in its treasury.

Stratford reached Constantinople on 28 January 1832, making the journey from the Dardanelles by steamer for the first time. The steamer caused a sensation as it moved up the Bosporus, none of the spectators knowing that this modern wonder had both run out of coal and been aground in the Sea of Marmora. The British embassy having burned down in 1831, with the total loss of its archives, Stratford took up residence in the old summer house, now grievously cold under a burden of fresh snow, and until August, when he left Constantinople with his mission accomplished, he did his paper work either there or at the consulate-general. The governor of the Bosporus village of Anadolu Kavak was ordered by the Porte to provide the British envoy with firewood, and as he sat by a great brass stove and planned his diplomatic offensive concerning Greece, he found a spare hour to recommend to Palmerston the construction of a new embassy, on the ruins of the old, keeping the price down by getting the plans drawn up by some young man just completing his architectural studies.[27] Stratford wanted to get his tasks over quickly, and to get away again before the plague made its appearance with the hot weather in July, so he laid his plans with some completeness for a sharp and effective assault. The Ottomans, he knew, were 'uneasy' over his arrival, and having accepted the minimal frontiers of Greece laid down by the Tories, they declared these were 'never to be changed'. So why had Sir Stratford Canning come, the *reis effendi* asked John Mandeville, the chargé d'affaires? Behind this question, Mandeville and Stratford could easily discern the Porte's rising anxiety over the Egyptian invasion of Syria, begun two months before. Could the Sultan's ministers surrender over Greece as well as in Syria and Algeria? Or might surrender over Greece be obtained by offers of help in Syria?

Stratford began by taking over complete charge of the embassy, a move for which Palmerston had given him discretion. Mandeville, he said, was 'the best person in the world', but it was best that the Ottomans should know who they were dealing with, and that there should be no divided command. Next, he took up the old problem of communication with the Porte, and here, he said, 'a stumbling-block of large dimensions lay at my very door'. Since the dissolution of the Levant Company in 1825, the nominal first dragoman, Francis Chabert, had been an object of suspicion in the embassy, and Stratford blamed him for his own failure to bring the Sultan over in 1827 to a policy of reason and concession towards the Greeks. There was, indeed, no doubt about Chabert's perfidy, but sacking a man with 35 years' experience of the British embassy behind him seemed more dangerous than keeping him, and Stratford now decided to use him for all the formal work but to conduct his most intimate and confidential intercourse with the Porte through others.

> Delicacy was out of the question: my opinion of his character was no secret. I told him at our first meeting in so many words that it was unchanged; that nevertheless I would not make a scandal without fresh cause; the sole test of his conduct, in my judgement, would be a success; if my ship went down, his boat should infallibly share its fate. He bowed, and silently accepted the terms.[28]

Frederick Pisani, nominally third dragoman, was entrusted with the most important official transactions at the Porte, and given a slice of Chabert's salary for his labours. Thus Chabert arranged Stratford's audiences and negotiated the dates of conferences, but Pisani was the public negotiator. But, beyond even Pisani, there was a triumvirate of unofficial negotiators, made up of two Scots and a Fanariot of Bulgarian extraction. Doctor Samuel MacGuffog was embassy physician and occasionally consultant to Sultan Mahmud II himself; David Urquhart, a 26-year-old who had fought for Greece but was now an incipient Turcophile, had been picked up in Paris as a potential commissioner in Stratford's Greek frontier negotiation.

The third confidential agent, and much the most important, was Stefanaki Vogorides, best introduced in Stratford's own words:

In a quarter of Stamboul, called the Fanar, there lived a Greek with whom I had long been acquainted. He possessed that sort of talent which, used with much patient and timed discretion, had gradually earned him a position of some consequence among the leading Turks, and even a degree of influence at the Seraglio. I had reason to believe him well disposed towards the English interests. . . . I made up my mind, therefore, to throw out a line for his co-operation . . . we agreed to meet. His house, at some considerable distance up the Golden Horn, was to be the scene of our interview. I promised to go at night, and he undertook to send his own boat for my conveyance. The night appointed for my visit chanced to be most boisterous. A strong north gale with driving rain blew down the harbour. I had to walk no small distance to the water, and then to embark alone on its troubled waves. On board I crouched in utter darkness under my umbrella.[29]

The meeting went off satisfactorily, and Vogorides became Stratford's intermediary with the Sultan, MacGuffog his go-between with the grand vizier, Reshid Pasha, who was currently in Albania but whose consent to the frontier modification of Greece would be essential. Urquhart, incidentally, had some, but not much, Turkish. Stratford himself, by some strange perversity of the will, never acquired any.

It is natural to wonder why the channels of communication were so carefully prepared for a task still bearing the signs of 'a fool's errand' and why, in particular, such care went into the establishment of a secret line to the Sultan when all the usual channels were still unrestrictedly open. The answer is that Stratford was looking far beyond the Greek question alone, and was excited by the unprecedented accessibility of the Sultan himself, of which he was told many stories.

There was also a change in Stratford's own approach to Ottoman statesmen. In previous stays at Constantinople, he was largely content to leave the cultivation of the *reis effendi* or the officers of the divan to the discretion of his dragomans, and to ease negotiations with gifts or trickles of secret service money, but British expenditure of this sort had never been great nor was much value placed on personal relations with the senior Ottomans. This is very apparent from the anonymity of the latter in Stratford's earlier dispatches and letters: he dealt with names, not with the men, until 1827. From 1832, there is a change, and he shows far greater acquaintance with the officials of the Porte as individuals. In the age of turbans and long robes, now quickly passing away, he left the group picture blurred and indistinct; in the new era of tight trousers, elasticated boots, and the fez, he focused the picture with greater care, and the faces and personalities came up more sharply in his correspondence. He also spent £1,500 on them in 1832 alone, a lot of money from the man who wanted the embassy rebuilt as cheaply as possible. The Sultan, however, was the main object of his interest.

Other embassies, notably the French, had always courted the Sultans more sedulously than the British, as in the case of Selim III and Sébastiani, but more recent and homely examples of royal accessibility for Stratford to notice were the attendance of Mahmud II at embassy receptions, and hunts in the Belgrade Forest with mixed parties of Ottomans and Europeans. Mahmud II's harem now sailed the Bosporus in open boats, no longer in close-latticed barges. Mahmud II danced with Baroness Ottenfels publicly, one of many acts of defiance against Muslim tradition which made the European colony wonder if he was 'cracked', to use Consul-General John Cartwright's description. Previously, cultivating the Sultan personally seemed as improbable and impertinent to Stratford as inviting the king of England to dinner, but in 1832 it suddenly appeared as the means of producing and controlling a transformation of the Ottoman state, rescuing it from religious fanaticism, social barbarism, and economic paralysis, and making of it a harmonious and prosperous empire strong enough to resist enemies and hold the respect of friends.[30]

Britain, the most economically advanced and politically sophisticated of European countries, would be the patient teacher, and the Ottoman Empire the tenacious pupil. It was an almost exact anticipation of Kipling's *White Man's Burden*, and at the personal and individual level, Stratford saw himself as mentor to the 'half devil and half child', Sultan Mahmud II. He was driven on by his own intense religiousness, by his high faith in the material and spiritual benefits of British civilization, and by the sheer magnificence of the challenge. Patriotism, too, was a prominent ingredient in his attitude, and it was patriotism of the most comprehensive sort. Britain was, preeminently, the land of 'progress', in every meaning of the word; the rising trajectory of her economic power drew up every virtue in its wake, encouraging in the individual the personal virtues of honesty, hard work, and self-discipline, and demanding from him a public sense of duty and responsibility to others. Stratford was always talking about 'duty', and for the great mass of mankind he meant the stoical duty of acceptance, while for the social and political élite he meant the duty to justify this trust. The Ottoman Empire could only be transformed for the better by following such an example, beginning, no doubt, by accepting the free-trading, economic policy of Britain. In no single document are the foregoing ideas woven together in complete fashion, but there is no shortage of letters and dispatches from which to assemble them. Two other possibilities for transplantation were never mentioned by Stratford. The first was constitutional government, since he saw no justification for transferring political power to the Sultan's subjects. The other was the invisible empire of culture, exempt from decay, 'the imperishable empire of our arts and our morals, our literature and our laws' which Lord Macaulay hoped would flourish in India.

The crux of everything was the sincerity of the Sultan as a reformer; many people were cynical of Mahmud II's capacity, as when an embassy employee told Stratford 'that there is something not quite right about the Sultan's mind I almost feel convinced of'. But even the scoffers were more than a little impressed by the possibility that 'Providence [might be] working a change in this extraordinary people by means of a madman'. Cartwright made the interesting point that he now hardly ever saw an Ottoman army officer over 30, and that they at least seemed to be entirely loyal, whatever old fanatics might think and do. The junior officers in the army, but a few prominent ministers too, were becoming recklessly western, and between them and the old guard of royal advisers a violent confrontation seemed inevitable, sooner or later. The dragomans told Stratford that older Ottoman pashas and their families, conservative but not bigoted people, were worried about the seeming collapse of private standards since 1826, and a former *reis effendi*, Mehmed Said Pertev, himself a reformer by nature, admitted to Pisani that the general populace was as fanatical and reactionary as ever and would give its support to anyone brave enough to defy Mahmud II. The Sultan himself seemed unconcerned: he 'pardons rebels, protects Christians, jokes with the dragomans, and makes love to his private secretary'.[31] At moments of unrest, he went to the barracks or the mosque where trouble had occurred, alone and unarmed, dispersing the trouble-makers with his irresistible dignity, and he made a point, as Abdulhamid II did after him, of coining stories and anecdotes to his own advantage, and circulating them in Constantinople. Not all of them were counterfeit, and it seems that he really did go incognito to the defaulters' prison at the Arsenal, only avoiding arrest by revealing the imperial decoration under his cloak. But to what extent the Sultan, however brave and daring in his own ways, remained a serious reformer, Stratford could not at first say,[32] and he was anxious to press Mahmud II to take up the war in Syria seriously, to settle the Greek frontier promptly, and to carry forward a programme of reforms, both military and civil, which would rescue the empire from the insubordination of pashas and dependence on doubtful European friends.

> I was received very graciously by the Sultan, and with circumstances of more than usual distinction. All the gentlemen with me were admitted into his presence and introduced separately to him, and he gave me a diamond snuff-box and a horse, &c. The box I hesitated to accept, but seeing a look of rising annoyance, I thought it best to take it, subject to the king's permission. I was right in supposing they were a little afraid of me from the recollection of past circumstances, and I have laboured hard to overcome the impression, and I really believe with the fullest success . . . you may therefore consider the outworks as carried, but a hard struggle remains for the citadel.[33]

Well before his audience with the Sultan, Stratford was receiving military information from the Porte about the war in Syria, and saying the outcome of the Greek negotiation seemed 'favourable'; a few days after it, he reported that the *reis effendi*, Suleyman Necib Bey, and the minister of war wished 'to sound me as to an *alliance*'.[34] In reply, Stratford sent the minister of war some suggestions for combating the Egyptian onslaught which had just been drawn up by Captain F.R. Chesney, newly arrived from his first navigational survey of the Euphrates.[35] He also managed to arrange a personal interview between Pisani and the Sultan, in which the latter was informed that the British ambassador 'trusted him to set things right about Greece'. The response was prompt enough, and the Greek conferences began in April. The frontier negotiation was concluded successfully by 21 July,[36] and it was the easiest negotiation of Stratford's entire career. The Sultan himself told

Ahmet Pasha of his pleasure that all had gone so well, and he made only a brief objection to the loss of Zeitoun, which Stratford overcame. The latter was highly gratified that 'a large and unexpected increase of the demands of the allies upon his territory' was accepted with such good grace, and he felt that his relations with the officials at the Porte so improved that 'the ancient feeling of affection towards Great Britain has greatly revived in the court and . . . cabinet in Constantinople'. The minister of war was particularly pro-British. In the same period, Stratford adopted a tone of disapproval of Muhammad Ali, and besides urging the kaptan pasha to adopt Chesney's plan of an attack on Alexandria, thus causing Ibrahim to withdraw from Syria, he advised the ruler of Egypt directly to capitulate and so prevent the enfeeblement of the empire of which he was supposed to be a senior viceroy.[37]

Palmerston, of course, recognized from an early stage that the outcome of the Greek negotiation would be affected by the Syrian war: 'This expedition of the pasha of Egypt must one should think render the Sultan a little more disposed to oblige us, as it shows him a nearer perspective of the possibility of wanting our aid.' But he was not ready to take sides between Mahmud II and Muhammad Ali just yet, and told Stratford not to go beyond expressing to Mahmud II 'our general wishes to maintain and uphold him, as an ancient ally and old friend, and as an important element in the balance of power in Europe'. The foreign secretary added that the pasha of Egypt had likewise been sent 'vague and general assurances of good will'. In the event that Russia were 'to try to bully him' (Mahmud II), Britain would hope that all the great powers would draw together to meet the situation.[38] So far as practical measures went, Palmerston concentrated on answering Stratford's plea for the prompt provision of a king for Greece, and in February that country's crown was finally offered to Prince Otto. The possibility of reforming and modernizing the Ottoman state was not, as yet, a topic of much interest to the foreign secretary, nor had Stratford any authority to discuss it formally. As has been seen, however, he had gone beyond Palmerston's neutrality over the Ottoman-Egyptian war, and the fall of Acre on 27 May, which caused a sensation at Constantinople and was 'whispered about for the twentieth time' before being confessed, led him to hint to Ottoman ministers more strongly than previously of the possibility of British help, and to urge a swift overhaul of the military departments as the first step in a general programme of reform.[39]

Stratford did not himself see Mahmud II between his audience on arrival and his audience of departure, nor did he often see Vogorides, to whom his ideas and instructions were carried by MacGuffog. Vogorides also had his own opinions and views, and he alone can have convinced Stratford that, far from being 'cracked', Mahmud II wished to undertake far-reaching reforms after the defeat of the Egyptians. Furthermore, he drew Stratford on to promise as much as he dared concerning eventual British aid, by revealing the Sultan's dire need and the existence of a fanatical group in the divan, led by Pertev Effendi, which was pressing hard for an accommodation with the ruler of Egypt. How Stratford shaped his case can be seen in the following typical letter, to MacGuffog:

Instead of having my feet in hot water [Stratford had a very persistent cough in 1832] I am sitting up to the chin in ink. A messenger came in from England this morning and has given me as much to do as my ride hitherto enables me to digest. It is now your turn to be tormented. Let our friend [Vogorides] know of the messenger, and tell him that I cannot give him a greater proof of confidence than by sending him the enclosed bulletin. Read it over to him, and if he wishes it, let him take notes of its contents, but I should not like him to have a copy of it.

Your next object – illustrious Plenipo! – must be to learn the impression made upon our friend's mind by the conversation of yesterday, and to ascertain what he has done, or means to do in the way of reporting. If he wishes to see it, and there be still time, I can send him some notes in aid of his report [to Mahmud II]; but I am inclined to think he will understand the proper mode of proceeding better than I do. In talking of this, you may let out that I had expected rather more from the proposed interview. No want of friendly expression, it is true, but I confess that I had expected something more distinct in the way of overtures to Great Britain and more of progress towards a settlement of the grand affair. I repeat that these delays are ruinous. Tell him it is because I want to see the Porte more free to advance his present system of improvement – favourable alike to the preservation of her own power, and to the happiness of her Christian subjects, that I am anxious for her to lose no time in coming to an agreement with us. I want to see her in a situation to receive the full tide of European civilization, to enlist the whole force of the country in support of its independence, to take her proper place in the general councils of Europe, and to base her military and financial systems on the only true foundations of security for persons and property. Beg of him to reserve this picture, and to imagine the Sultan wasting the remains of his strength in civil war with Egypt, alienating himself from his natural and most tried friends by rejecting their proposals, making himself unpopular at home by half-measures of innovation, without carrying them far enough to acquire confidence and sympathy abroad, and left to struggle as he best may in the coils which cunning aided by superior discipline has wound so dextrously around him. I say that it would be better for him to revive the janizaries, to resume the turbans and pelisses of ancient times, and to demand the restoration of Greece. The choice lies between *fanaticism* and *discipline*; there is no middle line.[40]

The letter illustrates well the almost subsidiary importance of the Greek frontier in Stratford's thinking: the Sultan, he argued, could not seriously withhold Europe's request when his empire stood in such dire need of help from a European source. And as Palmerston cautioned against offering anything beyond general good wishes, Stratford's purpose was to get Mahmud II to take the initiative by appealing directly to London for an alliance – hence the ambassador's need, expressed above, for 'something more distinct in the way of overtures', and his wish that the Ottomans should hurry 'in coming to an agreement with us'. After that, Stratford's views on *how* the Ottomans should be reformed were much more vague. The conclusion of the letter to MacGuffog, suggesting that the Sultan must either press forward or return to the days of the janizaries, was a prevalent idea in Constantinople at that time. The more debatable notion, that Mahmud II only needed to take the decision in order to 'receive the full tide of European civilization' (and Christian civilization at that), was peculiarly the ideal of Stratford, and of the Christian missionaries now about to put in an appearance in Ottoman lands. Old residents in the East were less confident that the dismantling of a theocratic empire was mainly an administrative task, or that Ottomans would, in the course of time, come to see and accept the moral superiority of Christianity over Islam. David Urquhart, very much under Stratford's influence at this time, but taking every opportunity to think and look for himself, was presently to repudiate his chief's ideas, and to seek a revival of Ottoman strength in a refurbishing, and not a jettisoning, of old Ottoman institutions, currently in decay or disuse. The

Urquhartian remedy was conceivably the best one. Most men who actually went to the Ottoman Empire thought so. But Stratford's remedy was the one which won most supporters for the empire in Britain, from men of action as well as visionaries, and the argument that Russia would obstruct Ottoman 'progress', because of her preference for a weak and incompetent neighbour, shaped the thinking of a generation and helped to provide the shouting majorities of the Crimean War.

Stratford kept up as steady a pressure upon Palmerston in London as upon the Sultan in Constantinople, reminding him of the strength of Russia's influence in the Ottoman Empire since Adrianople. The Russians were showing restraint, not pressing for the indemnity to which the treaty of Adrianople entitled them, and Stratford believed a secret treaty between the two countries was 'by no means impossible'. At the same time, he thought it impossible that Russia could have permanently relinquished her designs in Asia, and he sent home information, gathered by Urquhart, on the Russian penetration of Transcaucasia. 'The Russians, no doubt, act on a system in this country. Having obtained immense advantages by the late war, they may well be content to rest on their oars awhile. The game must be *bagged*, before the fire burns up again.' The Ottoman Empire, however, was stirring from a long sleep, and might yet save itself, or make itself worth saving by others.

> The Turks have undergone a complete metamorphosis since I was last here, at least as to costume. They are now in a middle state from turbans to hats, from petticoats to breeches. How far these changes may extend below the surface I will not take upon myself to say. . . . I know no conceivable substitute [for the empire's former strength] but civilization in the sense of Christendom. Can he [the Sultan] attain it? I have my doubts. At all events it must be an arduous and a slow process, if not an impracticable one. The chance would have been better, if it had been fairly taken before Navarin[o], and the treaty of London, and the Russian war. This was our daily entreaty to the Sultan, but he would not hear.

How could the transformation now be effected, and would it be in time? 'Can the Koran stretch to this point? Will the ever watchful Eagle of the North allow it? I should say "Yes" to the former question more readily than the latter. Meanwhile, *taxes, poverty,* and *discontentment.*' For the time being, however, Stratford felt the balance of influence was fairly well restored. Russian power was unquestionable, but British goodwill had been made clear and was, he believed, appreciated. The Russians certainly had no immediate plans to worry the British government: 'Think of our having a report that a Russian squadron is to come down to Constantinople.'[41] Stratford was quite sure the Russian squadron was merely sweeping the Black Sea for pirates.

Mahmud II was slow to take Stratford's advice, and the latter left Constantinople in August before Mavrojeni, the Ottoman chargé d'affaires in Vienna, set out for London to solicit a British alliance, but Stratford did all he could to prepare the way and ease the negotiation. In March 1832, before the Greek negotiation actually began, he informed Palmerston that 'the great end and aim of the Sultan's exertions is the formation of a military force, capable of maintaining his authority at home, and of enabling him to recover the station, which he has lost for the present, with respect to foreign countries'. He went on to suggest that

> the time is near at hand, or perhaps already has come, when it is necessary that a decided line of policy should be adopted and steadily pursued with respect to this country. The Turkish Empire is evidently hastening to dissolution, and an approach to the civilization of Christendom affords the only chance of keeping it together for any length of time.

A little later, in May, Palmerston was nudged again with the following:

> The Sultan and a few of his most favoured adherents are daily opening their eyes more and more to the weaknesses of this empire, and to the necessity of seeking support in some well-chosen foreign alliance, in order to obtain leisure for completing their military establishments, and counsel for proceeding with their present system of improvement on sound principles.

Anticipating the terrible alarm and confusion in Ottoman councils which was actually to prevail when Ibrahim Pasha, after besieging successfully the Acre citadel which had once defied Napoleon, began to advance on Constantinople, he hinted that unless Britain extended her hand to the Ottomans now, the Sultan might be driven into the arms of Russia in his search for protection. 'If ever they [the Ottomans] form an alliance with that power, fear and helplessness will drive them into it.' The spot where just such an alliance was to be signed in the forthcoming year of 1833, Unkiar Skelessi, was visible from Stratford's house, and the Russian ships, whose appearance in the Bosporus seemed to him an 'absurd' and remote chance in mid-1832, were actually there when his successor, Viscount Ponsonby, reached his post in 1833. Stratford's last dispatch of this mission, written on 9 August, only three days after his farewell audience with the Sultan, was on this same, most pressing, theme. This time, he said, an alliance had been solicited by the Sultan himself, and it was high time 'that those powers whose interests are at all involved in its [the Ottoman Empire's] fate should lose no time in adopting towards it a steady systematic course of policy in one sense or the other.' His greatest assault on Whig inaction was made in a famous memorandum, written on 19 December, after his return to London, and circulated among Cabinet ministers. It failed to budge them.[42]

The Greek negotiation, then, was unquestionably clinched by a strong, if unauthorized, intimation that British assistance would be available in the moment of crisis if Mahmud II asked London for it.[43] It was also helped along by the perennial Ottoman need for cash, and the Sultan's negotiators were forever balancing expected income from Greece against the indemnities owing to Russia. Hence they fussed very little over the loss of Acarnania, but bargained hard over the compensation for it. It was essentially Stratford's negotiation, and because of his secret dealings with the Sultan behind the scenes, it was also his success. He had Palmerston's authority to accept less than the Arta-Volo line, but managed to get all he had ever hoped for, except Crete. His colleagues, the French chargé d'affaires and the Russian envoy, were both under orders to let him take the lead, an arrangement which flattered his pride and which he could never quite believe genuinely reflected the attitudes of Paris and St Petersburg. By nature suspicious, he looked for secret Russian opposition to the enlargement of Greece. Yet the Frenchman was very pleasant and helpful, and he had to admit that the Russian, 'if he is instructed to deceive us . . . does it inimitably well'. He maintained his vigilance to the end, and came away convinced that his colleagues were not as innocent as they made out. They were not. Nor, of course, was Stratford. All three watched the unfolding Ottoman–Egyptian confrontation with keen interest. Stratford was so anxious to create an Anglo-Ottoman *entente*, and promote an alliance, that the Greek negotiation only received two pages in his voluminous memoirs; the French embassy supported him over Greece but privately strove for the role of mediator between the Sultan and his rebel viceroy; the Russian embassy, Stratford recalled, 'contradicted in the handsomest manner those sinister reports which prevailed on my arrival' at Constantinople.[44] The Russians watched the advance of Ibrahim Pasha to Homs, then Hama, then Aleppo, and finally through the defiles of the Taurus Mountains with close concern and, on the strength of reports from Constantinople, laid those plans for intervention which produced, first, the Muraviev mission and, next, the offer of armed aid to the Sultan.

Throughout the Greek negotiation, Stratford got much support from the tough and illiterate minister of war, Husrev, a pillar of the movement for military reform who was ready, with characteristic boldness, to see the Ottoman Empire cut her losses in Greece, and get on with the war in the south. But Husrev, a youthful 76, had his opponents, including the grand vizier, Reshid Pasha, whose conservative ways were already casting their spell over the impressionable Urquhart and, in the usual way, an immovable grand vizier could usually rely on the support of the ulema and the high ecclesiastical party.[45] Mahmud II himself, however, was quite prepared to surrender the debated lands north of Corinth, already largely populated by Greeks, mainly it appears because of the substantial amount of land there coming under the designation of *vakf*, and whose revenues he was anxious to appropriate to his own purposes. *Vakf* was land or property providing income, by way of rent or revenue, for religious purposes, and was ordinarily administered by religious men of appropriate status. Mahmud II, consciously following the example of Muhammad Ali in Egypt, was trying to divert all *vakf* revenues to the state treasury, and set up a special department of state to collect and administer them. Its director at the time of Stratford's 1832 mission was the pliant Elhaj Said Effendi, whose duty it was to value the *vakf* to be surrendered in Greece as highly as possible, so that his master could claim a proportionately large compensation.[46] The compensation as finally fixed was 40 million piastres, or about £450,000. Stratford briefly hoped Britain might agree to foot this bill, but it was Russia who finally did so, deducting it from the indemnity owed her by the Ottomans. By early July, Mahmud II had consented to give up the land, and the Turkish population was to return by the end of the year. The Ottoman ministers tried to write some extra advantages for their country into the settlement, such as a limitation of the Greek forces and, more absurdly, a decree that Greece should be neutral in wars involving the Ottoman Empire. Stratford simply consented to refer these to London, where they were rejected. The evacuation of the Turkish populations from Attica, Acarnania, and the islands was an untidy affair extending across some years, and the maps defining the frontier were not, in fact, exchanged before 1835.

At the end of his mission, Stratford sent out invitations to dinner to the officials with whom he had worked most closely, an arrangement he considered to be an innovation though Gordon had entertained senior officials before him. In accepting, Husrev asked Stratford to promote a new phase of Anglo-Ottoman cordiality, and at the actual dinner – which seems to have been overshadowed by the drinking – again pressed the matter of an alliance. To him, as to the *reis effendi*, Stratford promised to do his best to persuade the British government to support the Ottoman Empire 'so long as the system of the Porte tends to improvement founded on mildness, equity, and civilization'.[47]

On 6 August, he bade farewell to Mahmud II, whom he never saw again. He knew in advance that the Sultan proposed to send an agent to London to ask for an alliance 'and that the occasion would be used to apprize me of his Majesty's reliance on the good will of England'. Vogorides and Stratford crossed the Bosporus to meet the Sultan, who had no attendant at the interview. The details of what passed were never committed to paper, and Stratford left a record of the circumstances but little of the substance of the meeting beyond the fact of the request for an alliance. Mahmud II was very gracious, met Stratford standing up, and concluded the occasion by investing him with the highest Ottoman honour, the Sultan's portrait in a diamond-studded medallion, on a gold chain.[48]

Only Vogorides lifts the veil for us: in one of his last hasty notes to the departing ambassador, he wrote that Stratford had agreed to promote the alliance in return for the Sultan's promise to facilitate 'la question de la navigation et de la civilisation depuis la Golphe de Basra jusqu'aux environs de Halep'. Vogorides, having had ample opportunity to learn something of the proud and vain spirit of the British special envoy, phrased his farewell accordingly. 'Peut-être il est réservé au nom et à la famille de l'illustré Canning de devenir le moteur et l'organe d'un projet qui dans les temps réalisera la réunion des diverses communions dans cette partie du monde.'[49] By this, Vogorides meant the reunification of the Ottoman Empire in all its ancient vigour, and therefore the suppression of Muhammad Ali's dynasty.

While accepting the compliment as being no more than was his due, Stratford virtually broke with his Fanariot accomplice at the moment of his departure. Though he did not get Crete or Samos for Greece, he imagined that it was his own influence alone which got the latter island for Vogorides, who became its prince for the next 20 years, and Stratford was furious to discover that Vogorides was not ready to promulgate a constitution from the moment of his accession. There was no time to expostulate with the new prince, and Stratford had to content himself with bundling ashore an antique statue which Vogorides had presented to him, leaving it to MacGuffog to put things right with a man who had been at the very heart of the Greek negotiation throughout.[50] The episode is instructive: it typifies Stratford's egotism that he should have thought Mahmud II conferred the princedom of Samos on Vogorides to gratify the British envoy, and that he should minimize that great personal influence which Vogorides both previously and subsequently enjoyed at the palace; by the return of the statue, he offended and lost a valuable associate for the sake of an obscure and doubtful principle; but most serious of all is the expectation that Vogorides, on receiving the gift of Samos, should have provided his Greek subjects with a constitution, for this reveals Stratford as a man with a dangerously simple view of the world, also a man who could believe constitutions could be for Greeks but never Ottomans. Vogorides was not without his own ideals, as he later showed in the precarious fight to establish a Bulgarian church in Constantinople, and his neglect of his new charge after 1832 was preferable to the attentions Samos would have received from an Ottoman governor. His failure to grant the constitution Stratford wanted was attributed to deceit and despotic instincts, and it never occurred to the latter that it might be dangerous, futile, and even irrelevant, to try to promote such a cause. It is very possible that Vogorides accepted the sins of the world too easily. It is yet more certain that Stratford refused to compromise with the actual world in order to advance an ideal one.

He came home to Britain, having seen the beginnings of a transformation of the Ottoman Empire, and convinced by his interviews with Mahmud II that further dramatic and beneficent changes were at hand. The consuls, like R.W. Brant in Smyrna and Francis and James Charnaud in Salonika, were very pro-Ottoman and confirmed his optimism as often as they could. He had been loyal to the Greek policy of his cousin, been recalled when it was no longer fashionable, and finally carried it to its conclusion under the Whigs. But he was glad to escape from it now, and significantly told the *reis effendi* before leaving Constantinople that the Greek settlement made it possible for Britain again to resume her 'former liberty' regarding relations with the Ottoman Empire. During the Greek revolt, humanitarian feeling came before all political calculation: whatever else, complacent reactionaries could not be allowed to grind the rebels back into the ground. The later, unheroic squabbles of free Greece, however, did much to restore his fundamental respect for authority, even Ottoman authority, so long as it maintained itself by decent and civilized means, and when he got home he found himself sufficiently in disagreement with Whig theorizing about governmental authority to commence that rightward movement which was soon to take him into the ranks of the conservative supporters of Peel. Tory foreign policy had been fossilized; Whigs in home affairs seemed too headstrong, with the aristocrats unable to restrain the radicals and the theorists. The Canningites did not carry the weight he originally hoped for, except in the one sphere of foreign affairs, where Palmerston seemed to have a free hand. And in that sphere, Stratford hoped it might be possible to initiate a new phase in Eastern policy, in which the old Tory instinct for aiding the Ottomans might be rationalized along lines the reformist Whigs would approve. Russophobia was making strides in Britain in 1832, and stood in no need of the returning minister's advocacy. But Turcophilism needed a firmer justification than this, if it was to become a positive sentiment in Britain.

How justified was Stratford's optimism about the Ottoman Empire, and what, to date, had Mahmud II achieved? In 1826, he destroyed the janizaries, justified his action in a printed book, deposed a *Shaykh ul-Islam* who resisted him, entrusted the formation of his new army to Husrev Pasha who, as war minister, abolished traditional flowing uniforms and put his new soldiers into jackets, breeches, boots, and the fez. But these achievements, like the suppression of the dervishes, were contributions to the establishment of royal authority, itself the true preliminary to reform, and it remained to be seen what else Mahmud II would attempt. When Stratford first arrived in 1832, he learned that the *vakf* were being taken over, to strengthen the imperial financial resources, and there were rumours that a census was in hand, as a means for exacting men and taxes from the people on a more systematic basis. There was even a newspaper, *Takvimi Vekayi*, and there was also a new medical school. A few army cadets had been to France for officer-training, and in the Ottoman capital itself a school of military music was opened under Donizetti Pasha, brother of the famous composer.[51] The *Moniteur Ottoman*, the official gazette, besides being published in French, was introducing its readers to a wider world – *Voyage aux chutes de Niagara* runs a headline – and providing local news and gossip about personalities. These beginnings convinced Stratford of Mahmud II's sincerity and wisdom, and he was greatly impressed by the decline of fanaticism in the streets of Constantinople. A European could now wander in the bazaars, even penetrate the slave-market, unmolested.

Other observers were less impressed,[52] and preferred to wait for weightier evidence of true regeneration. Mahmud II's most important measures were still in the future in 1832. It is also of note that Mahmud shared Stratford's optimistic inclination to minimize the difficulties that lay ahead, and shared, too, his failure to calculate the possible effects on a superstitious, bigoted people of western ideas and innovations. Mahmud II had been brought up within the confines of the palace, and knew little of the world of real men. It is no surprise that a despot accustomed to having his way within a small circle, and an idealistic diplomat who never saw beneath the superficialities of Eastern life, exaggerated what the will of one man might achieve, whenever it turned upon the problems of an entire society. Of Mahmud II, Slade was later to write, he 'took the mask for the man, the rind for the fruit', and he went on to explain that his 'blind adoption of forms' created disgust and anger among a people to whom they were utterly alien. Stratford, likewise, did not examine the situation with sufficient care and found the 'blind adoption of forms' enormously promising. The sight of the royal harem in open boats was for him 'a strong indication of the Sultan's intention to proceed still further with his present system of reform', and he said every Ottoman minister he knew personally wanted to exchange 'the civilization of Christendom for the bigotry of an exclusive and sanguinary disease'.[53] It is difficult to take this seriously, and perhaps Stratford just did not recognize courtesy and restraint when they were presented to him. He was overjoyed at the sight of Ottomans in European clothes, and it required an Ottoman to warn him that the people themselves were no different. He spoke of 'la question de navigation et de la civilisation' with disarming confidence, and had some hazy image of the Eastern peoples standing at the knee of a mother-figure who would raise them in Christian as well as western ways. Yet even Mahmud II intended to be selective about what he took from Europe, though Stratford never saw it, and a speech the Sultan made in 1838 on the opening of a new medical school admonished the students: 'You will study scientific medicine in French . . . my purpose in having you taught in French is not to educate you in the French language; it is to teach you scientific medicine and little by little to take it into our language.'[54]

In Britain, Stratford was asked soon after his arrival to comment on the pro-Egyptian opinions of Samuel Briggs, head of a British firm which argued that the Whigs ought to support Muhammad Ali in his Syrian adventure, as a truly enlightened Oriental reformer. Knowing that Mavrojeni was soon due in London, Stratford replied:

> I agree with him [Briggs] that the pasha of Egypt's enterprize has an immediate bearing on our foreign interests, and you are aware of my opinion that the present state of Turkey requires to be considered by Govt. [sic] deliberately and comprehensively with the least possible delay. But I cannot quite understand how the Sultan's dominions are to be made a more efficient barrier against Russia by the loss of Syria and Egypt.

Muhammad Ali was a reformer, to be sure, but as 'the pasha intends to reorganize his state on the Mussulman principle, it is clear that Christianity and civilization have most to hope for from his Imperial competitor'. Stratford also challenged Briggs' contention that Muhammad Ali would be content with Syria alone, and if Britain did *not* rescue the Sultan, what could be more convenient for Russia? Briggs maintained a pertinacious championship of Muhammad through a series of interviews at the Foreign Office for several months more, but the opinions of Stratford and an array of other experts on the East slowly moved Palmerston into the Sultan's camp.[55]

Stratford returned to London in a minor blaze of glory and congratulation. Palmerston was very pleased with his 'successful and brilliant mission', and Gally Knight had 'a great mind to write the *Canningiad*, an epic in 20 books, to give it immortality'.[56] William IV sent a special letter of approval to the man who was now the doyen of his diplomatic corps, and a peerage could not be far off. Inevitably, the shelved problem of appointing Stratford to St Petersburg was taken up again, and as anti-Russian feeling in Britain had hardened during the intervening year, the previous inclination to oblige the tsar was perceptibly diminished. On 29 September, Grey himself wrote to Palmerston: 'We must now hold very firm language there, and the sooner Stratford Canning can go the better.'[57] On 15 October, the king heartily endorsed the proposed appointment, and on 30 October it was announced in the *London Gazette*. Stratford had the gratification of knowing that Nesselrode hinted that he would welcome Sir Robert Gordon, but that Palmerston had refused to send him. Nevertheless, it is a little hard to understand why Gordon, an energetic pro-Ottoman, would have been preferred to Stratford, who worked faithfully at Poros and the Porte with his Russian colleagues.

There were some men beginning to discern in Stratford a watchful guardian of British interests in the East, such as Chesney, who was now in Britain, and who wrote,

> I am glad of what is in the Gazette for your sake, and I may add John Bull's, who will (if I mistake not) know *what the Bear is about*, and be a match for his course amidst the rocks and lairs of northern politics; and I am only sorry that your Excellency cannot be, like Sir Boyle Roche's bird, in two places at once – Stamboul as well as Petersburg.[58]

But it was not fear of the hunter that caused the Bear to reject Stratford, as Lane-Poole romantically suggests, and while the government never clearly revealed why it would not have Stratford, the balance of the existing information on the question, and particularly the correspondence of John Bligh, the chargé d'affaires at St Petersburg, suggests strongly that neither Nicholas I nor Nesselrode nor Orlov nor the patriotic party at court wanted a relative of Canning, and, *ipso facto*, an arch-critic of neo-Holy Alliance policies in Europe, badgering them over Belgium and other international questions. Nesselrode spoke of the 'temper and *touchiness* of which . . . we should have to witness instances every day', and the Lievens advised him to stand firmly against the appointment 'and teach these islanders manners'. The princess said Palmerston had promised her in 1831 never to raise Stratford's name again, which the foreign secretary strenuously denied, and she tried to extract from Grey the desired revocation. Prince Lieven said he had authority to offer Stratford one of the highest decorations of the Russian empire if the nomination was suppressed, but Grey stood firm, and said the offer 'did not accord well with the objection now made to Canning'. At the end of January 1833, a formal notification arrived from Russia to the effect that Stratford would not be received. By then, Stratford was in Spain on a temporary mission, and over the intervening miles, he stolidly refused to give up his Russian appointment, saying his 'good name' was at stake, and had already suffered enough. In May, he came home again, went over all the arguments with Palmerston, and once more stood firm. Yet in light of the Russian attitude, he cannot have wanted to go to St Petersburg except to win the game of principle, and it was presumably with his consent that Palmerston made a final offer through Bligh to withdraw Stratford after a short time if only the tsar would accept him temporarily.[59]

It failed, and on 18 July, Stratford was told that neither he nor any other ambassador was going to represent Britain in Russia. Bligh would stay on as chargé d'affaires. To his friend, Planta, Stratford expressed his mystification at the Russian attitude, but added, 'Palmerston is ready to do anything for the protection of my *character* and *interests*', a reference, perhaps, to his own request that Palmerston should get him a peerage from Grey. Planta, himself a sturdy Russophobe, took the same line as Chesney, and wrote in his solacing reply:

> After much reflection, I cannot conceive a reason why the E. of R. should take this line, except this: that having now his chief attention turned on Turkey [this was the month of Unkiar Skelessi], he does not wish to have as ambassador with him from this country one who is thoroughly acquainted with the whole policy of Russia towards Turkey, who best knows the remaining resources of the Porte, if she have any, and who has already dealt with and thwarted Russia in her earlier transactions with Turkey. Now these are the qualities which make you the fittest man in England now to fill the embassy to Russia, and is it not somewhat too bad then that *they* should be permitted to *prevent* your going there? . . . As to this producing the recall of the Lievens, Gioia, gioia! if it does.[60]

The incident was over. Russia did not get a British ambassador, Stratford did not get a peerage from Grey, and in 1834, the tsar withdrew the Lievens. Stratford resumed his experimentation with a parliamentary career as a 'liberal conservative' for King's Lynn from 1834 until 1841. He spoke rarely, and very rarely well. The Eastern Question brought him forth only once, in 1838 when he moved for a select committee on the *Vixen* episode. Yet in December 1832, when the dispute over his nomination to St Petersburg was at its height, he submitted a memorandum for the consideration of the Grey cabinet, which shows in its contents an increasing preoccupation with the Eastern Question, and an anxious desire that Britain should become its arbiter.

The memorandum was written under, for Stratford, very trying circumstances. It was penned in Paris, when he was on his way to Spain, and at a time when he would have much preferred to stay in London to assist Mavrojeni, just arrived in London to plead for an Anglo-Ottoman alliance. An alliance was perhaps not to be expected, but British naval help was a possibility. In the Levant, the Egyptians were approaching the climax of their successful campaign, and the Ottomans sustained the great defeat at Konya on 21 December, two days after Stratford sent off his memorandum to London. Of Palmerston's sympathy for the Ottoman cause, Stratford was in no doubt, and his own sentiments, even his phrases, echo in the following letter from the foreign secretary to Earl Granville:

I think it in the general interest of all Europe except Russia to uphold the Sultan's power against the pasha. The Turk is a better reformer than the Egyptian because the first reforms from principle and conviction and from political motives, the second merely upon a mercantile speculation. But Mehmet Ali should still be left in possession of Egypt and if he wants to extend himself let him go up the Nile.[61]

But others in the Cabinet were more pro-Egyptian, or at least more doubtful of the Ottoman Empire's hopes of survival. Holland was for encouraging Muhammad Ali, while Grey himself thought the collapse of the Ottoman Empire 'nearly certain'. Mavrojeni's appeal for naval aid or alliance was refused in London before the news of Konya arrived. Stratford's memorandum and the news of the battle were both available to the Cabinet when Namik Pasha, of the Ottoman Imperial household, followed up Mavrojeni's failure with a second plea for help in January 1833.

The memorandum runs as follows:

The Turkish Empire has reached, in its decline, that critical point, at which it must either revive and commence a fresh era of prosperity, or fall into a state of complete dissolution. To Great Britain the fate of this empire can never be indifferent. It would affect the interests of her trade and East Indian possessions, even if it were unconnected with the maintenance of her relative power in Europe. Nearer and more pressing duties may forbid His Majesty's government to take an active part in the contest which now agitates Turkey; but the issues of a struggle so likely to prove decisive of the Sultan's independence, can hardly be overlooked and left to chance on any sound principles of English policy.

Often as the Sultan and his predecessors have had occasion to maintain their authority by force of arms, they have always done so with ultimate success, except in the recent instance of the Greeks. But the Egyptian war, though originating in the same vicious system of government, which has caused so many convulsions in Turkey, is far more dangerous to the Porte than any preceding rebellion, whether it be considered with reference to the character and resources of Mehemet Ali, or to the difficulties of the Sultan's position. The pasha, however, if he succeed in the end, will not be able to carry his point without a severe and protracted contest. Already overstrained by his exertions, he can only sustain them by imposing additional burdens on Egypt and Syria, increasing thereby the hazard and odium inseparable from the prosecution of this enterprise. His sovereign, who has publicly branded him as a rebel and outlaw, is urged by the strongest motives to reject such terms of compromise as, on any probable supposition, it would agree with the views or safety of the pasha to offer of his own accord. If Mehemet Ali be superior in point of capacity, if he can dispose more completely of the resources of his country, and exhibit a higher degree of discipline in his fleet and army, the Sultan, on the other hand, has those advantages, which belong to an acknowledged right, and a greater extent of territory. He cannot be blind to the consequences of allowing his vassal to form a separate sovereignty within the limits of his empire. The erection of Syria and Egypt into an independent state would in fact cut off the communication between Constantinople and Mecca, and while it weakened Mahmoud's title to the Caliphate, would place the most important parts of Arabia and Mesopotamia under the control of his enemy.

The extraordinary progress made by Ibrahim Pasha during the last campaign has given rise to an idea that the capital itself is not beyond his reach. In Turkey no kind or description of revolution is impossible. But the Egyptian army has paused in its career. The Sultan has had time to repair, in some measure, his losses; and the grand vizier at the head of a considerable force, composed in part of new levies, and partly of the Albanian troops, which he commanded with so much credit in Bosnia, will afford a rallying point for the remains of the army defeated under Hussein Pasha, and, if not strong enough to attack the Egyptian cantonments, will at least be able to make a stand in the fastnesses of Mount Taurus. But let us suppose an extreme case. The vizier, no doubt, may experience the fate of his predecessor; his army may be dispersed; the country may rise in favour of the Egyptians; and Ibrahim Pasha, encouraged by these circumstances, may possibly follow up his victory even to the shores of the Bosporus, and dictate the most humiliating terms to the Sultan.

In this case one of two results would be unavoidable. The Sultan must either abandon his throne altogether, or consent to such a reduction of his empire as would leave Mehemet Ali in permanent possession of Egypt and Syria with all the country behind those provinces as far as the Persian frontier. Supposing the triumphant viceroy to occupy and maintain himself on the vacant throne of Constantinople, it is evident that he would be placed towards the powers of Europe in the same position as the Sultan, with the additional weakness belonging to an usurped title, and the necessity of flattering the religious prejudices of the Turks. The interests of England and of Christendom would gain little by such a change. Whatever price the chief of a new dynasty would be willing to pay for recognition, could equally be obtained from the reigning Sultan in return for support and co-operation. Supposing the contest to terminate in the formation of a separate government under the sceptre of Mehemet Ali or of Ibrahim Pasha, the Sultan, deprived of so large a portion of his empire, and degraded in the opinion of his subjects, would find it more difficult than ever either to make head against the encroachments of Russia, or to carry on that system of improvement, which is become essential to the maintenance of his independence.

If the contending parties were left to themselves, it is but too probable that a long and arduous war would drain their respective resources, and, by adding another cause of desolation to those which have long worn down the Turkish Empire, render it an easy prey to the first invader. Nor is it in this respect alone that a protracted contest in the Mediterranean provinces of Turkey would be detrimental to European interests. The necessities of both parties would oblige them to employ every kind of extortion and violence injurious to life and property, and it is difficult to conceive how commerce more than civilization could expand, or even exist, under such a pressure.

So many indeed and great are the evils which this contest is likely to generate in its progress, that it becomes a duty to enquire by what means Great Britain, either alone or in concert with any of her allies, may best contribute to hasten its termination. No pretext for interference is wanting. The Sultan and the pasha have both appealed to the friendly and equitable disposition of the British cabinet, but with this difference, that the former applies for our assistance, and the latter for our mediation. It is not surprising that the Sultan, whose honour and independence are at stake, should look for succour to that power, which has once already been the instrument of restoring Egypt to the Porte; nor is it less natural, that Mehemet Ali should reckon, however erroneously, upon Great Britain for the means of securing to him that independence, of which the Greek insurrection has probably given him the idea and the occasion.

Unfortunately this very consideration indisposes the Sultan to every kind of foreign interference unaccompanied with a moral or physical co-operation in his favour. He must necessarily feel that his plain unquestionable interest is to put down the pasha of Egypt, and to re-establish his own authority in that province and Syria. What he wants is the effectual aid of Great Britain for the accomplishment of this purpose, and there is little doubt, that, if His Majesty's government could find in the present circumstances of the Turkish Empire adequate motives for acceding to this request, the presence of a British squadron would suffice to ensure success. [Or. *Is even this quite certain?*]

The principal difficulties, with which the Sultan has to contend in directing his operations against Mehemet Ali, arise out of the distant and insulated position of Egypt, the ease with which Syria can be defended against an army invading it from the north, and the disadvantage of having a fleet, which though superior in numerical force to that of Egypt is by no means so well manned and manoeuvred.

With the assistance of a British squadron there is great reason to believe that the Sultan would easily surmount these obstacles. Instead of attacking the Egyptian forces in Syria, he might send an expedition by sea against Egypt itself. To the east of Damietta the coast affords facilities for landing troops, and an invasion properly directed on that side would not only compel Ibrahim Pasha to retreat, but would also menace Cairo, and bring into the field all those, who, secretly attached to the Sultan's cause, are nevertheless kept down at present by the want of support and the fear of punishment.

Whatever just or insuperable objections may be raised on the score of expense, or on any other account, to the participation of Great Britain in this measure, the probable result of it would be beneficial in no small degree to her interests. The very attempt, indeed, would give her an important influence in the counsels of the divan. That influence would operate most powerfully in promoting the progress of reform and civilization throughout Turkey; and the spirit of improvement, thus encouraged and directed, could hardly fail to revive the overlaid resources of a country so rich in natural advantages. [*We rescued Egypt once for Turkey. We acquired, or supposed that we acquired influence in this divan. What was the beneficial result? Certainly no progress in civilization or reform nor any such improvement of Turkish measures as is here contemplated.*] The treaty of alliance, which would naturally be formed to regulate the operations of the combined forces, and to provide for the reception and refreshment of the British squadron, might also contain stipulations in favour of any specified concession desired to indemnify our merchants at Alexandria for any losses arising out of the participation of Great Britain in the contest. The Sultan's pardon and a suitable provision for Mehemet Ali and his son Ibrahim, in the event of their overthrow, might be secured by means of the same instrument.

It is obvious, that, as far as Great Britain is concerned, the only ground on which this plan could be recommended, is the necessity of interfering to rescue the Turkish Empire from a war, which threatens to lay it at the feet of a power already too great for the general interests and liberties of Europe. [*This is most just and true.*] It is impossible at the same time to contemplate such a necessity without an increased feeling of regret that a contest fraught with such consequences should ever have commenced; and hence arises an anxious desire to discover some means of restoring matters, as nearly as may be practicable, to the state in which they stood before the pasha's attempt upon Acre.

If it be true, as the Sultan alleges, that Mehemet Ali has embarked in an enterprise of mere ambition; if he has taken advantage of his sovereign's embarrassments with the sole view of establishing an independent sovereignty for himself, and his family, there is evidently no middle course; he must either succeed altogether or fail altogether. [*Do not see that this conclusion follows from the premises.*] The question in that case is, whether the object of enabling the Sultan to hasten the conclusion of the war by an attack upon Egypt, be sufficient to overbalance the objections which His Majesty's government may entertain in general to extending their interference in foreign quarrels. Of their right to interfere upon an invitation from the Sultan there can be no doubt; and it is probable that the mode of interference suggested above would prove effectual.

But to judge impartially of the viceroy's motives, we must call to mind the situation in which he was placed before his expedition into Syria. The main object of the Sultan's internal policy throughout his reign has been the suppression of all minor authorities, which had acquired in any degree an abusive power of checking his own. [*Is authority built on the forcible suppression of minor authorities – and if not, in what would the pasha's usurped authority differ from the Sultan's, if successful, but in degree? Both would be usurpation.*] Having destroyed the janizaries, who formed the great obstacle to his designs, and having reconciled himself to the loss of Greece, that perilous bone of contention between him and Christendom, his views were turned to the establishment of a more regular system of administration in the provinces of his empire, and to the cultivation of a better understanding with the powers of Europe, and principally with Great Britain. Such being the case, it is far from improbable that Mehemet Ali may have looked with apprehension to the moment, when measures arising out of this policy would be applied to Egypt, which he had advanced, during an administration of twenty years, from a state of confusion and comparative poverty, to a degree of improvement, in point of order and production, which filled his coffers, and placed him at the head of a considerable military and naval force. He might have thought that the Sultan's designs, coinciding with his necessities, would shortly lead to the spoliation of these fruits of his eminent capacity for government, and therefore that it would be better to avail himself of the latter, while there was yet time, in order to increase his means of resisting the execution of the former at his expense. Upon this supposition prudence and not ambition would be the motive of his conduct; security, rather than aggrandizement, his object. In a question of so much difficulty and complication, it may, therefore, be worth while to ascertain how far a reasonable security, consistent with what is due to the rights and character of the Sultan, might by possibility be obtained from him by means of British interference.

To go at once to the point, it is clear that the pasha cannot be left in possession of Syria, on any imaginable terms whatever, without a considerable loss of credit, if not of strength, to the Sultan's government. His right to retain possession either of Syria or of Egypt without the Sultan's consent can only be the right of force. [*What other has the Sultan?*] The obvious inference is that no arrangement intended to give security to the pasha can be fairly proposed to the Porte, unless it be attended with the recall of the Egyptian forces from Syria. Nor is it likely that any proposal would prove effectual, which should not be accompanied with a distinct understanding as to the amount of revenue, and the contingent of troops and ships that the pasha would be ready henceforward to hold at the Sultan's disposal, in consideration of his continuing to hold the viceroyalty of Egypt for life, and co-operating with the Sultan for the advancement of those plans of reform, upon the execution of which the best and only hope of maintaining the independence of the Turkish Empire, and improving the condition of its inhabitants, may be truly said to depend. An arrangement comprising these points, and concluded under the sanction, though not necessarily with the guarantee, of Great Britain, might be expected to allay the pasha's apprehensions, supposing his present conduct to have originated rather in them than in any ambitious impulse. But in order to reconcile the Sultan's mind to a transaction which, at best, would be far from palatable to a prince of his temper and policy, something more than the recollection of his disasters in the late campaign would be necessary. He would no doubt expect of Great Britain to declare herself openly in favour of his cause, and to follow up that declaration with measures tending to uphold his authority in the eyes of his subjects, and to facilitate his operations against the Egyptian forces. The most obvious measures of this description are a prohibition to His Majesty's subjects to convey provisions or warlike stores to Egypt and Syria [*i.e. with a view to remote and precarious advantages to our commerce, to begin by cramping and prohibiting that which exists with Egypt and Syria*], the establishment of cruisers on the coast to prevent the importation of those articles, the recall of all British subjects serving under the pasha, an arrangement for introducing engineers and naval officers into the Sultan's service, and a refusal to acknowledge the Egyptian flag. To these might be added such diplomatic proceedings at the courts of Persia and Greece, and at Baghdad, and in those parts of Syria which are not actually occupied by Ibrahim Pasha, as would counteract the intrigues of Mehemet Ali, and contribute to the promotion of the Sultan's interests in those quarters.

Great Britain by adopting these measures, or measures like these, might perhaps be able to gain in a sufficient degree the confidence of the Sultan; but much would still remain to be done in order to bring the viceroy of Egypt into an arrangement on the above mentioned terms. It would be necessary, in the first place, to extinguish his hope of our consenting to the accomplishment of his schemes of independence, in the second, to provide in some degree for Ibrahim Pasha's interests, and, in the third, to soften his mortification at the loss of Syria by making some change in the authorities of that country more acceptable to him than the reinstatement of those whom he has forcibly removed. On the second and third of these points, it would of course be advisable to consult the views and feelings of the viceroy himself, but as far as conjecture may be hazarded, it is not impossible that an immediate transfer of the government of Candia to Ibrahim Pasha, or a promise of the reversion of that of Eygpt to him during his life time on the same conditions under which it is proposed that Mehemet Ali should hold it in future, would be satisfactory on that point; and that as to Syria, the Sultan might be induced to consign the pashalic of Acre to one of Mehemet Ali's grandsons, provided no Egyptian troops were allowed to remain there, and that the fortress of Acre were garrisoned by a detachment of the Sultan's guard, and commanded by a governor enjoying his confidence.

The effect of this plan, if it were carried into execution, would be to restore the matters in question as nearly as possible to their former state. It is grounded on the threefold persuasion that nothing but absolute necessity would induce the Sultan to consent to the union of the two provinces of Egypt and Syria under Mehemet Ali; that his efforts to avert that necessity would exhaust his resources, and render the independence of his empire still more precarious than now; and, finally, that His Majesty's government might either find insuperable objections to co-operating with the Sultan by means of an auxiliary squadron, or, at all events, that they would prefer withholding that kind of assistance until the experiment of milder measures had been made without success. The very apprehension of their recurring eventually to such an extremity would doubtless contribute to produce in the viceroy's mind a disposition favourable to the acceptance of their proposals.

How far it may be practicable to render the proposed alliance respecting Egypt, on either of the preceding suppositions, available to the acquisition of any exclusive advantage for Great Britain, is by no means so clear as the benefit which would in all probability accrue from it to the general interests of Europe and of Turkey itself. It is not to be doubted that our support, and more particularly our assistance under such circumstances, would secure the confidence and gratitude of the Sultan, and that he would be ready to make any reasonable sacrifice in return for such important aids. But the Porte is so bound by her treaties with the principal European powers, that no commercial privilege granted to one could long be withheld from the others, and it would be difficult to point out any special object of interest not coming under that head, unless it were the grant of certain facilities for navigating the River Euphrates by steam, with a view to the promotion of a more direct intercourse with India; the feasibility of which very important project, though probable in the highest degree, has not yet been submitted to actual experiment; or the privilege of obtaining ship-timber from the extensive forests of Turkey, which could only be of value to Great Britain in the event of her being engaged in a naval war in some degree similar to the last. But it stands to reason that the same motives which induce the Sultan to court an alliance with Great Britain would render the existence of that alliance favourable to the promotion of our interests in Turkey. Nor can it be a British and a European object not to uphold the Turkish Empire as a barrier against encroachments from the north, and if the Sultan's independence be endangered by the changes of a contest indefinitely prolonged against Egypt, and the consequent interruption of measures essential to its maintenance, there are sufficient motives for acceding, under proper restrictions, to the Sultan's overture without the additional inducement of a special or exclusive British interest.

Another part of the subject remains to be examined, and it is one which embraces such various and extensive considerations as scarcely to find place in a memoir grounded on the presumed facility of access to local information. The question of British interference in the Egyptian contest is, however, indissolubly connected with the policy of other courts respecting Turkey. Nor is it possible to arrive at a satisfactory conclusion on the subject, without referring in some measure to the opposition or concurrence which Great Britain would have to expect from them in the event of her determining to support the Sultan's cause, or to offer her mediation between him and the pasha of Egypt. But it is by no means necessary to go over the whole ground of inquiry on this occasion. What can be stated with some degree of confidence, or prospect of utility, it is not difficult to bring within a narrow compass.

There is no doubt that the Sultan would in any emergency look with preference to the counsels or assistance of Great Britain. No Christian state ranks so high in his estimation either for power, or for good faith. If England were to take up the affair of Egypt in concert with France, he would not perhaps reject their joint interference accompanied with the support of his cause, but in all probability he would only consent to it from deference to His Majesty's government. Many acts of France during the last forty years, concluding with the occupation of Algiers, have rendered the Porte extremely mistrustful of that power. The concurrence of France in the supposed case could therefore be desirable to Great Britain, only as it might tend to allay jealousy, or enable her to operate more effectually on the pasha of Egypt. The motives which at present prevail with the French ministers to cultivate the good-will and confidence of England, might possibly suffice to reconcile them to her single interference in the affairs of Turkey; but the counteraction, however disguised, of a power like France could hardly fail to increase the difficulties already existing, and it is well known that the French cabinet has long regarded the Levant, and Syria and Egypt in particular, with more than common interest. [*Surely it would be very strange if it did – should we be easily reconciled to the single interference of France? Yet France is not by position and actual connection more directly interested in Turkish affairs than ourselves?*]

Of the two remaining powers, whose disposition with respect to Turkey is of any immediate consequence, Austria would no doubt behold with satisfaction the influence and energy of Great Britain employed in support of the Sultan's authority and the preservation of his empire from dismemberment. It is equally clear that a similar interference for such purposes could never be agreeable to Russia, although the feelings, which it would be likely to excite in that quarter, might soften in proportion as British influence was pointed to the overthrow of rebellion; and the court of St. Petersburg, though no less adverse to our interference than to the Sultan's application for it, could hardly, with due regard to its own principles and professions of peace, step forward to *oppose* its exercise. [*Perhaps not, but would she or could she be entirely neutral and passive on such an occasion – America is not glanced at but she has commerce in those parts and by interfering will sanction her right of interfering too.*]

To return to the main question, there is no denying that whether it be contemplated with reference to a single or to a joint interference, the difficulties are great, the hazards considerable. In one respect, however, the prospect is clear. Let Mehemet Ali succeed in constituting an independent state, and a great and irretrievable step is made towards the dismemberment of the Turkish Empire. That empire may fall to pieces at all events; and he must be a bold man who would undertake to answer for its being saved by any effort of human policy. But His Majesty's government may rest assured that to leave it to itself is to leave it to its enemies.[62]

This memorandum, assembling in one document the various arguments submitted by Stratford to his government during the earlier months of 1832, failed in its main purpose, to produce a British intervention in the war in the Levant. Namik Pasha, like Mavrojeni, was sent away empty-handed. Penned in December, the memorandum had come before the Grey Cabinet at an unpropitious moment, for a general election took place that very month in Britain. Although the Whigs emerged with 320 seats against the Tories' 150, there were two other substantial groups to be considered, the Radicals and the Irish members, each about 70 strong: neither would give Grey a blank cheque for military expenditure. If there was money to spare, there were causes at home to absorb it, and the Sultan was unlikely to take precedence over the chance to cut the poor-rate, the imminent possibility of having to compensate the Anglican establishment in Ireland or the West Indian plantocracy for inroads upon their power and status, the relief of thousands of families in Britain ravaged in 1832 by cholera, or the cost of projected municipal reforms.

From the tactical point of view, too, the Tories would savage a ministry, sprinkled with former philhellenes, the moment it asked for a naval augmentation to assist the Ottomans. Inside the Cabinet, a few who hailed with pleasure 'the untoward event' of Navarino in 1827, remained true to former sentiments, and were readier to see Muhammad Ali become the strong man in the Levant than colleagues who saw Russia as the more likely beneficiary of an Ottoman collapse. But the men who guessed the outcome of events most accurately were too slow to act, and only Palmerston was ready to take his fears of a Russian intervention in the East to a logical conclusion, and demand parliamentary support for a swift naval action in the Mediterranean. Nothing was done, and as he told Ponsonby later on, 'a postponed decision became practically a negative'.[63]

This was the more unfortunate as Russia, as well as Austria and France, were expecting a British lead. When none was forthcoming, and with Ibrahim Pasha within a few days' march of the important city of Bursa, the Russian ambassador at Constantinople was ordered to proffer Russian ships and men to the Sultan, while General Muraviev travelled to Egypt to express the tsar's displeasure. The offer of help was accepted. On 4 February, a fast cutter dashed from the Bosporus to bring Russian warships from Sebastopol, and the first of these dropped anchor in the Golden Horn on the 20th. The protests of the French chargé d'affaires were cut short with the unanswerable Turkish proverb: He who falls in the sea embraces even a serpent. The Egyptian advance was halted, and an accommodation arranged between the Sultan and the rebel pasha by the convention of Kutahiya in April. The Russian warships were withdrawn and the tents of the Russian regiments melted away from the Asiatic headlands of the Bosporus. But from 1833 until 1841, the Ottoman Empire was considered, in Paris and London, to be a mere Russian protectorate, with Mahmud II reduced to the humiliating role of an obsequious doorkeeper of the Straits. This relationship was believed to have been established by the treaty of Unkiar Skelessi, signed in July 1833: it was Russia's pound of flesh for staving off the Egyptian onslaught. Looking back over the details of this swift change in the balance of influence at Constantinople, Palmerston pronounced British inactivity to have been 'a tremendous blunder', the greatest miscalculation in the field of foreign affairs ever made by a British Cabinet. He put most of the blame on Grey.[64]

Stratford's memorandum of 19 December 1832 came too late and too soon, too late to turn the ministry from its mood of reticence, too soon to insert itself into the great debate on the Eastern question, now at hand. The memorandum was also too general in character, an invitation to action based on principles and Russophobic intuitions rather than an examination of accumulated details. Other men, nevertheless, were at hand to provide precisely these details, and during the rest of the 1830s they banished the traditional and picturesque impressions of the barbaric pageantries of old Turkey, and gave the Sultan's empire a new image and a new importance. They were not disinterested historical investigators, otherwise von Hammer's great work, the most important individual contribution ever made to Ottoman studies, would have met with greater acclaim than it did, and perhaps even been translated; they were Turcophiles who set out to show that common problems confronted all states, and that while the Ottoman Empire rather lagged behind other countries in dealing with these, there was no inherent reason why her rulers should not solve them successfully, given the time and the guidance.[65] A rejuvenated Ottoman Empire would be a logical friend for Britain; she would stay the Russian penetration of central Asia, and consequently check the tsarist threat to the security of British India, while perhaps providing Britain herself with access routes to the Indian peninsula by way of Suez and Mesopotamia. As a virtually free-trade empire, devoid of industrial enterprises of her own, she was a potential market of the highest value to the British exporter, and as a Muslim despotism ruling millions of Christian peoples, she was an outstanding challenge to the missionary, the educator, and the humanist. The earlier writers – Maundrell, Dallaway, Jonas Hanway, Hobhouse, James Morier, Knolles, Niebuhr, Buckingham – on whom the generation of the young Stratford was reared, described an exotic social scene they had no thought of changing; the later ones treated it as an oriental predicament which could be rectified, and once rectified, protected.

NOTES

1. Palmerston to Stratford, 7 March 1833, FO 352/25B/2; Lane-Poole, *Life*, ii. 20.
2. Bagot to Palmerston, 5 June 1832, in Charles Webster, *The Foreign Policy of Palmerston, 1830–1841* (London, 1951), i. 322, n. 2; Lane-Poole, *Life*, ii. 19, 21.
3. Gordon to Aberdeen, 16 Sept. 1829, FO 78/181; *Despatches of Wellington*, vi. 98, 107, 108, 110, 119, 152, 192; Sir Arthur Gordon Stanmore, *The Earl of Aberdeen* (New York, 1893), pp. 75–91.
4. Gordon to Aberdeen, 26 Aug. 1829, FO 78/180; Lady F. Balfour, *Life of George, Fourth Earl of Aberdeen* (London, 1922), p. 237; Crawley, *Greek Independence*, p. 164.
5. R.J. Kerner, 'Russia's New Policy in the Near East after the Peace of Adrianople', *Cambridge Historical Journal*, v (1937), 280–90; S. Turan, '1829 Edirne Antlasmasi', *Dilve Tarih-Cografiva Fakultesi Derqisi*, ix (1951), 111–51.
6. Lord Ellenborough, *A Political Diary*, ed. Lord Colchester (London, 1881), 13 Aug. 1829; Crawley, *Greek Independence*, pp. 172–3; V.J. Puryear, *France and the Levant* (Berkeley, 1941), pp. 76–9.
7. *Despatches of Wellington*, vi. 192; Balfour, *Aberdeen*, p. 240.
8. Palmerston to Stratford, 26 Sept. 1831, FO 352/25B/2.
9. Palmerston to Stratford, 26 Sept. 1831, FO 352/25B/2; Stratford to Palmerston, 9 Nov. 1831, Add. MSS 48493. In the latter Stratford offered not to go if Gordon would be very upset. Gordon was, and Stratford still went. See memoirs, in Lane-Poole, *Life*, i. 494, 'I begged to be excused, but friends were urgent that I should accept'.
10. Crawley, *Greek Independence*, p. 169.
11. Palmerston to Dawkins, 28 Dec. 1830, FO 32/9.
12. Memoirs, in Lane-Poole, *Life*, i. 494.
13. Palmerston to Stratford, 16 Nov. 1831, FO 352/25B/2.
14. Stratford to Palmerston, 21 Nov. 1831, FO 352/25A/1.
15. Stratford to Lady Canning, 17 Dec. 1831, Lane-Poole, *Life*, i. 496.
16. Stratford to Palmerston, 21 Nov. 1831, Add. MSS 48493. The agent employed by Stratford as his liaison with the grand vizier was the young Scots philhellene, David Urquhart, soon to become famous as an ardent pro-Turk.
17. Memoirs, in Lane-Poole, *Life*, i. 496.
18. Crawley, *Greek Independence*, p. 197; William P. Kaldis, *John Capodistrias and the Modern Greek State* (Madison, Wisc., 1963), pp. 109–13.
19. Stratford to Palmerston, 26 Dec. 1831, 13 Jan. 1832, Add. MSS 48493.
20. Stratford to Palmerston, 13 Jan., 14 Feb. 1832, ibid.
21. Stratford to Palmerston, 16 and 21 Nov. 1831, ibid.; also 26 Dec. 1831, FO 352/25A/1. Lane-Poole, *Life*, i. 496, in quoting this last letter to Palmerston,

could not bring himself to quote Stratford's more critical comments about the Greeks, and left them out, e.g., 'It really seems to me that Greeks have left this country for places under the Turkish sway, in disgust'.

22. Trikoupis to Stratford, 31 Dec. 1831; Mavrocordates to Stratford, [n.d.], FO 352/24B/5.
23. Stratford to Backhouse, 26 Dec. 1831, FO 352/25B/2; same to Palmerston, 28 Dec. 1831, Add. MSS 48493.
24. Stratford to Palmerston, 10 and 12 Jan. 1832, FO 352/25A/1.
25. Stratford to Backhouse, 28 Oct. 1832, FO 352/25B/2, wrote, 'any nomination is better than none'. Greece had been run for long enough by quarrelsome committees of senators. Throughout the negotiation over the frontiers, Dawkins wrote pessimistic accounts, chiefly about the shortage of funds in Greece. See Dawkins to Stratford, 10, 12, and 19 Jan., 16 Feb., 23 March, 19 and 23 April, 1 and 29 May 1832, FO 352/25B/2.
26. Stratford to Lady Canning, 16 Jan. 1832, Lane-Poole, *Life*, i. 501–3.
27. Mandeville to Stratford, 24 Dec. 1831, FO 352/24A/1; Stratford to Palmerston, 1 and 14 Feb. 1832, FO 352/25A/1; Chabert to Stratford, 3 and 9 Feb. 1832, FO 352/24A/2; Stratford to FO, 19 Dec. 1832, FO 78/211.
28. Memoirs, in Lane-Poole, *Life*, i. 509. For Chabert's betrayal of British embassy policies in 1826, and his subsequent exposure, see also pp. 10–11.
29. Memoirs, in Lane-Poole, *Life*, i. 506. The phrase to the effect that Stratford 'had long been acquainted' with Vogorides can be discounted. In his papers for the year 1832, he is unsure how to spell the name of his intermediary, and had rarely been in the 'Fanal', as he called it. For this remarkable Fanariot family, see J.C. Filitti, 'Notice sur les Vogoridi', *Revue historique de Sud-Est Europe*, vi (1927), 314.
30. Stratford to Palmerston, 9 June 1832, FO 78/210.
31. Stratford to Adair, 29 March 1832, FO 352/25B/4.
32. Stratford to Granville, 14 Feb. 1832, FO 352/25B/4.
33. Stratford to Lady Canning, 24 March 1832, Lane-Poole, *Life*, i. 503.
34. Stratford to Palmerston, 9 Aug. 1832, Add. MSS 48493.
35. Stratford to Palmerston, 28 March 1832, FO 352/25A/1; Chesney to Stratford, 12 March 1832, FO 352/24A/2.
36. Pisani's reports on the Greek negotiations are in Pisani to Stratford, 19 and 24 April, 2, 3, 27, and 29 May, 4, 6, 11, 15, 16, and 17 June, 2, 10, and 16 July 1832, FO 352/25C/8; Stratford to Palmerston, 17 May, FO 78/210; 22 July 1832, FO 78/211; Lane-Poole, *Life*, i. 511.
37. Stratford to Barker, 10 March 1832, FO 352/25B/4.
38. Palmerston to Stratford, 20 Feb. 1832, FO 352/25B/2.
39. Stratford to Palmerston, 30 April, 11 May 1832, FO 78/210; 22 and 23 July 1832, FO 78/211.
40. Stratford to MacGuffog, 30 March 1832, Lane-Poole, *Life*, i. 507.
41. Stratford to Palmerston, 14 Feb., 28 March 1832, FO 352/25A/1.
42. Stratford to Palmerston, 7 March, 17 May 1832, FO 352/25A/1; Stratford to Granville, 23 July 1832, FO 352/25B/4; Stratford to Palmerston, 9 Aug. 1832, FO 78/211; memo, in Stratford to Palmerston, 19 Dec. 1832, FO 78/211.
43. Stratford to Palmerston, 11 and 17 May 1832, FO 78/210; Lane-Poole, *Life*, i. 512.
44. Stratford to Heytesbury, 22 July 1832, FO 352/25B/4.
45. Stratford to Palmerston, 17 May 1832, FO 78/210.
46. Bernard Lewis, *The Emergence of Modern Turkey* (London, 1961), p. 91.

47. Stratford to Pisani, 9 and 26 July 1832, FO 352/24A/2.
48. Stratford to Palmerston, 7 and 10 Aug. 1832, FO 352/25A/1; Lane-Poole, *Life*, i. 512–14.
49. Vogorides to Stratford, 1 Sept. 1832, FO 352/24B/4.
50. Memoirs, in Lane-Poole, *Life*, i. 515; Stratford to MacGuffog, 13 Aug. 1832, FO 352/24A/2.
51. Lewis, *Turkey*, pp. 75–101, 435; E.Z. Karal, *Osmanli Interatorluqunda ilk nufus sayimi* (Ankara, 1943) deals with the first census in 1831.
52. Including Urquhart, still in his anti-Turkish phase. Urquhart had discovered slavery to be very common in Albania, Macedonia, and Thessaly, and he wanted Greece to be as big as Stratford could make it in order to liberate these unfortunates. In the capital, Stratford employed him to study the continuing extent of slavery there, with a view to securing the release of all Greeks now that they were citizens of a new, independent state. Urquhart, who lived in the *Fenar* at this time, was helped by some local Greeks with his investigation, and he concluded that Constantinople had a total of about 10,000 slaves of all races and nationalities. The usual travellers' estimate was nearer 30,000. The discovery that Balkan Christians employed slaves at least as freely as the Ottomans amazed Urquhart and began that swing in his sentiments which by 1834 was complete. In Egri Kapi, a Turkish suburb, he found 170 slaves; far fewer *per capita* of population than in contemporary Spitalfields, Boston, or St Petersburg. Urquhart to Stratford, 9 March 1832, FO 352/24A/1.
53. A. Slade, *Record of Travels in Turkey . . . in the Years 1828, 1830 and 1831* (London, 1832) ii. 210; Stratford to Palmerston, 7 Aug. 1832, FO 352/25A/1.
54. Lewis, *Turkey*, p. 83.
55. Backhouse to Stratford, 10 Oct. 1832, Stratford to Backhouse, 14 Oct. 1832, FO 352/25B/2. The prosperity of Muhammad Ali and the firm of Briggs and Company rose together and the strongly anti-Greek, anti-Ottoman firm is discussed in F.S. Rodkey, 'The Attempts of Briggs and Co. to Guide British Policy in the Levant in the Interest of Mahomet Ali', *Journal of Modern History*, v (1933), 338.
56. Knight to Stratford, 18 Sept. 1832, FO 352/25C/9; Palmerston to Stratford, 19 Oct. 1832, FO 352/25B/2; Lane-Poole, *Life*, i. 517.
57. Grey to Palmerston, 29 Sept. 1832, Webster, *Palmerston*, i. 323.
58. Chesney to Stratford, 2 Nov. 1832, Lane-Poole, *Life*, ii. 18.
59. Lane-Poole, *Life*, ii. 20. See also Webster, *Palmerston*, ii. 320–32, and Franklin A. Walker, 'The Rejection of Stratford Canning by Nicholas I', *Bulletin of the Institute of Historical Research*, xl (1967), 50–64.
60. Stratford to Planta, 20 July 1833, Planta to Stratford, 23 July 1833, Lane-Poole, *Life*, ii. 21–2.
61. Palmerston to Granville, 6 Nov. 1832, Broadlands MSS GC/GR/1439. In further letters of 30 Nov., 4 and 11 Dec., Palmerston's expanding comprehension of Near Eastern geopolitics is very clear to see. Besides the dangers for Britain from an Egyptian kingdom embracing Syria and Baghdad, he saw Russia as the only possible beneficiary.
62. Memo, in Stratford to Palmerston, 19 Dec. 1832, FO 78/211. The memorandum has been printed in full as Appendix V to Crawley's *Greek Independence*. The italicized comments in square brackets were attributed by Crawley to Palmerston, as indeed they were long ago in W. Alison Phillips, *Cambridge Modern History*, x (Cambridge, 1907) 551, 852. But the handwriting is unlike Palmerston's and the question of authorship was reopened, though not

answered in M. Vereté, 'Palmerston and the Levant Crisis, 1832', *Journal of Modern History*, xxiv (1952), 143–51. Tentatively, Vereté assigns authorship to Holland. [He was right. The handwriting is clearly Holland's. Ed.]
63. Palmerston to Ponsonby, private, 22 Aug. 1834, Broadlands MSS GC/PO/607.
64. Palmerston to Lamb, 22 May 1838; encl. in Palmerston to Holland, 8 March 1840, Webster, *Palmerston*, ii. 283–4.
65. *Quarterly Review* (1833), p. 283, contains a review of the latest, eighth volume of J. von Hammer-Purgstall, *Geschichte des Osmanischen Reiches* (Budapest, 1827–35), and begins with a topical contemporary reference: 'This extensive and valuable work, before it is terminated, may perhaps comprehend the whole drama of the Ottoman greatness . . . if we may judge from the signs of the times, one more concluding volume may describe its fall'. The alarm was fashionable, as was the scepticism about Ottoman reformability: 'the Turk can only be formidable as a Turk.' If any country can rise, 'midway, as it were, between Asiatic and European civilization, the chances seem at present in . . . favour of Egypt'. In government circles, this became heretical thinking from the very year, 1833.

CHAPTER III

The Sick Man and the British Physician

If a classic is a permanently contemporary book, then Alexander Kinglake's *Eothen* is one, and should be required reading for anyone concerned with the difficulties of mutual understanding which arise when one state regarding itself as 'modern' seeks to establish a tutelary relationship with another which it perceives as unregenerate in a 'traditional' sense. *Eothen* was published in 1844, at a time when growing numbers of Kinglake's countrymen were seeking, with a rising sense of urgency, cures for the ailments of the 'sick man of Europe', that is, for the Ottoman Sultan's decrepit empire. Kinglake did not deny the possibility of total recovery, but simply suggested that, being fundamentally ignorant of the condition he sought to cure, the British physician might kill the sick man prematurely or, what was possibly worse, find himself treating a terminal condition whose progress could only be delayed. It was not more information that was needed; it was greater insight into the patient's past. Thus *Eothen*, which Richard Burton would later call 'that book of books' about the East, was, as it remains, a cautionary tale, with a special message for reformers prone to the 'sociologistic error' of thinking history is dismissable or, as Wilbert Moore puts it, of supposing that 'history began yesterday, if not this morning'.[1]

Eothen opens with 'the Traveller' – Kinglake himself – waiting to cross the river Sava at 'Semlin' (Zemun), surrounded by friends who shake his hand 'as if we had been departing from this life'. Some such possibility may have been in their minds for, although Kinglake travelled in 1834, a journey into the Ottoman Empire was still attended by unpredictable risks. Nearby, 'the unveiled faces of women shone in the light of day'; opposite, the first minarets of Serbia speared the sky. Once across the Sava, the impact of an utterly alien culture was far greater than Kinglake had ever expected. In the suburbs of Belgrade he at once encountered 'real, substantial, incontrovertible turbans' and was deeply affected by the faces beneath: 'the faces of men – but they had nothing for you – no welcome – no wonder – no wrath – no scorn', nor the least interest in Kinglake who concluded these must be Turks 'of the proud old school' – a dwindling breed if one could believe Great Britain's latest expert on the East, David Urquhart, who was currently assuring his countrymen that all Turks nowadays exhibited 'the strongest desire of instruction and respect for our customs and institutions'.[2]

Perhaps it was Kinglake's misfortune only to meet, or only recognize, members of 'the proud old school'. While in regions where people were 'carefully shot and carelessly buried', he concealed his amazement and dismay. Once home again, he wrote a book about people rather than places which, though couched in the language of farce and exploiting many theatrical moments, coincides more often than not with the less humorous, more detailed warnings of those contemporaries who had also visited the East and believed Urquhart was a wild optimist. Old 'Moostapha Pasha', the pasha of Belgrade, is jocularly compared by Kinglake with Jove – 'like Jove too in the midst of his [tobacco] clouds' – but no reader could miss the intended conclusion that this courteous, indolent 'Osmanlee' gentleman, nominally supreme in an effectively independent Ottoman province, and who knew 'the armies of the English ride upon the vapours of boiling cauldrons', was unfitted by his general ignorance of the world for high office, even in the East. 'Moostapha' was not pure invention, and was probably inspired by that grand vizier whom William Wittman heard in 1800 disputing the roundness of the earth with the argument that ships navigating a sphere would be forever sliding uncontrollably into the wrong harbours, the same official General Koehler met at Jaffa, before marching against Jean Baptiste Kléber in Egypt, delightedly sailing a toy boat while his soldiers, conscientiously camped on a fetid graveyard, died like flies.[3]

Modern research has uncovered far more active, concerned bureaucrats than Kinglake ever knew about, and certain statesmen, parliamentarians, and publicists in Great Britain were, by 1833, coming to feel that these committed Ottomans might yet pull their imperial master's dominions into the modern age. More remarkable still, some British leaders were disposed to establish a supportive alignment between the most industrialized state then existing and this decadent agricultural empire camped on the southeast corner of Europe.[4] But it was precisely this last point which concerned Kinglake for, to him and perhaps a majority of British people who thought about the matter at all, old 'Moostapha' represented not a dying past but a powerfully entrenched array of ultra-conservative interests and attitudes, more ready for British aid than British advice. If these interests were impressed by the fact that 'the ships of the English swarmed like flies', they also recalled warily that in India the 'lumber rooms [of British merchants] are filled with ancient thrones'. Kinglake believed Englishmen should also be wary of what they were taking on. Mahmud II had been twice rescued, in 1833 and 1840, from the consequences of military defeat by the upstart viceroy of Egypt, Muhammad Ali. Were British policy-makers aware that supporting Mahmud II's successor, the boy-sultan Abdulmejid, in the development of those 'new institutions' mentioned in the famous reform-proclamation that coincided with his accession, would require from them a far more continuous intervention in the *domestic* affairs of the Ottoman Empire than was consistent with the British principle of 'non-intervention in the domestic affairs of other states'? Kinglake was very sceptical about the inevitable 'passing of traditional society', and thought the subject deserved far more attention.[5]

As increasing references in British parliamentary debates during the middle third of the century to the 'integrity' and the 'independence' of the Ottoman Empire show, a first concern was for Ottoman security in the face of external enemies. But, until the collapse of British sympathy for the Ottomans during the post-Crimean disillusionment, there was also much talk about 'the sick man' – incidentally, a metaphor in use long before a Russian tsar gave it axiomatic status in 1853[6] – and it is important to know what outsiders like the British thought the internal debilities of the Ottoman state actually were, before it can be asked whether outside advice was relevant to Ottoman needs and, if relevant, why it nevertheless failed to save the Sultan's empire. Kemal Karpat warns against expecting nineteenth-century Europeans to have produced 'objective studies of the [*sic*] Ottoman society in the hour of doom', and it is obviously probable that westerners, gratified by the prospect of Ottoman collapse, would exaggerate as well as find supporting evidence for its imminence.[7] But stereotyping Europeans is no more sensible than stereotyping other people, and it is important to recognize that, before the dictated peace of Adrianople in 1829, and the loss of Greece by 1831, much western opinion was a good deal more tolerant of the Ottoman regime than of, say, the wider world of Islam. Far from predicting an early 'doom' for the empire, British ambassadors and travellers were simply astonished by the extent of political disorder and regional insubordination, assumed it had always been much the same, and concluded that it might go on a long time yet. When the earl of Aberdeen spoke of a baffling 'occult force' that seemed to keep Ottoman power alive, he was perplexed but by no means disappointed that it should be so. The Ottoman Empire was of great international convenience.

The doomsday attitude is really a generational matter, and there are two main reasons for its growth after about 1840. The first is that as the deism of the early gentleman-traveller gave place to the sectarian heat and national pride of the middle-class Victorian, the latter expressed much more loudly his *hope* that the Sultan's dominion would fall, and was distressed, on moral grounds, by his own government's efforts to frustrate the rise of Balkan nationalism. The second is that the generalized prejudice against Islam crystallized into a particularized detestation of the Ottoman regime itself when, despite all promises of improved performance, the Ottomans seemed to be wilfully falling behind in that 'march of civilization' in which so many comfortable Victorians were able to believe so fervently. Thus the pre-Victorian, pre-*Eothen* literature which Karpat so understandably distrusts is by no means all hostile, and while it exhibits much ignorance and misunderstanding, is not particularly malicious. It comes nowhere near explaining, it is true, how once vigorous Sultans 'raised a universal empire, holding together in a single framework of order and administration, and a single loyalty to a ruling family, many different regions – many different ethnic groups – different religious communities – and different social orders',[8] and its authors would have regarded the very modern opinion that the Ottoman Empire was once 'the best governed state the world had seen since the decline of Rome' as a ludicrous mistake.[9]

What that literature does do, however, is to supply us with an abundant corpus of information on latter-day Ottoman society. Like any such literature, it discloses a great deal about the viewer as well as the viewed. Although this literature is greatly in need of the correctives now being drawn from Ottoman archival sources, it is striking how much modern research still locates itself unconsciously within a framework of nineteenth-century questions, and sometimes even assumptions – an unintended compliment no doubt. And, of course, until governments in Great Britain began to assemble data for themselves,[10] a largely sporadic, amateur literature provided the working knowledge on which men in office shaped their opinions about the East. If, over the years, the accumulation of knowledge, particularly of the treatment of subject Christians, hardened opinion in some quarters against Ottoman rule, that dislike was, until 1856, outpaced in Great Britain by fear of Russia's believed designs at Ottoman expense.

By the time of *Eothen*'s publication, a middle-aged European would have experienced little difficulty in assembling 200 titles, mainly in English and French, but also in Dutch, German, Italian, Magyar, and Russian, of books written during his lifetime on some aspect of life in the Ottoman East.[11] As today, he would have found it harder to assemble the books than the titles. If there is any one characteristic binding most of these works in a single category, it is the absence of historical perspective, which is why they were collectively responsible for establishing the idea of 'the unchanging East'. Short on history and long on anecdote, their descriptions imprisoned eastern people in motionless dioramas of the market place, the village, the pasha's court, and so forth. This static view is partly to be blamed on the surviving prestige of elderly but unchallenged 'authorities' on the Ottoman past like Laonicus Chalcocondylas, Richard Knolles, Augier de Busbecq, and Joseph de Tournefort; an Ottoman gentleman reading Clarendon's *History of the Rebellion* in 1815 would be as similarly misled if he closed that work supposing nothing much had happened since in England. No one before Baron Joseph von Hammer-Purgstall (excepting Sir William Jones) had the linguistic skills, commitment, or historical perspective to attempt a study of the Turks comparable in detail, insight, and continuity with Gibbon's *Decline and Fall*.[12] But another extremely persuasive cause of the impression of timelessness is at once apparent if we consider the work of the contemporary artists;

examining, for instance, Thomas Allom's crowded street scenes, David Roberts's landscapes, Sir David Wilkie's *Oriental Sketches*. In his search for authenticity for his biblical paintings, Wilkie simply went East and drew landscapes, villages, and costumes, which, to the casual eye, had not altered in two millenia. Constantinople, with hardly a factory chimney in sight before 1841, appeared – at least from a distance – to be an Arabian Nights' stage set. Palestine was as Christ knew it. Until the coming of Muhammad Ali, Egypt changed little, the ways of life seemingly immemorial. For so universally static a state of things, some fundamental and comprehensive simple explanation seemed essential; perhaps in the innate delinquency of the Ottomans, perhaps Islam, perhaps the climate. This last explanation had a pretension to be scientific and carried the endorsement of Montesquieu, and Thomas Thornton, a long-term resident of Constantinople who discerned as much movement in eastern society as any other, was exceptional in asking sceptically what great climatic change could be invoked to explain the difference between the vigorous, expansionist era of Suleiman the Magnificent and the feebleness and inefficiency of the empire of Selim III. Montesquieu, Thornton was suggesting, would really no longer do, as he seemed 'to attribute to climate and geographical situation what should rather be sought in social institutions, in government, in religion and domestic economy'.[13]

Without surrendering entirely the hierarchical view of peoples himself – he speaks of 'the licentiousness of the Greek' and the 'softness of the Syrian' – Thornton was severe on such unsatisfactory critics of the Turks as Baron François de Tott and François Pouqueville. He broke new ground with explanations of his own by blaming the *ayan* for the enfeeblement of the Ottoman Empire and delineating – not very well – the financial resources of the Sultans, and so belongs to that small group, including Felix de Beaujour, Louis Auguste Mériage, E.C. Clarke, Antoine Juchereau de Saint-Denis, Count Constantin Volney, William Leake, and Sir Adolphus Slade, whose members picked a middle way between, on the one hand, merely moral reprobation and, on the other, an exaggerated regard for the integrity of tradition. Such authors sensed that the Ottoman Turks had not really decapitated history, either that of the Balkan Christians or the Arabs, in 1453 or any other date earlier or later, but were an imperial people with a remarkable past, and a more recent experience of generalized debility and decline still eluding detailed description or explanation. Thus for most, particularly British, writers, the Ottoman Empire was a clock without hands, and it did not often occur to them that it might be Great Britain herself, undergoing unusually dynamic social changes, which might be untypical of the age; much of Europe was as rural as the Ottoman provinces, whereas few regions of the Continent were as industrialized as central England.[14]

★ ★ ★

Certain topics commanded special interest and comment in the literature of the early nineteenth century. By no means exhausting the catalogue of Ottoman ailments which scholars identify today, it was these few *in combination* which led so many people to the conclusion that the Ottoman Empire was a large state incapable of measuring up to European assumptions about the meaning of great power. The topics, which we shall look at in turn, include the phenomenon of depopulation, the ubiquity of rural poverty and agricultural backwardness (producing what a modern writer has labelled 'a low-level equilibrium trap'),[15] a widespread failure of the rule of imperial law, a rudimentary network of commercial activity in which, however, Ottomans seemed to play a negligible part, and – underlying all – a capricious, avaricious, but impotent central government. Obviously, none exerted a constant effect across an empire so diversified by geography, history, and deliberate imperial policies, and none was unknown in contemporary Europe. Yet had the many different observers and authors been able to pool their information more effectively, they must have concluded that the Ottoman crisis was deeper still than it superficially seemed to be.

The mix of data which has come down to us is the work of military experts, consuls, comfortable gentlemen, amateur historians, bureaucrats, statisticians, and merchants. British writers acquired a reputation, and not with British readers only, for the accuracy of their information, particularly their geographical and economic data: as physiocratic as any Frenchman once abroad, they were particularly severe and illuminating when discussing the misuse or neglect of land.[16] Much of the best French writing was the work of Napoleon's intelligence officers and political analysts, several of whom complimented Volney by emulating his sociological approach and sense of social structure: where Volney studied Ottoman Asia, his uniformed successors wrote tellingly about Albania, one of Napoleon's intended stepping-stones to the East.[17] Austrians give the strongest impression of an innate understanding of much that came within their observation, perhaps because their own Military Frontier districts, contiguous with the Ottoman lands, so resembled territories just across the border, but even more because further instalments of the Ottoman inheritance appeared to be within Austria's grasp: Ion Dragasanu and Johann Demian best typify the authoritative Austrian writers, with their better opportunities for extended Balkan travel and study.[18] Von Hammer-Purgstall's great history, appearing between 1827 and 1834, was the product of an Austrian official also.

There were also some insiders to the Ottoman situation who wrote about it but their observations, by their official nature, either did not pass into general circulation or did so only after a long delay: such people included Ottoman Muslim bureaucrats making conscious comparisons with Europe, Christian public servants of the Ottoman state, and European consuls of long residence in the East with their special insights into the world of trade.[19] Predictably, the bulk of contemporary literature concerns the Balkans, as Greece, sometimes with a small excursion to Constantinople in addition, was the end of the *haj* for so many Europeans. That was a circumstance of the highest importance; concern for the condition of the subject Christians became coupled with the unproven assumption that subject Muslims in the unvisited Asian wing of the empire were probably better off and more loyal, both false impressions. Predictably again, the final jigsaw still lacks many pieces, even today.

★ ★ ★

Beginning with depopulation, it is instructive to plot on a map the nearly abandoned or deserted areas which the books record, noticing in the process their sheer number, size, and distribution. There was a justified expectation that the north-west angle of the empire, near Kinglake's point of entry, should exhibit the neglect of a much-controverted frontier zone, the scene of forced and voluntary migrations over the centuries, and that the mountains of Bosnia and Montenegro should support only thin populations, but it was a constant surprise for men who believed populated, productive land to be the measure of state wealth to find eminently cultivatable land deserted, even in the main valleys of the Serbian Morava, the upper Vardar, the lower Maritsa, and in undrained pockets of the middle Danube itself. William Wilkinson, British consul at Bucharest after 1815, wrote in his *Account of the Principalities* that only one-sixth of Wallachia was cultivated in spite of 'the almost incredible richness of the soil'. Kinglake, on his diagonal journey to Constantinople, observed empty villages and derelict fields. South of Adrianople he navigated his way *by compass* across a vast wilderness to the very gates of a city as populous as Paris. In place of intensive cultivation to feed the capital, arriving Europeans recollected the felled tree trunks which were the 'roads', the squelching miseries of hovel-towns like Corlu and Silivria. Robert Walsh, a British embassy chaplain, riding the much-used route from the Dardanelles to Constantinople in 1829, was amazed that 'in a journey half of the length of the Hellespont I did not see a single human habitation, and this in the finest climate, the most fertile soil, and once [in Byzantine days] the most populous region in the world'. The marquis of Chateaubriand, his emotions deeply involved as he rode through an area once prosperous with city-states, was in consternation at the condition of the Morea, which was 'in general uncultivated, bare, monotonous, wild . . . no husbandmen . . . no carts . . . no teams of oxen'. Here, flagstone trails a yard wide were the roads. Thirty years after Chateaubriand, James Baillie Fraser was still warning of the dangers of getting lost: 'once you go astray, there is no such thing as finding the track again.' It is fair to summarize the general situation with Fraser's succinct remark about 'the [unexpected] absence of man, the rarity of villages, the paucity of cultivation'.

The same story was also found true of Ottoman Anatolia by the much smaller band of travellers there. Beyond the plain of Iznik, only a few hours' ride beyond Constantinople, 'a rich grassland such as would make the mouth of a Leicester farmer water with envy', the areas of emptiness grew larger, distances between towns expanded, food and shelter were harder to find. In spite of large prairies east of Kutahya, peasant poverty looked worse than ever. It was not only that 'science' was wanting and that 'routine and habit preside over agricultural operations', Abdolonyme Ubicini

The Sick Man and the British Physician 81

reported, 'there is an actual want of hands'. The journeys of Ali Bey, Fraser, Austen Henry Layard, Charles Macfarlane, Frederick Burnaby, and A.F. Townsend, spanning the whole century, repeat the powerful impression of thousands of small, impoverished villages, standing still or getting smaller, with good, untilled land nearby. Similar conditions were reported in Syria, inland from the urbanized coastal belt of the Fertile Crescent, and as far as Iraq.[20]

Travellers neither understood all they saw nor saw all that was significant about the countryside, but in two major guesses about population trends they have been upheld by later research: first, that within a confusing redistribution of Balkan peoples the Muslims seemed to be migrating to the towns in the process of draining out of the Balkans altogether, and second, that an absolute decline in numbers was also taking place in Ottoman Asia, including the Arab lands. It was difficult to quantify either view, rare instances being Chateaubriand's discovery of only six of the 80 villages which Pellegrin counted around Coron in 1719; Amadée Chaumette des Fossés' estimates of declining Muslim numbers in Bosnian towns; several British reports on the flight of Muslim refugees from revolutionary Greece after 1821; and Macfarlane's habitual counting of children in mixed Christian-Muslim villages during his Anatolian journeys: 'it was rare to find a Turkish family raising more than one child. We seldom saw two . . . three was unheard of.' Other evidence of depopulation was more circumstantial, and in the form of empty Muslim villages, dilapidated *hans*, neglected graveyards, the infiltration of Muslim districts by growing numbers of Christians: this sort of evidence is massive in aggregate.[21]

Speculation about the causes of this demographic haemorrhage, which permitted the population of Hungary, one-quarter that of the Ottoman Balkans in 1700, to overtake it by 1800, conventionally began with a repetition of Pouqueville's triple explanation – polygamy, venereal disease, and widespread abortion among Muslims. This last was, for instance, Macfarlane's explanation for the small Anatolian family. Of the ravages of malaria, specific children's diseases, and famines, very little usable data is to be found. The scattered information about plague, on the other hand, is impressive, and made more so by the refusal of Muslims to take special precautions against it: old residents of

Constantinople said that special prayers were never arranged against plague until the death rate reached a thousand a day. A growing British interest in quarantine required Levant Company consuls to report the incidence of plague in their neighbourhoods, and the latter leave little doubt but that ships and caravans were the great carriers, and ports and trading towns the chief victims. John Barker reported 8,000 deaths in Aleppo in 1814, while 20,000 died of plague in Malta, a node of the Levant trade, between 1810 and 1812. Salonika and the east Balkan towns suffered regularly. Constantinople lost a few thousand people annually, for which reason the embassy staffs moved to the Bosporus villages in June for four months. A further cause of Muslim depopulation was, of course, the battle casualties in the numerous wars against Austrians, Russians, and Persians, following the reversal of the imperial Ottoman tide in 1699: only Muslims fought under the banners of Islam by this date.[22]

In the Balkans particularly, what appeared regionally to be a decline in total numbers, Muslim and Christian, might occasionally be no more than a moment in a long process of population redistribution, and a steady upturn in absolute Christian numbers is only certain from the later stages of the Serbian and Greek wars for independence. A visible cause of population depletion *and* disarray was the devastation of the Nish-Kragujevatz plain for a dozen years after 1804, Ottoman armies burning guerrillas' homes and the Serbs retaliating by expelling 'almost the entire Moslem element from the Pashalik of Belgrade'. The former *sipahi* landlords retreated to the greater safety of garrison towns elsewhere. Less easy to recognize, though John Cam Hobhouse and the French glimpsed it, was the outward movement of the Muslim Albanians, beginning before 1800, propelled by the violence and insecurity generated by the long and savage career of Ali Pasha of Janina, and drawn by the prospect of victimizing Greek sedentarists of the Vardar and Struma plains.[23] Besides allowing Muhammad Ali of Egypt to call himself an Albanian though born in Kavalla in Thrace, the Albanian migration out of the Berat-Argyrocastro region produced the desolation Chateaubriand saw in the Piraeus, where he recollected 'a Turkish customs officer . . . the lonely sentinel of the coast and a model of stupid patience'. Albanians also pushed Bulgar pastoralists out of the Rhodope foothills on to the plain of Sofia after about 1790. Parasitic banditry could not, however, tear the web of trade on the plains as easily as in the hills, nor was it in its interests to do so. Hence the upturn in Christian numbers was a true reflection of cautiously rising morale and prospects, and the effects of the change were visible even in lands still held firmly by the Ottomans after Serbia and Greece had broken away: Wyburn put the Moldavian and Wallachian populations respectively at one and a half and one million in 1820, whereas by 1839 Felix Colson calculated the joint populations to total 3.8 million.

By contrast, Muslim birth rates, anywhere in the empire, rarely rose above one per cent and in 1815 Egypt had a population of 2.5 million, Syria 2 million, and Anatolia perhaps 6 or 7 million. Iraq had under 1 million. The later upturn in Asia, after 1840, was the result of refugee Muslim immigration from Russia, and to a much lesser extent from the Balkan area. By 1853, Ubicini would conclude that the Ottoman Balkans contained 15.5 million people, of whom only one-seventh were now Muslim; Anatolia had 10.7 million; the Arab lands, excluding Africa, 5.3 million. The general decline in Muslim numbers led the British to press for the admission of Christians to the imperial armies, while the unfavourable Balkan ratio, so ominous to the continuance of Ottoman power there, led them to recommend, first, full Christian participation within an expanded meaning of *Osmanlilik* (Ottoman citizenship)[24] and second, full Christian independence.

★ ★ ★

Turning to agriculture, the resigned spirit of pastoralists and cultivators alike also drew much comment. While Serbs could often seem sturdy and well-fed, Montenegrins flashily dressed on saints' days, and Anatolian Kurds confidently anti-Ottoman, peasant life everywhere in the empire was usually hard and poor, with a large proportion of peasants voluntarily distributed on poor soils and in austere mountain landscapes as a way of escaping oppressive officials. Had Volney been able to survey more widely he would have found that, of the three extant ploughs – the prehistoric, earth-scratching *ard*, and its wood and metal successors – the first was much the commonest east of Trieste for most of the century, without becoming totally unfamiliar in Iberia, Scotland, and Ireland. But while urban demands for more foodstuffs compelled more efficient farming in Europe, the Frenchman found the typical plough in Syria to consist of 'a branch of a tree cut below a bifurcation'. Similar instruments which 'seemed to have come out of Noah's ark' prevailed in Croatia, Serbia, Bosnia, and the Principalities. Across all provinces too, clothing, bedding, footwear, looms, locks, tools, and houses were predominantly home-made or village-made. Harnesses of the Roman kind, throttling the work animal, were as widespread as the biblical threshing sledge. The Catalonian forge fired the metal-work of rural specialists from the Macedonian *zadruga* to the villages of north Iraq. Westerners who recommended crop-rotation or cross-breeding, both of which were occasionally practised in the vicinity of the more prosperous Danubian towns but hardly at all in Anatolia, were usually answered with the significant reaction, 'What we have is enough'. Islamic fatalism, or a peasant sloth in the case of Christians, were commonly adduced to explain this attitude, but a far better one lay in God-given and man-made disincentives operational over a long time,[25] chiefly high levels of taxation and insecurity.

A significant detail, frequently reported, was that peasants were wont to fly and hide from strangers on horseback, fearing bandits or tax-collectors. Furthermore, they took pains to increase their isolation, tearing up road-beds, settling out of sight of the roads trod by their natural opponents: thus, 'in the interior parts of the country there are neither roads nor canals, nor even bridges over . . . the rivers and torrents'. With so few needs that could not be produced at home, only items like glass, saddlery, and weapons induced peasants to go beyond those local fairs, catering to their social needs as much as to the exchange of commodities, to the riskier money transactions of large-town markets like Janina, Uzunjova, Sofia, Trebizond, Konya, Aleppo, or Damascus.[26] Nor was the 'revolution of rising expectations' automatically released by political liberation from Ottoman control. Even at the end of the century, when 86 per cent of Serbs were still poor peasants, Albanians continued to be described as 'savages', Croats as 'ignorant animals', Romanian farmers as being 'as superstitious as a Red Indian', and Turks as the most benighted of all peasants. Outsiders very rarely saw revolutionary material in such people.

And yet to outsiders looking for evidence of 'progress', as in later times they might seek out signs of 'development', it is of the utmost significance that the harsh Balkan situation seemed somewhat redeemed by a degree of primitive commercial activity and hesitant urbanization which held out a prospect of eventual economic betterment for increasing numbers of its peoples, whereas the interior Anatolian situation not only appeared, but actually was closer to being stationary, stubbornly retaining what Ibrahim Yasa calls 'the all pervading feudal mentality'. Any expectation that the Asian homeland of the master-race must be peopled by a free peasantry enjoying a marginally better life than was available to subject Christians therefore had to be discarded. Indeed, a prior journey across the Balkan mosaic of costumes, language, and religions only served to intensify the surprise occasioned by the uniformities of the depressed way of life found on the high, bleak plateau which was the 'ethnic reservoir' of the Ottomans. High mountain ranges to north and south unbreached by any great rivers except the Kizil Irmak and the infant Euphrates, and to the west the diagonal ranges (NW–SE) of the Ala Dag and Erciyes Dag, isolated this plateau from the outside, diminished any migratory incentive of its people, and committed the poor highlanders living on it to a subsistence livelihood based on a destructive pastoralism. Everything seemed everywhere the same to the few Europeans traversing high Anatolia before 1830, and though they do not explicitly tell us so, their information coincides remarkably on the position of the line to the west of which a greater affluence with an Aegean orientation began to appear: the line in question connected Bursa, Eskishehir, Kutahya, Afyon, Konya, Eregli. West of this line we hear of some, though few, pockets of intensive, commercial agriculture; of occasional ploughs and even wheeled vehicles; of mixed populations whose disagreements the authorities could not quite contain; of some awareness of the politics of Constantinople and Europe.[27]

To the east, travellers noted the shabby dignity of the peasantry, a peculiar wantlessness and lack of curiosity about tomorrow or the wider world. As the predominance of Islam seemed less challenged here, there was a readier friendliness in the villages though also less food. Women were more often unveiled; their children notably fewer. Many people were incapacitated by illness and no one seemed rich, or even in comfortable circumstances. There was no commercial agriculture to widen the gap between a few leading families and the rest. Very few visitors blamed the peasant exclusively for his depressed condition, though it was usual to comment on the overgrazed hills, the neglect of good land, the old irrigation systems and water wheels, the extravagant wastage of the meagre crops by inefficient harvesting, and the diminishing oak forests. Some said the Turk was really a nomad, without agricultural traditions, or suggested that the dullards stayed home while active peasants went off to the army. And yet, Europeans kept concluding, 'one is bound to like him [the Anatolian peasant], if only for his courage and simplicity, and his blind fidelity and loyalty', qualities many thought disappearing in Europe under the industrial impact.[28]

Most surprisingly, Anatolian peasants, particularly in the *Tanzimat* years, were ready to discuss their grievances, even with infidels:[29]

> The Oda-Bashi and the other notables of the village spent the evening with us, and were scarcely less communicative than the men of Musal [a village near Bursa]. They complained of their Agha, who, it appeared, lived away at Kutayah, of the ushurjees, and of the collectors of the Saliane, saying that Mussulmans could no longer live in a Mussulman country. . . . There were several villages in the valley all bearing the same name, all inhabited exclusively by Turks, and all poor, hungry, and going to pieces. . . . It was poorer than the poorest village I ever saw – even in the interior of Sicily; yet the cornland, which stretched for many miles from north to south, was excellent, and the valley was well watered. . . . It ought to have supported in abundance and comfort a thick population, but the thinnest was starving. . . . Some Turks had abandoned their villages, and were migrating with their little stocks towards the lower part of the plain of Bursar; their Agha came down after them . . . tufekjees drove the poor people back to their villages, threatening to shoot or hang them if they tried another flight. In spite, however, of all of this vigilance and rigour many families do disappear, and villages are annually deserted.

Poor Turks, in other words, obtained no discernible *economic* advantage from membership in the Faithful, and Volney, with his usual insight, observed that whereas in Europe the cities 'are in some measure the overflow of the countryside', in Ottoman Asia 'they are the result of its desertion'. The scattered towns were unable to absorb rural refugees who, in their turn, were unwilling to return to the conditions which had driven them from the countryside in the first place, the insecurity, the cul-de-sac of crop-mortgaging, share-cropping, and forced labour, the inexorable demands for tithe and *ondalik* in bad as well as in better years. It was because so many people were ready to invest in his distress that the peasant was so often to be found, defeated and uprooted, smoking away the long afternoons in the dusty coffee-houses of comfortless towns. The Anatolian peasant class was the last of its kind, as well as the poorest, eventually to be liberated from Ottoman control. 'Who else can arrest the Anatolian death?', D. E. Hogarth could still ask a century after Volney's analysis, adding, 'Not the Ottoman rejuvenated by any political alchemy'. The Ottoman bureaucracy alone was not, of course, entirely responsible for this 'living death', as we shall see.[30]

Anatolia, then, was decreasingly able to supply all the manpower needed for imperial armies, or a large agricultural surplus sufficient to finance major imperial efforts elsewhere in a loosening empire. Outsiders, without being able to assemble confirmatory data, guessed that the diminished means for dealing with the political centrifugalism of Serbia after 1804 and Greece after 1821, or with the chronic insubordination of the Arab provinces of Syria, Lebanon, and Iraq, was probably the authentic Ottoman 'sickness', from which other debilities developed. Beneath the defeats inflicted by Russia between 1774 and 1829, and the search for a reliable European ally during the Napoleonic age, lay an impoverishing contest between a desperate central government in Constantinople and a kaleidoscope of regional interests frustrating its pursuit of greater control over the scale and regularity of state income. These interests sought to curtail, by sharing in, the ultimate imperial prerogative to tax, and the Ottoman government was itself to blame for having initiated the ruinous practice of tax-farming in the first place. The spread of tax-farming (notably from the mid-eighteenth century) accounted more than any other cause for the disruption of the order that had formerly ruled in the provinces. But what rendered the pursuit of agriculture difficult, and in many cases finally impossible, was the provincial anarchy that resulted from the weakening control by the central government, and the consequent emergence of petty dynasts. The reciprocal advantages which centre and periphery could offer each other, not religious or other meanings of loyalty, had become the precarious foundation of the Ottoman state.[31]

The parallel which came most readily to European observers was with the nation-building phase of their own histories, in which the ideas of an encompassing territoriality and a unifying loyalty had only been realized on the ruins of the local pretensions of the 'overmighty subject'. It was from such a comparison, in detail inexact but in substance usable enough, that those references to oriental 'feudalism' emerged which today's scholars rather dislike. By preventing the establishment of a more direct connection between imperial bureaucrats and the mass of small proprietors across the empire, the 'dynasts' impoverished the Ottoman state, checked the prospects – always doubtful enough – for establishing *Osmanlilik*, and, in Asia as much as in Balkan Europe, prepared the way for political separatist movements. We can now begin to see where the comparison with an earlier, feudal Europe was perhaps most misleading: European commentators had the historical actualities of the East the wrong way round. Without ever seeking a centralized character on the European pattern, the Ottoman state had, nevertheless, in its great days been a well-ordered agglomeration of regional jurisdictions, the *sipahi-timar* system providing the essential framework of state security, taxation, and the rule of law. The old Ottoman preference for a cellular rather than a unitary administrative structure showed at every turn, in the *millet* organization, the *imaret* method of propagating the growth of towns, and the zoning of the towns themselves under self-regulating trade-guilds. By the early nineteenth century, the disorder which Europeans took as proof that Ottomans could conquer but not rule was, in reality, a once great decentralized pattern now in disarray, which, in its decay, had come to resemble the early disorder of feudal Europe. The ancient glue, compounded of crusading faith, confidence, loyalty, and common interest was gone. It is as easy to see why Ottoman reformers, in their search for a basis of reintegration, should have looked to the past as it is to understand why westerners wanted a Selim III or a Mahmud II to dismantle old structures, remove rebellious rural *derebeys*, reduce the disloyal pretensions of the *ayan*, those string-pullers of urban politics across the empire, and begin anew. But was it too late for that?

The individuals and groups personifying regional independence were very numerous, came in all sizes, were Christian as well as Muslim, stood somewhere along a spectrum between a modest autonomy and a defiant isolation, and fascinated European visitors who were caught between approving their vigorous example and reprobating their doubtful loyalty to the will of Constantinople. That some were held in high local esteem in their own localities was freely acknowledged, and notably by consuls like John Barker of Aleppo, who had small faith in the ability of pashas sent from Constantinople to do their duty in manly fashion. Some radiated an impressive charisma, Ali Pasha of Janina convincing Byron and Hobhouse in 1809 that oriental chivalry still flourished, while Muhammad Ali of Egypt, with his plans for a state-regulated economy, convinced John Bowring in 1837 that the light of Benthamite utilitarianism had reached the Orient. And yet if some of the provincial *derebeys*, *ayan*, and self-made dictators seemed, by their very example, to be part of the Ottoman solution, most seemed to be part, and a major part, of the Ottoman problem.[32] Constantinople might divide local rivals against each other, loading with honours and official duties men it could not capture or discipline, but was that the problem solved or, as the most discerning Europeans concluded, the problem deferred? It is a sombre fact that most of the regional despots who survived longest, during that heyday for their kind which ran from about 1750 to 1820, were not the Sultan's allies but his opponents, and much money that ran into their pockets should have gone into his. The rising scale of their authority can be sampled quickly.

David Urquhart, travelling in the Cassandra peninsula near Salonika, met the head of the Anastasi family.[33] 'The Pasha promises me the captainship of the whole country if I can clear it of robbers', the sometime *klepht* explained, but this could only be done by negotiating with the robbers since to seize them would violate the local political ethic. 'I therefore cannot proceed against the robbers until the Pasha gives me his word that he will not require that any of them be given up.' Anastasi got the job and paid the robbers small stipends to become local guardians of the civil peace. Higher up the scale comes a small clan like the Küçük Ali,[34] with a field force of about 200 brigands, holding the strategic corners round the gulf of Alexandretta for about a century until 1865. The Küçük Ali victimized local villages, infidel travellers, and the Constantinople contingent of the *haj* to Mecca. A humiliation rather than a threat to official authority, the high points of their turbulent record were the capture of an incautious grand vizier in 1800, and a nominal resistance to the invasion of Anatolia by Ibrahim Pasha in 1832. A much larger confederation was that of the Canikli, whose power base was on the Black Sea coast round Trebizond: disgraced and decimated on imperial orders for once surrendering eastern fortresses to Catherine II's invading forces, survivors of the Canikli negotiated their way back into imperial favour through personal contacts in the divan at Constantinople, were disgraced a second time by Selim III for resisting his military reforms, defeated the armies sent against them, refused to negotiate with an ex-grand vizier sent to placate them, extended their dominion as far west as Bursa, and outlived Selim III himself. In their campaigns against the rival family of Capanoglu, the Canikli are said by a modern writer to have garrisoned Trebizond, their main base, with 50,000 men and to have had an expeditionary force of similar size. Certainly, travellers could everywhere see the widespread ruin left by the great, interfamilial struggles in northern Anatolia: 'our host', one traveller wrote in 1848:

> pointed out to our notice a solitary house, now in ruins . . . the strong abode of one of those Dere-Beys, or Lords of the Valleys, whose atrocities are related, and it is to be hoped exaggerated, in the popular traditions of the country. The Dere Bey of Billijik set the feeble government of the Sultan at defiance for many years; but – as the boldest and cunningest of Orientals do – he fell at last into a wretched trap, and, quietly submitting to kismet, he had his head taken off in his own strong house. [It] went to Constantinople at the saddle-bow of a Bostanjee.[35]

Not all rebels were losers. In 1802, the British ambassador, returning to Constantinople from an archaeological jaunt, found the capital besieged by a rebel pasha, all European ships in the harbour ready to sail, and a note from his own chargé d'affaires predicting the fall of the Ottoman Empire into 'numberless, petty, piratical states'.[36] In fact, the insubordinate pasha had to be bought off with the governorship of Silistria. In 1803, another former rebel, Djezzar Pasha of Acre, was promoted to Damascus to deal with the Wahabi menace. By 1807, it was Selim III himself who was the loser, murdered in his own capital, a victim of conspiracies against his plans to modernize his armies, conspiracies in which the plotters included the highest officials of the state, the most reactionary elements of the Constantinople population, and yet other pasha-rebels who would not allow taxing or recruiting in their jurisdictions, nor the Sultan's orders to be promulgated there. The courageous Mahmud II brought the Anatolian *derebeys* to heel by 1820, removed untrustworthy public servants, and finally crushed the janizaries in 1826, but even then there remained despots some of whom not only outlived Mahmud II but whose breakaway dynasties – in Egypt and Arabia – survived beyond the collapse of the Ottoman family itself. Mahmud II's most famous contemporaries, and nominal subjects, were Ali Pasha of Janina (executed in 1820), the 'Prince of the Druses' in Lebanon (deposed in 1840), and Muhammad Ali of Egypt who died in 1849. When Sultans faltered and upstarts flourished, the curious asked if a Sultan was really anything more than another regional authority, whose balancing function as *primus inter pares* derived from his possession of Constantinople, and the prestige which accrued to the head of a dynasty and a Caliph. Given the malversations of pashas, the independence of *derebeys*, and the extortions of tax-farmers, enquirers looked with special interest at the urban economy as an imperial resource perhaps easier to supervise, regulate, and tax[37] than the almost inaccessible rural economy of the provinces.

★ ★ ★

In general, the designation of 'city' was reserved for Asian rather than Balkan centres of population, a misleading tendency since it was ancient Smyrna, Aleppo, Baghdad, and Damascus which were commercially static or in decline, and Balkan towns like Belgrade, Bucharest, Jassy, and Salonika which were in the ascendant. Once-famous Alexandria was but a reminder of the transience of human greatness, 'one third forsaken . . . another third occupied by sepulchres'.[38] The main urban centres in Asia disappointed, reflecting the neglect and dilapidation of the surrounding countryside. The impression of universal decay is wonderfully caught in Allom's drawings of Bursa or Galibert's of Smyrna, and it was usual for visitors to comment on the fact that the most imposing public buildings of the empire were survivals from a wealthier past. 'Now it is worthy of remark that all these fountains, all these hans, all these bridges are of the earliest time of the empire, and are falling into ruin. I cannot recollect having seen one single modern fabric.'[39] The neglect of military fortifications was particularly alarming and, in different years, the French and British were employed to do perfunctory repairs at the Dardanelles.

It was also usual for the same pockets of specialized enterprise to be listed by travellers and consuls: in Asia, Erzerum, and Damascus for blades, Van for jewellery, Usak and Smyrna for carpets; among textile centres, Baghdad for calicoes, Usküdar for muslins, Diarbekir for velvet, Ankara for mohair, Lebanon, Bursa, and Aleppo for silks; in most towns, there were soap factories and some glass-making; ships were constructed at Constantinople, Gelibolu, and Rhodes, leather goods at Canak, weapons at Damascus and Dolmabahce; copper was mined at Tokat, some coal on the Black Sea, some silver at Trebizond. And yet no list, however long, added up in western calculations to a significant system of manufacturing and commerce capable of financing increasing state programmes of, for instance, army and navy reform. Missing from the countryside was the improving landlord; missing from the Ottoman city was the Muslim capitalist entrepreneur. Beirut would be raised to prominence by Christians, Trebizond by Europeans. Missing from both settings was the communications pattern to facilitate the commercialization of agriculture and an easy flow of urban produce. Coastal trade was hampered by poor harbours, undredged and unmapped channels, unlit headlands. The curious equilibrium of the economy of the port of Smyrna and its hinterland, and the puzzling lack of the familiar, western infrastructure, was described extensively in 1812 by Christophe Aubin, agent for a British business firm,[40] with a special interest in eastern textiles.

Aubin's discoveries can be rearranged sequentially, and taken to apply widely in Ottoman Asia. The countryside, being both poor yet self-sufficient as to everyday needs, gave little stimulus to urban production; cities, therefore, despite a certain historical prestige, contained only a small part of the overall population, and apart from a very few, were just towns of moderate size; the urban population, in its turn, contained fewer artisans and craftsmen than porters, guards, domestic servants, vendors, and workless peasants; as money was short, credit had to be long, and the craftsman often expected the purchaser to provide his own raw materials; the craft-guilds, admirable for their quality control and concern for members, nevertheless balanced supply against demand to hold prices up, and obstructed innovation; the craftsman was often the entrepreneur also, familiar only with the needs of an essentially local market. Any adventurous entrepreneurial activity involving more money and larger risks fell, by default, into the hands of Europeans or Ottoman-Greeks and Armenians, who traded with each other, crystallized into a 'Levantine bourgeoisie', and oriented their activities not to the Muslim-controlled bazaar but to the importing opportunities of foreign trade. Dealing in luxury imports, they put little new money into general circulation. The imperial Ottoman government inhibited capital accumulation by skimming off too much in taxes on *transactions* (that is, sales taxes, purchase taxes) and taking less than it might from *commodity values*; lastly, since no foreign trader in his senses would want fast-depreciating Ottoman 'light moneys', there would always be a balance of trade problem. Most ominously for the future, the West wanted very few manufactured goods from the Ottoman East, beyond the much envied, much copied products of the textile industry; once these were surpassed, as Aubin predicted with complete clarity, only raw materials would be exportable to Europe.[41]

Within 30 years of his writing, the best, most extensive industry of the Levant provinces, based on hand operations and the beginnings of a true proletariat (selling its labour rather than a product), was annihilated. Poor communications deferred the fate of the interior manufacturing towns briefly, but eventually spinning and weaving came almost to a complete halt in Aleppo, Amasia, Aintab, Bursa, Baghdad, Beirut, Damascus, Hama, Mardin, Mosul, and Urfa. With the approaching end of a primitive commercial development based on agriculture (food processing, cash crops, textiles), an impatient reformer like Mahmud II moved to the experimental introduction of industrial machine practices aimed at the final stages of manufacture, an enormously costly step in which Muslims played a small part and western capital, eventually, a large one.[42]

While Anatolia was topographically a cul-de-sac, the Balkan area was enabled by its arterial rivers to escape a similar economic confinement, and to undertake the commercialization of animal farming and the development of cash crops to a degree unknown in Ottoman Asia, possessing to its north growing European markets which were far more populous, lucrative, and demanding than those of Persia or the Fertile Crescent. This economic transformation, beginning in the early eighteenth century, was financed up to 1840 by men comprehensively called 'Greeks', but in fact – and in turn – by Austrians, Ottoman Jews, mainland Greeks (before the revolution of 1821), island Greeks, and Serb and Bulgarian merchant interests. An overview of the literature finds British writers strangely incurious, with one or two exceptions, about the details and implications of this general development until after it drew in the Ionian sea-traders, whose islands Great Britain controlled in the last years of the Napoleonic struggle and annexed in 1815. Archaeological enthusiasts, who wrote so much, hardly noticed the contemporary towns; consular agents, well qualified to write, sent their reports of the changing urban scene, until 1825, exclusively to the Levant Company's headquarters in London; the only British people who knew much about the mercantile and proto-capitalist endeavours of the emergent Balkan merchant-trader class were the resident merchants trading under the Levant Company's monopoly in Smyrna, Constantinople, Salonika, and Patras, who did not compete very successfully with them.[43]

For certain kinds of information, therefore, we have largely to depend, as fortunately we may, on Austrian and Balkan authors; for information, for instance, on changing Muslim–Christian relationships at every level, as the traditional status, landed wealth, numerical strength, and distribution of the former community were modified by the emergence of what was, in effect, a new social and economic class among the infidels. As ever, when an old political dispensation begins to crumble, many people, interests, and loyalties are caught in the middle with difficult choices to make: the Ottoman landed gentry found the *ciflik* system disintegrating around them, and tried to stave off the inflation caused by a growing money economy by raising rents or finding legal expedients for tethering peasants to the soil; those Ottoman political auxiliaries known as 'the Christian Turks' – Greek primates, Serbian *primucar*, Bulgarian *corbaci*, Rumanian *boyars*,

The Sick Man and the British Physician 95

Orthodox bishops – had to contemplate the wisdom of realigning their political loyalties by becoming good nationalists; the Greek clergy were deeply divided between aristocrats of the Orthodox church loyal to the Ottoman establishment, and village priests who closely identified themselves with their impoverished neighbours. There were prospects as well as problems. Ivan Geshov's 'peaceful invaders' – ordinary Christian folk with a little money, a special craft, or just a competence in the Greek *lingua franca* of the Balkan trade – began transplanting themselves beyond the confines of their traditional linguistic and ethnic groupings, becoming townsmen among the Ottomans in Belgrade, Sofia, Sarajevo, Novi Bazar, Yambol, and Tatar Pazarjik, as well as giving life to new places. Ottoman pashas, able to offer some security in their areas of jurisdiction, accepted migrant refugees, occasionally fleeing from Ottoman misgovernment elsewhere. Haji Mustafa, a governor of Belgrade, armed and used his Christian *rayas* to suppress the janizary dissidents under his nominal rule and, on account of his unusual benevolence, was remembered as the 'Mother of the Serbs'.[44]

Through all the turbulence and political dislocation, Aubin could still report on the incredibly long mule-trains wending northwards from southern ports in 1812 to the markets of the Danube and beyond, illustrating the pressing need for more wheeled vehicles and for improved roads. Besides drawing much western Anatolian produce to the Balkan fairs, and obtaining 'a great part of the internal maritime commerce of Turkey', the Balkan traders were able 'at length to share in the exchange of the corn, oil, silk, and other products of Greece for the manufactured goods and colonial produce of the European nations'. In fact, only Ottoman merchants were missing from the fairs T. Stoianovich has mapped so patiently,[45] while even Persians travelled to the largest of them all, the great fair at Pest. Whether the truth is that the dwindling Muslims positively preferred an enclosed trading system of their own, or lacked the language skills and contacts essential to join any other, it was supposed that what they really lacked was any sophisticated experience of money as a commercial lubricant and, indeed, that they might just lack money.

Muslim merchants by their apparent inactivity, and pashas by revelations of their occasional dependency on their Christians, thus tempted men of special luck or energy like Karageorge and Milovanovic, both successful pig-traders, to move through trade to politics.[46] The same story was repeated in the Aegean, where the notion that the Turk was neither farmer nor merchant was enlarged by the belief that he was not a sailor either. The once totally deserted islands of Spetsia and Psara, with financing from Smyrna, became centres of a thriving shipbuilding industry whose vessels, converted to war purposes in 1821, smashed the Ottoman hold on southern Greece; these islands made Greek independence. Thus the Ottoman authorities were prevented by internal and disabling difficulties, and not only by foreign diplomats, from really capitalizing on the Napoleonic years, when the Levant seas rarely saw French, British, or Austrian merchant ships. By contrast, the Greeks, using the Russian carrying trade from the Black Sea as their nursery for sailors, raised a fleet of 615 vessels crewed by over 37,000 men.[47] Whether Greeks would become as politically sensitized as Serbs was long controverted. Henry Holland, travelling in 1812, concluded that they might not. 'The active spirit of the Greeks, deprived in great measure of political or national objects, has taken a general direction towards commerce. But, fettered in this respect also, by their condition on the continent of Greece, they emigrate in considerable numbers to the adjacent countries.' But Holland concluded his reflection by adding that, if any factor *could* make the difference, the commercial renascence in the Balkans, with the glimpses it allowed into a wider, freer world, would produce 'the independent consciousness of power which is necessary as a step to their future liberation'.[48] Holland's countrymen took small notice of such possibilities until after 1825, but until then were more disposed to see the modern Greeks as troublesome pirates than sharers of the Protestant ethic.

★ ★ ★

Goethe has the revellers in Auerbach's *Keller* singing, 'The dear old Holy Roman Empire, how does it hang together?'. By 1815, it no longer did so, but a similar question impressed itself on the consciousness of every curious man examining that other ramshackle polity, the Ottoman Empire, a similarly extensive state with similarly uncertain means for disciplining and shaping its own destiny. The Napoleonic age of upheaval proportioned some of

Europe's contempt as it watched, sometimes with chagrin, sometimes with relief, as the Ottoman Sultan survived unscathed while many illustrious European thrones trembled and fell in humiliation. Several powers even found it useful to join the Ottomans in alliance, at different moments. No further forward in systematic knowledge of Ottoman resources, statesmen could only guess at the empire's chances of a reprieve after 1815 as Russia became more enmeshed in the conservative–revolutionary confrontation in the West. With Russia thus tied down, might the Ottoman Empire float free, at least long enough to put its house in order against any resumption of the eighteenth-century pressures and defeats it had endured? Certainly, there is in the literature, as there was in the chancelleries, a grudging respect for the endurance of a power deemed, in most conventional respects, contemptible, as if it possessed some secret, beyond the political mechanics which raised and lowered western powers in the scale of nations. Turcophilism, that improbable growth, would rise from this unpromising beginning. Until it did, guesses about the central weakness of the Ottoman power were obligatory for every author.

Some 'explanations' were merely abusive, but most were not. A common opinion, which western writers tended to pass from one to the other, anticipated what L.S. Stavrianos calls 'dynastic degeneration': it postulated that the first ten Sultans were vigorous leaders whose successors retreated from the battlefield to the narrower challenges of the harem, thus taking the dynasty out of the mainstream of public affairs, leaving the state a body without a head.[49] Some writers, perhaps after hoping for a constitutional explanation in Mouradja D'Ohsson's magnificent folio volumes, complete by 1824, concluded that Ottoman government had become elaborately organized deadlock.[50] Thomas Thornton believed the main problem was not a shortage of money so much as an attitude towards money: the Ottomans were adhering to the discredited notion that a full treasure-chest means power.[51] Anticipating one of Halil Inalcik's modern concerns, William Eton blamed much on the fixity of men in functions within the 'circle of equity', writing that 'every man is supposed to know his own business or profession, with which it is esteemed foolish and improper for any other person to interfere'; in short, occupational and social immobility.[52] William Wittman blamed all on backward military technology, having watched an Ottoman army leave Constantinople to fight the French in 1798: 'some of them were enveloped in curious network coats of mail of steel, others wore yellow dresses, decorated with ribbons . . . and brass helmets on their heads . . . armed with spears and lances'; the wild janizaries were the problem, Wittman and other western experts believed.[53] Once the spearhead of conquest, they had now domesticated themselves; fighting less, rebelling more, contesting *civil* authority in Ottoman towns from Belgrade to Aleppo, and in general disturbing the civilian context from which an earlier, celibate discipline had segregated them.[54] It is no wonder westerners thought the destruction of this decadent order in 1826 was a major 'reform'. The baleful issue of tax-farming, with major resultant loss to the imperial treasury, was, perhaps, the most repeated criticism of the Ottoman administrative system: when a British official calculated the final indemnity independent Greece should pay the Sultan in 1831, he first computed the taxes Greeks had paid, then said one-eighth of this sum would well represent what traditionally reached Constantinople.[55]

It will be noticed that these were objective speculations about the Ottoman state, though the language in which they were expressed was not without passion and reprobation. It was left to Volney, of all people, to offer an intemperate opinion for his time, though it would have a growing following in after years. This was the view of Islam as the great corrupter: 'no one was more ignorant than Mahomed [and] of the absurd compositions ever produced, none is more truly wretched than his book.'[56] About the only later theory which went unanticipated in the first third of the nineteenth century was the A.H. Merriman-Lybyer red-herring which proposes that the Ottoman Empire was brought down as Muslims replaced Christians in the bureaucratic woodwork, a theory, as we can well acknowledge, which would have appealed to the superiority complexes of not a few British readers, among others, had it been offered them.[57]

The attempt to bring the Ottoman Empire into a tutelary relationship with Great Britain belongs to the middle third of the nineteenth century, and to a later instalment of this study. Governments were not, to begin with, much drawn to the novelty of guiding the processes of 'reform' and 'modernization' in the

Ottoman case, though they faced the same challenge with steady confidence in that other arena which they now had to themselves, India. So it was not really the difficulties which daunted British ministers but the possible size of the bill, in terms of their relations with other powers. It is an important fact that most British ambassadors at Constantinople became pro-Ottoman while their masters in London havered: most of them eventually came home, if not exactly in disgrace, then certainly not to high praise. Lord Palmerston was the only true Ottoman zealot to appear in the highest office at home. The assumption common to virtually all Englishmen was, of course, that the East would only enter the modern world by methods determined by outsiders: to take a practical illustration, industrial development would not make sense as that was a race already won, by westerners. Orientals should take note. Unaware of the stubborn power of traditions in their own society – how many British 'reformers' really measured the conservative influence upon British legislation of their own *ulema* in the House of Lords? – there was a strong inclination to think that any traditional society can, under guidance, break through the restraints of its own conventional thinking, and find its due place in the world order. The Ottomans were not, however, Queen Victoria's 'dear Indians'. They were independent and they were heathens, and if knowledge is power, it is still not a patch on prejudice. An increasing number of the queen's subjects disliked the Ottomans the more they heard about them, so that would-be reformers and modernizers of the empire from outside were also always at the mercy of fluctuations in their fellow-countrymen's fears of Russia, or general regard for the Ottomans. One Englishman, looking at the need for regenerating the Ottoman Empire in 1812, asked 'Can the Koran stretch to this point? Will the ever watchful eagle of the North [Russia] allow it?' It never occurred to him to ask if he or his countrymen, seeing the East prismatically through their own shifting anxieties and interests, could ever hope to recognize with any certainty what truly needed to be done.

NOTES

1. H. Gorvett-Smith, *Kinglake's Eothen* (London, n.d.); W.E. Moore, *The Impact*

of Industry (Englewood Cliffs, N.J., 1965), p. 15.
2. Eothen, pp. 9–13, passim; the only biography of Urquhart is Gertrude Robinson, David Urquhart: Some Chapters in the Life of a Victorian Knight Errant of Justice and Liberty (Oxford, 1920), but see M.H. Jenks, 'The Activities and Influence of David Urquhart, 1833–56' (Ph.D. dissertation, London, 1964).
3. Eothen, p. 17; W. Wittman, Travels in Turkey (London, 1803), p. 133; Koehler to Elgin, 4 July 1800, Elgin MSS. Koehler was head of the British military mission to the Turkish army in Palestine, and died of plague himself in December 1800. Elgin was British ambassador at Constantinople. The grand vizier in question was Yusuf Ziya Pasha, for whom see A.G. Gould, 'Lords or Bandits? The Derebeys of Cilicia', International Journal of Middle East Studies, vii (1976), 487; S. Shaw, Between Old and New: The Ottoman Empire under Selim III, 1789–1807 (Cambridge, Mass., 1971), pp. 244–85.
4. Bolsover, 'Lord Ponsonby and the Eastern Question', is still one of the best introductions to the genesis of the supportive alignment, along with F.S. Rodkey, 'Lord Palmerston and the Rejuvenation of Turkey, 1830–1839', Journal Modern History, i (1929), 570–93; ii (1930), 193–225; see also, Webster, 'Urquhart, Ponsonby and Palmerston'.
5. Eothen, p. 18.
6. For example, a British dragoman in 1836 wrote: 'The sultan may be compared, with propriety, to an infirm man, supported by crutches; withdraw them and he must fall'; Early Correspondence of Richard Wood, ed. Allan Cunningham (London, 1966), p. 87.
7. 'Introduction', in The Ottoman State and Its Place in World History, ed. K. Karpat (Leiden, 1974), p. 4.
8. A.H. Hourani, 'The Ottoman Background of the Modern Middle East', in ibid., p. 68.
9. C. Issawi, Economic History of the Middle East, 1800–1914 (Chicago, 1966), p. 23.
10. In 1789, the under-secretary at the Foreign Office, J. Bland Burges, said, 'the immense number of despatches which come from and go to foreign courts are piled up in large presses, but no note of them taken, nor is there even an index to them . . . it would be a Herculean task to put things right'; Letters of Correspondence of J.B. Burges, ed. J. Hutton (London 1885), pp. 131–2. The eventual 'Hercules' wrote about his experiences in E. Hertslet, Recollections of the Old Foreign Office (London, 1911). In Constantinople, the archives of the embassy were, until 1800, in the hands of the Levant Company and Lord Elgin, who arrived in that year as ambassador, had great difficulty in obtaining custody of them.
11. An excellent, though by no means complete, catalogue of such works is Shirley H. Weber's Voyages and Travels Made in the Near East . . . in the Gennadius Library in Athens (Princeton, 1952).
12. L. Chalcocondylas, De origine et rebus gestis (Basileae, 1556), the first European study of Ottoman history, more commonly found in French translation as L'histoire de la décadence de l'empire grec et établissement de celuy des Turcs (in Paris editions of 1584 and 1662); R. Knolles, Generall Historie of the Turkes (London, 1610), more usually found in the revision of Sir Paul Rycaut, in 2 or 3 volumes (London, 1687–1700); A.G. de Busbecq, Legationis Turcicae (Paris, 1589), translated into English by C.T. Forster and F.H. Blackburne Daniell as Life and Letters of Ogier Ghislain de Busbecq (London, 1881); J.P. de Tournefort, Rélation d'un Voyage du Levant (Paris, 1717); J. von Hammer-Purgstall, Geschichte des

Osmanischen Reiches (Pest, 1827–35).
13. T. Thornton, *The Present State of Turkey* (London, 1809), ii. 106, 163, 189.
14. Baron de Tott, *Mémoires sur les Turcs* (Amsterdam, n.d.); F.C.H.L. Pouqueville, *Voyage en Morée à Constantinople, en Albanie* (Paris, 1805); F. Beaujour, *A View of the Commerce of Greece . . . from 1787 to 1797* (London, 1800); A. Boppe, *La Mission de l'Adjutant-commandant Mériage à Vidin* (Paris, 1886); A. Juchereau de Saint-Denis, *Révolutions de Constantinople, en 1807 et 1808* (Paris, 1819); E.D. Clarke, *Travels in Various Countries of Europe, Asia, and Africa* (Cambridge, 1810); C.F. Volney, *Travels through Syria and Egypt* (London, 1787); W.M. Leake, *Travels in the Morea* (London, 1830); A. Slade, *Record of Travels in Turkey, Greece . . . in the Years 1829, 1830 and 1831* (London, 1832).
15. R.R. Nelson, 'A Theory of the Low Level Equilibrium Trap in Underdeveloped Economies', *American Economic Review*, xlvi (1956), 894–908.
16. See the two works written far apart by Charles Macfarlane, *Turkey and Its Destiny* (London, 1850), which estimates the changes visible since his previous *Constantinople in 1828* (London, 1829); Sir J. Gardner Wilkinson, *Dalmatia and Montenegro* (London, 1848); Walsh, *A Residence*; W. Wilkinson, *An Account of the Principalities of Wallachia and Moldavia* (London, 1820); J.B. Fraser, *A Winter's Journey from Constantinople to Teheran* (London, 1838).
17. J. Bessières, *Mémoire sur la Vie et la Puissance d'Ali Pacha* (Paris, 1820); G.A. Olivier, *Voyage dans l'Empire Othoman* (Paris, 1801). For later discussion of French involvement in the area see A. Boppe, *L'Albanie et Napoléon, 1797–1814* (Paris, 1914); P. Pisani, *La Dalmatie de 1797 à 1815* (Paris, 1893); P. Skok, 'Le mouvement illyrien et les Français', *Le Monde slave*, xii (1935); A. de Gardane, *Journal d'un voyage dans la Turquie d'Asie et la Perse* (Paris, 1809); A. Chaumette des Fossés, *Voyage en Bosnie dans . . . 1807 et 1808* (Paris, 1822); and, perhaps best of all, C. Pertusier, *La Bosnie* (Paris, 1822), which uses the accounts of other French officers in the area.
18. I.C. Dragasanu, *Peregrinual Transilvan* (Bucharest, 1842); J.A. Demian, *Statistiche Beschreibung der Militär-Grenze* (Vienna, 1806). Dragasanu was a Romanian by birth but an Austrian subject, while Demian was an Austrian army officer. Extracts from their work, in English, are in D. Warriner, *Contrasts in Emerging Societies* (London, 1965), p. 145 *et seq.*, p. 324 *et seq.*
19. For the views of the Ottoman ambassador at Paris between 1802 and 1806, see E.Z. Karal, *Halet Efendinin Paris Büyük Elciligi* (Constantinople, 1940); B. Lewis, *Emergence of Modern Turkey* (London, 1961), discusses the *Impact of the West* in ch. 3, with quotations from the court historians; N. Soutzo [N. Soutsos], *Notions Statistiques sur la Moldavie* (Jassy, 1849), is by a scion of one of the Fanariot families, on which see M.P. Zallony, *Essai sur les Fanariotes* (Marseilles, 1824), and also Cyril Mango, 'The Phanariots and the Byzantine Tradition' in *The Struggle for Greek Independence*, ed. R. Clogg (London, 1973); among consuls, W. Wilkinson, British consul at Bucharest between 1814 and 1818, wrote *An Account of the Principalities of Wallachia and Moldavia* in 1820, and E. Poujade, French consul-general at Bucharest for some years before the Crimean War, produced his *Chrétiens et Turcs* (Paris, 1859); John Galt, *Letters from the Levant* (London, 1813).
20. Warriner, *Contrasts in Emerging Societies*, pp. 142, 167; *Eothen*, p. 32, 'I was always conning over my maps and fancied that I knew pretty well my line'; Walsh, *A Residence*, i. 212; F. Chateaubriand, *Travels in Greece, Palestine* (New York, 1814), p. 176; Fraser, *Winter's Journey*, pp. 104, 138; A. Ubicini, *Letters on Turkey*, trans. Lady Easthope (London, 1856), i. 325; Badia y Leyblich,

Travels of Ali Bey (London, 1816), passim; A.H. Layard, Early Adventures in Persia, Susiana, and Babylonia (London, 1887), passim; F. Burnaby, On Horseback through Asia Minor (London, 1877), p. 84; A.F. Townshend, A Military Consul in Turkey (London, 1910), passim. Macfarlane, Turkey and Its Destiny, i. 32 refers to 'hundreds of thousands of acres [which] lay untilled . . . for centuries untouched by the plough'.

21. Chateaubriand, Travels in Greece, p. 72; Chaumette des Fossés, Voyage en Bosnie, pp. 33, 41; Macfarlane, Turkey and Its Destiny, i. 231, 235–6, 244, 316; Fraser, A Winter's Journey, p. 31. On the other hand, Hobhouse, Travels in Albania, rarely mentions Turkish villagers north-west of Corinth.

22. Pouqueville, Voyage en Morée, i. 265; see also on Pouqueville, the long and stimulating article by T. Stoianovich, 'The Conquering Orthodox Balkan Merchant', Journal of Economic History, xx (1960), 234–313, which considers the prevalence of abortion as an economic measure. On the effects of plague, and related matters of quarantine, see Thornton, The Present State of Turkey, ii. 208, et seq.; Wittman, Travels in Turkey, pp. 75, 277; E.B.B. Barker, Turkey under the Last Five Sultans (London, 1876), p. 164; Walsh, A Residence, i. 64. An important early work on plague is A.F. Bulard, De la Peste Orientale (Paris, 1839).

23. An interesting comparison can be made between Hobhouse, Travels in Albania, pp. 96–116, and the excellent study, D.N. Skiotis, 'From Bandit to Pasha: First Steps in the Rise to Power of Ali of Tepelen, 1750–1784', International Journal of Middle East Studies, ii (1971), 219–44; early travellers often exaggerated, whereas Skiotis shows that Hobhouse's data was often on the conservative side, both with reference to Ali Pasha's wealth and the number of his armed supporters. For the agricultural system and the forms of tenure, see T. Stoianovich, 'Land Tenure and Related Sectors of the Balkan Economy, 1600–1800', Journal of Economic History, xiii (1953), 398–411; for the destruction by Ali Pasha and his father of Moscopolis, possibly the largest of all Balkan towns in 1788, see Stoianovich, 'Orthodox Merchant', p. 252. One of the best and most instructive accounts of Albania after the age of Ali Pasha is in D. Urquhart, The Spirit of the East (London, 1839), pp. 202–319, a journey made after Urquhart was wounded in the Greek war for independence.

24. Chateaubriand, Travels in Greece, p. 157; Warriner, Contrasts in Emerging Societies, pp. 142, 170; Issawi, Economic History, pp. 3, 17 n.; the first Ottoman census of 1831 is examined critically by E.Z. Karal, Ilk Nüfus Sayimi (Ankara, 1943); for army recruitment policies, and the effect of refugee immigration in holding up the Asian population of the empire, see S.J. and E.K. Shaw, History of the Ottoman Empire and Modern Turkey (Cambridge, 1977), ii. 100, 116–17; Ubicini, Letters on Turkey, i. 18; for a discussion of the general reliability of nineteenth-century censuses and their varying principles of calculation, see C. Issawi, 'The Ottoman Empire in the European Economy 1600–1914', in Ottoman State, ed. K. Karpat, especially pp. 107–10, where Issawi argues that the empire contained about one-fifth of the population of Europe in 1500 but only seven per cent by 1880.

25. Hobhouse, Travels in Albania, i. ch. 12; Volney, Travels through Syria, ii. ch. 37; Wittman, Travels in Turkey, p. 27; Macfarlane, Turkey and Its Destiny, i. 66; Warriner, Contrasts in Emerging Societies, p. 86.

26. Macfarlane, Turkey and Its Destiny, i. 261, 278, 284; Ubicini, Letters on Turkey, i. 266, 281, 332; Wittman, Travels in Turkey, pp. 218–21; Barker, Last Five Sultans, p. 76; Stoianovich, 'Orthodox Merchant', passim. On roads see V.

Monro, *Summer Ramble in Syria* (London, 1835), ii. 262; also Macfarlane, *Turkey and Its Destiny*, i. 49, 137, 148, 154, 157.
27. Ibrahim Yasa, *Studies in Turkish Local Government* (Ankara, 1955), p. 75; Carle C. Zimmerman, 'Rural Development in Turkey', in *Sociology of Underdevelopment*, ed. Carle C. Zimmerman (Toronto, 1970); R.H. Pfaff, 'Disengagement from Tradition in Turkey', in *Political Modernization*, ed. C.E. Welch (Belmont, Cal., 1969), p. 105 *et seq*. Zimmerman, 'Rural Development', p. 254, says Turkey has 34,063 independent villages (as against the *bucak*, or group of villages) in which the average population was 414. Many are located on the hill flanks, which seemed perverse to travellers a century and a half ago, but which was a balance of temperature, security, and amenities. Bandits could be seen, plains temperatures and insects avoided, land naturally drained, and upper forests made more accessible. The soil was often poor, but offset by proximity to grazing and fuel. Examples of the dividing line between western-oriented Anatolia and the east are very numerous: Macfarlane, *Turkey and Its Destiny*, i. 151, *et seq*., comments on the good crops of potato and turnips to the west; Monro, *Summer Ramble in Syria*, p. 286, on a journey from Egypt, noticed 'the first vehicle that I had seen since I left Europe [excluding Cairo] . . . the wheels were circular pieces of wood; animals were fed on chopped straw to the east, and so lost condition sharply, or were killed off, but haystacks were occasionally noticed to the west'; see also, Ubicini, *Letters on Turkey*, i. 258, 315; Volney, *Travels through Syria*, ch. 39. Volney is another who says he never saw a wheeled vehicle in all Syria.
28. D.G. Hogarth, *A Wandering Scholar in the Levant* (London, 1896), p. 69.
29. Macfarlane, *Turkey and Its Destiny*, i. 252 *et seq*.
30. Wittman, *Travels in Turkey*, pp. 218–21; Barker, *Last Five Sultans*, p. 16 *et seq*.; Hogarth, *Wandering Scholars*, p. 90. The tax system, and the modes of taxcalculation – beyond the familiar idea that Christians paid a special tax to 'keep their heads' – was largely unknown to western travellers: there is also very slight discussion of the legalities of land-ownership, tenant rights, or rents; cadastral surveys only began after the Crimean War, in Bursa in 1858 and Janina in 1859, and only ended in 1908. The surveys are discussed in G. Young, *Corps de Droit Ottoman* (Oxford, 1905–6), vi. 93–100; see also the comprehensive description of tax changes in S. Shaw, 'The Nineteenth Century Ottoman Tax Reforms and Revenue System', *International Journal of Middle East Studies*, vi (1975), 421–59.
31. *Islamic Society and the West*, ed. H.A.R. Gibb and H. Bowen (Oxford, 1963), i. part I. 256.
32. Skiotis, 'From Bandit to Pasha', *passim*.
33. D. Urquhart, *The Spirit of the East*, ii. 107; both Urquhart, ibid., ii. 142–57, and Robert Curzon, *Visits to Monasteries in the Levant* (London, 1865), p. 278, were captured by bandits.
34. Besides Monro, *Summer Ramble in Syria*, ii. 300–8, who describes having to cross the Gulf to avoid the Küçük Ali robbers, see A.G. Gould, 'Lords or Bandits?'; Shaw, *Selim III*, pp. 212–17.
35. Ibid., p. 285.
36. Mary Elgin to Dowager Lady Elgin, 12 Jan. 1802, Elgin MSS; Straton, chargé d'affaires, to Elgin, 29 May 1802, ibid., in which he says the rebel Pasvanoglu is master of Wallachia, will soon take Bucharest, then Constantinople, depose Selim III, and murder all the leading officials of state. On 29 Aug. 1802, Straton reported that the rebel had been bought off; Chateaubriand, *Travels in Greece*,

describes (p. 385) how Djezzar Pasha of Acre raided across the Jordan for sheep and camels, doubled their market price, and forcibly sold them to the principal butchers of Jerusalem.
37. Data on the Sultan's income were very hard to obtain, and made more so by the existence of various treasuries, of which the sultan's privy purse (*cep-i humayun*) was but one. Elgin MSS 60/16/18 contains a detailed estimate for 1798 which puts the entire income of the Ottoman government at only 32,250,000 piastres, or about £2,500,000; Thornton, *The Present State of Turkey*, ii. ch. 5, put the total income of the state at £3,375,000, adding that as much as £20,000,000 more was raised and spent in the provinces. Ubicini, *Letters on Turkey*, i. 266, claims, on the basis of French embassy information, that 'during several years' the tithes, land-taxes, poll-taxes, customs receipts, indirect taxes, tributes from Egypt, Moldavia, Wallachia, and Serbia had totalled between £6 and 7 million. This refers to the pre-Crimean years. For comparison, the net income of Great Britain stood at £13,214,053 in 1784.
38. Chateaubriand, *Travels in Greece*, p. 400; Monro, *Summer Ramble in Syria*, p. 222 for Aleppo, p. 275 for Eregli, p. 286 for Konya; Barker, *Last Five Sultans*, p. 185 for Aleppo; Fraser, *Winter's Journey*, p. 114 for Sofia, p. 135 for Edirne, whose British consul told him it was 'one of the biggest towns in European Turkey', p. 190 for Bolu, p. 204 for Amasya, p. 251 for Erzerum, in which 'half the houses are in ruins, the other half in the most squalid disrepair', p. 282 for Bayazid; Badia y Leyblick, *Ali Bey*, p. 12 for Cairo, p. 30 for Suez, p. 40 for Jidda, pp. 94–105 for Mecca, pp. 214–27 for Jerusalem, pp. 264–82 for Damascus, pp. 291–3 for Hama, p. 296 for Aleppo, p. 312 for Konya, pp. 326–50 for Constantinople, p. 370 for Edirne, p. 372 for Bucharest; Wittman, *Travels in Turkey*, p. 15, thought Constantinople had 400,000 people; W. Eton, *Survey of the Turkish Empire* (London, 1799), p. 287, estimated the all-time maximum was 300,000; Hobhouse, *Travels in Albania*, rejects the idea of one million in 1810, but offers no figure of his own; Macfarlane, *Turkey and Its Destiny*, i. 105, noticed the decline of population since his earlier visit, in the Muslim districts of the city. Shaw, *Ottoman Empire*, ii. 241, shows earlier figures to have been inflated, and from Ottoman records offers for Constantinople a population of 391,00 *adults* in 1844; 430,000 in 1856; 547,437 in 1878. As many as 100,000 may have been foreign residents. Ahmed Lutfi, *Tarihi Lutfi* (Constantinople, 1290–1328 A.H.), put the adult male population of Constantinople in 1826 (i. 289, ii. 175, iii. 142–6) at 45,000 Muslims; 30,000 Armenians; 20,000 Greeks. For distribution of people by ethnicity, religion, nationality, see Ubicini, *Letters on Turkey*, i. 18–19, 24, who put the city's population at 891,000 in 1844. The largest Balkan city was Salonika, with 100,000 in 1832 according to J.E. De Kay, *Sketches of Turkey in 1831 and 1832* (New York, 1833), p. 172. The next largest Balkan urban centre was, most people agreed, Belgrade, with 50,000 people in 1825. See Stoianovich 'Orthodox Merchant', p. 249. For comparison, J.R. McCulloch, *A Dictionary, Practical, Theoretical and Historical of Commerce* (London, 1834), p. 834, estimates some other city populations as follows: London, Paris, 1,500,000; Berlin, 436,000; Vienna, 486,000; St Petersburg, 492,000.
39. Chateaubriand, *Travels in Greece*, p. 76; Fraser, *Winter's Journey*, pp. 71, 77, 157, thought Constantinople the most oriental city, more so than any in Persia: 'it puts me in mind of the Arabian Nights Entertainments more than any of the Persian or Indian capitals.' Fraser describes old Ottoman ruins in many places, e.g. Tokat (p. 207); Monro, *Summer Ramble in Syria* ii. 305, speaks of Isnik

'contracted to a rude village, shrinking within the circle of its walls'; the broken bridges of Bursa are described in Macfarlane, *Turkey and Its Destiny*, i. 130. More significant, Macfarlane and others notice modern public buildings, of the age of Mahmud II, falling into decay.

40. Allan Cunningham, 'The Levant Trade in 1812: The Journal of Christophe Aubin', *Archivum Ottomanicum*, viii (1983), 1–126.
41. The raw materials were predominantly natural products, such as cotton, medicinal herbs, fruits, mohair, raw silk, animal skins, natural dyes, vallonia for tanning; minerals were believed to exist in great quantity, but rarely found. See Ubicini, *Letters on Turkey*, i. 274, for a typically unfounded piece of optimism.
42. The stages of decline are easily sampled. Barker, *Last Five Sultans*, p. 25, writes about the Baghdad convoys, 3,000 camels strong, arriving twice each year carrying textiles from India, around 1805. Then, in the 1830s, a British consular report (Issawi, *Economic History*, p. 41), refers to British textiles, in great quantity, having 'entirely superseded the importation via the Persian Gulf of a similar quantity from the East Indies'. That development allowed Urquhart (*Turkey and Its Resources* [London, 1833], pp. 141–4) to assert that British 'cottons and muslins, calicoes, chintzes, etc. are, if not better, infinitely cheaper than those of the East', and to predict a highly beneficial readjustment of Ottoman economic goals, in which Great Britain should persuade the Sultans to 'turn their attention to cultivation'. They had the lands and the climate. 'The village which was isolated before "is rescued": cultivation extends, wealth accumulates, instruction follows, desire for new objects increases, produce is raised. England's looms have called this prosperity into existence but she *must* sell at the lowest possible prices to enable the Turkish peasant to buy.' The last stage but one is described by Ubicini, *Letters on Turkey*, pp. 339–43; by 1848, Bursa and Diarbekir were producing one-tenth of their output of 30 years before; the Scutari–Tirnovo looms numbered 2,000 in 1812 but 200 in 1841; Aleppo's 40,000 looms, producing £1,000,000 worth of textiles per annum at one time, produced only £75,000 worth in 1853. 'The same decay is observable in the old manufacturing towns of Syria and Arabian Iraq.' The last stage is that the peasant remained where he was, and Urquhart's rescue operation never touched him. See also E.C. Clark, 'The Ottoman Industrial Revolution', *International Journal of Middle East Studies*, v (1974), 65–76.
43. In the early years of the Greek war for independence, Levant Company merchants lost many cargoes to Greek pirates, as did the Austrians, and it was company pressure on the foreign secretary, Canning – who was also MP for the port of Liverpool – which brought him to recognize the Greeks as belligerents, thus exempting British vessels from their depredations.
44. For collusion between the Armenian church hierarchy and the *derebeys* of Anatolia, see Gould, 'Lords or Bandits?', pp. 495–6; P. Sherrard, 'Church, State and the Greek War of Independence', in *Greek Independence*, ed. Clogg, pp. 182–200; for Geshov's 'peaceful invaders', see the quotations in Warriner, *Contrasts in Emerging Societies*, pp. 260–7. Geshov, from a Plovdiv textile family, studied in Manchester under Jevons, was condemned to death by the Ottomans, but survived to become prime minister of Bulgaria in 1911.
45. Stoianovich, 'Orthodox Merchant', pp. 261, 280–1, 299, explains that Ottoman Jews often took out Austrian citizenship, much as Greeks in the Black Sea trade obtained Russian passports, a process, like the Capitulatory regime in general, which took more and more originally Ottoman subjects, many of

them merchants, under the umbrella of extraterritorial privileges, thus giving them great advantages over – for instance – Muslim merchants.
46. Stoianovich, 'Orthodox Merchant', pp. 282, 307; J.M. Halpern, *A Serbian Village* (New York, 1958); the Serbian export trade in livestock to the Habsburg empire in 1800 was worth 3 million francs.
47. G.B. Leon, *Greek Merchant Marine* (Athens, 1972), pp. 32–3; Hydra had 99 vessels by 1806, 186 by 1820. The wealth of the Hydriots collapsed from 7,750,000 piastres in 1816 to 1,375,000 piastres in 1820, as British and French merchantmen reappeared in the Levant. The growth of trade is in N. Svoronos, *Le Commerce de Salonique au XVIIIe siècle* (Paris, 1956).
48. H. Holland, *Travels in the Ionian Islands, Albania . . . during the years 1812 and 1813* (London, 1815), pp. 148, 530; Hobhouse, *Travels in Albania*, ii. 597, also doubted if the Greek people had the necessary 'feeling and spirit', and thought the upper clergy would damp down any insubordination. The conjunction of mercantile and political energy in the *Filiki Eteria* is discussed by G.D. Frangos in *Greek Independence*, ed. Clogg, ch. 4, who points to Odessa as a logical starting point for political agitation.
49. Stavrianos, *The Balkans since 1453* (New York, 1965), p. 118.
50. I.M. D'Ohsson, *Tableau général de l'empire Othoman* (Paris, 1788–1824).
51. Thornton, *Present State of Turkey*, ii. ch. 5, mentions most of the current European criticisms; although 'rivers of wealth . . . flow through every province', not enough reached Constantinople. Too much money, besides being locally raised, was locally spent, with insufficient auditing to show how it was spent. There was still too much inefficiency in the processes by which payments-in-kind, such as the annual tribute of 500,000 sheep and 80,000 goats and oxen from the Principalities, or the hemp from the Black Sea towns, was converted into state income. Depreciating the coinage by retaining the face value but lowering the precious-metal content of successive coin issues was seen as the cardinal sin. Under Mahmud II, the process carried on, so that the 'form and name of the Ottoman Turkish piastre or its equivalent to the pound sterling fell from 23 in 1814 to 104 in 1829'; B. Lewis, *Emergence of Modern Turkey*, p. 108.
52. Eton, *Survey*, p. 203. The 'circle of equity', was a theory of social equilibrium which postulated the mutual dependency of men classified by occupation, and the resultant dangers whenever men ceased to recognize or accept their due position within the 'circle'. A practical example of disequilibrium was the deterioration of the *sipahi-timar* system whereby a military group lost sight of its true function and became a hereditary landed interest, thus merging with the *re'aya*, the food producers. The janizary infantrymen took the same direction as the *sipahi* cavalrymen, with catastrophic results for the Ottoman state. Halil Inalcik, writing in *The Ottoman State*, ed. Karpat, p. 54, stresses that the 'circle of equity' did not immobilize capitalistic activity. On the contrary, a typical piece of advice for the conscientious ruler, who upholds the circle, says, 'look with favour on the merchants . . . always care for them; let no one harass them for through their trading the land becomes prosperous'. See also N. Itzkovitz, *Ottoman Empire and Islamic Tradition* (New York, 1972), ch. 4. Nevertheless, the distressed condition of the peasantry suggests that it was another element whose position in the 'circle' had been allowed to deteriorate through lack of paternalistic rule.
53. Wittman, *Travels in Turkey*, p. 9.
54. N.M. Penzer, *The Harem* (Philadelphia, n.d.), pp. 89–93; Lewis, *Turkey*, pp. 75–81.

55. Stratford Canning, British delegate at the Poros conference in 1829; his calculations are in his own private papers, FO 352/22/4/5.
56. As mentioned earlier in the text, Islam came in for much heavy criticism as 'a false creed' (even Sale, the Koran's excellent translator, thought of it as a falsehood); the Ottomans were incompetent but might survive; ordinary Turks were admired.
57. A.H. Lybyer, *The Government of the Ottoman Empire in the Time of Suleiman the Magnificent* (Cambridge, Mass., 1913); R.B. Merriman, *Suleiman the Magnificent* (New York, 1966). Arnold Toynbee retained always his belief that 'the Ottoman Empire's success was largely due to the policy of drawing . . . on the ability of its Christian subjects', and seems also to have accepted the Lybyer corollary.

CHAPTER IV

Stratford Canning and the *Tanzimat*

Numerous British writers, from Alexander Kinglake to Harold Temperley, have linked the name of Stratford Canning so confidently with the genesis and progress of the Ottoman reform movement that their readers are to be excused for imagining that but for him there would have been no reforms. In his famous *History*, Kinglake portrays Stratford as the lonely defender of British interests in the East, but also sees the ambassador as a man determined, in 1854, to encircle another great achievement – the renascence of the Ottoman Empire – with the guardian arm of Britain. When Canning returned to the endangered empire in 1853, 'the event spread a sense of safety but also a sense of awe . . . it was the angry return of a king whose realm had been suffered to fall into a danger'.[1]

Now Stratford, who first went to the Ottoman Empire in 1808 and was still writing letters to *The Times* about the so-called Eastern Question after the congress of Berlin in 1878, had the inestimable advantage of outliving all his critics; and when he died in 1880, Dean Stanley in his funeral oration described him as 'the best bulwark against its [the Ottoman Empire's] ruin'.[2] The great reputation passed on, substantially intact, of a vigilant watchman, the opponent of greedy emperors from Napoleon I to Nicholas II of Russia, and the patient counsellor of Sultans, whom he set patiently upon the path of civilization and change, chiding, guiding, warning, helping. Tennyson described him as 'the Voice of England in the East', being no more able than anyone else to recollect what an embarrassing as well as commanding voice it had once been. In 1888, Stanley Lane-Poole produced the inevitable and authorized biography: the Foreign Office did the authorizing. Fifty years later, Stratford's own estimate of his place in the Ottoman reform movement, which in his memoirs – a priceless document which Lane-Poole lost – he claimed to have originated, was still good enough for H.W.V. Temperley. After enjoying – if that is the word – the full run of Stratford's correspondence, both public and private, Temperley found it possible to conclude that the age of the *Tanzimat* reforms got under way 'with Reshid as captain and Stratford as pilot'.[3]

This brings us to the Ottoman point of view. In *Tanzimat*, a large publication which appeared in 1940 in Constantinople to mark the centenary of the Ottoman reform movement, the contributing authors described the renascence of their country in great detail, yet with a trivial number of references to Stratford.[4] The general implication of the work is that Stratford occasionally encouraged Ottoman statesmen who were toiling at the slowly revolving wheel of change, but without putting his own shoulder to it. To adapt Temperley's metaphor, they saw Stratford neither as captain nor as pilot, but as a first-class passenger who was rather free with his advice.

Such a diminution of reputation may be due to one or more of a variety of explanations, ranging from the possibility of chauvinism in the authors of *Tanzimat*, to the opposite extreme which would postulate that Stratford's reputation, in this particular regard, is totally undeserved. A great limitation upon the chances of examining this problem profitably has been the tendency of Ottoman historians to write of the nineteenth-century reform period purely in terms of domestic history, while British writers have treated the reforms almost as an offshoot of British foreign policy. Neither is sufficient.[5]

The first critical students of the *Tanzimat* epoch were the philosophical writers of the so-called Young Ottoman school, men who arrived at a limited understanding of the recent past of their country because they were only interested in, and so only asked questions about, a part of it. As a result of their highly subjective inquisition, reformers like Ali Pasha and Fuad Pasha were blamed for abandoning the inspiration and social guidance inherent in the wisdom of Islam in favour of a shallow version of western manners and forms. Even Reshid Pasha, patron of both these reformers, was regarded by his Young Ottoman critics as having been too much under the influence of European secularism, though redeemed by a greater respect for his Sultan than his disciples possessed as well as by a greater caution in his nature.[6] The Young Ottomans were far less able, incidentally, to postulate very clearly just what practical measures of reform the wisdom of Islam might actually allow in the mid-nineteenth century and yet this is precisely the area in which they should have carried on active investigation. If Reshid Ali, and Fuad were on the 'wrong' lines, what would have been 'right'?[7]

Throughout their criticisms, the Young Ottomans imply that a moral reinvigoration of the Ottoman state, and not merely an administrative overhaul, was obtainable without the need for any major concessions either to European secularist thinking in matters of law and individual rights, or to those European notions of territorial sovereignty which already infused the political thinking of a good half of the Sultan's subjects, notably in the Balkans. Was this actually realistic, however desirable, at any stage after 1774, let alone 1839? Was there an Ottoman solution to the predicament of the Ottoman state which could remove the civil and legal disabilities of the millets and raise non-Muslim communities in the empire above the status of second-class citizenship in which, if they were lucky, they lived, *while at the same time* preserving intact the traditional Islamic foundations of the state? It is, of course, arguable that a reformist policy had no obligation to countenance the interests of the Christian millets, since these were composed of unbelievers who had perversely refused the light of Islam, thus voluntarily embracing inferior status. A good deal of this way of thought is discernible in the thinking of the Young Ottomans[8] and clearer still in the attitudes of the Young Turks later on, concerning whose views on modernism and reform a British ambassador said that they resembled crushing the subject peoples in an Ottoman pestle.

Reshid Pasha and his successors did not have a free hand to 'reform' as they pleased. The Ottoman Empire was neither British India nor the American South, places where external pressures and opinions could be disregarded, at least for the time being. If this external pressure adversely affected the character of what was done in the name of reform, producing, in one recent commentator's view, a 'disequilibrium in Ottoman society',[9] it may be asserted, nevertheless, that without such external pressure there would have been far less reform of whatever description. Ironically, therefore, infidel Europe was the real motor of the Ottoman reform movement, insofar as this movement means anything beyond military reorganization and overhaul of the imperial administration in Constantinople and the vilayets. Stratford Canning, who was neither an impartial nor an unprejudiced observer, wished as much as any Ottoman patriot to see the empire survive, reform, and flourish. Disqualified, as he undoubtedly was, as an outsider and an alien, he nevertheless gave immense attention to the modernization of the Ottoman Empire; his professional career, for instance, encompassed the whole *life* of Reshid Pasha.

Stratford's invariable conclusion was that the empire could only survive through *Europeanization*, a view which all the Ottoman reform ministers came to share to a greater or lesser degree. To Stratford, the disestablishment of Islam was also an essential step, but in this regard the reformers were less able to share his thinking and also more afraid of the strength of Ottoman conservative feeling. Both ambassador and reformers were at one in suspecting that the greatest obstacle to the survival of the empire was the dominant millet itself, that is, the Muslim Ottomans who saw no reason for compromise with the conquered people within the empire or the European states beyond. Unlike Stratford Canning, the Young Ottomans believed that the genius of Islam would permit a controlled modernization; from Europe one could borrow things without needing to borrow ideas. The Young Turks, at the threshold of the twentieth century, were less sure of this, and one of them, Kemal Pasha, did not believe it at all. Canning could not have trained a more faithful intellectual descendant than the first president of the Ottoman Republic turned out to be.

It must not be assumed that Stratford's solicitude for the cause of reform was enjoined upon him by British governments because, on balance, he was criticized rather than approved for persisting with the question instead of concentrating upon his diplomatic duties. The typical governmental attitude was that of the earl of Aberdeen, who detested Stratford and who told the ambassador, 'it is quite enough to govern England, and if we are to regulate the affairs of Turkey also I fear the task will be too heavy'. Later on he added, 'I fear you must abandon your notions of regenerating the Ottoman Empire. The corruption and misgovernment in every dep[artmen]t may be enormous; but provided they attend to our complaints I am decidedly of the opinion that we ought not to interfere in the domestic details of their administration.'[10] This kind of fatalism drove Stratford into transports of violent anger, and he was happiest when serving Viscount Palmerston, a foreign secretary who was ready to bully Ottoman ministers and who did not believe, as Aberdeen did, that even an unregenerate Ottoman Empire would be saved by 'a principle of vitality, an occult force', which had kept it going against all predictions for a long time already. Unfortunately for Stratford, the great turning-points in his career found Aberdeen, or Sir Robert Peel, or the earl of Derby in power, and not the easy-going Palmerston, and these men kept him in the East because, embarrassment though he was over Ottoman reform, he would have been a bigger one in Parliament, as they all privately agreed.

Within Stratford's career there is a great watershed at 1829. For over 20 years before that he was a hostile critic of the Ottomans, believing them incapable of reform and destined to retreat into Asia like a glacier retreating in a warmer climatological epoch. Nor did he think hostile neighbours would be responsible. 'Destruction will not come upon this Empire from the north or from the south [from Russia or Egypt]; it is rotten at the heart, the seat of corruption is in the government itself. Conscious of their weakness and slaves to the janizaries', Ottoman ministers strutted in a dream world, and the Sultan was clearly powerless.[11] This judgement also reflected the opinion of British official circles in London; and Viscount Castlereagh, in 1815, was the last senior minister to think of giving the Ottoman Empire a territorial guarantee and a place in the European concert of powers without asking her to qualify for admission by reforming herself. After him, and until 1829, upholding the Ottoman Empire looked too much like upholding a corpse. Opinion changed gradually but most noticeably after the Russian-dictated peace of Adrianople of that year. The old hostility towards Russia was now joined by the new sentiment of Turcophilism. The 1830s produced a wave of travel books which did much to shape the thinking of the shouting majorities of the Crimean War period; and in 1831 Stratford Canning opened his personal assault upon the Ottoman authorities in Constantinople, urging them to mend their ways and repair their empire.

Before this, Stratford had often expressed great doubts about the capacity of the Ottomans to reform themselves: the conjunction of an Asiatic origin and their religion was a fatal disadvantage. As a young whipper-snapper in 1808, he had written, 'they are, almost to a man, proud, ignorant, sly, jealous, and cruel, each . . . cringing to his superiors, quarrelling with his equals, preying upon his dependants, and indiscriminently [sic] cheating them all'. He added graciously, 'There are doubtless some exceptions',[12] but over a long public life he made little attempt to find them, and his enduring attitude is expressed in two particular slogans which recur in his private letters, one to the effect that 'the turcs [sic] are no more to be treated like other people than other people are to be treated like turcs',[13] and the other asserting that 'all turcs are more or less children'. This view became so ingrained that Stratford could never quite believe that Reshid Pasha was not of Greek parentage and, as is well known, he treated all Ottoman ministers with substantial contempt. They also had to meet him on his terms, for he made a point of never learning Turkish beyond the word *bakalim*, which he liked to use with theatrical effect upon terrified junior officials at the Porte. And if he did not get his own way, Stratford simply crossed the road from the Porte to the Sultan himself in the Topkapi Saray. By 1831 the once-aloof Mahmud II was ready to meet him half-way.

The great debate in Ottoman court circles over the causes of imperial decline had been going on for generations before Mahmud II's accession in 1808. Indeed it accelerated that accession, for both Selim III and Mustafa IV were liquidated in quick succession in the struggle between the janizaries and the military reformer Mustafa Alemdar. The janizaries kept the whip-hand until their own annihilation in 1826, an event which Stratford Canning actually witnessed. What Mahmud II meant by reform could not be disclosed before that momentous event, and there were no visible changes in the ruling institution until after it. The effervescence caused by the French Revolution had subsided long ago, leaving a sediment of secular ideas in a few Ottoman minds, but historians can still only guess at its effects upon the lonely, courageous, and inscrutable Mahmud II. If the Martinique beauty, Aimée Dubucq, was genuinely the mother of Mahmud II, and if she introduced him to contemporary French ideas, it is very odd that she should have done so without teaching her son French.[14] Mahmud II did, however, make one significant innovation in the 1820s which was to extend Stratford's opportunities greatly in the years immediately ahead, and this was to raise up a new corps of bureaucrats. The practical result is well expressed by G. Rosen where he writes, 'The status of servants of the government changed from that of slaves to the Sultan to that of servants to the state'.[15]

Mahmud II had no wish to do violence to the main prejudices or ideas of his ulema and his people, and a survey of Stratford's dispatches during the 1820s reveals that the positions of power were still being filled by anti-western ministers, that is, by ministers ready to borrow western *things* while rejecting the contamination of western *ideas*. Such ministers therefore anticipated the Young Ottoman error and supposed that intellectual seepage from Europe could be filtered to make it safe for Muslims. Mahmud II was himself still thinking in this mistaken way in 1838 when, at the opening of a new medical school, he said to the first entrants: 'You will study scientific medicine in French . . . my purpose is not to educate you in the French language . . . work to acquire a knowledge of medicine . . . and strive gradually to take it into Turkish.'[16]

The generation of young bureaucrats brought into his service during the Greek War of Independence was intended by Mahmud II to provide those auxiliaries who would be faithful to him when the janizaries were broken and who, after that event, would help to reaffirm his power over the semi-independent provinces and their unruly derebeys. Like many a European sovereign, Mahmud II was confronted by all the debilitating difficulties posed by 'the overmighty subject'; and, as in Europe, the centralization of royal power required a new breed of loyal public servants. One commentator has claimed that these men in the Ottoman Empire grew up in 'an ideological vacuum',[17] relegating Islam to the position of a personal religion, and so thinking in terms of new political institutions severed from the shaping influence of religious law. This is an exaggeration of their isolation within their community with its moral and intellectual traditions. On the other hand, it underplays their difficulties as they outgrew royal control and came face to face, as fully fledged ministers, with the power of the European embassies, these latter demanding better treatment of subject Christians, or the concession of Ottoman lands as the price of peace, or making similar and equally unpalatable demands as the condition of friendship.

Military reform was not in itself sufficient, as Mahmud II learned between 1826, his year of hope, and 1829, the year of self-analysis. The treaty of Adrianople, which dismayed Europe, also served to underline for Mahmud II the power of domestic opposition surviving against him. He dealt successfully with many of the derebeys, notably in the Black Sea pashaliks, in Smyrna, Salonika, and the south of Anatolia; but Constantinople was as critical in Ottoman history as Paris in that of France, and in the capital the coalition of ulema and reactionary political families was an unexpectedly stubborn obstacle. Even among the reformers there were some, like Husrev Pasha, who hesitated uncertainly once the new army had been created. And they hesitated even more when that new army was trounced by Count Diebitsch in the campaigns of 1828. Stratford said that many patriotic Muslims of an enlightened turn of mind thought Mahmud II was 'not so much actuated by comprehensive views of national improvement as by motives of self-preservation and absolute dominion'. What would have been excusable in a devout Sultan was suspect in this one. The abolition of the dervishes, including the Bektasi order, like the forced declaration of the royal supremacy by the *Shaykh ul-Islam*, pointed unmistakably to increasingly secularist policies, whatever the personal disposition of the sovereign.

When Stratford went East again in 1831, he was eager to see all the changes which people already described as characterizing the new Ottoman Empire. In the short interval since he last left the country, after Navarino in 1827, European observers told of fezes and stambouline frock-coats in place of turbans and flowing robes, of a greater tolerance for the millets and a decline in the old fanaticism, of a Sultan who was a madman through whom God might be producing beneficent change 'in this extraordinary people'. Stratford was greatly excited by the prospect of directing Mahmud II into more serious activities, and he envisaged leading an antiquated theocracy towards a capitalist economy, a decent and honest public administration, and some kind of ecumenical government in which the leaders of the millets would all draw together in one large privy council. It might be as well to emphasize at this point that Stratford was totally opposed to the introduction of parliamentary practice into the Ottoman Empire, and he remained so all his life.

Mahmud II was badly in need of help of all kinds. By 1828, his new army was over 100,000 strong under its new official commander, the serasker. That had cost a lot of money. So too had the reclassification of the offices of state in terms of membership and function, and so too had the establishment of the new bureaucracy with its uniforms and fixed salaries. Various expedients were tried in order to raise the money to pay for these changes. The holders of janizary hereditary pensions had to repurchase them. The master of the mint was elevated to the divan, a sure sign of imminent devaluation; the *harac*[18] was raised from 12 to 36 piastres a year; and a new duty of two and one-half per cent was put on imports. None of these devices paid for the administrative revisions, the cost of the Greek war, or offset spiralling prices.

At first, Stratford thought his mission to the Ottoman Empire to obtain a settlement of the frontiers of Greece might prove 'a fool's errand', as he told Palmerston, but the latter rightly suspected that the Egyptian invasion of Syria would have Mahmud II 'conceding on the side of Greece'. The fool's errand turned into a great opportunity. As soon as he reached Constantinople, Stratford was hurried into the royal presence and treated with great affability by a sovereign before whom, in the old fanatical days, he had been thrown on the floor with pinioned arms. This time he was given a snuff-box and a horse, and within a few weeks the Greek boundary question was settled, the Sultan getting – in theory – a compensation from Greece of 40,000,000 piastres.

There was a price to be paid, and it was not the settlement of the Greek frontiers. During those six months of 1832, Canning urged reform on all the ministers with whom he came in contact: on the tough old serasker, Husrev Pasha; on the grand vizier, Reshid Mehmed Pasha; on the *reis effendi*, Süleiman Necib; on the former *reis effendi*, Mehmed Said Pertev, a very able and worried person, who told Stratford the populace would still give its support to any reaction against the Sultan. There was a response from all of these men and also from Tahir Pasha, the defterdar, or treasury chief, who wanted British financial aid, and the naval chief, Halil Rifat. A junior attached to the *reis effendi*'s staff was also much impressed with Stratford; this was Mustafa Reshid Effendi (soon pasha) who next met the ambassador in London in 1839, the year of the *Tanzimat* decree. What, in talking to these men, did Stratford mean by reform? Primarily, an agricultural revolution, thus giving the

Ottoman Empire some purchasing power to buy more extensively from Europe; second, a fiscal revolution in the form of a rational and equitable system of taxes in place of the rigours and uncertainties of tax-farming; and third, the removal of the disabilities on Christians so that they would be able to enjoy equal citizenship and equal opportunity while remaining loyal subjects of the empire.

This meaning of 'reform' was put in various ways but never ambiguously, as the following directive, sent to Dr MacGuffog, physician to the British embassy and the Porte, for communication to the Sultan, makes plain:

> Tell him it is because I want to see the Porte more free to advance his present system of improvement – favourable alike to the preservation of her own power, and the happiness of her Christian subjects – that I am anxious for her to lose no time. . . . I want to see her in a situation to receive the full tide of European civilization . . to take her proper place in the general councils of Europe, and to base her military and financial systems on the only true foundations. . . . The choice lies between *fanaticism* and *discipline*; there is no middle line.[19]

Britain, in fact, was the only disinterested friend to whom the Sultan could look, and it would be her responsibility to lift the moral and intellectual as well as the economic standards of the Ottoman Empire: 'Every engine which goes forth must be accompanied by its honest John Bunyan.'

The treaty with Britain, which Stratford encouraged Ottoman leaders to expect, never came to pass; and Mavrojeni and, after him, Namik Pasha were sent away from London empty-handed. Canning was vastly incensed by the stupidity, as he saw it, of the British government and wrote on 19 December 1832 a famous memorandum on the need to support the Ottoman Empire. Two days later the Sultan's armies were defeated by the Egyptians at Konya, and the Sultan accepted from Russia the aid Britain withheld. In his remonstrations with the Whig government, which was still trying to decide whom to back between the Ottoman Empire and Egypt, Stratford gives an interesting explanation for his preference. 'I cannot quite understand how the Sultan's dominions are to be made a more efficient barrier against Russia by the loss of Syria and Egypt. . . . [As] the pasha [of Egypt] intends to reorganize his state on the Mussulman principle, it is clear that Christianity and civilization have most to hope from his Imperial competitor.'[20] This argument carried little weight with the Whigs, but it became an obsession with Stratford after 1832 and seems to have had something to do with his second marriage to an extremely pious and determined 17-year-old who worshipped him and saw him as the light of Asia. Nor did Stratford forget that Husrev Pasha had asked him to inaugurate a new phase in the Ottoman Empire's foreign relations, that the leading ministers had dined with him before his departure, and that he had indiscreetly pledged British aid.

It is fairly clear that each man was, in his way, sincere about the policy of Anglo-Ottoman collaboration and that each thought the transformation of the Ottoman Empire was feasible, even in the teeth of popular resistance. Until his death in 1839, and in spite of the treaty signed with Russia at Unkiar Skelessi, Mahmud II looked to Britain of the great powers, while France, whose influence had before his reign been paramount at Constantinople, lost all ground by her championship of Muhammad Ali of Egypt. The British opportunity was thus a very real one, and Viscount Ponsonby, Stratford's successor as ambassador, encouraged the reformist ministers as much as the Whig government would allow. The Ottoman reformers themselves were split into factions, and they lost ground in public esteem on many counts ranging from their European habits to their truculence towards the ulema. Akif, a *reis effendi* who was subservient to the Sultan, intrigued against the reformers until Ponsonby got him disgraced. In his turn, Akif persuaded the Sultan to bring down Pertev, the patron of Reshid Pasha, for his outspoken criticism of Mahmud II. Pertev was bowstrung, and the execution had a great effect on men who were just beginning to sense the extent of their own emancipation and power. Reshid pursued Akif and had him disgraced in 1838. In 1839, Reshid was in London trying to extract that same alliance which had been withheld from Namik Pasha seven years before.[21]

The outline of the famous Gülhane decree was drafted by Reshid in his residence in Bryanston Square and, according to Stratford, submitted to him before anyone else.

I remember that he opened himself on the subject of reforms in

Turkey. . . . He asked me when and how the promoters of the system ought to begin. I replied, '*At the beginning.*' 'What do you mean by the *beginning*?' he said. 'Security of life and property, of course,' I rejoined. 'Would you not add the protection of honour?' he asked. 'No doubt,' I said, but in truth I wondered what he meant by honour among Turks.[22]

After that and two or three further interviews, Stratford did not see Reshid again until 1843 when the latter returned from Paris and settled in Balta Liman. Palmerston was more encouraging than the ambassador and was sure that if the Ottoman Empire nationalized her administration and disciplined her pashas, 'there would be an end to all the nonsense which people talked about Turkey being in decay'. All the Sultan had to do was to ensure that his 'institutions and laws should adapt themselves to the changes which take place in the habits of the people'. He made it sound very easy, yet if adaptation had waited on the changing habits of the Ottoman people, there would have been no *Tanzimat* at all. As for the 'nonsense' about decay, the defeat of the Ottomans at Nezib, the surrender of their fleet by treachery, and the sudden death of Mahmud II showed that the danger was real enough. Reshid hurried home, and on 3 November 1839 read out the *Hatt-i Humayun* at Gülhane.

The decree had something in it for everyone, so that men as different as Palmerston and Prince Metternich could send their congratulations to Reshid. Western liberals found contrition in its first paragraph where the deterioration of recent times and the decline of prosperity are candidly attributed to the collapse of the rule of law. Even better, there was a promise of 'nouvelles institutions' and of three new principles for future action: security of life, honour, and property; just and scientific taxation; and military recruitment by methods which would be 'également régulier'. On the other hand, Metternich was consoled that administrative efficiency had been placed above abstractions about liberty and democracy.[23] Stratford was pleased that there was 'no question of transferring any portion of power from the sovereign to his subjects', and he appreciated Reshid's clarification that the Gülhane proclamation involved no 'connivance with European constitutionalism'. In truth, the decree comes much closer to the spirit of Magna Carta than men who casually compared it with that document actually realized. In each case, the authors of these famous documents, one British and one Ottoman, assumed that the general weal would be promoted by initially securing the position and interests of a small but powerful class at the expense of the ruling dynasty.

The members of this new class were far from secure even under a boy Sultan as ineffective as Abdulmejid, and although a good deal of prominence has been given to their arrogance, this is no real measure of their power as distinct from their pretensions. It was, indeed, a major misfortune in Stratford's eyes that Mahmud II had gone. He was in no doubt that the reformers in the Ottoman Empire still had too many domestic opponents to be very effective unless they had some friend or ally – such as himself – who could not be intimidated by the threats of the old reactionaries. What the situation most needed was a great Sultan – 'the master mind, the gigantic hands, that grasp and press and mould at will the scattered elements of Empire'. But as no such person existed and the Gülhane decree had been publicly proclaimed, Stratford was determined that its principles should survive and flourish. Estimating his actual achievement is difficult; but it is beyond question that he, more than any other individual ambassador, was responsible for the expulsion of the idle, old grand vizier, Rauf Pasha, for breaking the power of Riza, the Sultan's favourite in 1845 and, above all, for the restoration in 1846 of Reshid himself, who had been turned out of office in 1841, allowed to return home in 1843, but largely kept in the background for the next two years.[24]

Stratford fought with the reformers as often as with the reactionaries, so anxious was he to get practical things done. He regarded Sarim, the *reis effendi* in 1841, as 'a liar'; he called Sadik Rifat, Sarim's successor, 'a beast' and 'Metternich's pet', a man who 'seeks truth at the bottom of his brandy bottle'. Safeti Pasha, the minister of finance, swindled his royal master and because of him the empire 'gallops downhill'.[25] The Sultan was weak and afraid of the popular prejudices of his people. Stratford's impatience was that of someone determined to see the Ottoman Empire on the right path before he retired. Approaching 60, he wrote of 'the bitter feeling of disappointment under which I came here in my autumnal days'. His quarrels with the reformers were intended to drive them on, not inhibit them. But with the banishment of Reshid in 1841, the followers he left behind were reluctant to rely for their principal prop on a foreigner; and this reluctance explains two features of the period between 1841 and 1851.

In the first place and in spite of all that has been written about the reforms that flowed from the Gülhane proclamation, the general view of all the western embassies in Constantinople was that the Sultan failed to back his more enlightened ministers, thus making it possible for the reactionaries to dismantle those reforms. Second, because Stratford Canning was now obsessed with the cause of reform to a degree which his London superiors found irritating and dangerous, he was encouraged by the supineness (as he saw it) of the reformers to impose his own meaning of reform upon theirs. We can take these points in turn, because they are very important.

The first reforms to flow from the 1839 decree reflect Reshid's mind, not Stratford's, whatever the latter may have claimed. Reshid and his friends committed the ruling institution to their cause by making the late Sultan's creation, the council of justice, the directing agency for the *Tanzimat* reforms. They were likewise careful to compromise the reluctant reformer, Serasker Husrev Pasha, with the presidency of this council. In March 1840 the provincial administrators were disciplined with a notification that the future way to promotion was through obedience and efficiency. Provincial defterdars, fiscal officers, were appointed to eliminate tax-farming and to raise instead only authorized taxes. This was a great blow at the corruption of pashas, and the tax-farmers who were their tools.[26]

Many other things were outlined and promulgated; one firman promised an Ottoman bank; another, a new currency. In May 1840 came a new penal code, the *Kanun-i Ceraim*, drawn up by a legislative committee. Resting for the most part on Koranic ideas and norms, the code nevertheless contained a statement to the effect that all Ottoman subjects were equal before the law – a declaration of immense portent and one showing the unresolved confusions of the reformist imagination. It was of the essence of the *Seriat* to discriminate against the infidel and protect the faithful. Strangely, it was not on this issue that the reactionaries clashed with and triumphed over Reshid. They raised the cry of blasphemy when he was asked in full divan if his new proposals for a commercial code were against the Holy Law. Reshid felt he was on safe ground by saying that matters of trade and commerce were merely secular matters, but he was wrong and he was dismissed. It is no surprise to find Reshid still feeling that reform itself must wait a little longer until the citadel of royal power was breached. Looking back, he told Palmerston that the 'tyrannie insupportable' of Mahmud II had led merely to 'prétendues réformes'.

After 1841 the idea of paying pashas regular salaries and controlling them was given up in favour of tax-farming again. The Penal Code of May 1840, despite the fanfare about equality before the law, brought no serious improvements before the Crimean War. The firman promising the Ottoman Bank brought forth no such institution. The first paper currency was a failure, and ordinary Ottoman people hoarded their coinage by preference. Stratford fought the reactionaries tooth and nail and shrugged off Aberdeen's warnings by writing, 'The duty of opposing a system so radically opposed to our commercial interests, political views, and moral principles, chiefly falls upon this embassy'. Whenever it was suggested to him that falling out with everybody might be strategically unwise, he said he could not give up simply because 'our maxims are little understood, our honesty is inconvenient, our advice is unpalatable'.[27] After all, in the years of peril Britain had stood by the Ottoman Empire – in 1812, in 1832, in 1838, in 1841 – so her own disinterestedness could not be misunderstood. Or so he imagined.

Stratford was a friend and Stratford was an embarrassment. Among the new men of Reshid Pasha's following, he came to know Ali and, after 1844, Fuad, the two men of the future. Both could see his honesty; both were strongly impressed by the white fury with which this strange man could offer his friendship; and they had to concede that at times he brought off diplomatic triumphs which no other contemporary European representative at the Porte could contrive. Yet, oddly, his support was two-edged, and in Constantinople one could be guilty by association with him. Reshid was the sole Turk on social terms with Stratford, who exchanged very frank letters with him only. The Canning children gave a Christmas party for those of Reshid one year, and Stratford saw this as a social revolution and a token of a better future, little realizing that some of his own staff, like Austen Henry Layard, were already on more familiar terms with intellectuals such as Ahmed Vefik and stayed in their homes. But for Ottomans, it was possible to be too closely identified with the British ambassador, particularly after the apostasy affair.[28]

It has been said above that Stratford tried to impose his meaning of reform more as the years went by. People who spotted the divergence of British and Ottoman views on what was practically possible advised him to give up, but his response to this was, 'God's will be done'. He pressed on, telling his government that a handful of Ottoman bigots must not wreck an empire. 'We are too far advanced to retreat, and I proceed on the belief that you [that is Aberdeen] are resolved to force Justice if she cannot be won.' For a picture of Stratford 'forcing Justice', one may look most profitably at the apostasy problem.[29]

Conversion to Islam presented no difficulties, but reconversion to any other creed was fraught with danger and carried the capital penalty. Ottoman jurists were as reluctant to apply the full rigour of the law as were their British counterparts before Robert Peel overhauled the criminal law, but on occasion they found it impossible to resist a wave of Muslim feeling and some tragic and bloody verdict was given. For Stratford, this became the acid test of the Ottoman reformist conscience; and as most of the reformers were in varying degrees of eclipse in 1843, he set himself up as their conscience and moved in to the attack when two executions for apostasy were brought to his attention.[30] In earlier times Stratford had seen plenty of evidence of judicial murder in the Ottoman Empire. He had seen the Alemdar himself, 40 years before, suspended by one leg in the public market place, and through the intervening years he had from time to time been stricken by some new revelation of the dark and violent side of the Ottoman soul. But the spirit of Muslim pride had, as even Stratford admitted, cooled imperceptibly; and in 1843 he wanted no less than an official repudiation of the practice of execution for apostasy from Islam. Though he claimed that he was only seeking a promise of civilized behaviour, he was actually fighting a highly controversial encounter on behalf of religious equality; and when he finally extracted a document conceding the theoretical abolition of execution for apostasy, he exultingly informed his brother that he had slipped his dagger between the ribs of 'the false Prophet' – which makes one wonder if religious equality was all Stratford wanted. He did not, of course, stop anti-Christian persecution in the Ottoman Empire, as Bulgarian atrocities and Armenian massacres attest; but it was a sign of changed times that an ambassador could make the attempt at all, could bully the Sultan personally, and could, in the last symbolic and triumphant interview with Rifat, take a copy of the memorandum he intended to send to London as the authoritative statement of Ottoman concessions and stuff it down the shirtfront of that long-suffering minister. Furthermore, the secularization of Ottoman law, to which he contributed so powerfully, went on after he took leave in 1846. When he returned again in 1848 he found the *Ticaret Mahkemesi* (the mixed commercial court) operating alongside the yet more significant mixed tribunals. In these, a mixed Muslim and Christian bench heard civil and criminal cases involving litigants from different millets. At large, the Europeans in the empire were speaking of railways – the first of which, running from Smyrna to Aydin, was opened by Stratford – and canals, of commercial treaties and the closer integration of the Ottoman Empire in Europe. In 1850 the Protestant millet was recognized.[31]

The reader may be beginning to feel that the isolation of Stratford's reformist enthusiasms from the general matrix of his life as a diplomat involved in all the manifold crises of the Eastern Question – Greece, the Egyptian invasion of Syria, the Lebanese crises of 1841–46, the Russians in the Principalities, the Hungarian refugees difficulty, the friction with Austria over Bosnia, Ottoman–Persian quarrels, the rising squabbles over the Holy Places – does some violence to history as it actually happened. After 1841, however, it is precisely the obsession with reform which dominates the ambassador's thinking. There was only an Eastern Question because the Ottoman Empire was the 'sick man'. Cure the 'sick man' and the Eastern Question would disappear. Students of the Crimean War period have constantly failed to appraise Stratford's prior interest in reform when they have tried to assess his responsibility for the start of that struggle, and yet this is the very key to the man's attitudes and the key to his response to Prince Menshikov and the Sultan's ministers in 1853.

Before the mid-century, Stratford was optimistic of the chance for reform and of what might be achieved by his own rising power.

I assist in turning wicked functionaries into good ones, gripping extortioners into pleasing collectors, bigoted Musulmans into easy latitudinarians . . . sometimes an ill-favoured vizier, who growls and snarls . . . might be taught by a sound bastinadoing to walk steadily in the right path . . . individuals are protected under the new constitution in their lives, fortunes and honour.[32]

He was even found saying, before coming home on leave in 1851, 'all the leading questions, in which I have been engaged, are either completely or virtually settled'.

The prospect of success made him jealously watchful of other European interference, and it was to avoid his swift wrath that Aberdeen had told him nothing of the fateful conversations in London in 1844 with Nicholas I over the future of the Ottoman Empire. For to Lord Aberdeen, Stratford's maundering about reforming 'the crapulous barbarians' had gone on long enough. But for the ambassador, Britain's role was clear. 'Our duty, our vocation is not to enslave but to set free. . . . Our task is to lead the way and to direct the march of other nations.' The difficulty, nevertheless, was how to encourage and to coerce the Ottomans; and Stratford came to believe in 1847 that the only hope for the future was to offer her a defensive alliance with Britain, 'proportioned to the advancement of Turkey in European civilization'. Palmerston, back in power, was all for reform also but declined to offer rewards. The Sultan's best reward would be his independence of foreign influence, and in Reshid and Ali he had 'instruments well adapted to work out his own generous and enlightened intentions'. He was sure 'an equalization of the two races' (Muslim and Christian) was their intention and was firm that Europe would accept no other outcome. A Christian must enjoy 'the fullest liberty to exert his industry'. Stratford, of course, agreed with the ends Palmerston had in view, but could not accept the proposition that the Ottoman Empire would achieve them unaided.[33]

Back in the Ottoman Empire again in 1851, Stratford's morale suddenly took an extraordinary plunge. The explanation is far from clear, but it is as if his optimism, sustained through so many years, suddenly broke either because of age, gout, or some unexpected experience. The British archives and Stratford's letters show only the dispatch to the provinces of a commission to examine the operation of the *Tanzimat-i Hayriye*. Ali Pasha and Reshid sent the commission out with very extensive powers to look into the application of law, the use of torture, and the existence of brigandage and corruption. Stratford had a copy of the commission's terms of reference. Then, on 7 February, there arrived information of 'atrocious massacres' in Rumelia, and this seems to have taken Stratford by surprise and to have desolated him.[34]

On that same day he wrote a very important dispatch to London. We may take it as the final crystallization of all his experience in the Ottoman Empire, his last testament on the subject of reform. 'The cloud which has long gathered over the destinies of Turkey [continues] to thicken into hopeless gloom. . . . The exertions of Reshid Pasha, sustained and stimulated by British counsels, are unequal to the task of either producing unanimity in the Cabinet, or of removing the scruples of the Seraglio.' Exhausted by his long efforts, Stratford wrote that he had no choice but to give up the cause for ever. In explanation he continued:

> *the master mischief in this country is dominant religion.* . . . That is the real Leviathan which 'floating many a rood', overlays the prostrate energies of Turkey. Though altogether effete as a principle of national strength and reviving power, the spirit of Islamism, thus perverted, lives in the supremacy of the conquering race and in the prejudices engendered by a long tyrannical domination. It may not be too much to say that the progress of the empire towards a firm re-establishment of its prosperity and independence is to be measured by the degree of its emancipation from that source of injustice and weakness.

Islam at the private level was one thing, but at the level of the state the double standard of treatment it prescribed for Ottoman subjects invited *and justified* the policy of territorial dismemberment which countries like Russia, Austria, and France had at various times advanced. It was useless for the Ottomans to protest that they could not be expected to legislate for their own 'diminished ascendancy' because that ascendancy had diminished already and would get smaller yet. What was at the bottom of Ottoman incorrigibility? Besides the blind adherence to Islam, there was 'the backwardness of the Turks in knowledge of every description, their general unfitness for competition with their Christian fellow-subjects, the consequent fewness of those who are properly qualified for office'. What had been done during his Eastern career had, he wrote, been achieved far less by Gülhane than by 'Greece, Adrianople, and Egypt', that is, by external pressures rather than an inner volition. Reformers were few, obscurantists many, the Sultan weak, enemies numerous.[35]

Within a year the Holy Places dispute began to assume dangerous proportions. Stratford, on leave, hurried back to his threatened kingdom in the East. His professional obligation to defend the Ottoman Empire from external threat mingled indistinguishably with his ancient desire to reinvigorate her from within. Everyone in London should have seen this, and probably all the Ottoman ministers did. He had often demanded of his superiors in London the power to offer the Ottoman Empire an alliance in return for a guaranteed programme of reform, and he had often demanded reform of the Ottomans as the price of British goodwill and protection. In 1853 the Ottomans needed his help as never before, and they knew his price. He, in his turn, saw the emergence of an unexpected and unprecedented opportunity to bring off the impossible. The Ottomans were not dishonest in hinting that his price would be paid when the war was over: after all, the Ottoman diplomats of 1853 were the same men as the Ottoman reformers, and they were serious about reform even if not in the same ways as Stratford. It is still often and unwarrantedly said that Stratford was the catalyst of the Crimean War because he encouraged the Ottoman leaders to stand firm against Russia instead of forcing them into a more concessionary attitude towards a tsar who only wanted a decent way of retreat; but it is at least as likely from the evidence we have that the Ottoman leadership met Stratford half-way and in a kindred spirit, hinting by glance and nuance that if Britain stood firmly with 'her ancient ally', she would not be disappointed by the empire's domestic regeneration after the war. Even then, any such silent pact between the British ambassador and the Ottoman ministers can never be construed as precipitating a war which actually took a further year to proceed beyond the declaration of hostilities to actual conflict. Courts and governments which do not know how to retreat from an unwanted war with a year in which to do it demonstrate nothing so clearly as their own total incapacity. No one can be more to blame than they.

It is clear then that we must question whether Stratford Canning was a fit emissary for the situation of 1853, if the ultimate purpose was peace at any price; but if the purpose was the defence of the Ottoman Empire, then there could be no more resolute person to hand. To the early reformers of the *Tanzimat* he had given immense encouragement; to the later ones, he helped provide the chance of a new start after 1856. By then, his own influence was on the wane and the race between reform and territorial disintegration was to go against the Ottoman Empire, in part at least because the cause which mattered so much to him was regarded more fatalistically by his successors as something beyond the control of Europeans.

NOTES

1. Lane Poole, *Life*, ii. 247.
2. Ibid., p. 466.
3. Temperley, *Crimea*.
4. Turkish Ministry of Education, *Tanzimat* (Constantinople, 1940).
5. S. Mardin, *Genesis of Young Ottoman Thought* (Princeton, 1962), has a useful discussion in its Introduction. Oddly, the rest of the book ignores its fruitful commencement.
6. Ibid., pp. 107–14.
7. See, for instance, how superficial Namik Kemal could be and how often he spoke of 'the people' yet clearly was thinking of Muslims only. His strictures on the West could also be very shallow. See his writing in *Hürriyet*, 7 Sept., 10 Oct., 28 Dec. 1868. For Ziya Pasha on the 'unfathomable sea of the Seriat', see *Hürriyet*, 5 April 1869.
8. Mardin, *Genesis*, p. 117, calls this anti-European hostility 'cultural and religious puritanism'.
9. Ibid., p. 118.
10. Stratford to Aberdeen, 20 Jan. 1845, Add. MSS 43139.
11. 27 April 1809, quoted in Lane-Poole, *Life*, i. 51.
12. To Richard Wellesley, 19 Oct. 1808, ibid., p. 42.
13. Stratford to Aberdeen, 2 May, 21 Dec. 1844, 12 Feb. 1845, Add. MSS 43139.
14. Lewis, *Turkey*, p. 76.
15. G. Rosen, *Geschichte der Türkei* (Leipzig, 1866), i. 302.
16. Lewis, *Turkey*, p. 83.
17. Mardin, *Genesis*, p. 118.
18. *Harac* was a head tax on Christians in lieu of military service.
19. Lane-Poole, *Life*, i. 508; Canning to MacGuffog, 30 March 1832, FO 352/24A/2.
20. Stratford to Backhouse (permanent-under-secretary, Foreign Office), 14 Oct. 1832, FO 352/25.
21. Mardin, *Genesis*, pp. 155–61.
22. Lane-Poole, *Life*, ii. 105.
23. C. Baysun, 'Mustafa Resit Pasa', *Tanzimat*, p. 731 *et seq.*; Mardin, *Genesis*, p. 105 *et seq*.

24. Stratford to Aberdeen, 28 Dec. 1844, 12 Feb., 13 and 23 Oct. 1845, Add. MSS 43139. Reshid, in a letter of 20 May 1843, asked Stratford for a letter which could be used in emergency to get him taken on board any British ship; see Lane-Poole, *Life*, ii. 109.
25. Stratford to Aberdeen, 1 April, 2 May, 4 Nov. 1844, Add. MSS 43139. 'I might have used the late crisis [over apostasy] to shake and perhaps to overset the ministry, but thought you would not like so bold an experiment.'
26. J.H. Kramers, 'Tanzimat', *Encyclopedia of Islam*, 1st ed., iv. 656–60; Mardin, *Genesis*, p. 163.
27. Stratford to Aberdeen, 26 April 1845, Add. MSS 43139.
28. Stratford to Aberdeen, 1 July 1845, ibid.
29. Stratford to Aberdeen, 28 Dec. 1844, Add. MSS 43139; Aberdeen to Stratford, 6 April, 6 June 1846, FO 78/635.
30. The Apostasy case is in FO 97/413; Lane-Poole, *Life*, ii. ch. 18.
31. Stratford to Palmerston, 24 Oct. 1850, FO 97/413; Lane-Poole, *Life*, ii. 96, n.
32. Stratford to Rev. Canning, 2 Dec. 1845, ibid., ii. 143.
33. Palmerston to Stratford, 30 Oct. 1847, FO 78/691.
34. Stratford to Palmerston, 20 Jan. 1850, FO 97/413.
35. Stratford to Palmerston, 7 Feb. 1850, FO 97/413.

CHAPTER V

The Preliminaries of the Crimean War

In the ceremony raising him to a viscountcy in 1852, Lord Stratford de Redcliffe was congratulated by Queen Victoria on the conclusion of 'the ill advised and long pending question of the Syrian shrines', and thanked for enabling his government to give undivided attention to events just across the Channel, a sentiment which allowed him to ponder, however fleetingly as he knelt before Her Majesty, the ease with which France could always supplant Russia in British fears. Only two years before, Russia had been a great villain, but in the train returning him to London after the ceremony, the new peer had time to read the papers he bought on Windsor platform, and to see for himself how truly the earl of Malmesbury, the current foreign minister, had spoken to him of the 'universal apprehension' of 'the French'. Popular terminology and imagination are instructive. Russia, represented in the cartoons of the period as a crowned bear, was equated with the will of one man, the tsar. But the same newspapers usually referred to 'the French' rather than to any individual leader, crowned or otherwise. The duke of Wellington, now near to death, said the tsar was an insincere man, 'a Greek of the lower Empire', but went on to concede that Muscovite ambitions, though broad, had some rationale, and even some limits, whereas 'the French' would chase prestige wherever it led them. The tsar was greatly disliked for suppressing political freedom in eastern Europe, but the French were as suspect as reformed tipplers, collectively unpredictable if exposed once more to the aroma of Napoleonic revisionism. And now that they had a Napoleonic president, notoriously contemplating the revival of monarchy, Stratford was quite amazed at the anxieties of the strongest of nations: ' "Panic" pamphlets were again issued broadcast . . . panic letters and speeches succeeded one another in the newspapers [and a people] communicating their fears to one another, persuaded themselves that the dreaded hour had at last come.'[1]

The 'dreaded hour' only came at the end of 1852, but the preceding months in Britain were marked by real hysteria as the prince-president in Paris attempted to prepare his own people and the governments of Europe psychologically for the revival of kingship in France. A mere four years after the removal of Louis-Philippe such an eventuality might have been welcomed across the Continent as a blow to Jacobin radicalism and a sign of reassuring stability, but for the name and temperament of the man determined to bring it about. When he moved his official residence to the Élysée, and repudiated his English mistress, plain Mrs Howard, when his head appeared on the republican coinage, when the Great Napoleon was accorded the numeral 'Premier' and bishops began to intone prayers for 'Louis-Napoleon', the great powers began to recall their obligation, dating back to 1815, to forbid a Napoleonic resurrection. French nationalism seemed on the march again, and Stratford was amazed that Count Buol, the Austrian foreign minister, should show the courage to summon the powers to demand a confirmation of France's peaceful intentions before recognizing any new Napoleon. The tsar of Russia, who had at intervals been trying to quarantine France and draw Britain to his side at least since 1829, was ready to try the same again, and Louis-Napoleon was quick to challenge the initiative, reminding the British ambassador at Paris, Lord Cowley, of the futility and hypocrisy of a situation in which John Bull, 'who had never seen a drop of blood spilled and read of 1688 as a romance', could believe *The Times* when it described him as an enemy of popular government. Was he not France's choice, raised to power by a far wider franchise than British legislatures would ever risk? Was Britain really going to heed lessons on constitutionalism from the European despotisms?

The British papers were certainly deeply impressed with developments in France, some editors proposing the recall of the Lisbon squadron to guard the Channel. Others reported that French visitors to the Great Exhibition had been in the habit of appraising the strength and disposition of Britain's defensive arrangements on behalf of their government, as they travelled between Dover and London. Even sensible people who refused to be stampeded must, nevertheless, have been concerned as well as amused by the disclosure of Ducos, the French minister of marine, that there had been at one time an official plot to kidnap Queen Victoria from the Isle of Wight, a scenario rich in theatrical potential. The unemployed Lord Palmerston kept his powder dry by playing war games and writing memoranda on the importance of the screw-steamer. Lord Raglan, a general who had never commanded in wartime but would get his chance soon, spent the summer of 1852 planning the defence of London against a French invasion. Queen Victoria, so often more steadfast than her ministers, thought it could do no harm that July to mute the customary celebrations on the anniversary of Waterloo. These scattered tokens of national insecurity can be multiplied almost infinitely, making it impossible to identify the spirit of defeatism with any particular British administration.

The prince-president threw his weight around a good deal in 1852, sending a French ambassador to his post at Constantinople on a warship that violated the 1841 Straits Convention, threatening force to resolve the Tunisian crisis in July, and reopening in November the question of 'the Syrian shrines' which Queen Victoria prematurely supposed to have been terminated. Emboldened with an imperial title, there was great speculation on what this new Napoleon might attempt next. Nothing, from Corfu to Australia, escaped his acquisitive eye. He promised a Piedmontese general to 'faire quelque chose pour l'Italie' in good time. King Leopold of Belgium feared for his kingdom and advised his niece that Britain would find 'its most powerful ally in Russia'. Palmerston believed trouble could come anywhere, *except* in the Near East where Britain and France had squabbled for years 'like two men in Love with the same woman'.[2] Russian opinion, on the other hand, though divided at the very highest level of the tsar's entourage, expected French provocations in the East as in Europe unless Britain and Russia stood firmly together, and thought the time had clearly come to blow the dust off the famous memorandum of 1844, the document in which the two governments agreed to the principle of prior consultation at any time when the disintegration of the Ottoman Empire 'appeared imminent'. For, as Count Nesselrode put it, 'there are many reasons which might recommend the East as a preferred object of attack'.

Well before the Aberdeen–Russell coalition came to power in December, Baron Philip Brunnov, the Russian ambassador, was shocked by a confession of the aged Scottish peer destined soon to be prime minister. 'If he [Louis-Napoleon] thinks we are divided he will fall on us', Aberdeen said, going on to explain that if Britain were actually invaded, '50,000 Frenchmen would beat 50,000 Englishmen'. Brunnov could hardly believe his ears, but his chief, Nesselrode, took the former statement as urgent proof that he and Aberdeen should revive the intimacy of 1844. The trouble was that the earl of Derby was actually in power in late 1852, but in his *Précis historique de la Question des Saints-Lieux*, written at Tsar Nicholas's command, in which he laments that French ambassadors at Constantinople were coercing the Ottomans to disregard their international obligations, Nesselrode has a subsection entitled *Angleterre*, in which he discusses the responsive diplomacy of the novice foreign minister in London, Malmesbury. Reputedly a personal friend of Louis-Napoleon, Malmesbury had nevertheless expressed special gratitude for Russia's prompt offer of 60,000 troops to defend Belgium if needed, and had in return co-operated cordially with Russia in drafting treaties to regulate the Danish and Greek successions. It could do no harm to seek Malmesbury's personal reaction to the famous 1844 memorandum. Brunnov was in for a disappointment: Malmesbury played safe, simply saying the memorandum was important but lacked treaty force. When Brunnov turned to Derby, the prime minister flippantly told him he was lucky not to find himself dealing with Stratford.

The irony is that Brunnov may have been very unlucky, for while British prime ministers *always* found it unseasonable to discuss the imminence of Ottoman collapse, Stratford as foreign minister would have been ready for a dialogue with Russia over the *Tanzimat* programme as the price the Ottomans must be forced to pay for immunity from partition. The old ambassador, furthermore, believed the Russians were entitled to some redress over the Holy Places, and when Brunnov met him one day on the steps of the Foreign Office, and asked him what he thought of the tsar's plan to send Prince Menshikov to demand redress from the Sultan, he was astonished when Stratford shot back, 'J'aime bien voir à Constantinople votre Admiral [Menshikov bore the title of Prince-Admiral] que votre flotte'.[3] The Russian government did not give up easily, persisting in assuming that in 1844 Britain had undertaken, in Nesselrode's words, 'to have an understanding with

Russia [about the East] before agreeing with all the other courts of Europe'. On the basis of this faith, another princely Russian, Gorchakov, was sent to London in late 1852, while Derby still held the reins of government. He came, and saw, and almost conquered. At a dinner at the United Services Club, he concluded a toast with the cry, 'Mais avant tout, vive la vieille et glorieuse Angleterre'. His voice of thunder, Malmesbury remembered, 'had an electrical effect', for the audience which roared its applause knew a great development was imminent in Paris. On 4 December 1852, Napoleon III was proclaimed at last. On the 17th, Derby fell from power. On the 28th, the earl of Aberdeen became prime minister. Between the fall of the Conservatives and the installation of the first Liberal coalition, a ceremony in distant Palestine was also to have its effect on the international situation: 'On Wednesday, the 22nd of the same month, the Latin Patriarch [of Jerusalem] with joy and a great ceremony replaced the glittering star in the sanctuary of Bethlehem, and at the same time the key of the great door of the church, together with the keys of the sacred manger, was handed over to the Latins.'[4] The symbolic challenge to Russia was great. On 9 January 1853, the tsar took the initiative into his own hands and opened the famous conversations with the British ambassador, Sir Hamilton Seymour. Even so, a year after his speech, Gorchakov was not co-ordinating Anglo-Russian military arrangements against France. He was organizing the defences of Sebastopol against the British and French combined.

★ ★ ★

The tsar's four talks with the British ambassador at St Petersburg have often been dissected for verbal content without sufficient regard for this broader and preceding historical context. By the narrow approach, the best analyst of the conversations had no difficulty in indicting Nicholas I as 'plotter' and 'blunderer', and it is quite true that the royal exercise in candour ricocheted back in the most unfortunate way.[5] He was not as candid as he pretended and had wider territorial ambitions in the East than he disclosed. Nevertheless, the tsar, in his fear for the European balance of power, and indignation over the French challenge to his presumed and prior right of intervention in Ottoman affairs, pressed Aberdeen through Brunnov as well as Seymour to listen to him seriously; thus Brunnov said his government fully expected France under Napoleon III to overturn Europe's repose and also reach out to 'Maroc, Tunisie, l'Egypte, la Palestine, la Syrie, Candie'. The guess was good. In the course of the following years, France fought Russia, Austria, and Prussia, in turn, and became very active in the loosening of Ottoman authority. But the tsar was not taken seriously because he posed for Britain the awkward question of choosing between two powers she distrusted equally. 'We must take care not to burn our fingers for either party', warned the foreign secretary, Lord John Russell, and at least one authority has remarked on the misfortune that 'this great possibility should have been presented to the foreign office when Lord John Russell was in possession of it'.[6] A way out of an awkward dilemma was to treat the tsar as unhinged by illness as well as ambition: it was an open secret in the British cabinet that he had only two years to live. In turn, this belief led men to suppose that procrastination must be good diplomacy. Russell's expedient was to refute the suggestion that the Ottoman Empire was in a state of collapse, and to argue for leaving it alone. Aberdeen's earliest expedient was just as dangerous; to give the tsar his head temporarily, trusting to Brunnov, a mere ambassador, to restrain his sovereign from demanding so much of the Ottomans that it would antagonize France. 'Every day renders more certain,' he incautiously told the Russian, 'the impossibility of any European sympathy with a [Turkish] system founded on ignorance and ferocity.' No one, it will be noticed, was particularly ready to restrain or lecture 'the French'.

When the curtain went up on the first Seymour conversations, Nicholas I sermonized the British ambassador on the need for a clear Anglo-Russian understanding. 'If England and I agree,' he began, 'I care little for the rest, or what others do and think.' Nesselrode, excluded from the talks but knowing all about them, was unhappy that the tsar should disclose his own thinking in too much detail, but Nicholas I plunged on, believing as sovereigns often do, that they have special insight as well as exceptional authority. Using imagery which was to pass into history, he told Seymour: 'We have a sick man on our hands, a man gravely ill; it will be a great misfortune if he [the Ottoman Sultan] slips through our hands, especially before the necessary arrangements are made.'

With the Ottoman Empire 'falling to pieces', the time so long foreseen by Russia but ignored by Britain had come. Without specifically excluding France by name, Nicholas I stressed that 'England and Russia should come to a perfectly good understanding . . . and that neither should take any decisive step of which the other is not appraised'. Speaking as a 'gentleman and a friend', he sought to remove old fears by stressing that the grand ambitions of Catherine II's time belonged to the past. Russia could not allow Britain or France to take Constantinople, but no longer coveted possession herself. In the turmoil of an Ottoman collapse, Russia might take the capital temporarily (*en depositaire*) but there was no question of her seeking to retain it for ever (*en propriétaire*). Its obvious destiny was to become a great international city. In only one blunt remark did the tsar reveal the enemy he most feared: if the French sent an expedition to the East, he said, he would order his troops into Ottoman territory. Seymour was sardonically amused by what he had heard, and advised Nicholas I that the British would probably react in their habitual fashion, objecting, 'as a general rule, to take engagements upon possible eventualities'. In a private letter accompanying his report to London of the first two conversations, he advised Russell that a friendly response would be enough. Britain obviously could not say what she would do in a hypothetical situation, but perhaps the foreign secretary could ease the tsar's apprehensions by stressing what Britain would *not* do.[7]

Seymour's first reports of his conversations with the tsar caused only slight concern in London and the Cabinet consensus was that a soothing reply would be sufficient. Aberdeen found nothing in the conversations, he said, 'to justify reproaches of territorial aggression, or hostile ambition' on the part of Russia.[8] Charles Greville, to whom Seymour's dispatches were shown quite improperly by the earl of Clarendon, thought the tsar was simply overwrought about 'a string of conditions about shrines and other ecclesiastical trifles'.[9] Only the queen seems, from the start, to have estimated the tsar's personal effort to win Britain to his side at its real value: 'The Russians accuse us of being too French,' she said, 'and the French accuse us of being too Russian.'[10] However, no one in London was anxious to provoke the French, and everyone was determined to expect the best from Napoleon III. When the latter grandly offered to placate the world in a speech in which he proclaimed, 'the Empire means peace and when France desires it the world is at rest', the British government seized on the first part of the statement, while the tsar fumed over the implications of the rest.

Anyone who feels that Nicholas I lived in an apocalyptic world of his own imagining must recognize how anxiously men in London were also rearranging international appearances to match their desires. A good example of it will be found in *The Times* for February 1853, where Russell engaged in a correspondence with Lord Mount-Edgcumbe to belittle the idea that French naval preparations threatened anyone. But the sorriest instance of all was provided by Aberdeen, who Brunnov accurately said possessed 'peu de courage pour affronter une crise'.[11] Here was a chance, indeed an obligation, to repair, at least in part, that 'state of perfectly unparalled isolation [so] pregnant with danger' in which the prime minister said his Cabinet colleague, Lord Palmerston, had left Britain a year before. It was Aberdeen's first opportunity to show leadership in foreign policy; instead, his inactivity was pregnant with danger. He would not choose between France and Russia. To Brunnov he expressed his fears of the Eastern Question getting out of hand, but to Queen Victoria, who might have required some diplomatic action, he wrote fatuously: 'Lord Aberdeen does not think there is anything very new in this demonstration by the Emperor [of Russia]. It is essentially the same language he has held for some years, although, perhaps the present difficulties of the Ottoman Empire [with Russia, France, Austria] may have rendered him more anxious on the subject.'[12] Aberdeen even refused a suggestion of Russell's that a circular supporting the principle of Ottoman integrity should go out from London to all powers, saying that 'everybody knows' Britain's attitude on that matter. The prime minister was sure Russia would behave; the foreign secretary, that France would too.

In the spacious, private correspondence of these two men on domestic politics, nothing was too small for their attention, so that they discussed at length and anxiously the suitability of calling their coalition the 'Conservative Progress' party, and the solemn responsibility of offering office to an aspirant before he had proved he was a regular communicant of the Anglican Church, but in early 1853, when the international situation was very challenging, each tried to abdicate by saying the other was having too much of his own way: Aberdeen said he had really been tricked into leading the government; Russell, that he had never served in a worse. He wanted to give up the Foreign Office, so recently accepted, to concentrate on leading in the Commons. On 22 February, Russell carried out his threat, and handed the busiest department of state to Clarendon. One of his last acts was to 'read the rough draft of a proposed answer' to Seymour, which the Cabinet, 'with slight alterations . . . fully approved', a document which was to have exactly the opposite effect in Russia of the restraining one intended.[13]

Thoroughly sceptical of the wish or capacity of the Sultans to persist with the *Tanzimat* programme, Russell's colleagues prevented him from arguing that the Ottomans had an improving record as reformers. In his own office, Edmund Hammond's Eastern department also believed the Ottomans to be wilfully incorrigible. Austen Layard, one of Stratford's zealous supporters until 1851, agreed. W.E. Gladstone, too, was reluctant to support indefinite repression of the Balkan Christians. Aberdeen hated 'the barbarians' and grieved that his country should ever again be found on their side. In conclusion, Palmerston and Stratford had seemingly given them up as well. Incapable of becoming a great and civilized power, the Ottomans had opted to remain the great European nuisance. Russell's only remaining expedient was to argue that, left alone, they could lurch on, 'twenty, fifty, or a hundred years hence'; an appeal, therefore, for the Ottoman Empire to be treated as a power vacuum. He drew a comparison, in drafting his reply to Seymour, between 1853 and the situation in which Britain had found herself a century and a half previously, when Anglo-French prior arrangements concerning the disposal of the Spanish Empire were imperative because the king of Spain was childless and extremely sick. But prior partition plans in 1853 would only 'alarm and alienate the Sultan and stimulate all his enemies to increased violence'. In talking about taking Constantinople into his temporary custody, Nicholas I was obviously trying to be candid and collaborative, but even a move like that, explained in advance with the most pacific intentions, could expose the European peace to 'numberless hazards'. Britain preferred to assure the world of her general disinterestedness in the East by saying she 'renounced all intention or wish to hold Constantinople'. It was the unilateral action of, for instance, Austria in Montenegro, that could always produce a wider crisis. From all this, it is apparent that in the dispatch of 9 February, which Russell sent to Russia, he was trying to win Russia to an opinion, and not proclaiming a line of action, his hope being that the quarrels about Montenegro and the Holy Places could be disposed of as isolated problems. What he did not tell the tsar just yet was that Britain proposed to bring Stratford back into service to guide the Ottomans in the resolution of these difficulties.[14]

The tsar's reaction to these and other statements in Russell's dispatch are available to us because he scribbled them in the margins of his copy of the dispatch sent to Seymour. His basic response was one of gratification. Against the remark that the Montenegrin crisis 'may bring on war', he wrote, 'this war [sic] might easily end with the fall of the Ottoman Empire'. Against Russell's observation that 'increased violence' might result from a premature exposure of partition plans, he remarked: 'My aim is simply not to find myself in contradiction with England.' Against the advice not to take Constantinople, he wrote, 'the Russian Emperor no longer seeks to establish himself there'. The promise that Britain would never seek to occupy the Ottoman capital he marked as 'a precious assurance since it proves what perfect identity of intentions exists between England and Russia'. But there is one outstanding section of the dispatch which Russell's Cabinet colleagues ought never to have authorized, and which later historians, who appear to have spotted everything else in this famous correspondence, seem to have overlooked. In encouraging the tsar to show restraint in resolving the Holy Places dispute, Russell referred to 'that exceptional protection' over *the generality of Christians* in the Ottoman Empire which Nicholas I 'has found so burdensome and inconvenient, though no doubt prescribed by duty and *sanctioned by treaty*' (emphasis added).[15] What more could the tsar want to hear except a proposal of an Anglo-Russian alliance? If any reservations remained, they were removed by a dispatch from Brunnov reporting another example of Aberdeen's irresponsible and private prattling: Aberdeen had informed the Russian ambassador that the Ottoman government was the worst in the world and that the British people had little inclination to uphold it any more. 'Whether right or wrong,' Brunnov was delighted to hear, 'we advise the Turks to yield.'[16] On this the tsar wrote, 'The most remarkable dispatch of all: it explains the *unexpected success* [emphasis added] of our first steps'. In the light of such understanding, he talked more candidly still to Seymour in two further conversations, and, on Nesselrode's advice, sent Menshikov on his ill-fated mission to the Porte. Brunnov congratulated his royal master that a 'fatal alliance' of Britain and France was no longer to be feared. The tsar had, in his own words, 'obtained the guarantee against the future which I fear'.

To Seymour, Nicholas I expressed satisfaction with Russell's dispatch, and said he hoped it might be amplified not into an engagement which he knew he could not have, but at least into a fuller 'exchange of ideas'. Nicholas I meant territorial ideas, and it should occasion no surprise that he now felt freer than before to disclose some – not all – of his own.[17] The later two Seymour conversations, those following the receipt of Russell's reactions to the first two, now took place and were marked, respectively, by the tsar's revelation of his intention to send Menshikov to Constantinople, and his views on how the Ottoman Empire might be partitioned in the event of its collapse. Seymour was unwilling to receive details of such proposals, which he found alarming, but since he could not refuse to listen gravely, he satirized the situation as follows:

> I, Nicholas, by the grace of God and so forth, not willing to incur the risk of war, and desirous not to compromise my character for magnanimity, will never seize upon Turkey; but I will destroy her independence. I will reduce her to vassalage . . . by a process that is perfectly familiar to us, as it is the same that was employed with so much success against Poland. The danger is that England and France will foregather for the purpose of preventing this consummation. I will, therefore, show a decided preference for one of these powers and will do my best to disunite them.[18]

Russell, to whom this was written privately, was also sent in official dispatches details of the sort of 'vassalage' Nicholas I had in mind for parts of the Ottoman Empire. The tsar told Seymour that his first intention was certainly to uphold the Sultan: in fact, he had sent an offer of help 'little more than a month ago [in December 1852]' in which Russian aid was proffered 'for resisting the menaces of the French'. He was also sending Menshikov to hold the Ottoman authorities firmly to the letter of existing treaties with Russia, particularly where Russia's rights to protect the Orthodox Christians were concerned. But should all fail, should the French bluster the Ottomans into further capitulations, humiliating Russia, then it seemed proper that Serbia, Bulgaria, and the Principalities should obtain independence, albeit 'under my protection'. Then came a hint which, 40 years later, Lord Salisbury wished Britain had taken. The tsar said he would understand if British interests dictated the annexation of Cyprus and Egypt. Seymour reproved this excess of candour to the extent his position allowed, saying stiffly that as long as the eastern Mediterranean routes to India remained open, Britain had no wish for actual territory along them. Even so, Seymour was very surprised at Nicholas I's silence regarding Austria and France. The former's remonstrance with the Ottoman government over Montenegro showed the considerable recovery in her morale since 1848, when Russian troops retrieved Hungary for her. To pretend France would demand nothing from a liquidation of the Sultan's empire was even more unrealistic.

★ ★ ★

On 5 February, and so before the Cabinet approved the reply to Seymour's report of his first conversations with the tsar, Russell proposed the reappointment of Stratford de Redcliffe to the Constantinople embassy: 'Lord Stratford will go back for a short time if we wish it, and for my part I think it very expedient.' He cautioned that the old ambassador was only 'ready [not willing] to go'.[19] Aberdeen assented reluctantly. Probably both ministers would have preferred to send Layard to the East – 'he is so very well informed' – either with the rank of minister to take over from Colonel Hugh Rose, or as secretary of embassy to Stratford, over whom they imagined he might exert some restraining influence.[20] But Layard, as a new MP, intended to be conscientious about his parliamentary duties, and turned down all offers including the consul-general's post in Egypt, while deciding to go out with his old chief for a brief glimpse of old haunts. In later times, Russell defended the appointment of Stratford on two grounds: the first, that other men half-afraid of him had also neglected opportunities to remove him, and the second, that nobody else was so qualified to help France and Russia to settle their quarrel about the Holy Places. It is certainly true that the diplomatic men already in, or about to go to, Constantinople, were relative lightweights: the Russian embassy was in the hands of a counsellor, Ozerov; Nesselrode unkindly called the Austrian, Baron Karl von Bruck, no more than 'a Trieste grocer'; the Prussian minister was a polite nonentity; Count Vincent Benedetti, of future fame, was holding the French legation between the departure of the marquis de Lavalette, withdrawn for stirring up the Holy Places question, and the appearance of new appointee, de la Cour. Constantine Musurus, the Sultan's resident minister in London, told Russell that Stratford was by elimination the only man with enough knowledge and authority to steer the Sultan safely between the rival claims of France and Russia. Colloredo, the Austrian minister to London, took the same line, and pressed for Stratford's return.

It is Aberdeen's agreement to the appointment which is the most surprising circumstance. One does not perhaps expect him to have had the imagination to send Lord Cowley back East again, thus allowing Stratford to have the nominal spell in charge of the Paris embassy he so coveted. Perhaps the prime minister surveyed the spectrum of Cabinet opinion on the Eastern Question and saw no harm in appointing to a brief mission an elderly man whose nomination would please Palmerston, now cut out of foreign affairs, Russell, the admiring Clarendon, and one or two other Cabinet ministers. What was afterwards forgotten by all was that, at the time of Stratford's re-employment, the Montenegro question seemed more immediate and threatening than any other. The Holy Places dispute only seems of importance to men looking back on this fateful year because it was the problem which led, against all expectations, to war. We may, of course, dismiss the idea, which stubbornly survived Alexander Kinglake's times, that Stratford was sent back to Constantinople to do battle with Menshikov. He was expected, in the beginning, to be the hammer of the Ottomans, not the flail of the Russians.[21]

It is even harder is it to understand why Stratford himself agreed to another Eastern mission. He now had a home in Frant; a town house in Grosvenor Square; and there was the prospect of an interesting yet leisurely political life in the House of Lords. His gout bothered him at times, and always would, but on the other hand, no change of climate seemed to help it. There was also his cough, always worse in London than in the Levant, but after so many years accepted as a mannerism rather than an ailment. It rarely put him to bed. There are two real reasons for his return to Constantinople, the first of which he was unable to recognize. The city was irresistible to him as to so many other men. They cursed it, but they went back, drawn by the glinting, sun-laden dust of the noisy streets, or the eternal dream which is the Bosporus. The researcher eventually recognizes the cycle of Stratford's discontent: he would begin to regret his return to the East after the first week there; he would feel the nostalgia for it after three months in England. Constantinople was the most meaningful place in his world. The second point is that he was a professional – Queen Victoria's most seasoned career diplomat – and he set out again in 1853 because he saw the final chance to give his arduous career design and significance. What, in practical terms, he hoped to achieve is visible in the memorandum Russell asked him to draw up as the basis of his instructions.

Stratford's memorandum passed over the Montenegrin question in a short paragraph; it did not much matter whether 'the defence of Montenegro may be prolonged or terminates in the complete subjugation of the Mountaineers'. The Holy Places quarrel, now three years old, was much more critical because 'the Porte is unavoidably exposed to the rival pretensions of France and Russia, each animated by a political interest as well as religious zeal . . . threatened from both sides, and unable to satisfy one party without displeasing the other, the Sultan is evidently placed in a position of embarrassment and danger'. Did the great powers realize, the memorandum asked, that in 'the present state of Europe, and France in particular, the Levant may become the opening ground of war?' Whether they understood it or not, if the Sultan, in his powerlessness, resigned himself to these outside pressures, 'the dismemberment of Turkey' would be the result. Only Britain had the power and authority to forbid such a calamity and, if the Sultan was to be induced to put his fate in British hands, then the Cabinet must 'empower their representative at Constantinople to encourage the Porte, should its independence be menaced, by assurances of prompt and effective aid on the approach of danger'. In return, the Ottoman government must, in its turn, 'give proof of the capability and determination to carry punctually into effect and to extend that much vaunted system of improvement particularly in the essential branches of justice, revenue, roads, police, and military defence'. Otherwise, the memorandum concluded, the persistence of the Ottoman ministers with their 'present course of rashness, vacillation, and disorder [will alienate] the sympathies of the British Nation [making it impossible] to shelter them from the impending storm'.[22]

There was nothing here that Stratford had not been saying, in an infinity of variations, for many years past. There were Foreign Office clerks in its Eastern division, grown old reading such ideas, who could have anticipated them word for word. But truisms do not necessarily become less true through repetition, even if they seem to do so. Unfortunately, the message that the Ottomans should be taught to stand on their own feet in order to keep predators at bay was addressed to a head of government whose desire was to trust the predators to go hungry. Aberdeen – who said he 'should as soon think of preferring the Koran to the Bible as of comparing the Christianity and civilization of Russia to the fanaticism and immorality of the Turks',[23] and was always upset by the counter-suggestion that Russian 'civilization' was a brutal sham whereas Ottoman 'progress', though halting, was at least real – naturally read Stratford's memorandum with more than ordinary care. He liked the admonitions, but not the suggestion that the Ottomans might, in some circumstances, be plucked from the sort of quarantine in which the prime minister thought they were best kept. 'It may be necessary,' he commented, 'to give them moral support, and to endeavour to prolong their existence but we ought to regard as the greatest misfortune any engagement which compelled us to take up arms for the Turks.' Consequently, when Russell reported that Stratford would like to be given some discretionary control over the squadron of the Mediterranean fleet at Malta – adding wryly, 'This you will hardly like' – Aberdeen would have none of it. If Stratford got control of warships, he would assuredly find some excuse to use them: 'The assurances of prompt and effective aid on the approach of danger,' the prime minister replied, 'given by us to the Porte, would in all probability produce war. These barbarians hate us all and would be delighted [to embroil us] with the other powers of Christendom.'[24]

The instructions drawn up by Russell concentrated on the Holy

Places question, but also contain a lengthy *excursus* about Russian forbearance, no doubt inspired by the first Seymour conversations. Since the days of Catherine II, and down to 1829, each Russo-Ottoman encounter terminated in 'the aggrandisement of Russia, and the depression of the Mahometan power'. In this period, 'the conquest of Constantinople [was in Russia] a favourite object of national ambition', while millions of Balkan Christians longed 'to reverse the triumphs of the fifteenth century'. But since then, Russell wrote, Russia had come to realize that 'any attempt to cut the knot . . . would unite against her all the powers of Europe. The Emperor Nicholas is conscious of this difficulty and with a moderation at once magnanimous and wise is content to forgo the prospect of this brilliant prize.' Stratford's task was thus to pour oil on troubled waters, for both Russia and France had exhibited 'a dictatorial if not menacing attitude' over the Holy Places. Exerting moral influence only, he was expected to persuade Napoleon III to recognize the tsar's 'moderation' and 'superior claims'. The recent refusal by Britain of an alliance, solicited by France, was to be courteously re-explained, and her 'cordial co-operation' in 'maintaining Turkish integrity' was to be earnestly required. In Vienna, assurances of an abiding concern for maintaining peace in the Levant were to be given and asked, and Austria's collaboration in resolving the question of the Holy Places was to be secured. Here, Russell was writing under the influence of Aberdeen, who was particularly anxious to close the gap between Britain and Austria. At the Porte, the Ottoman ministers would be reminded that 'the crisis is one which requires the utmost prudence on their part, and confidence in the sincerity and soundness of the advice they will receive from you, to resolve it favourably for their future peace and independence'. In accordance with Stratford's memorandum, the Sultan's government was also to remember that chronic mal-administration was a fundamental cause of foreign complaints, and that Christian revolts were predictable unless the long-promised reform programme was genuinely and soon put into effect.[25]

Stratford had written his memorandum; Aberdeen commented thereon; Russell drew up the provisional instructions; Clarendon, succeeding Russell, put them into final form, and signed them. But the last word was still Aberdeen's. To Clarendon, as to his predecessor, Aberdeen stressed that 'we ought not to trust the disposal of the Mediterranean fleet – which is peace or war – to the discretion of any man'. Stratford therefore, could have power to call the Malta squadron to readiness, but not to direct it to sail without authority from London.[26] This conditional authority over the fleet was, in fact, all Stratford wanted, or needed; the shadow, for once, was as good as the substance. With Stratford preparing to leave England, Aberdeen urged Brunnov to have Menshikov's mission, of which only London as yet knew the facts, brought to a conclusion before Stratford arrived. When one adds this private advice to the effect of Russell's dispatch to Russia of 9 February, it is easy to see why the tsar felt he had been encouraged by the European power he respected most to raise his tone in his dealings with the contemptible Turk.

Meanwhile, Clarendon was having his difficulties with the cactus personality of the ambassador. 'Lord Stratford is too bad, his temper is ungovernable, and I believe he is more *in* a passion than *out* of one. He would have quarrelled with me and thrown up the mission half a dozen times before he went *if I had let him* [emphasis added].'[27] Control of the fleet does not seem at any point to have been the issue. On the other hand, Stratford, who was not called 'Jupiter' by his attachés for nothing, badly wanted to go to his post by way of St Petersburg, so that he could eventually appear among the Ottomans bearing the mandate of all Europe. There was a personal aspect to this request. For many years, Stratford had been convinced that it was Nesselrode who had nurtured the tsar's opinion of him as dangerous. Like many strong, vain men of his kind, Stratford badly wished, at this last high point of his career, to stand well with Nicholas I personally, and was sure he could accomplish it. Clarendon referred the idea to Aberdeen. Aberdeen passed it to Brunnov. Brunnov, marvelling at such 'megalomania', turned it down flat.[28] More irritating still to Stratford than this disappointment was the open hostility of the ministry towards the Ottomans, which was going to make his diplomacy impossibly difficult. Henry Reeve, the able leader writer of *The Times*, was in and out of the Foreign Office repeatedly, making it plain that his paper was 'not disposed to embark in a campaign for the integrity and independence of that ancient fiction, the Turkish Empire'. *The Times* was as good as Reeve's word; it launched in February a barrage against Ottoman misgovernment, leading Stratford to remind Clarendon that the Sultan would have no reason for trusting British advice, if treated by the government and press like 'a patient universally given over and fit only for dissection'.[29] Was it not dissection he was going out to prevent? Clarendon – or Aberdeen – was amazingly tactless and unrepentant, and actually gave a Foreign Office official, Henry Parrish, the task of re-educating the old man to see that Britain's past policy towards the Ottoman Empire was 'a mighty delusion involving the suppression of truth and the acceptance of falsity in its stead'. Parrish was not very successful,[30] and Stratford was furious. Sent a volume by 'one of the profoundest investigators into Mussulman Affairs', he returned it with the pages uncut. By the time Clarendon finally got him on the way, Stratford was laying about him with some vigour and, as the foreign secretary said, threatening almost daily not to go. He secured Rose's removal, and even had the embassy architect, whose tastes he disliked, recalled, before he set forth.

★ ★ ★

Stratford at last left England on 7 March, accompanied by his private secretary, Lord Sheffield; by that resourceful manipulator of long leaves in England, the elderly Count Pisani; by Charles Alison, the oriental secretary, now much restored in health; and by his former protégé, the new MP for Aylesbury, Austen Henry Layard. With instructions to call at Paris and Vienna, Stratford made the most of his opportunities, staying in Paris until 17 March, reaching Dresden three days after that, Vienna by the 23rd, and Constantinople only on 5 April. While he was on his journey, the situation in Constantinople was being transfigured in the most threatening way by Menshikov, whose mission had not in the beginning raised much speculation in London, or anywhere else except the Porte. Whenever anyone asked what Menshikov was about, Brunnov was at hand to provide a soothing reply. Thus Greville understood from Clarendon that Menshikov's business did not run beyond 'a string of conditions about shrines and other ecclesiastical trifles'.[31] Clarendon also sent a note to overtake Stratford which said, 'Count Nesselrode has positively assured Sir H[amilton] Seymour that beyond the Holy Places Prince Menshikov has no demands to make on the Porte'.[32] On 18 April, *The Times* produced the rather troubling news that Menshikov had raised with his Ottoman hosts a demand for 'an official acknowledgement of the protectorate of the tsar over the Greek schismatists', and on the 19th London heard that the Ottoman foreign minister had resigned.[33] Meeting the usually amiable Clarendon at Buckingham Palace, Brunnov was greeted with the accusing remark, 'I see Menshikov has turned the Turkish government out'.[34]

The 19th also brought very stirring news from the Admiralty. A telegraph had come in from Vice-Admiral Dundas at Malta, reporting that he had been urged by the chargé d'affaires at Constantinople, Colonel Rose, to come at once to the Straits. Dundas was unwilling to oblige without a direct order from London. An additional report from Cowley, in Paris, said the French Toulon squadron, which had also been called to the East by Benedetti, was actually going, which it did on the 25th. On the 20th, a quartet of ministers – Aberdeen, Clarendon, Russell, and Palmerston – met at the Admiralty to decide what to do. Russell was already in an agitated, aggressive mood, for as leader of the House he would have to defend the administration's decisions. He was in no doubt about what should happen:

> The emperor of Russia is clearly bent on accomplishing the destruction of Turkey and *he must be resisted.* . . . The vast preparations at Sebastopol show a foregone purpose. . . . In case I am right in this conjecture the crisis is very serious. My opinion is that, in case of the invasion of Turkey by Russia on any pretence, we ought to send a messenger and *demand* the evacuation of Turkish territory, and, in case of refusal, to enforce this demand both in the Baltic as well as in the Dardanelles. We should of course enter into concert with France.[35]

This was strong talk for a man who, so shortly before, had been giving a sympathetic hearing to the Seymour conversations, but Russell felt a strong sense of betrayal, and it frightened Brunnov very much. Fortunately for him, the tsar received the benefit of the doubt, and on the supposition that Menshikov had been heavy-handed but the tsar was a 'Gentleman' to be trusted, Dundas was approved for sitting still. Brunnov congratulated the prime minister, saying: 'As long as you and Nesselrode are at the helm I am confident that we shall steer off the Oriental rock.'[36] It was certainly unfortunate that Menshikov's clumsiness had let the

French off the chain. On the other hand, Britain had refused to act with her, so the western powers were now divided. What Brunnov seems not to have recognized was that Nesselrode, the practising Anglican, was no more captain of the Slavophile ship in Russia than Aberdeen was the head of his new Liberal team, at least where foreign affairs were concerned. 'It was certainly unfortunate,' Clarendon hastily wrote to Stratford, 'that you should not have been on the spot when he [Menshikov] arrived. I am sure under the grave circumstances of the case you will not lose an unnecessary moment in getting to Constantinople.'[37] What had Menshikov been instructed to do, and what had he done?

Though not quite as large as Brunnov, the 'hippopotamus' of the Russian diplomatic service, Menshikov was the equal of Nicholas I in bulk, and an adherent of the strong, Stroganov tradition in Russian diplomacy, rather than of the gentler school of Orlov and Titov. He was chosen in that eventful month, December 1852, to reverse the victory won at Constantinople by the French. As Nesselrode, who first suggested the mission and the man, explained the situation, 'the key of the church of Bethlehem has been made over to the Latins so as publicly to demonstrate their supremacy in the East. The mischief is done. It is now necessary to remedy it.' Count Leiningen was winning his encounter on behalf of Austria by threats. France had done the same. Why not Russia also? The British, especially, understood Russia's situation, and for as long as they did so, who else mattered? Malmesbury, when foreign secretary in 1852, had freely admitted to Brunnov that Nicholas I was 'a kind of Pope' to the Christians of the East, more able to accept Napoleon III's numeral than to tolerate in him some such title as 'Protector of the Eastern Catholics'. Clarendon made the same point to Stratford: the tsar was not 'a free agent in the question of the *Lieux Saints*. His Majesty is compelled by the feelings of his people to give every protection to his co-religionaires.'[38] Russell had agreed, in his reply to the first Seymour conversations. Seymour lamented in later years that the persuasive, supple Orlov was not chosen for the fateful mission, and Harold Temperley, by a re-arrangement of personalities, has written that 'had Nicholas been weak, Aberdeen strong, or Menshikov tactful, there might have been no war'.[39] This misses the whole point. Menshikov was selected precisely because he would know how to terrorize the polite, decadent Ottomans into surrender. Reports of his style, it is true, varied, and Vitzthum called him 'a tall stately old gentleman of stiff soldierlike deportment and exceedingly courteous', but Clarendon received the more common impression that Menshikov, besides disapproving of Nesselrode's cosmopolitan manners, detested the French, was an intensely patriotic Russian, and could be 'remarkable for bitter sarcasm'. He habitually 'liked to make jokes and *donner le change* upon serious matters'.[40] No one ever seems to have noticed the resemblance to Stratford, though the clash of two similar personalities was to be no small part of the tragic outcome at Constantinople.

If there was controversy over the man, there were positive dangers in the instructions with which Nicholas I instructed Nesselrode to provide him. These were devised, the Russian chancellor believed, in the knowledge that Russia could have 'entière confiance' in Britain while possessing 'une solidarité parfaite' with Austria and Prussia. France had demonstrated her mischievous potential often enough already; and the chances of Napoleon III wishing to overturn the territorial *status quo* in the East were high. Menshikov would not show either belligerence or fear in his dealings with the French embassy. As for the Ottomans, and particularly the reformist modernizers – 'ces présomptueux régénérateurs' – it was clearly their policy to embroil the European states with one another. The task, Menshikov was told in the preamble to his orders, was consequently to secure from the mischievous Ottomans 'reparation for the past and adequate guarantees for the future'. With the position in the East restored to the situation of a year before – the situation before the French had worked their mischief – the leading conservative powers would be in a position thereafter to preserve the old *status quo*, which had stood since 1841, and in many of its details since 1829, against any further French challenge.[41]

In practical terms, this meant Menshikov would refuse to negotiate with Fuad Pasha, the Ottoman foreign minister who had surrendered to the French, and seek to redress the balance of privileges and concessions through persons allegedly ready to deal more honourably with Russia – Sultan Abdulmejid, his mother, and a number of right-minded officials of the imperial household. As to the demands to be made, two were inflexible, and the third discretionary. By the first, the Ottoman government would confirm the return of Russia's privileges in the Holy Places in the appropriate firmans. Sufficient as 'reparation for the past', the firmans would only become adequate as 'guarantees for the future' when embodied in a contractual document, possessing 'the force of a treaty', to be called, in Turkish, a sened (convention). Menshikov's second demand would therefore be for just such a sened, by which the Ottoman government would be held accountable hereafter for any neglect of the privileges and rights of the Orthodox church in the East. The sened would convert all former Orthodox privileges into treaty rights. The third contingent demand was left to Menshikov's discretion. If he found the Ottomans afraid to agree to a sened out of fear of France, he might offer them a secret, defensive treaty, to run for a number of years. He would only conclude such a treaty *after* a sened was duly signed. So that there should be no mistake about what was most wanted, Nesselrode provided Menshikov with a draft sened, to which only the smallest modifications would be acceptable.[42]

What is most striking about this six-point document is that the Holy Places' requirements – concerning the much debated keys, rights of access to holy buildings, repair of the decrepit cupola over the Holy Sepulchre, the precedence of Greek over Latin religious services, demolition of Muslim houses to provide land for a Russian hostelry, etc. – are relegated to the bottom three places. As Nesselrode had assured the British, and others too, that the Holy Places comprised Menshikov's sole business, the first three items of the sened require particular attention, and the more so as the debate over their meaning soon carried quarrelling governments along the road to war.

The modern analyst has to ask himself whether these much controverted clauses went significantly beyond Russia's existing treaties with the Porte, or were simply reasonable expedients for holding the Ottomans to pre-existing commitments. The first clause of the draft sened required that the Orthodox rite should be protected 'in all its churches', with the Russian embassy in Constantinople retaining its traditional right to make representations on behalf of the Orthodox churches and clergy in Constantinople and other towns and places in the empire. By the second clause, the four Orthodox patriarchs of the Ottoman

Empire – of Constantinople, Antioch, Jerusalem, and Alexandria – would, along with their metropolitans, bishops, and lesser clergy, exercise their traditional spiritual functions and enjoy their traditional immunities and privileges, without obstruction. By the third clause, once elected, the patriarchs would retain office *for life*, unless guilty of disloyalty to the Sultan or oppression of their own people. For some time to come, and with considerable vehemence, Nesselrode would insist that Russia was *not* asking for any new right or privilege, simply the observance of those already existing. If the Russian chancellor's interpretation proved to be correct, there was no reason why Menshikov and the returning Stratford should disagree. Indeed, they were expected by their superiors to collaborate in resolving the crisis over the Holy Places. But there was room for some British suspicion. If Menshikov was only seeking a means for holding the Ottomans to the fulfilment of past agreements, and the honouring of the arrangements to be made over the Palestine shrines, why could London not have a copy of his instructions? It is time to see how Menshikov presented his case, and how it was received.

★ ★ ★

Menshikov reached the Bosporus in early March, on a warship with the appropriate name, *Thunderer*. He was accompanied by the Russian naval commander for the Black Sea, senior army staff officers, and Nesselrode's son for secretary. According to Rose, he also brought almost unlimited secret service money. And yet, for some days, no one could say why Menshikov was coming. Ozerov, with whom Rose dined twice a week, and was on the best of terms, had at first known only that a visitor was on the way, but was ignorant of his identity or purpose. He was later able to provide the name, but said his understanding was that Menshikov was paying a private visit. Fuad Pasha at the Porte had no information. Rose began to worry when the news came down to him of the size of the entourage which had come ashore at Buyukdere, virtually opposite the British summer residence, and, in the light of the good relations with Russia on which Russell was insisting, he wondered if there was some secret development afoot which the Foreign Office had neglected to bring to his attention. This was evidently on the Ottomans' minds too, particularly when Menshikov went into action. His orders gave him 'a wide latitude . . . as to language, by turns friendly and threatening', and he decided to begin with a show of resolution.

The style in which he presented his credentials on 4 March has often been told. Visiting the offices of the Porte, in civilian clothes rather than diplomatic uniform, Menshikov would not consent to be received formally by the foreign minister, Fuad, and waited outside for the grand vizier to come to him.[43] Reshid Pasha, the former holder of that high office, just might have obliged, but Mehemet Ali Pasha, the present incumbent, and a brother-in-law to the Sultan, had little regard for Europeans, least of all rude ones, and a rude Russian was for him the worst of the breed. When Menshikov finally entered the Porte, he strode past the open door of Fuad's reception room, and Ozerov himself admitted later to Rose that Menshikov loudly told his half-scandalized, half-disbelieving following of Ottoman officials that their foreign minister was 'a rascal, a fool, and a liar'. The grand vizier received Menshikov coolly, yet properly, but Fuad resigned later in the day, to be replaced by Rifaat Pasha, much distrusted at the British embassy as a pro-Russian. So at least Menshikov had obtained a quick result. The Dutch representative, Baron Mollerus, was as mystified as his hosts by such tempestuous proceedings, but made the cogent observation that Menshikov must work quickly, whatever his undisclosed purposes might be, since 'once aided by the advice of Lord Stratford, they [the Ottoman ministers] would follow no impulse but his'. The English tyrant's popularity would come surging back once the officials of the Porte felt renewed danger from Russia. Even without waiting for Stratford, they appealed for Rose's advice and intercession on the very afternoon of this first fracas with Menshikov.

There was much more to Hugh Rose than Stratford could ever allow. His ideals for the Ottoman Empire were considerably less exalted than Stratford's, running to railways and capital investment rather than civil rights, but he was a courteous and helpful man, fluent in Arabic, good in Turkish, and much liked by his hosts. Drawing on his personal knowledge of Jerusalem, he did much to damp down the smouldering argument between the French and Russian embassies about the Holy Places, seeing no reason why the French should not use the keys they had been given to the Virgin's

Tomb, nor why the Russians should not have publicly promulgated the firman conferring on them custodianship of Orthodox visitors to the sacred shrines of the Holy City. He applauded the disposition of the French to allow others to repair the rickety cupola of the Holy Sepulchre and, on the other hand, could sit at Ozerov's hospitable board, Martens in hand, arguing against the Russian pretension – much older than Menshikov's current mission – to be the protector of the Greek Orthodox subjects of the Sultans. To his own government, Rose had also rather courageously declared that Sultan Abdulmejid had been placed in an impossible position by the great powers, 'cowered [sic] and humiliated before his own subjects by menaces, forced to give contradictory and dishonourable decisions, and then accused of perfidy by those who have driven him to it'.[44] Stratford cannot have been very pleased to read this while browsing in the Foreign Office records in 1852, but it was the sort of sentiment which explained why the Ottoman ministers looked to Rose for aid.

The grand vizier was with Fuad when Rose called, and explained that Menshikov had claimed, in his first stormy scene, that there was no point in looking to Britain for aid as she was in full agreement with Russian aims. If this were so, Mehemet Ali Pasha said, then it looked like an arrangement 'to destroy Turkish independence'. On his desk lay recent issues of *The Times*, with the more anti-Ottoman editorials marked in pen. Rose could promise nothing on the 4th, being as mystified as his hosts, and regretfully declined a request to get the Malta squadron sent to Vourla Bay. Going back to the embassy, Rose tried to assemble some sort of sense from the mass of incoming consular and newspaper reports. What *were* the Russians up to? There had to be more to their new Russian visit than just the Palestine quarrel. James Yeames, from Odessa, reported the assembly there of Russian troops for embarkation. From Galatz, there was a vice-consular report that the towns of the Principalities were being alerted to provision 60,000 Russian troops in the near future. From Canak, at the Dardanelles, came the news of a Russian steamer, the *Bessarabia*, taking soundings in the Straits. Remembering that only two weeks before the Austrians had dispatched 10,000 troops to Dalmatian Kotor to underline Count Leiningen's demands, and looking again at the nature of Menshikov's entourage, Rose decided on the night of the 4th that 'a new treaty of Hunkiar Skelessi' or 'something worse' was about to be demanded by Russia. Once the idea got into his head he could not resist it: 'If Russia once possesses and fortifies the Dardanelles and the Bosporus, then she will have a key which she values more than that of Bethlehem. She will have the key to the East.' Looking at the recent history of Palestine, 'the minarets are disappearing and the churches are rising . . . the Crescent is on the wane'.

It was Captain John Hay, of the *Wasp* war-steamer, who pointed to a practical way in which the Ottomans might be assisted. The Malta squadron was due to sail for Corfu on spring exercises on 20 March. Why did not Rose invite Vice-Admiral Dundas to cruise to 'the bay of Smyrna' (Fuad's 'Vourla') instead? The French minister was more than ready for such a measure, and on the 6th both men telegraphed for help. Thus Rose, by his own confession, did what he could 'to strengthen the Turkish and weaken the Russian position' without knowing what Menshikov actually wanted. He spent the rest of March trying to find out.[45]

Dundas, as mentioned, refused to move to Vourla. His superiors in London approved, and Clarendon thought Rose's attempt to make the Eastern Question 'seem black, is not very successful'. It had, nevertheless, split the western powers, for the French minister's appeal was answered positively. The Toulon squadron sailed for the eastern Mediterranean. Brunnov thought everything had blown over, asking Aberdeen: 'Is it not strange that the wisdom of an admiral should come to the rescue of diplomatic haste?' Menshikov was blamed for being hot-blooded, Rose for his impetuosity.[46] No one blamed the tsar, yet. When the news got about that the French squadron had actually sailed from Toulon, British officials were furious with Napoleon III for escalating international tensions so rashly. Baron Kisilev, the Russian ambassador, received the sympathy of both the transient Stratford and the resident British minister, Cowley, who notified the Foreign Office: 'Luckily, we have sensible people to deal with in the Russians who will not mind this little French puerility.' Clarendon agreed: 'They [the French] and they alone are the authors of this mischief in the East.'[47] Much of the anger and criticism soon to swirl round the head of Stratford was the result of his revelation that the tsar was not as innocent as he at first seemed. But for the moment, he too thought Paris the centre of irresponsible mischief.

★ ★ ★

During his few days in Paris, Stratford struggled between fascination and disapproval, like everyone else. France itself was divided, with the emperor's adversaries telling the ambassador 'his system has no basis and cannot last', while adherents asked what better alternative existed. 'In general, as might have been expected, the Emperor is a blackamoor to the former and almost an angel of light to the latter', and his advent to supreme power was a blow to constitutionalism as well as radicalism. He preferred to draw his support from the popular will of the opaque masses, thus separating himself 'from all the talents and almost all the moral principle of his country'. Unable, as Stratford saw it, to command the allegiance of the politically sophisticated elements in French society, Napoleon III would be a variable quantity in international affairs, and Britain ought not to expect him routinely to provide 'a stable element of resistance to any dangerous combination of the anti-constitutional powers'. 'It may be doubted whether his co-operation even in the East can be accepted by us without some shades of caution; nor would it apparently be safe to rely on his goodwill, unable as Her Majesty's government must be to remove all causes of difference with him.' This was a reference to the freedom of the British press to be as hostile to Napoleon III as it pleased, as well as to the political sanctuary England provided for plotters against his life.[48]

At the foreign ministry, Drouyn de Lhys told Stratford that the French minister had just stepped ashore at Toulon, and introduced him to de la Cour, the new French ambassador to the Ottoman Empire. He and Stratford were to reach Constantinople on the same day, 5 April. On Continental politics, Drouyn said his government was sure Russia and Austria were in league in the East, and that Buol knew all about Menshikov's mission; Britain and France must watch the situation and consult. On 10 March the British party dined at the Tuileries. Stratford recalled:

> The emperor took me into an adjoining apartment and, when we were seated, entered into conversation at some length, though rather in a desultory manner, on political affairs.
>
> He began by expressing his satisfaction at finding that there was nothing to prevent the two governments from acting together in the

East, and that both agreed in wishing to uphold the Ottoman Empire. He seemed to think that Austria had treated the Porte rather sharply in the late transactions at Constantinople and he made some enquiries regarding what I understood to have been settled about the Turkish claims in the *Bocche de Cattaro*. He spoke of the Holy Places and threw the blame of engaging in that question on the *parti pretre* of the Montalembert school and the legislative assembly. He desired nothing better than to finish the affair. He was not disposed to make difficulties so long as his honour was uncompromised; and he would not object to the maintenance of the Sultan's firman [favouring Russia], supposing France to retain what had been previously accorded. He talked of Egypt as having been an object of some difference between the two governments. He understood that we only wanted the railway [across Suez] for our communications with India, and he had declared his mind to people who seemed to forget that England, not France, possessed extensive territories in the country. He said that he had no wish to make the Mediterranean a *French lake* – to use a well-known expression – but that he should like to see it made a *European* one. He did not explain the meaning of this phrase. If he meant that the shores of the Mediterranean should be in the hands of Christendom, the dream is rather colossal. Syria came next into consideration. I recommended a strict adherence to existing arrangements. He acquiesced, like a man who knew little of the subject. He showed some curiosity respecting the Sultan's character, nothing that implied belief in the probability of Turkish regeneration. The Emperor then touched upon several topics unconnected with the East. . . . Reverting for a moment, as he rose and walked towards the Empress's drawing room, to the affairs of Turkey, he declared his wishes to be in favour of Turkish independence and the progress of civilization.[49]

Stratford spoke very little: 'Throughout our conversation, it was my object rather to learn the Emperor's opinions rather than to hazard any of my own.' This paid a dividend as, on the 16th, in a second interview, Napoleon confirmed the idea 'that if the Turkish Empire fell to pieces, he should like to see the shores of the Mediterranean, now occupied by the Turks, partitioned among several powers of Christendom'. But the emperor did reiterate regarding the Holy Places that 'it was France's duty to be foremost in concession, as France had been the first to cause that embarrassing question'.[50] Leaving Paris on the 18th without knowing of the dispatch of the French fleet – it left Toulon six days later – Stratford was increasingly suspicious of Menshikov, and whether his train was boiling dry outside Frankfurt or struggling through the snows of Bohemia, his thoughts were leaping ahead. 'I am very anxious to know more and be on the spot. If the Menshikov act of the play continues till we reach the Bosporus, there may be room for much.'[51] In Brno, 'an old German newspaper, stewed to rags, has yielded up a report that Menshikov's Ultimatum has been rejected'. In Vienna, he heard more details of the deposition of Fuad Pasha, the sailing of the French fleet, and the withholding of the British. But what the Menshikov 'Ultimatum' was, none could say.

What, then, of Austria, so widely believed to be afraid of Napoleon III? Stratford's Vienna interviews were brief, formal, useful. Buol, wallowing around in the shoes of office left behind by the departed Metternich and Bach, was remembered in the British diplomatic service as the only foreign diplomat ever thrown bodily out of his office by a British foreign secretary. To Stratford's eye he exuded incompetence. Stratford had always, since his cousin's lifetime, suspected Austria's diplomatic reliability and effective power. He recognized the events of 1848 as underlining her deficiencies and was content now simply to obtain Buol's assurance that the Montenegrin disagreement with the Ottomans was over, and that Austria, like Britain, expected Menshikov's visit to the Porte to be restricted in purpose to the Holy Places quarrel.

Four days out of Trieste, on HMS *Fury*, Stratford's party passed the Dardanelles, where Stephen Pisani, Etienne's nephew, was waiting for him with the latest news. The Ottoman ministers were keeping outsiders at bay, but there was a decided rumour. 'The Russian demands and accompanying demonstrations seem to mean the acquirement once and for all of a preponderating influence with all the Greeks in their train, or some act of territorial encroachment by way of substitute.' If Menshikov failed to obtain some sort of treaty concession, Russia might take over the Principalities, on whose frontiers her troops were massed. Thus Stratford informed his wife, adding, 'I also learn that the grand vizier, though negotiating secretly [with Menshikov], intends to wait for my arrival before taking a decision', and the stern believer in God's Will expressed his rising excitement by biblical allusion:

> The prospect is more than enough to make one nervous; but there is hope to be derived from the best of books, and possibly a pebble from the wayside may be found once more the most effectual weapon against any armed colossus. My pebble is the simple truth,

but I must stoop to pick it up where the heavens lie reflected on smooth flowing water. Do you understand my metaphors?[52]

On the morning of 5 April, a month after Menshikov's arrival, Stratford's war steamer dropped anchor off Pera. The first boat load of visitors brought Rose in uniform, the attachés, the faithful Étienne Pisani, and the leaders of the British mercantile community. Layard shook hands with Rose, a bad sign. The merchants had been terrorized by Rose's sending for the Malta squadron, and let Stratford know they were very relieved to have him back: 'His frigid caution,' *The Times*' local correspondent believed, 'would counsel the Porte to take no effective steps in a military sense.' No one saw anything strange about a Russo-French quarrel being patched up by the returned British ambassador. Who else? Rose himself acknowledged that even the Orthodox folk in the Ottoman capital were far more concerned about French warships appearing beneath their windows than about shrines in Jerusalem: they too were glad Stratford was back.

Stratford could not resist an immediate show of vigorous purpose to underline his return to full authority. It was, after all, *his* embassy. Almost as soon as his horse was led away, he was at the familiar blue desk, with the globed lamps at the corners, giving orders: Étienne instantly to the Porte to arrange an audience with the Sultan for the 7th; a note of greetings to the grand vizier; Stephen Pisani with personal messages to Fuad; Sheffield to bring copies of Rose's recent dispatches; Rose to pack.[53] The attachés bustled about nervously, trying to look conscientious and busy. They knew he was cross about the appointments and promotions made during his recent absence.

> Others, old friends, now out of office, send messages to me . . . but I keep personally at a distance, wishing not to excite suspicion at the Porte. . . . Reshid, I guess, is itching to recover his place; but he has no right to be in a hurry, and I must have large explanations with him and strong pledges [favouring reform] before I can even wish to see him restored to office.

First things first. At the end of the first day back, Stratford scribbled a short note to his wife: 'How strange! and without you? It cannot be, yet so it is.'[54] Coming back for only a month or two, he was to remain there for five years more. It was the story of his life.

It was typical of his vanity, and carefully cultivated image of omniscience, that Stratford should pretend to Clarendon in an early dispatch that he uncovered Menshikov's secrets for himself and by his own methods. This was very unfair to Hugh Rose, whose undercover work had already revealed a great deal. Menshikov had been followed everywhere, and trailed once to the private residence of Husrev Pasha, an ancient intriguer who had helped to negotiate the sensational and pro-Russian treaty of 1833. This, of course, confirmed Rose's worst fears. Working closely together, Rose and Benedetti also explored the possibility that Menshikov was on an exercise in economic subversion, with the newly founded Ottoman Bank, set up by British capitalists, its intended victim. When confronted directly about this, as he was on two occasions, Menshikov baffled his pursuers with an enigmatic silence. The Holy Places problem, he said, was 'tout à fait secondaire' to his main duty.[55]

The real reason the western embassies at first established so little was that, for almost three weeks after his first stormy appearance at the Porte, Menshikov attempted virtually nothing, a leisurely style which suggests he had no fear of the returning Stratford, of whose good disposition he received reports from Paris and Vienna. It was only on 22 March that Menshikov raised his psychological warfare to the highest level of intensity. On that day, he stood impassively by his dragoman while the six points of Nesselrode's proposed sened were read out to Rifaat Pasha, in the presence of the grand vizier. Rifaat, as Menshikov later reported home, became 'visibly gloomier', 'appeared greatly upset', and by the recital's end 'was unable to make any reply'. To brace the foreign minister's courage, the possibility of an alliance was touched upon briefly. Sending for the Russian dragoman, Argyropoulos, a few days later, Rifaat made it as clear as he could that the grand council, while prepared to make some declaration about the Holy Places entirely satisfying Russia's demands about Palestine, could never consider the idea of a contractual agreement. 'In the name of God, be moderate,' Rifaat pleaded. In practical terms, the dragoman reported back to his ambassador, he 'begs you to desist from the idea of a *sened*'. Remembering Nesselrode's injunction to vary his tactics, Menshikov decided to let the sened drop out of sight for the moment, telling

The Preliminaries of the Crimean War

Nesselrode he would only return to 'the guarantee we need for the future' after clearing up the Holy Places problems. As this decision was taken well before Stratford stepped ashore on 5 April, it disposes of the common belief, praised by some historians and deplored by others, that it was he who cleverly disjointed the question of the Holy Places from that of the sened, the better to expose the illegitimacy of the latter demand. Nicholas I himself approved Menshikov's strategy, while pencilling on the dispatch reporting it that a 'crisis of compulsion' would have to be brought on if the Ottomans proved recalcitrant for too long.[56] And as fear began to loosen Rifaat's tongue after 22 March, a reasonably accurate knowledge of Menshikov's demands was available to Stratford when he resumed control of the embassy. All he now required was an actual copy of the document Menshikov had allegedly left with his hosts, and how this came into his hands is best told in the words of Etienne Pisani, his first dragoman.

> All my endeavours to induce Rifaat Pasha to let me have copy of the *Note Verbale* given him by Prince Menshikov proved fruitless. He even refused to let me see it, and pretends that the Note in question was drawn up in Turkish; whereas I can assure your lordship that it is not the case, because I have ascertained from good authority that the original of the Note containing the several demands of Russia was kept by Rifaat Pasha himself. Having pressed upon his Excellency to comply with my request, he finally told me very plainly that he was not authorized to communicate the papers presented by the Russian embassy to anyone, and were he to do so, that would have for certain the effect of giving cause to a suspension of relations between the Russian embassy and the Porte. I observed to his Excellency that his behaviour on this occasion was an unequivocal proof of his want of confidence in the British embassy. [At this, Rifaat allegedly capitulated, and began to talk.] The demands upon which Prince Menshikov insists are the following:
> He demands to have the privileges formerly granted by the Porte to the patriarchates and the Greek clergy confirmed in a treaty to be concluded between Russia and the Porte; the right to Russia of interfering in matters connected with the Orthodox religion, *and an exclusive protectorate over those who profess it*, and the appointment of the Greek patriarch of Constantinople for life, and independent of the Porte's sanction. What they want, in fact is a revision of the treaty of Kainarji, which they say is not explicit enough. . . . Rifaat Pasha pretends that he said to Mr Argyropoulos, that if what Russia demands from the Porte was, as they contend, grounded upon some

undoubted right, why do they so earnestly recommend secrecy?. . .
While I was taking leave of Rifaat Pasha, he entreated me most
urgently to call again tomorrow and *let him know what answer he was
to give* [emphasis added] to Prince Menshikov when he calls on
Saturday.

[But the next day, the 8th, Stratford heard that the divan had not
waited for his advice and had made its own decision.] The grand
vizier informed me that the council, after I left the Porte, had
unanimously decided that the demands put forward by Russia were
inadmissable and the grant of them would be tantamount to a
distinct division of the empire, and they came to the conclusion that
the answer to be given to the Russian ambassador at the interview,
which is to take place tomorrow at Rifaat Pasha's house would be,
that until the pending question of the Holy Places was definitively
brought to a solution, the Porte could not enter in any new
discussion respecting the other points which remain to be examined
afterwards.

[As to the long-withheld papers presented to the Porte by
Menshikov] I am requested [by the grand vizier] to assure your
Lordship that on Sunday, the latest on Monday, you will be
furnished with copies of the papers in question. I think it incumbent
upon me to tell your Lordship confidentially that the great objection
of Rifaat Pasha to let you have those papers is, that Mr Argyropoulos
repeated to him over and over again that, were a single paper,
communicated to the Porte by Prince Menshikov, to be given to any
embassy, and especially to your Lordship, such a proceeding would
be considered as a breach of faith, and the consequences would be a
suspension of relations.[57]

Thus by 9 April, only four days after his return, and three weeks
after *The Times* report of a Russian 'protectorate' over the Orthodox
subjects of the Sultan being required, Stratford de Redcliffe had a
French translation of the sened on his desk, Menshikov having,
contrary to Pisani's information, presented his six points in a
Turkish original so that there would be no dispute about the
wording he wanted. Interpreting the document's significance for
Clarendon's benefit, Stratford observed that, contrary to Nesselrode's insistence that the Holy Places were Menshikov's only
concern, he was demanding

> a remodelling of the Greek patriarchate in Constantinople so as to
> make the election of the patriarchs henceforward an appointment for
> life, independent of the Porte . . . and a most clear and comprehensive
> definition of [the] Russian right under treaty to protect the Greek and

Armenian subjects of the Porte in religious matters: and . . . the conclusion of a formal agreement, comprising these points between the two governments.[58]

Menshikov had also proposed an alliance, Stratford added, 'but receiving no encouragement [from the Ottomans], had desisted from the overture'. While London might choose to go on trusting the tsar, Stratford did not for a moment believe demands as detailed as those which lay before him lacked authorization from St Petersburg. That Russia wanted some means for holding the Ottomans to promises they had made, he found 'reasonable'. But to seek to exact a proper performance from them by means of a treaty seemed to him futile, improper, and potentially dangerous, and he felt 'a mystery hangs over the intentions of Russia'. Until he received fresh orders from London, he would press the Ottomans to settle the Holy Places dispute with the greatest possible dispatch, but to concede nothing beyond unless it were some kind of declaration of good intent to pacify Russia.

The stage was now set for a contest between two very imperious men, and it is important to recognize the qualities Menshikov and Stratford de Redcliffe shared in common: conceit, ill temper, intense patriotism, and an extreme dislike for the role of second fiddle. To Menshikov, the Englishman was of a lower social order, a mere diplomat. To Stratford, the Russian was a clumsy bureaucrat and imperial yes-man, an intruder in a game he would never master. The possibility of their collaboration went out of the window almost immediately, assisted by accidents of time and timing for which no one was really responsible. Menshikov was ill in bed when Stratford began his official round of visits, but the latter was convinced the postponement of their meeting was deliberate. In his turn, Menshikov was brought the story – a true one – that on presenting his credentials to the Porte, Stratford promptly retreated to a quiet corner with the grand vizier and Rifaat, there to converse in animated whispers. As the Englishman's contempt for Mehemet Ali Pasha's private life had once been notorious in Constantinople, their sudden mutual confidence irritated Menshikov and, when the two envoys finally met, their encounter could be nothing but coolly polite. Menshikov knew Stratford had the terms of the sened; Stratford knew

Menshikov had forbidden the Ottomans to reveal them. First round to Stratford. They discussed the Holy Places, which, Menshikov reported home, Stratford understood to the tiniest detail. Unfortunately, the occasion concluded with a long lecture by Stratford, in which he made plain his view that none of the great powers should any longer be coercing the Ottomans unilaterally, and all should be jointly requiring greater attention to trade, agriculture, communications, and a charter of subject-Christian liberties. These ideas had absolutely no appeal to Menshikov, but at least the lines were now drawn, and each man knew he could only succeed at the expense of the other.

There was, nevertheless, an important trend in Menshikov's conduct which the personal aspects of the rising quarrel should not be allowed to conceal, and that was the progressive reduction of his demands. He mentioned an alliance to the Ottomans at an early stage of his negotiations, which Stratford duly reported, but he never mentioned the idea again, which Stratford seems not to have noticed. Though promising to return to the sened in the course of time, he dropped the contentious matter of life appointments for the four patriarchs when he did so. There was, in the end, as in the beginning, only one clause of the sened Menshikov dare not abandon, and that was the first one, which, by a fatal shorthand, was already known in Europe as the Russian 'protectorate' over the Greek Orthodox people of the Ottoman Empire. And yet even this was amenable to rewording, in order to remove its most obnoxious character, and by the time he left Constantinople in May, Menshikov was ready to consider almost any formula, as we shall see. But the role of conciliator did not come easily to Stratford, and he did not mind too much if Menshikov, once he started to lose, should fall completely flat on his face. By aligning himself rather obviously behind the Ottomans, instead of between them and Menshikov, he neglected diplomacy's cardinal operational principle, which is to maintain bridges for the defeated to retreat over while keeping their self-respect. The evidence suggests that this might have been done. None of this takes heavy blame away from Menshikov. It only requires Stratford to share it.

The Holy Places altercation between France and Russia was resolved within three weeks of Stratford's return. Again, Stratford's vanity led him to report, and his admirers to suppose, that his was a single-handed achievement. In practice, Menshikov wanted to get it out of the way quickly so that the firmans pronouncing full reparation to Russia could be incorporated in the sened, to which he was anxious to return. The new French ambassador, de la Cour, with orders to accommodate Menshikov, deferred informally to Stratford's superior knowledge of the question, but was sensible enough to deal directly with Menshikov in a friendly fashion. It is difficult perhaps for a modern reader to have much patience with the minutiae with which the three embassies grappled industriously and, at last, successfully. Even Kinglake, writing for a more earnest and pious age, could claim that Stratford's skilful mediation between the interests of Britain and France 'prevented the vain and presumptuous Russian from seeing the minuteness and inanity of the things which he was gaining'. Kinglake goes on:

> For the Greek patriarch to be authorized to watch the mending of a dilapidated roof – for the Greek votaries to have the first hour of the day at a tomb – and finally for the doorkeeper of a church to be always Greek, though without any right of keeping out his opponents – these things might be trifles, but awarded to all the Russias through the stately mediation of the English ambassador, they seemed to gain in size and majesty: and for the moment, perhaps, the sensations of the Prince were nearly the same as if he were receiving the surrender of a province or the engagements of a great alliance.'[59]

Menshikov was not so foolish, nor Stratford so artful, as this version of the facts would suggest. Stratford's self-importance led him to say: 'I thought it was time for me to adopt a more prominent part in reconciling the adverse parties',[60] and it is only fair to add that, at the end of three weeks of exchanging papers on the allocation of custodial privileges in Palestine, Menshikov and de la Cour sealed their agreement with a handshake in Stratford's study in acknowledgement of his help.

The negotiation succeeded expeditiously, nevertheless, mainly because it had a following wind. Napoleon III, now strong enough to face down the legislative assembly, was also strong enough to face Russia on bigger issues than the Palestine shrines. While negotiating graciously with Menshikov, de la Cour knew perfectly well that the Toulon squadron was at Besika. Menshikov needed a settlement in order to proceed to bigger things. As for Stratford, the testimony of his dispatches and private letters shows that his mind too was, from the start, on the larger problem, although, until the matter of the shrines was concluded, he and Menshikov 'both avoided entering into a discussion [about the sened] which might have proved irritating'.[61] In London, Russell understood 'that Stratford was behaving very well'. Clarendon was directly encouraging: 'There is general satisfaction in knowing you are on the spot and confidence that you will prevent catastrophe.' If Menshikov tried to obtain concessions beyond those connected with Palestine, it would be 'a violation of all that should be binding on a sovereign and a gentleman'.[62]

Menshikov could not quite wait until the Ottomans issued the relevant firmans about the Holy Places before reverting to the subject of his sened. The Ottoman ministers, as Rifaat candidly informed him, were confused by his mixture of 'embraces and pistol-shots', and were unwilling to sign any further document with him having 'the force of a treaty'. This proved to Menshikov that the Porte had 'abandoned itself more blindly than ever to the British ambassador's arguments', for who else could have corrupted them into fearing such reasonable and legitimate demands as the sened would embody? It was therefore very important to push the Ottomans into the final concession before their resistance hardened further. Menshikov heard that in the council the official he had insulted, Fuad, and the highly intelligent Ali were the core of resistance to his pressure. The really dangerous circumstance was that Menshikov thought Stratford should mind his own business, the sened being a direct Russo-Ottoman subject of negotiation, and an instrument for holding the Ottomans to existing agreements, not for the acquisition of new advantages. His instructions said he was to 'clarify and define' the meaning of certain clauses of the treaty of 1774 (clauses 7, 8, 14, 16), but that otherwise he was only to demand 'le maintien de ce qui existe depuis plusieurs siècles'. And when Menshikov approached the Ottomans once again on 19 April, while the firmans concerning Palestine were still at the drafting stage at the Porte, he reiterated that, while requiring a sened which must be 'prompte et éclatant', he sought no new political concessions.

Stratford found this view perplexing and worrying when Rifaat

Pasha told him about it, for the first, controversial clause of the sened was to his mind quite incompatible with the Russian claim that it only 'clarified and defined' the 1774 treaty. The first clause in Nesselrode's original draft sened, it will be remembered, declared 'that the Orthodox religion shall be protected in all its churches, and Russian representatives in Constantinople will, as in the past, have the right to make representations on behalf of the churches and clergy, in Constantinople and other towns and places'. Coupled to the demand that the four patriarchs, elected 'according to the laws, regulations, and usages of the Oriental Church', would be irremovable by the Ottoman authorities, this virtual 'protectorate' over 15 million Orthodox subjects of the Sultan seemed to Stratford to run far beyond the stipulations of the 1774 treaty, of which, he said, clause seven 'allows of a limited Russian interference on behalf of one particular church [in Galata] and its ministers, and of no direct protection at all'; clause eight related to the affairs of Russian pilgrims; clause 14 again to the Galata Orthodox establishment; and clause 16 had reference only to Wallachia.

Unable, as he felt, to talk the matter out candidly with Menshikov, Stratford tried to explain his point of view to Ozerov, the Russian first secretary, on 25 April. 'I know you want something more resounding and solemn', he said, than a simple Ottoman promise of good behaviour for the future, 'but that is neither right nor fair. Far better to take your stand on any violation of treaty, whereas a new right will bring western opposition and Turkish resistance.' Ozerov knew Stratford well enough to answer with some warmth, saying it was 'scandalous' for the Englishman, whose influence over the Ottomans was famous, to complain against Russia's present negotiation as an improper intrusion in their domestic affairs. The spirited Russian counsellor went on to make a very measured defence of Russia's manifest policy of restraint since 1829. 'Believe me,' Stratford pleaded in response, 'the note you will receive will satisfy you entirely, because it will contain formal assurances for the future.' But what, Ozerov retorted, would be the value attachable to one more Ottoman promise? Russia already possessed the 'protectorate' which so frightened Stratford. It was hers by custom and treaty. Why should not Menshikov have confirmation of such a situation in the form of a sened? Menshikov himself was high in morale and, interestingly, did not think the British would obstruct him to the end. He was sure the sened would soon be his. 'Let us hope so,' ran the tsar's comment on this report. 'But let us not be too confident. We have much to fear from Redcliffe.'[63]

Ironically, each of the two ambassadorial rivals thought he was being responsible and reasonable, with little need to conceal his behaviour but for the factious opposition of the other. As the Holy Places problems came nearer to settlement, Stratford abandoned his original view that the Ottomans need offer nothing beyond, and recognized that the safest way for them to refuse a Russian sened was to offer a document of their own. Hearing the very promising rumour that Menshikov was ready to abandon his claim for life-appointments for the patriarchs, he pushed them to understand that there would be 'eventual danger in mortifying and irritating Russia by too complete a refusal'. They ought, therefore, to go to the very limit of giving Menshikov the most generous form of words he could possibly desire so long as there was no 'extension of influence having the virtual force of a protectorate to be exercised exclusively by a foreign power over the most important and numerous class of the Sultan's tributary subjects'. In trying to write such a formula himself, Stratford told his wife, 'my brain is half on fire, and my fingers worn to the quick. I get up at five. I work the live-long day, and I fall asleep before I reach my bed.' He even kept his distance from the Ottoman ministers, so as not to antagonize Menshikov, a considerable strain for a man who enjoyed the drama of highly charged interviews. 'I have only been out three times [since arrival] to any of them: once to the padishah, once to the grand vizier, and once to the same person and Rifaat, the latter having called upon me.'[64]

But all this was vain for, as Menshikov reminded the Ottomans, they ought to be negotiating about an exclusively Russo-Ottoman matter with *him*, and no one else; 'the Porte was doing a very objectionable thing,' Argyropoulos complained, 'which is to consult and act upon the advice of the British ambassador, and they had better abstain from so doing in future.' The grand vizier allegedly replied that 'no one could prevent their showing regard and respect to one who on every occasion evinced so much good will . . . and who takes so much interest in the promotion and welfare of this country'. It was Layard, who quit Constantinople for England about this time, who put his finger on the shortcoming in Stratford's personal style: he 'suspects everything and everyone and only has one end – his own selfish views'. Layard saw nothing wrong with the policy of supporting 'the Turkish Empire in its present state until the Christian population may be ready to succeed the Mussulman'.[65] But Stratford saw only one way of doing things, and nearly everyone who ever met him, while finding much to admire, also discovered that he exuded a self-righteous infallibility like embalming fluid. He showed this very clearly in considering the consequences of not actually winning Menshikov to his point of view. 'No hostilities would ensue,' he blandly declared, 'but a coldness and perhaps a suspension of diplomatic relations embarrassing and occasionally endangering the Porte.'[66]

Stratford's complacency was constantly sustained by Clarendon in this period, who not only sent congratulations for his 'most judicious advice' over the Palestine shrines, but agreed the time had come for the Ottoman government to give 'some pledge that practicable reforms and particularly as regards the treatment of Christians shall be carried out as well as promised'.[67] The suggestion suited Stratford remarkably well, and he translated it to Rifaat Pasha in the following way:

> The true remedy for this evil [Russian intervention in Ottoman affairs] is in the Sultan's own hands. Now is the time for solemnly confirming by his own authority and proclamation all the privileges hitherto conferred upon the rayas of every description, including Greek, with such *precision* and *completeness* as may throw all foreign influence into the shade, and revive the sympathies of Europe, and most particularly of the English people, in favour of Turkey.'[68]

In short, a new *Gulhane* decree, promulgated by the Sultan's sovereign will and offered to the major powers of Europe in the interests of all his Christians, rather than a sened, proffered by Russia for the imperial signature, on behalf of the Orthodox rite alone. There was only one problem, which Stratford's 'selfish views' allowed him to overlook. It was a '*guarantee* for the future' Menshikov wanted; not an empty Ottoman promise. Only a sened would do.

It was to obtain one, after two months of tedious negotiation, but at last with the Holy Places firmans in his pocket, that Menshikov returned to the charge on 5 May.[69] Lane-Poole writes that, with the Holy Places question settled, Menshikov 'now found himself standing on empty air . . . obliged to create a grievance out of nothing'; Temperley, who has written in the greatest detail on the period, claims that, on 5 May, Stratford 'learned at last the full meaning of the Russian demands' and appealed to Ozerov 'in vain' against them.[70] It is true that Stratford was able to treat the demands of 5 May as an 'ultimatum', for Menshikov attached a five-day time-fuse to his peremptory requirement for the long-delayed sened, after which he would terminate diplomatic relations. But to see Menshikov as the villain of the piece evading the wise suggestions of a resourceful colleague is a total misrepresentation of the facts, and thus of the meaning of the facts. Menshikov delivered his ultimatum on 5 May, but on the next day, being again confined to his bed, sent Ozerov to explain in person to Stratford the impossibility of his going home with the firmans alone. Far from concealing his requirement, he asked Stratford to help him obtain it, but the latter told Ozerov that if the British government itself ordered him to obtain the sened, he would resign.[71] The two ambassadors met on the 8th, with Stratford complaining against 'an innovation altogether disproportionate to the chief cause of your embassy'. Later the same day, the Ottomans were advised by him to refuse the demand for a sened as 'illegal'. When Rifaat notified Argyropoulos on the 10th that the sened was indeed refused, Menshikov naturally put the negative down to 'the violent and passionate opposition of Lord Redcliffe', and he was quite right.[72] This was doubly infuriating because, in the same way that Stratford tried hard, but irrelevantly, to devise the right form of words to be offered by the Ottomans, Menshikov lowered his terms also, hoping they would be accepted, a fact no one seems to have recognized.

The first clause of Nesselrode's original draft sened, first read out on 22 March, had terrified the Ottomans. Its modification by Menshikov, as presented on 5 May, reads as follows:

> No changes will be made in the rights, privileges, and immunities enjoyed since ancient times by the churches, religious foundations, and Orthodox clergy in the territories of the Sublime Porte, which is pleased to support them on the basis of the *status quo*. All rights and

privileges granted to the other Christian rites in future will also apply to the Greek rite.[73]

Notice that neither Russia nor her embassy officials at Constantinople are any longer mentioned by name as having a custodial function over Orthodox interests. There is no sinister elastication of the treaty of 1774. With the clause concerning life appointments for the patriarchs now dropped completely, the Ottomans were really being asked to sign a document in which they would contract to keep their existing promises. The attempt which has been made to prove this sened as threatening in its terms as its predecessor does so by asserting, without justification, that the word 'churches' should be understood to mean the Orthodox people worshipping inside them. Stratford himself recognized the magnitude of Menshikov's concession. 'The real difficulty consists in this,' he wrote in a memorandum to the Porte: 'Russia requires the insertion of the aforesaid privileges in a sened having the force of a treaty, and would thus make herself the arbitress of all that concerns the Russo-Greek religion and clergy . . . it is highly desirable for the Sultan to have the exclusive credit of the concessions confirmed or extended by him.'[74] In conclusion, then, it was irrelevant for the two ambassadors to cudgel their brains for a form of words acceptable to both parties. The real issue dividing them was the sort of diplomatic instrument in which the words should be embodied, not the words themselves. From the Russian point of view, a new *Gulhane* would not be worth the paper it was written on. Stratford was really admitting the truth of this in resisting a sened so fiercely. Since the Ottomans were unlikely to keep their promises, a sened would indeed be a licence for constant Russian interference. The Ottomans were much happier with Stratford's plan for a new and solemn promise of good behaviour by the Sultan to the High Court of Europe; they knew very well the judges would never agree if they were hauled before it.

With his ultimatum close to running out on the 10th, and half-expecting a refusal, Menshikov switched his attack from the ministers to the Sultan himself, requesting an interview for 13 May. The appeal was made, not through official channels at the Porte but through carefully selected persons, in the first instance (on about the 7th) the minister of finance, Namik Bey, and on the fateful

10th itself through the most famous, if temporarily unemployed, Ottoman minister-of-state, Reshid Pasha the reformer, a man Menshikov was quite ready to acknowledge was 'not very favourable to Russia'. There had, however, been contacts between him and the Russian embassy in the months of Stratford's absence in England, and there is some, equivocal, evidence that Reshid was the person who inspired the idea that a sened might be the most effective diplomatic instrument for concluding the Holy Places altercation. In return, there are clearer signs that Reshid hoped to obtain a return to high office through Russian aid, his old patron, Stratford, having, as he imagined in 1852, left the East for ever. Menshikov's interview, however novel and procedurally improper, was duly arranged, and his defence for it could well have been that there was a precedent in a reception he knew the British ambassador had enjoyed on the 9th, a reception intended to be confidential if not exactly secret, but which managed to remain neither.

It was after visiting Menshikov on the 8th that Stratford had returned to Pera to find a note from Rifaat awaiting him. In the event that relations with Russia worsened – a hint, surely, that Menshikov was about to have his demands rejected – could the Ottoman Empire depend on British naval support? Too wise to answer so leading a question in writing, Stratford called on Rifaat in person, at whose house, as he expected, he met the grand vizier. To the reiterated question, he replied that he 'considered the position in its present stage to be one of a moral character, and consequently that its difficulties and hazards, whatever they might be, should be rather met by acts of a similar description than by demonstrations calculated to increase alarm and resentment'. Obscure enough in English, it is academic to guess what was transmitted, by way of Stratford's French and Rifaat's Turkish, to the ear of the monolingual grand vizier, but the intended message was that, with the ships far away and Menshikov near, it would be discreet to keep talking. Nevertheless, on 9 May, and with the Russian ultimatum due to expire on the morrow, Redcliffe obtained an audience with the Sultan, ostensibly to offer condolences on the death of his mother – a lady on whom the Russian embassy had pinned considerable hopes – but in reality to

> apprize his Majesty, what I had reserved for his private ear, in order

that his ministers might take their decision without any bias from without, namely, that in the event of imminent danger, I was instructed to request the commander of Her Majesty's force in the Mediterranean to hold his squadron in readiness.[75]

This was very far from being a blank cheque, and Musurus, the Ottoman minister in London, was in a position to assure his government that Aberdeen was unlikely ever to sign one. But it is also unlikely that the sorrowing Sultan neglected to pass the reassurance to his brother-in-law, the grand vizier, or that it had no effect whatever as 'bias from without' on the deliberations in the grand council that very evening, which led next morning to Rifaat's refusal of a sened. On receiving the rejection, Menshikov extended the expiry of his ultimatum to the 14th.

On the 13th, Menshikov was received in his turn by the Sultan. The only person present besides the imperial interpreter, Nureddin Bey, was a close confidant of the Sultan, Edhem Pasha. With the second period of the ultimatum running out, Menshikov reminded Abdulmejid of the gravity of the moment. A 'guarantee for the future' was absolutely essential to Russia, and a new *Gülhane* decree, of which there was talk, was an unacceptable alternative. Having also heard of the qualified offer of the British fleet, Menshikov warned that any 'occupation maritime' by the western powers would serve to legitimate a Russian seizure of the Principalities. A change of ministers alone could resolve the impasse and the recall of Reshid Pasha to active service was strongly advised. To his intense gratification, Menshikov was told that the grand vizier and the foreign minister had both been dismissed earlier that morning, and he left the audience confident that the game was back in his hands. His pleasure was increased when he heard that Stratford greeted the news of Reshid's reappointment 'with an outburst of anger approaching dementia'.[76] But the reconstruction ought to have warned Menshikov. Reading the list of ministers next morning, Stratford noticed with relief that nearly all of them held 'opinions adverse to the extreme demands of Russia'.[77] Rifaat was raised to the presidency of the council, hardly a rustication. Mehemet Ali Pasha stepped down as grand vizier, but took over the ministry for war. The new head of government was Mustafa Pasha, a former governor of Crete and father of the current Ottoman minister to Paris, Veli Pasha. Though married to a Christian,

Mustafa was a devout Muslim and friend of the *Shaykh ul-Islam*. He was also, according to Slade, one of the 'présomptueux régénérateurs' whom Nesselrode detested, and foresaw an Ottoman imperial future which bound Muslim landholders and the Christian business classes together in partnership. One or two men – Namik, the minister of finance, and Fethi Ahmed Bey – were well disposed towards Russia and there was, of course, Reshid Pasha, back to office as foreign minister, but what chances had the latter of winning round his colleagues or, more problematical still, the larger grand council to which the ministerial council was an occasional adjunct? Menshikov hurried the pace in a 'severe' interview with Reshid Pasha on the 14th, the day the prolonged ultimatum expired.[78]

Reshid Pasha's loss of influence during his months of retirement is hard to estimate. Ottoman political figures were less obliging in keeping memoirs than their western equivalents. But the French-language newspapers of Constantinople were openly critical of Reshid and his family for their speculations and, more important, their pursuit of political rivals, several of whom now sat in the grand council. It is distinctly possible that Reshid Pasha was conscripted by his superiors, partly to placate Menshikov, but also to team up with the British ambassador against the Russian in an unpleasant negotiation with small prospect of success. After his bullying by Menshikov, Reshid went directly to see Stratford, who tried to steady him with the opinion that, however much Menshikov might threaten terrible consequences and the occupation of the Principalities, 'I felt certain that neither a declaration of war nor any act of open hostility was to be apprehended for the present'. Stratford recommended the now familiar strategy of yet another form of words, and a request for time for Reshid to study Rifaat's paperwork; 'time [too] not only in the interests of the Porte, but for the conveyance of information to friendly powers at a distance'. Very far from trusting the returned foreign minister, Stratford took the trouble to find out how Reshid performed at his first council meeting, also on the 14th, in the evening. He did, it seems, recommend submission and acceptance of a sened, but had got only slight support. Next morning, Reshid had to go back in person to Menshikov – now living on board a Russian war steamer at Buyukdere to underline his readiness to leave – and stress his need for more time.[79] To 'save the tsar's dignity', Menshikov officially suspended diplomatic relations with the Porte, but told Reshid he had until the 20th to produce the long-awaited sened or face 'the incalculable consequences and vast calamities which might result therefrom'.[80]

Reshid held Menshikov's confidence to the end of the fateful week: 'Reshid seems to me of good faith in respect to us,' he wrote home, 'in so far as a Turk is capable of it.'[81] Certainly, Reshid would have loved to succeed where his predecessor in office had failed, but he was not given enough time in which to plead a suspect case with the grand council. That body, which the British dragoman calculated to contain 48 members, consisted of the new ministers, but included also the leading ulema under the *Shaykh ul-Islam*, five provincial governors, and a sprinkling of retired, experienced ex-ministers such as Husrev Pasha, who was allegedly the recipient of Russian money as well as confidence. But there were some younger men there, too, like the patriotic and zealous *Tanzimat* figure, Fuad, whom Menshikov had insulted into resignation. Meeting on the 17th, the grand council refused to accept Reshid's argument that, since nothing was now being asked which had not been conceded to Russia already by the 1774 treaty of Kutchuk-Kainardji, there could be no harm in allowing Menshikov to have his sened. Three voted for Reshid's suggestion including, it seems, the *Shaykh ul-Islam* himself, but 42 turned it down. The Russian embassy blamed this crushing adverse vote on Stratford, who was charged with going round to many of the council members in person the night before the vote. The evidence from Stratford's own papers, however, suggests that he sent Mehemet Ali Pasha a form of words which could be offered to Menshikov in the format of a firman to soften the refusal of the sened.

On the 18th, Reshid again had to take the bad news to Menshikov, although official relations no longer existed between the Russian embassy and the Porte. His palliatives included a special firman, to be couched very much along the lines of Menshikov's preferred wording, but only addressed to the patriarch of Constantinople. There would even be a sened, and with the force of a treaty, though confined to ceding the site for a Russian church and hospice in Jerusalem. No further changes would be made in the balance of custodial privileges in Palestine without consultation with both France and Russia. Reshid cannot really have expected anything but the 'refusal, dry, clear, and strongly expressed', which he received. But Menshikov was curious. Perhaps these new arrangements could become a new basis for discussion. He asked to see them. They were still being drafted, he was told, but they could go to the grand council in the morning. This was too much and Menshikov virtually dismissed the Ottoman foreign minister; Reshid seemed ashamed of the propositions he had to make, and confessed his inability to control the situation. To cap Russian anger and disappointment, when Reshid's *caique* rowed away from the Buyukdere landing, Menshikov heard it was met by a second at the Tarabya corner. In the second sat Stratford. 'This,' Menshikov stormed to Nesselrode, 'is what the British have the effrontery to call the independence of Turkey.'[82]

Menshikov's mission was not quite over, and its most controversial moment in the entire seven-week passage-of-arms between the Russian and British ministers was at hand. It relates to the circumstances of Menshikov's actual departure on 21 May. No one doubted, after the 18th, that time was fast running out for him, and on the 19th he took a momentous decision to avoid going home empty-handed. He decided to surrender the principle on which he had been resisted for so long, that of insistence upon a sened with a contractual character. More than that, he diluted for the second time the wording of the highly debated first clause of Nesselrode's draft sened, in the hope that the grand council would recommend its acceptance verbatim to the Sultan. In its second modification, the clause now read:

> The Eastern Orthodox rite, its clergy, its churches, and its properties, will enjoy for the future and without any restraint, under the aegis of the Sultan, the privileges and immunities assured to it since ancient times, or which have been conferred upon it at different times by the Sultan's favour, and will also share in all advantages accorded other Christian rites.

Given as if by the spontaneous will of the Sultan, would such a wording have amounted any longer to the feared 'protectorate'? What ought the European ambassadors to have advised?

Stratford told Clarendon that the precise text was not available to them on the critical day because the Russian dragoman would not leave a copy of it in Reshid's hands, but on the basis of Reshid's recollection of it, he continued to object, speciously as one might think, to the Ottomans supplying any document 'having the force of a treaty' (which idea Menshikov had, as Stratford himself elsewhere acknowledged, surrendered in a 'conciliatory' spirit), and to warn against permitting the erasure 'of the limitation conveyed by the term spiritual as applied to the privileges and immunities of the Orthodox clergy'. What this last phrase meant is obscure, since 'the term spiritual' is nowhere in Menshikov's wording. And an incorrigibly suspicious watchdog like Stratford was probably not the best person to guide either Ottomans or less experienced colleagues through such a moment of opportunity. Only a few days before, he had said it was not the actual words that mattered but the principle of the sened. Now that the sened was surrendered, he reverted to the importance of words.[83] It was right to be extremely vigilant about the wording of any bilateral agreement, but Menshikov's final solution only asked the Ottomans, once more, to promise to keep past promises. If the form of words was wrong, or too open to interpretation and argument in the future, then more constructive behaviour was available to the Constantinople embassies than that they adopted under Stratford's influence.

When Reshid consulted him formally on the response to be given Menshikov, Stratford recommended that the matter should be raised with all the European representatives together. This was done, and the envoys replied that 'they do not feel themselves authorized under existing circumstances to provide an opinion'. Stratford's most resourceful apologist argues that 'they had to be non-committal, for if the ambassadors had urged Turkey to resist, they would have been compelled to defend her in case of attack'.[84] This singular and inaccurate remark ignores the numerous other expedients to which the Ottomans could have been urged. Also, Stratford did not need to call his colleagues together in solemn conclave to find out they had no opinion to offer, and it is surely more reasonable to suspect that he went through the performance of summoning them precisely because he knew in advance, and had even arranged in advance, the reply they would give. Their unhelpfulness to Reshid kept him under control; their unity warned Menshikov that he stood alone, and should think again before leaving; Stratford was nicely rescued from any appearance of isolated and vengeful behaviour. No refusal was sent Menshikov. Instead, the ambassadors sent one of their number, the Austrian chargé d'affaires, Baron de Kletzl, to offer him his colleagues' good offices and to invite him to receive 'the Porte's intended note'. But Menshikov was in no mood to be cajoled. He had heard that Etienne Pisani had been implored by Reshid Pasha to obtain Stratford's permission for him to accept both the form and wording of the final Russian note. 'Mettez-moi aux pieds de Lord Redcliffe, s'ecria-t-il c'est lui qui par sa résistance nous pousse dans l'abîme,' Reshid was supposed to have pleaded. That Reshid protected himself from Menshikov's wrath with this story seems proven.[85] That he himself exaggerated the dangers of the final Russian proposal in the course of relaying it to Stratford is also, from the fragmentary evidence, more than possible. But the rumour of Stratford's intransigence remained to haunt his reputation, deservedly.

It has been mentioned above that several diplomatic expedients might have saved the day, and one in particular should have commended itself to Stratford, to whom the other Constantinople diplomats were, sadly, far too deferential. Reshid could have been inspired to reply that he accepted the Russian form of words provisionally, subject to confirmation from the other great powers that the permanent acceptance involved no infraction or undue extension of existing international treaties like that of 1841. Had this resolve been conveyed to Menshikov by the European envoys in delegation, it is unlikely so vain a man would have been unresponsive. As it was, Europe was now committed to find the form of words which eluded the antagonists in the East. Reshid sent his son to see Menshikov on the 20th, but only to repeat the offer of the terms made on the 18th. Menshikov would not accept any change – not 'a single letter' – from his treacherous protégé. His mission was over.

Before we allow him to sail away and turn to the reactions of Europe, the reader may like to judge for himself the quality of the advice Reshid Pasha received from Stratford de Redcliffe. It was written on the evening of the 20th when, Stratford says, he was still anxious for an agreement. He deals, in turn, with the *form* of agreement Menshikov desires, its content, and how the Porte should answer.

The Preliminaries of the Crimean War

The *Projet* of an official Note or Declaration . . . should be examined with an earnest desire to make it an instrument of reconciliation. . . . Now the main essential points on which Pr[ince] Menshikov has hitherto insisted and which the Porte has determined to reject are the form of agreement having the force of a treaty, and the reference of [*sic*] the Sultan's confirmation of his Christian subjects' privileges [in an Ottoman promulgation] to the requisition and protection of Russia. The first subject of inquiry therefore is: Does the Note in letter or spirit contain those two objections? Take each of them in succession. With respect to the first, we perceive that the phrase of 'having the force of a treaty' does not appear in the Note. The words are expunged. Do their meaning and spirit remain? Now can anyone having the Note in his hand answer this question negatively? [No analysis follows: expected answer to this rhetorical question is thus, No].

As to the second objection, the whole tenor of the preamble goes to make the Sultan's declaration in favour of his Christian subjects an immediate consequence of Prince Menshikov's mission, and therefore no longer an act of grace on his part binding their affections to him and resting on his honour, as an independent sovereign pledged in the face of Europe, whose good will is essential to his safety, but as a deed of compliance with foreign dictation [the 'preamble' required the Sultan's promise to be addressed to the tsar: Stratford had hitherto agreed he should receive a statement, even one negotiated exclusively with Russia by an Ottoman emissary: now the ambassador objects that the document would not be addressed to Europe, only to one power in it: Russia 'dictates', Europe only 'pledges'].

If this be a mistaken view of the subject, let the error be made clear . . . the proposed amendment is a mere superficial change of forms and phrases, leaving the capital objects in reality as they are, and the Note would in spirit and practical effect be a sened without the name, a treaty without its formalities [forms and phrases, once the essence of the dispute, are now 'superficial'; disprove my guess, the ambassador challenges]. Next comes the question of a possible modification. But it is self-evident that any modification calculated to remove the Porte's objections would be deemed inadmissable by Russia.

What then is to be hoped from the new version?

The paper may go before the Sultan and his council. It may possibly be accepted by them, notwithstanding their previous decisions. Should such be the case, so flagrant an inconsistency would afford the Porte an escape of much convenience, some danger, and no small expense, but the responsibility of other consequences would rest with those who advised the measure, and more than a silent acquiescence could hardly be expected from one who, in concert with his colleagues, has hitherto approved the

Porte's resistance, coupled, as it has been, with forbearance and conciliation [pure Menshikovian blackmail: the Porte is an independent power, but if it behaves like one, it must bear the consequences].[86]

The ambassador explained his view of the situation rather differently for Clarendon's benefit:

> What Russia requires of the Porte would bear a strange appearance if the principle invoked in it were applied to other countries. . . . What would be thought in Europe if France or Austria were to demand a guarantee from Great Britain for the protection and good treatment of the Roman Catholic priesthood in Ireland? . . . Is there a canton in Switzerland endowed with so little spirit and foresight as to submit without a struggle to France asserting her right to take part in the protection of all the Roman Catholic churches and priests in that country? In Turkey, the dignitaries of the Greek or Orthodox church exercise in some degree the powers of civil magistrates. Russia, overstepping the spiritual limit declared by herself [in previous treaties] includes these powers in the sphere of privilege for the unalterable maintenance of which she seeks a treaty right. [What if the Ottomans complied, he asks?] The Russian embassy would be provoked by interested individuals to wield its power with a high hand and to apply it in a searching spirit; nor would the Porte be so humiliated by concession as not occasionally to struggle for the recovery of its lost ascendancy . . . the process of contention between force and weakness must terminate, sooner or later, in the hopeless subjection of the victim.[87]

It is in passages like these, replete with sonorous earnestness and somewhat clouded explanation, that Stratford worries the historian most. He writes of Russian inflexibility although Menshikov had changed his ground a good deal, giving up the secret alliance, surrendering the life appointments for the patriarchs, modifying the sened twice, giving it up altogether. He draws strained analogies between truly independent states and one whose independence had become increasingly more anomalous, not least through the purposes of Stratford himself, exerted over many years. What remains unfathomable is his own belief in the arguments he pressed so steadily. In one particular respect his campaign to persuade his superiors was especially well grounded, and that was his determination to test all Russian pretensions with a lawyer's care against the texts of existing treaties. His conservative peers at home, nearly all amateurs in foreign affairs, were most at ease intellectually when precedent could be invoked to guide them in this way. But regard for precedent and respect for custom are not far apart, and had the Russians argued more vigorously about their customary role in Orthodox affairs and their entitlement to refurbish it in 1853, they might have done much better with their London audience. Had not Russell, as foreign secretary, acknowledged the very thing Stratford was bent on resisting, Russia's *customary* championship of Orthodox interests? Aberdeen smirked at the idea of Ottoman independence. Stratford was rescued by the impetuosity of the tsar, by Nesselrode's perverse misinterpretation of Russia's treaty position in the East, and by the tendency of large numbers of Englishmen to know in advance what they were determined to believe about Russia.

★ ★ ★

Menshikov sailed from Buyukdere on 21 May, and confirmation of the event was in London six days later, a speed justifying the ambassador's arrangements for getting important news to the Marseilles telegraph by fast postal vessels. Stratford knew, of course, that his news would be an unpleasant surprise and that there would be 'those who will wish me at old Nick because I would not keep the peace by giving way to the new one'. While the implication of a success over Nicholas I should not go unnoticed, it would be wrong to accept a modern assertion that the wicked old man at Constantinople had been plotting the rupture of Russo-Ottoman relations all along so that he would have an excuse for panicking his superiors into sending British warships to the Bosporus. In his insensitive way, he was rather surprised when Menshikov finally left Constantinople, and fairly confident war would not ensue. It was a moment, he believed, for the British Cabinet to show solidarity in a large cause and to invite Russia, as a matter of great urgency, to reconnect herself to the other major powers in obtaining equality of citizenship for Ottoman Christians. She should put away her separate ambitions. He saw, he told Clarendon, 'no threat of immediate war, nor hint of an approaching occupation of the Principalities', but of his wife he asked: 'Will they look the crisis fairly in the face, and be wise enough, as well as great enough . . . to meet it firmly and settle it forever?'[88]

This was the moment when, the duke of Argyll wrote in his autobiography, 'we entered the rapids, and the roar of the distant cataract became slowly more and more audible to the ear'.[89] If that were true, Argyll had the best hearing in the Cabinet, since most of his colleagues remained engrossed with domestic concerns and did not notice the pace at which they were being carried to a crisis in foreign affairs. Contrary to what is often said, they were not whirled helplessly along by public opinion, nor coerced much by newspaper opinion, at this stage. Aberdeen affected considerable imperviousness to either sort of opinion, without denying numerous interviews and occasional inspired articles to Delane, the editor of *The Times*. Sir James Graham, at the Admiralty, was genuinely contemptuous, and not afraid of editors of any complexion. Palmerston thought *The Times*' anti-French attitudes 'idiotic', and evidently did not see they were changing; now at the Home Office, he brought the pressure of the *Morning Post*'s opinions on his colleagues whenever foreign policy was discussed, though it was a fairly open secret that the paper's editor, Peter Borthwick, enjoyed Palmerston's opinions as well as Walewski's money. Sidney Herbert, part-owner with the duke of Newcastle of the *Morning Chronicle*, was peacefully inclined, but dared not show excessive Russian sympathy in case the world unkindly reminded him that his mother was the daughter of the Russian general who took the Caucasus for Alexander I. Russell was very sensitive to the newspapers, less as a source of instruction than for what they said about his 'reputation', too often his main concern. Of all the Cabinet, Clarendon seemed to the Russian ambassador, Brunnov, 'extremely afraid, of the newspapers, of Parliament, and public opinion', an acute observation from a man not usually so perceptive. The foreign secretary said himself it was 'a well-known fact that *The Times* forms, guides, or reflects – no matter which – the public opinion of England', a rather narrow view of the location of 'public opinion'. It was this sensitivity, nevertheless, which Brunnov thought made Clarendon fearful he 'may seem more cowardly towards us [the Russians] than Palmerston would, were he in his place'.[90] Stratford, it may be added parenthetically, read *The Times* to see what Aberdeen and Clarendon were thinking, and as a kind of therapy for the release of his volcanic anger. In Constantinople, he kept *The Times*' correspondent at arms' length, and only occasionally fed his opinions, rather than information, to the *Morning Chronicle*, an unexpected choice. But, returning to the dialectic of Cabinet encounters, one is struck most by the extent to which the effective subcommittee on foreign affairs – Aberdeen, Clarendon, Graham, Palmerston, Russell – read the incoming dispatches from the major courts with conscientious regularity, rested their opinions mainly on that official correspondence, exchanged daily notes and often policy statements, jointly assisted in the drafting of outgoing dispatches, and invoked this or that newspaper to footnote a point of view.

There was only one Cabinet member with a truly exceptional source of information, Aberdeen himself. With Peel and the duke of Wellington both recently dead, he was the sole surviving British signatory of the 1844 memorandum which committed him – if no one else – to support Russia in her protection of the Orthodox religion, and to prior consultation with her, to the exclusion of France, on the affairs of the East.[91] His colleagues knew, and were uneasy about, his intimacy with the Russian ambassador at London, rightly suspected he was indiscreet and, worst of all, that he would dilute their expressions of concern at the current trend of Russian policy.

> Clarendon tells me he has no doubt Aberdeen has on various occasions held language in various quarters that was not prudent . . . and was calculated to give erroneous impressions as to the intentions of the government, and he thinks the Emperor [Nicholas] himself has been misled by what he may have heard [from Brunnov] of the disposition and sentiments of the prime minister.[92]

It was fairly predictable, under such circumstances, that Brunnov would try to counter Stratford's information with his own, supplied by Menshikov personally as well as from St Petersburg.

There is no truth in the assertion that 'no opportunity was given to Russia to make explanations as to why Menshikov had severed relations'.[93] Brunnov had copies of Stratford's instructions, as formerly of Rose's (though Parliament was refused them), but instead of providing Menshikov's, he spent his frequent visits to Argyll House denigrating the British ambassador at Constantinople. Brunnov, in Vilzthum's words, could affect 'a cordiality which was totally foreign to his nature', and made a strong, continuous impression on a prime minister ever anxious to remind his auditors that 'although perhaps we may continue for some time to come to talk with grave faces of [Ottoman] integrity and independence', Britain was 'under no obligation' to run to the aid of the Sultan.[94] Brunnov's message was simply that Menshikov was seeking no rights beyond those Russia already enjoyed, that Stratford was obstructing instead of helping him, and that the tsar had no intention of entering the Principalities. Perhaps Brunnov was genuinely misinformed, kept in the dark as, in varying degree, were Nesselrode, Orlov, and even Dolgorouky, the Russian minister of war. Whatever the truth, Brunnov succeeded in persuading Aberdeen of Stratford's misbehaviour, and Graham, that iron man who time would show was stuffed with straw, was also ready to be very stern with him. It was Graham's view that Stratford should stay out of Russia's legitimate business: 'Such temper and such manners are not the pledges or emblems of peace.'[95] The greatest resistance to all this came from the foreign secretary, and he continued to back his ambassador strongly, telling Stratford he had had 'a most anxious time and great responsibility' over the Holy Places and it was fortunate for England 'you are accustomed to both'. It was also Clarendon who dispersed the idea that Palmerston and Stratford were in confidential correspondence. He himself was Stratford's chief private correspondent, sending him literally hundreds of letters during the four years of their association. 'I have long seen that it was intended to attribute individually to you the failure of Prince Menshikov's mission, but I have defended you strongly, and shall continue to do so.' Clarendon kept his word for another four months, when his confidence in Stratford snapped briefly, but was soon mended. During the intense speculations of May, as the Cabinet awaited Stratford's dispatches to explain the rumoured departure of Menshikov, Clarendon tried to keep everyone calm saying, 'we think it better to wait for your view of matters before we do anything to commit this country'.[96]

On 16 May, Brunnov took details of Menshikov's instructions and the Nesselrode sened to Aberdeen, which led the suspicious to ask why now after so much secrecy, and to wonder what else was in store. As the presentation of these documents coincided with the arrival of Redcliffe's details of Menshikov's stormy demands of

5 May, here was a chance to test Stratford's alarms and speculations against the tsar's letter of accreditation, which notified Abdulmejid 'that the tranquillity of Turkey is wholly dependent on the immense majority of the population of the Orthodox Greek religion in the Ottoman Empire being protected from any molestation'. To ensure this tranquillity, the Porte 'must stay faithful to its engagements which date from the treaty of Kainardji granting to the Orthodox church that freedom of worship, that tranquillity of conscience, and that peaceable possession of rights, the inviolability of which Russia will never cease to watch over'. Now the treaty in question gave Russia no such supervisory authority and yet, in handing this material to Aberdeen, Brunnov claimed, as before, that Russia wanted nothing exclusive or new, only 'obtaining for the Greeks [i.e. the Orthodox subjects of the Sultan] some redress for the wrong which has been done them, and above all . . . securing them from further injury'. Menshikov, he said, had shown these papers to Stratford 'more than once', and, taking the material all together, Russia only asked that her religion 'should remain unrestricted, respected, and inviolable under Ottoman rule'.[97] Aberdeen, 'Russia's only friend' as Brunnov called him, sent the papers to Clarendon with the covering remark that he could see 'nothing new' or 'absolutely humiliating' to the Sultan in them. Stratford, he added, 'will scarcely allow the Porte to make [the sened] the grounds of a quarrel', thus echoing Brunnov's plea that Britain and Russia could surely never fall out 'about so very little'.[98] But Clarendon, deeply impressed with Stratford's interpretation of Menshikov's behaviour, disagreed with Aberdeen, and told Brunnov himself that he had been exchanging information with Walewski who told him 'it was the opinion of de la Cour at Constantinople and his [Walewski's] own that the convention [i.e., sened] if accepted, would be fatal to Turkish independence'.[99] Thus Stratford's strict interpretation prevailed with the more vigilant Cabinet members over Nesselrode's expansive meaning of the treaty of Kutchuk-Kainardji. Russell, too, after reading the sened, wrote: 'Every privilege of the Greek church (not of all Christians) is to be made a matter of engagement with Russia. It is intolerable. It is the way of the bear before he kills his victim.' 'Don't read this to Brunnov,' he added.[100] It was certainly the sened which caused the greatest consternation in Cabinet. 'You are quite wrong about it,'

Clarendon told Aberdeen, and after rereading it, Aberdeen had to agree that, if truly authorized by the tsar, it was 'quite unreasonable and ought to be resisted'.[101]

Aberdeen was now in a considerable fright: 'I cannot believe it will be necessary [to resist Russia] by war if the emperor should hitherto have been acting in good faith.'[102] In other words, Nicholas I might be in the wrong, but he must be helped to correct his error. Clarendon agreed: 'Get out of it as he may, backwards or forwards, he will have lost caste in Europe.' The tsar, however, was very far from penitent yet, belittled Seymour's information about Cabinet disagreements in London, and told the ambassador, 'You have been abroad too long, Sir Hamilton. All your countrymen think about is commerce.' Furthermore, Nesselrode now underwent a remarkable change of attitude: calling both Seymour and the French ambassador to his room, he told them 'he had never given any assurances that the question of the Holy Places was the only one which Prince Menshikov had to settle with the Porte, and that Russia intended to have the protectorate of the Greek religion in Turkey – and, moreover, would have it'. Western objections were 'unaccountable'. The western diplomats could hardly believe their ears. What he was now hearing, Seymour reported to Clarendon, ran completely 'contrary to the declarations made over and over again both to Your Lordship [by Brunnov] and myself'. On telling Nesselrode that a Russian sened would involve 'a very great extension of the rights secured to the Russian crown by the treaty of Kainardji', the reply he received was that the protectorate Russia intended to have formally recorded had been in effect 'for the last hundred years'.[103]

Stratford's dispatches announcing the withdrawal of Menshikov dropped into this superheated atmosphere in London, and it remained Russia's strategy to blame him for the Liberal Cabinet's state of unfounded apprehension:

> Unhappily, the ambassador of England was animated by [hostile] feelings towards us. An incurable mistrust, a vehement activity have characterized the whole of his conduct. . . . We are aware of the efforts which he employed with the Sultan, and also with the members of his council, to encourage him to resistance . . . by promising him the support and sympathies of Europe, if he granted to his subjects equality in the eyes of the law, and privileges more in accordance with the liberal habits of the West. Finally, at the last

moment, when Prince Menshikov had consented to abandon even the modified sened, and to content himself with a note, when Reshid Pasha himself . . . earnestly conjured the British ambassador not to oppose the acceptance of the note drawn up by Prince Menshikov, Lord Redcliffe prevented its acceptance by declaring that the note was equivalent to a treaty, and was inadmissable.[104]

More succinctly, Brunnov exclaimed to Aberdeen: 'It was *madness* on the part of Stratford to advise the Turks to reject the last note!' He had made 'retreat on our part impossible, while a timely acceptance of our modified proposal would have been so very safe and easy'.[105] Aberdeen was ready to believe this charge without question, and talked to Brunnov about the possibility of recalling Stratford; even Clarendon asked him to answer the accusation brought against him. Stratford would probably have found himself in a much tighter position but for Nesselrode's rash of pugnacious statements, the net effect of which was to lead most members of the British Cabinet to conclude that Menshikov had, after all, had official authority to snatch a sensational treaty at Constantinople, and had only been checked by the vigilance of Stratford.

'It is well known,' Lord Malmesbury noted, 'they [the Cabinet] are divided on the subject' of the Eastern Question, his informant being none other than Palmerston, whom he met riding in Pall Mall.

> Prince Menshikov, it is said, has left Constantinople. Lord Clarendon is very uneasy, but Lord Aberdeen, with childish obstinacy, refuses to believe that Russia intends any aggression, and will not send our fleet to Constantinople. [Palmerston] walked his horse by me till we got to Waterloo Place . . . between him and Lord Aberdeen there is a decided difference of opinion.

While everyone had been talking, Gorchakov had become Russian commander-in-chief in Bessarabia with two army corps under his direction. Merchant ships arriving at Constantinople and London brought news of concentrations of Russian troop-transports in the Crimea. There was growing fear for the continuity of British grain imports normally brought down the Danube. Parliamentary critics like Clanricarde and Layard, both friends of Stratford, had consented not to bring on debates for the moment but would not be kept at bay indefinitely. What excited Malmesbury most was that

Palmerston was now 'for decided measures; his policy quite agrees with ours'. The 'decided measures' meant primarily sending the Malta squadron, withheld in February, to join the French Toulon squadron in the Levant, as a gesture of support for the Sultan.[106]

Without any inside information to guide it, the parliamentary opposition was much more at the mercy of the newspapers than were the ministers. The first announcement of Menshikov's departure, though premature – *The Times* published it as a fact as early as 6 May – stirred the traditional distrust of Russia, first of all by the remarkably vituperative papers known as 'Gin and the Gospel', the *Morning Advertiser*, currently giving much space to the rabid Russophobia of David Urquhart, and, next in abusive power, *Bell's Weekly*, which would develop the idea of Aberdeen's guilt as 'the author of [the 1829 treaty of] Adrianople' and the lackey of the tsars. *The Globe*, with which Disraeli was associated, precociously proposed Aberdeen's impeachment for neglecting the national interest.[107] More restrained journals, while choosing to wait for more authentic information from the East, nevertheless worried Brunnov by moderating their formerly mistrusting view of the French. In this category were to be found the *Manchester Guardian*, the *Daily News*, the *Herald*, the *Morning Chronicle*, but, most notably *The Times*, the one paper which influenced any ministry by reason of its 50,000 readership and its reputation as the newspaper so many 'establishment' people, of whatever party, stood against the breakfast teapot. At first dismissed by the more radical, anti-Russian papers as 'our Hebrao-Austro-Russian contemporary', *The Times* was more amenable to the principle that the purpose of newspapers is to sell newspapers than many people understood, and Delane's sense of 'political meteorology' was drawing him from his anti-French hostility of 1852 to a very different stance by summer 1853. Sturdily retaining its principle that all talk of Ottoman 'reform' was just so much 'fudge', *The Times* dropped, quite abruptly, the associated hope that 'it may be the will of Providence to restore these provinces [of the Ottoman Balkans] and their miserable inhabitants to a purer faith and a milder sway'. By May, the paper was moving fitfully towards a pro-French, anti-Russian attitude: yet in the preceding year, some had actually called it 'Brunnov's organ'.

Much has been said of Stratford's alarmism; less of Seymour's, which was as great. Even when Menshikov left Constantinople, Stratford believed there was a chance of keeping the peace, and urged the Ottomans to send a delegate to Russia to resume the negotiation Menshikov had terminated. But Seymour's news was sombre. Hearing of Menshikov's arrival at Odessa, the tsar told the ambassador, 'We have no intention to commence war. But if blindness and obstinacy decided for the contrary, then we shall call God to our aid, and leave the decision of the struggle to Him, and march forward for the Church.'[108] More than that, while Seymour and Aberdeen were being lectured on Stratford's delinquencies, an ultimatum was on its way to the Ottomans. Addressed to Reshid Pasha and signed by Nesselrode, the document complained that the Sultan's ministers had refused to sign any document that would protect the Orthodox faith and churches in the Ottoman Empire. As a consequence, Russia had decided to occupy the Principalities unless, within eight days of receipt of the ultimatum, the Sultan met all Menshikov's demands 'without variation'. The Dutch ambassador at Constantinople was soon in possession of a copy of Nesselrode's demand and much struck by one sentence in it: 'We have found it needful to advance our armies . . . in order to show the Ottoman Porte to what its obstinacy might lead.'[109] So the Russians, the ambassador concluded, were actually on the march without waiting for an Ottoman reply. By the hazards of the postal system, a copy of the Russian ultimatum was in London by 5 June, before the original reached Constantinople, and 'there could not', Argyll later recollected, 'have been more agitation in Rome when Caesar crossed the Rubicon than in England when the armies of Nicholas crossed the Pruth'.[110] Brunnov, who had said the invasion would never take place, was treated as a deceiver. More important still, the blame the more trusting Cabinet members had been disposed to pin on the headstrong Menshikov was conclusively transferred to the tsar, making it extremely difficult for Aberdeen to claim there was anything meaningful left of the Anglo-Russian *entente* of 1844. The Cabinet, in any case, had taken a decision of its own, by ordering the British Malta squadron to join that of France in the Levant, sending the instruction simultaneously with, but quite independent of, Nesselrode's ultimatum to the Ottomans, at the very end of May.

The dispatch of the fleet, always a measure of great solemnity in

British eyes, was deeply disturbing to Aberdeen who resisted it as far as he could. Having admitted that Menshikov's terms, and the sened in particular, 'ought to be resisted', his own resistance to the fleet movement was necessarily on technical grounds, and he and Graham made much of the opinion of Sir Baldwin Walker, late of the Ottoman navy, that if the British squadron went up to the Bosporus, a Russian army, landing at Varna, would be quick to march to the Dardanelles and close the Straits against a return of the ships. Graham also invoked the adverse opinions of his brother, who commanded HMS *Rodney*. But this was just the sort of argument Palmerston revelled in and, drawing on the knowledge of the returned Rose, he dismissed Walker's ideas as 'visionary' and Graham's as 'twaddle'. It would take three days for Russia to offload a small army of 20,000 at Burgaz or Varna, and many additional days to bring another 20,000; should the Anglo-French squadrons choose to interrupt the process, 'the best day's grouse shooting you ever had in your life did not give you a better bag than our squadrons would realize'.[111] The Russians could not even begin to march on Constantinople if the Royal Navy destroyed the 30 bridges on the coast road from Burgaz.

What came out of the technical argument was, for Aberdeen, the alarming discovery that Palmerston was one of the more moderate members of the effective Cabinet. Russell, Granville, and Clarendon favoured sending the Malta squadron clean through the Straits to Constantinople; Palmerston was ready to be content with it at the Dardanelles, though he upset Aberdeen by wishing Stratford to control it. Stratford soon learned that the balance of opinion favoured action. To Cowley, in Paris, he wrote: 'The *opinions*, I see, in Downing Street, agree with ours. It remains for us to learn what the *course of conduct* will be.'[112] Brunnov was decidedly aware of Aberdeen losing ground, and tactlessly joined in the argument by challenging Palmerston himself: 'May not a sovereign avenge an insult by invading the territory of the party by whom the insult has been offered?' He was told in return: 'That does not apply in your case, you have received no affront, you have received full satisfaction on the question of the Holy Places, and the only thing you have now to complain of is that the Sultan has declined a convention which you had no right to propose to him.' Russia could not object if the British squadron sailed to the Levant; Britain and France were quite entitled to take precautions for the defence of a threatened Ottoman Empire.

The Cabinet debate, occupying the last few days of May, ranged over many aspects of the Eastern Question before Russell was able to say, 'I know of no one who is against it [the sailing of the Malta squadron] except Lord Aberdeen'.[113] More and more, it was Palmerston whose ideas predominated, his memoranda marked with the approving comments of colleagues, while the prime minister retreated tamely before him. Besides a long disquisition on the tsarist practice of noisily disowning unsuccessful emissaries while quietly accepting the success of others, Palmerston went on to steal Aberdeen's moral ground for argument, the worthiness or otherwise of the Ottoman cause.[114] Where Aberdeen weakly reminded his colleagues that Britain had no actual treaty commitment, Palmerston boldly claimed that it was exactly 'this broader difference between Christian and Mahometan' that the Cabinet should be discussing. If the welfare of Ottoman Christians was really Russia's concern, she should be working with the other powers, as Stratford said, not separately. It was unfortunate if the tsar forced Britain to take sides between Russia and the Ottoman Empire since in so many respects one was behind the other. Ottoman justice and corruption were no worse than Russian. From a liberal point of view, 'by far the largest number of the inhabitants of Russia are still slaves', whereas 'personal liberty is much more secure, and the press is more free in Turkey . . . the Sultan has no Siberia and no Poland with his dominions'. Written to Graham, Palmerston asked that this letter be handed on to Aberdeen, no doubt so that the prime minister should notice especially a passage which said, 'the party which followed the duke of Wellington [i.e. Aberdeen and the Peelites] did not think it inconsistent with general principles to take part in 1826–7 with the Turks against the Greeks, with Mohammedans against Christians'. The dispatch of the fleet would accord with the popular will of the British people, pacify Parliament, warn Russia, please France, and allow this very dangerous question to be safely internationalized. Beyond that point, Palmerston's solution coincided with Stratford's.

> The five powers might represent to the Porte that the only way of avoiding for the future questions of the most embarrassing nature

arising out of Christian complaints would be to place by an act of the Sultan's authority the Christian and Mussulman subjects of the Porte upon a footing of perfect equality in all matters civil and political, in short to pass an act of 'Christian Emancipation'.[115]

The final decision to send the fleet thus had little, if anything, to do with the pressure of public opinion, to which Clarendon alone makes regular reference, but a great deal to do with Aberdeen's anxiety to hold this experimental administration together. The back benches were full of restless men, several of whom, by a different turn of the political kaleidoscope, might have been in office. The Peelites, given their small overall numbers, were very prominent in the government, and Russell simply would not face disappointed Whigs in defence of a foreign policy he could not personally support. It was 'absolutely essential', he said, that the Malta squadron should sail to the Levant.[116] Clarendon, likewise, knew the burden of explanation in the Lords would fall on him, so little was Aberdeen's 'sneering' tone liked there. As the foreign secretary also believed the Menshikov episode would soon have to be laid before both Houses 'in a Blue Cover', he argued that the squadron must sail. 'I recommend this as the least measure that will satisfy public opinion and save the government from shame hereafter, if, as I firmly believe, the Russian hordes pour into Turkey from every side.'[117] There was more than a hint in the Cabinet altercation that France would wobble without a British show of resolution, and even some fear that, if Britain got into a confrontation without support, Russia would obtain help from the United States as well as Austria and Prussia. Aberdeen at last capitulated on 29 May, 'not objecting', as he put it, since the measure had become the clear will of the Cabinet, 'or at least part of it'.[118] It was another fateful moment: Aberdeen knew neither how to fight nor when to resign. Greville, who seems to have spent so much of his life at race-courses or on railway trains receiving confidences, was told the final details by a foreign secretary who could scarcely keep a secret longer than he could hold his breath. The plan was that 'seven Sail-of-the-Line' and '9 or 10 steamers of war', a very large task force, would rendezvous with the French squadron, presently at Vourla, at Besika Bay, off the outer Straits. The ships would sail 'towards the Turkish waters', but technically remain on the high seas. Vice-Admiral Dundas would 'comply with any requisition which he may receive from Her Majesty's ambassador' at the Porte.[119] Thus Redcliffe received in June the control of the fleet he had been denied in February. 'The emperor of Russia,' Greville prophesied, 'will be deeply mortified when he hears of this juncture . . . there is nothing he likes and dreads so much as the union of France and England.'[120] Though far from firmly established, that union was in formation.

There remained the question of the circumstance in which the ambassador could call the squadrons through the Straits, and Aberdeen was determined to hedge it in carefully. 'The authority given to Lord Stratford', he warned, 'is a fearful power to be placed in the hands of any minister' and he should not be 'permitted to employ the fleet for any other object than the defence of Constantinople'. Clarendon duly passed this on, but had great difficulty in explaining quite what was meant, and when it is remembered that the Russian provocations to which Britain was reacting were themselves aggravated by inexact statements of intent and requirement, the foreign secretary was dangerously imprecise. 'A declaration of war by Russia against Turkey, the embarkation of troops at Sebastopol, or *any other well established fact* [emphasis added] would . . . entirely justify Your Excellency in sending for the fleet.' Then follow the qualifications; that the Straits would only be passed 'on the express demand of the Sultan', and then only to protect the Ottoman Empire from 'an unprovoked attack, and in defence of her independence, which England is bound to maintain'.[121] The opportunities for a bold ambassador receiving such orders, like the problems for a cautious one, are immediately obvious. Had he so chosen, under the impulse of the burning thoughts of war the Russians claimed he harboured, Stratford could have persuaded the Sultan to treat the Russian occupation of the Principalities as 'an unprovoked attack' and, after prompting him to make 'an express demand' for help, could have provided it. The squadrons reached Besika Bay on 13 June. It is true the British agreed not to treat the Russian occupation of the Principalities as a *casus belli* for Britain when it got under way in July. But it was agreed at the same time that the Sultan's ministers were quite within their rights to see it as a *casus belli* for the Ottomans. It was, in fact, Stratford who persuaded them not to react belligerently to the

Russian invasion of Moldavia, using the quite brutal argument that they would be defeated if they did so.

The news of the sailing of the British squadron was leaked by *The Times* in early June, but seemed more than ever justified when the British heard of the Russian ultimatum to the Ottomans. As Nesselrode had always assured Aberdeen that Russia would take no positive action without consulting the British first, Aberdeen was unable to resist a Cabinet demand that a circular should go out to all the diplomatic corps explaining that the government 'actively approved' the advice Stratford had given the Ottomans, and that 'under the plea of confirming ancient treaties, further demands were put forward by the Russian ambassador, involving a protectorate of the Greek Church in Turkey, not only as regards the spiritual, but also the civil rights and immunities of its members'.[122] Britain thought the Ottoman authorities right to reject them. But what was to happen now? 'As we are drifting fast towards war', Aberdeen told Clarendon, it was important for the Cabinet 'to see where they are going'. He even raised 'the preposterous notion' that Dundas should be recalled in case the Russians were provoked by the movement of the British squadron to seize Constantinople. Clarendon panicked at this and wondered if there was a way 'to put the question back within the pale of negotiation'.[123] A Cabinet meeting on 5 June was so confused that Aberdeen told the queen he could not give her 'any intelligent account of discussion so desultory'. Stratford was told his tasks were heavier than ever: 'to maintain the independence of Turkey, to save the Russians from disgrace, and to keep the peace of Europe.'[124]

Palmerston remained almost alone for some days in his resolution and, punning grimly on the name of the Ottoman reformer-statesman, said the British government had 'our own wretched pasha'.[125] And he warned 'the wretched pasha' in question that the tsar was being misled 'step by step by the timidity of the British government' into 'mistaking our forbearance for irresolution'. In Palmerston's opinion, the Russian government had hit on the most ingenious mode of obtaining its ends.

> The emperor of Russia seems to have invented a new course of proceeding, to announce officially that he means to have war without declaring it. . . . [He intends on the one hand] to wrench by

force from the Turks the concession he asks and on the other to keep the Dardanelles and the Bosporus closed [to western fleets] on the pretence that the Porte is still at peace.[126]

Britain was hobbled by the treaty commitments of 1841 while Russia stepped neatly round them. Palmerston's irritation knew no bounds, and exploded into violent anger when a Russian circular put out on 20 June claimed, with obvious untruth, that Russia was only entering the Principalities because the Anglo-French fleets were now *within sight of Constantinople*. 'The best thing to be done,' he insisted in his briskest style, 'is that England and France should declare to the Russian emperor that his invasion of the Principalities . . . necessarily suspends and interrupts that peaceful state of the Turkish Empire which by the treaty of 1841 is the condition *sine qua non* of the closing of the Straits.' Consequently,

> the two powers [Britain and France] consider the Straits . . . open to their ships of war as long as the Russian troops shall remain within the Turkish frontier, and that the combined squadrons will accordingly proceed at once to the Bosporus. Nothing is to be gained with the Russian government, or indeed with any other, by anything which looks like hesitation and fear.[127]

This was absolutely consistent with a statement Palmerston had made to Brunnov in 1849: 'While the Porte remains at peace, the principle of the closure of the Straits stands.'[128]

For the moment, however, the Cabinet rested uneasily with what it had done. While Aberdeen promised to address Nesselrode 'in a tone of grave expostulation', and Palmerston inveighed against 'the robber who declares that he will not leave the house until the policeman shall have first retired', Clarendon set about bringing Austria into the role of general mediator, hoping fervently that 'the tsar would rather cross the Pruth [back into Russia] by a bridge made for him by his allies [at Vienna] than cross the Danube [southward] by a bridge of his own'.[129] The tsar had unquestionably been astonished and considerably intimidated by the British government's unexpected reaction to his adventurous and forceful diplomacy. Men as different as Delane and Urquhart, Charles Kingsley and Karl Marx, admittedly mere mortals beneath his notice, thought he was blundering into serious trouble. Aberdeen wanted the whole business resolved quickly with the aid of the conservative courts of Europe and hoped he would reach the end of the parliamentary session without the need for any great and public post-mortem.

★ ★ ★

Following the sailing of the British Malta squadron and the Russian decision to take the Principalities as 'material guarantees' of ultimate Ottoman acquiescence in the tsar's demands, the main courts of Europe made intensive efforts – more industrious than intelligible, more anxious than statesmanlike – to prevent the effective suspension of Russo-Ottoman relations on 17 June escalating into a continental war. Their activity seems, in retrospect, to be the final expression of the 1815 policy of preventive diplomacy, though Vienna in 1853 lacked the authority and resource under Buol's management which it had held under Metternich to assert itself as a true co-ordinating centre. There was very general irritation with the Ottomans who, according to *The Times*, were in themselves of no more account 'than the red Indians of Yucatan',[130] but the very circumstance that they were perceived as the cause of the crisis reflects the fears routinely evoked by any new instalment of the Eastern Question. No great power was prepared, and only Britain could afford, to fight a major war in 1853. Each, with the exception of Prussia, supposed it stood to lose, and perhaps lose seriously, if Russia effected a unilateral solution of her *imbroglio* with the Sultan. No power was absolutely certain of the support of any of the others.

The search for a peace formula was sincere, uncoordinated, and rather unreal; unreal because the statesmen became hopelessly entangled in a search for a form of words, some magic statement which had eluded the choleric Menshikov but which, once hit upon, all would recognize with cries of relief. It would rehabilitate Russian dignity without endangering Ottoman security. The process by which statesmen and diplomats lost their way, becoming mesmerized by words at the expense of the realities of which words are merely symbols, can be relived by any patient reader of the 1854 Blue Books, in which the various peace formulae – each but a short paragraph in length – can be laid side by side. The difficulty lies less in selecting that which best met Russian needs and *amour propre*, than in believing that any one of them made a whit of difference to her real power and influence. Much has been written about the 'drift to war' in 1853, with public opinion cast in the role of prime mover, much less about the massive failure of diplomatic professionalism. Stratford de Redcliffe was greatly offended by the ineptitude, as he saw it, as well as the plurality of plans: 'I reckon upon seven, exclusive of our own for Stamboul.' His first biographer calculated there were actually 11 schemes in the air at one time. 'When everyone else is dead,' the sardonic Charles Alison remarked, 'I intend to write an Oriental romance to be called *Les Milles et Une Notes.*'[131] It is unfortunate he never did, for the oriental romance became an occidental tragedy, and the guilty eventually looked back through their dismal record, less for an explanation than for a scapegoat. The turning point was seen to be the hopeful concoction of the Vienna Note, accepted by the tsar as the basis of peace. The scapegoat was Stratford, for allegedly persuading the Ottomans to refuse the formula the tsar had accepted. This traditional distribution – more accurately, concentration – of blame deserves more consideration.

The usual view has been that Stratford, as *doyen* of Queen Victoria's diplomatic service, head of her costliest foreign embassy, and a man of great insight into the workings of the Ottoman mentality, was at the height of his personal influence and power as the 1853 crisis unfolded; opinionated and inclined to insubordination, he should have been able to bully the Sultan's ministers into obedience whenever he chose. British patriots could feel safe that their Eastern interests were in such hands. When Europe managed to speak with one voice, as in July 1853, it too was entitled to expect this famous man to impose its united will upon the Ottoman ministers. The ambassador could scarcely complain. Had he not cultivated the legend of his omniscience and omnipotence through all his years at the Porte? Such narcissism ran in the family, as many people in British society well knew. But it was not a groundless vanity and the withdrawal of Menshikov with his tail between his legs seemed the latest demonstration of Stratford's enduring authority.

The reality in mid-1853 was not far from being the reverse of this supposed situation. For once, Stratford was not fighting running battles with his superiors, and was trusted by all at home except the prime minister. His behaviour during Menshikov's mission was stoutly defended at St Petersburg. But in Constantinople his influence was much less than once it had been, and a retrospect of his whole career suggests that, after 1851, it continued to shrink, little though he was disposed to admit it. The resistance to Menshikov, he admitted to Clarendon, 'may be steadied by foreign sympathies, but it most assuredly originates in the Porte's own intuitive apprehensions of future consequences, aided by traditions from the past'.[132] The Ottomans did not need Stratford to make them Russophobes. Alison believed Stratford was getting visibly older and very tired, and attached little importance to the return of Reshid Pasha to power, for he too was ailing and discredited among fellow Ottomans. Stratford cautiously resumed social calls at Reshid's home, but their most fruitful association lay in the past. The Sultan, too, was drinking himself into unreachable isolation, 'a kind of delirium', Stratford called it, 'which I am assured is next to madness'.[133] So there would be no more disciplining pashas through the throne. To Dean Stanley, on a visit from Britain, Stratford appeared positively dispirited and anxious, a shadow of his former, determined self. When Stanley asked Stratford if he thought the crisis with Russia would blow over safely, the old man replied cryptically: 'I feel it impossible to predict; sometimes I think it will pass over, sometimes I feel we are already on the verge of that most important event to which all the world has been looking for so many years, and that, after so many false cries, the wolf is come at last.'[134]

The decline in his morale and his authority, even in the short period since his return in April, is perhaps best explained by one of the acutest observers, not only of Stratford, but of the whole Constantinople scene. This was the naval expert, Adolphus Slade. In Slade's opinion, Stratford had almost done his work too well, and all Ottoman officials were anti-Russian. But there were two generations of such men, an older one to which Stratford's own career belonged, and a younger one less amenable to his sort of advice. Although 'Europeanized Turks', and in Slade's view 'a mean set in general without dignity or convictions, abased by the knowledge they have acquired of Frank power, [and] abject to and hating Franks in consequence', these younger men were already crowding the offices of the second rank, and about 60 out of 72 whose careers he examined were routinely anti-Russian, French educated, anti-British in varying degree, ready to promise good administration to silence importunate Europeans, but privately very opposed to any *Tanzimat* programme which sought to enlarge the civil right of Christians, whom they saw as a massive fifth-column ready to subvert the Ottoman imperium. They were not only cool towards Stratford, who had so often humiliated the most senior Ottoman officials, but distanced by an equal distrust from his collaborators such as Reshid Pasha, a man Slade described as a political 'jesuit', disposed 'to blow the trumpet as earnestly as he had [once] played the lute'. The new militancy of the second-rank officials was a factor in the calculations of several other first-rank men besides Reshid. Their brand of loyalty appealed to the new grand vizier with his 'firm belief in the excellence of Islam', and to a *Shaykh ul-Islam* disposed to recruit Christians for the army on the principle that 'men often took dogs with them to hunt game'. Even men with considerable, residual faith in the *Tanzimat* ideals, like Ali and Fuad, separated themselves from Reshid, and were polite rather than cordial in their dealings with the British.[135]

While Stratford's masters were calculating, in early June, the control he was to have over the Malta squadron, he was anxiously urging the new Ottoman ministry to treat Menshikov's departure not as a victory over Russia but as 'a fresh starting point for negotiation'. Drawing on the support of the other embassies of the 'European Confederacy', he strongly pressed for a swift promulgation of new firmans addressed to the heads of the different millets promising that 'the ancient conditions' conferred upon them would be 'for ever preserved from all prejudice'.[136] These firmans were issued on 7 June. Stratford's conduct anticipated his government's wishes exactly because the tsar, informed of London's agitation over Menshikov's mission, took advantage of his courtesy letter to Queen Victoria congratulating her on the birth of her child, Prince Leopold, to offer 'assurances about maintaining the Turkish Empire' and his abandonment of 'the notion of its speedy downfall', for he says his 'successor will carry out his policy'. The tsar agreed no single power should in future proceed against the Ottoman Empire alone. The letter caused great relief in the Cabinet. 'The Porte should in return', Clarendon told Stratford, 'give some pledge that practicable reforms and particularly as regards the treatment of Christians' would be promptly undertaken.[137]

But on 10 June, however, a Russian postal steamer entered the Bosporus, and Stratford guessed, correctly, that it brought some sort of ultimatum. Before it had dropped anchor, he was scribbling advice to Reshid Pasha: 'To maintain peace is an object of immense value to which many sacrifices may be made with honour and advantage. No effort offering the slightest chance of maintaining it can be neglected without regret.' Should the Russian communication threaten an occupation of the Principalities, as he expected, Reshid should prevent his colleagues from devising a pugnacious reply or issuing counter-challenges for a very simple, stark reason. In any large contest, the Ottoman Empire would be defeated at worst, and impoverished at best.[138]

The Nesselrode ultimatum accused Reshid Pasha personally of refusing 'to contract with the imperial court of Russia the slightest engagement calculated to reassure her of the intentions of the Ottoman government to protect the Orthodox faith and churches in Turkey. . . . His Majesty's dignity, the interest of his empire, the voice of his conscience, will not allow him to tolerate such conduct.' The Principalities would be taken, as 'moral guarantees' and 'material securities' unless, within eight days, the terms offered by Menshikov were accepted.[139] The grand council met that same night, with Etienne Pisani waiting in an outer lobby through the momentous session. Later he was told that Russia had indeed threatened an occupation of the Principalities and Stratford would be supplied confidentially with a copy of the council's draft reply on the morrow. The draft reply was duly forthcoming and shocked Stratford with its cold tone of resistance. It recapitulated the privileges recently confirmed in the firmans of 7 June and complained against the intended move into the Principalities as a breach of the peace and of international law. There was no reference to further Russo-Ottoman negotiations.

'I would submit', Stratford's next piece of advice ran, that the Ottoman government 'should secure another chance against the dangers and evils of war [and] at all events put itself still more completely in the right by intimating its readiness to send an embassy to St. Petersburg'. The emissary should give the tsar any form of words he wanted to end the current crisis, always remembering the one, critical qualification: 'You are aware that I can mean no other than that which the Porte has hitherto maintained – namely – the exclusion of all pretension to an engagement having the form of a treaty obligation towards Russia with respect to the privileges of the Orthodox Church.'[140] The Sultan was the benefactor of the Christians, not the tsar, and must be seen to be so. If this was expecting too much of Russian forbearance, it was endorsed by Clarendon who confirmed to his ambassador that 'our business is to spare his [the tsar's] dignity as much as possible, always bearing in mind *our main object* [emphasis added] of saving Turkey from his claws'.[141] When the final Ottoman reply was formulated, the British and French Mediterranean squadrons were at anchor in Besika Bay, and promises of Egyptian and Tunisian help were received in Constantinople on the next day, the 17th. Considering that Menshikov had not yet been gone a month, and that the grand council recognized the imminent seizure of the Principalities as an infraction of Ottoman sovereignty and a legitimate *casus belli*, the reply as finally sent was very restrained, formally protesting the coming occupation, drawing Russian attention to the firmans of the 7th as proof of the Sultan's good intent, and offering, in accordance with Stratford's suggestion, to send a negotiator to St Petersburg to draft a mutually satisfactory form of words.

As Menshikov had severed relations over a form of words, and as Brunnov had assured Aberdeen that Menshikov had agreed 'to content himself with a note' supplied by the Ottomans, Russian good faith was now put to the test, and failed. The Ottoman reply was found unsatisfactory by Ozerov, the counsellor left in charge of the embassy and its commercial staff. Ozerov evidently had no latitude to negotiate. He read the Ottoman reply to the ultimatum and, finding it was not a surrender, closed down his legation, boarded the windows, locked the gates, and sailed home with staff and archives. The Principalities were invaded on 7 July. The tsar issued a fiery manifesto calling on his people 'to go forth to fight for the Orthodox faith', an appeal given great prominence in the House of Lords as proof of the unreliability of a sovereign who said he wanted peace.[142] Assuming, like everyone else, that Stratford was behind everything the Ottomans said or did or wrote, Nesselrode retorted, on the subject of the Ottoman reply to his ultimatum: 'It was now asked that the emperor should give way, but really, when it comes to a personal question between an emperor and an ambassador, in his opinion it was for Lord Stratford and not for the emperor to give way.'[143] But it was Nesselrode's behaviour, much more than Stratford's, which sent ripples of consternation through Europe, so defiantly perverse and mistaken did his defence of the Russian position seem to be. 'In principle,' he asked the world, 'have we not ourselves, by our treaties of Kainardji and Adrianople, obtained the right of watching over the interests of our co-religionists in the Turkish provinces?' In reply the world said, with varying degrees of loudness, 'No'.[144]

'The emperor seems to be rendered ungovernable by finding for the first time that Europe *can* have an opinion of its own,' Clarendon wrote to Stratford. Fortunately, there was an avenue of hope. 'Austria and Prussia have both, *for them*, spoken boldly and his having asked for the good offices of Austria with the Porte is a proof that he finds it inconvenient to isolate himself.'[145] Stratford, however, took the tsar's action as proof that he personally was to be cut out of any further Russo-Ottoman negotiation, hardly an unexpected development, and he hoped Clarendon would 'not hear of a single Austrian mediation, but approve my notion of treating Bruck and Buol as we treated Kletzl, namely make them the mouthpiece of the quadruple understanding without exactly bringing the association into immediate contact with Russia'.[146] Clarendon's reply was eminently conciliatory as well as practical. Diplomats at all the leading courts should make a concerted effort to write a document of reconciliation. They might begin by reading carefully Menshikov's final demand and Reshid Pasha's final counter-offer, then proceed to suggest how the gap between the two statements might be bridged. 'What we want is an arrangement that shall be safe for the Porte.'[147] At whichever court the best egg was hatched was unimportant, and their recent experience as mediators between Menshikov and the Ottoman authorities gave Stratford and his colleagues an excellent chance of finding the urgently required formula. It becomes quite clear from such official encouragements that the unfortunately named 'Turkish ultimatum', devised by the Porte in collaboration with the local representatives of Austria, Britain, France, and Prussia in July was anything but an unauthorized 'side-show' or a solution 'initiated quite independently by Lord Stratford'.[148] More than that, the document sent to Vienna on 23 July should have enjoyed some degree of precedence over other proposals: it was an official statement issued by the Ottoman state, which would be required by international pressure to sign and implement the ultimately agreed form of reconciliation. As things turned out, the 'ultimatum' was not even taken into account at Vienna.[149]

The 'ultimatum' was painfully produced in Constantinople under the most difficult circumstances, extracted from a government which felt it had already negotiated enough with an active aggressor. 'The Russians are actually in the provinces,' Stratford told Eliza, 'and we must try to get them out without yielding the point in dispute. How is that to be done without war? . . . I tremble to think of it.'[150] The instability of the Ottoman administration was one problem. As soon as the Russians crossed the Pruth on 7 July, Sultan Abdulmejid impulsively dismissed his grand vizier of two months, Mustafa Pasha, and Reshid Pasha as well. As Redcliffe put it, 'I went bang down to the Padishah and put them in again', whereupon Reshid promptly became involved in a major row with old Mehemet Ali Pasha. Their sons were rivals for the hand of the Sultan's daughter. Continuous discussion of the crisis in the grand council was further complicated by the intervention in July of the *Kupbam Bayram* festival which closed the offices of the Porte for many days, and delay in itself was a large danger. The capital was ecstatic with excitement at the near prospect of a Russian war, and hardly the human context in which cool plans for keeping peace are laid. By the obscure mechanics of *jihad*, many thousands of Asian Muslims had mobilized themselves, and arrived unbidden in Constantinople to fight for their Sultan and their *umma*. Their numbers were swollen by the inflow of the first refugees from the Balkans, most of whom, being Christian, sought refuge and relief in Galata. Whenever he went out, Stratford saw them camped in the cemeteries and huddled in the churches. *The Times* correspondent put the total influx of people at over a quarter million, a number no government knew how to direct or discipline, except through the relief valve of a declaration of war or the swift promulgation of an honourable settlement with Russia.[151] 'The danger, expense, and annoyance would press sorely on the Porte after a time, and in a moment of impatience and alarm the coveted object might be irrevocably surrendered.'[152] Experienced Europeans expected at least civil commotion on a grand scale, whatever the government did, something like those Gordon Riots of 1780, which laid a traumatic memory on Londoners for decades afterwards.

Diplomats at more tranquil courts supposed that Stratford exaggerated the dangers, but such complaining would have been sharply redressed had they been able to wander *incognito*, as the bearded Alison did, in the seething streets.

> 'Tis a pity you can't see the Bosporus about Therapia, swarming with ships of war, and the opposite heights crowned with the green tents of the Egyptian camp. Constantinople itself has gone back fifty years, and the strangest figures swarm in from the distant provinces to have a cut at the Moscovite. Turbans, lances, maces, and battle-axes jostle each other in the narrow streets, and are bundled off immediately to the camp at Shumla for a quiet life.[153]

Worse, the city was patrolled by Albanian irregulars, an arrangement as hopeless as filling fire-buckets with petrol. Even the French-language newspapers – *Journal de Constantinople, Echo de l'Orient, Impartial de Smyrne* – addressed to a more westernized and mercantile Christian audience than were the clamant speeches of exalted *imams*, soberly informed readers who had much business to lose from a rupture of the peace that the Sultan had every right to refuse negotiation with a tsar whose belligerence was uncontrolled. Many Ottoman Christians, and not Muslims only, exhibited strong loyalist feelings in 1853, a possibility westerners had difficulty in accommodating among their preconceptions. It was in this atmosphere that the 'Turkish ultimatum' was devised.

The relationships between the European embassies were also quite changed after Menshikov left, and Stratford was put out to see his colleagues behaving as if each had come of age in Eastern affairs. They still exchanged plans and inspirations, and assembled periodically at the British legation, but it was Bruck, not Stratford, who brought forward the first plan, 'an improvisation of Count Buol's', for discussion, and it was de la Cour who scandalized Stratford most by spreading his wings and consulting the Ottomans for himself, 'talking to Reshid Pasha, without any previous intimation to me, of looking forward to the independence of the Danubian Principalities, and also of declaring all treaties respecting those provinces as abrogated by the [Russian] occupation'. Such radical talk could not possibly be the unauthorized chatter of a tyro diplomat, and Redcliffe sensed something of a reproach in the repeated comment of a few grand council members, who said 'France is wanting to get into a war while we [the British] are wanting to keep out of it.' He also saw danger in the four European representatives getting out of step, and felt the dangers of delay more acutely than the others. Time was not on the side of peace:

> Bruck asserts that he has no idea but that of securing the principle at stake [Ottoman independence]; yet his letter, as proposed to Reshid, contains a complete surrender of it. M. de la Cour is much inclined to run off the course in search of expedients, as he calls them, and like all Frenchmen, he attaches too much importance to rumours and secondary incidents. But in the main I presume he means the same thing that we do. . . . Delay will prove most fatal to Turkey if prolonged beyond a very few weeks, and I confess my own impression to be that if the next attempt at negotiation fails, there will be no room for half measures. . . . I am as much for peace as any man; but if the object at stake is to be maintained, as I think it ought, there should be a limit to attempts which can only prove nugatory in the end and turn to the benefit of uncompromising Russia.[154]

The Bruck plan was rejected by the Ottomans as too close in wording to the Menshikov ultimatum. 'This answer will be communicated, in the most civil manner, tomorrow, to Baron Bruck.'[155] The Ottoman ministers much preferred to concentrate on a protest against the Russian invasion, to the wording of which Stratford evidently contributed, in the hope that they would attach to it some more conciliatory statements. In this he was highly successful, to his great relief. In his papers, a scrap from Stephen Pisani, the dragoman, dated 10 July, says,

> Reshid Pasha is much pleased with the protest as amended by your lordship. It will be read in the council which is to be held tomorrow at the Porte, and subsequently submitted to the Sultan's sanction. As soon as his Majesty's pleasure will be given to it, Reshid Pasha will lose no time in communicating it officially to the representatives of the four power parties to the treaty of 1841.[156]

The protest was printed at the Porte on 15 July, and approved by 'the four' in Stratford's study on the 16th. The net result was the dispatch via Vienna of a bundle of documents – the protest, copies of the firmans confirming the privileges of the non-Muslim subjects of the Porte, the all-important communication to Russia which was to replace Menshikov's desired form of words and was described as a *projet de convention*, and a personal letter to Nesselrode from Reshid Pasha. Untidy though the 'Turkish ultimatum' may be, these documents collectively represented the ultimate concession the Sultan's ministers felt able to make, and all that Russia had originally demanded in her communications with the great powers.

The protest against the Russian occupation is a restrained and dignified statement. The letter to Nesselrode said that 'the ancient privileges of the religion professed by HM the emperor of Russia, and by the greater part of his subjects, have been confirmed in perpetuity; the Sublime Porte hopes that the Russian government will learn this with pleasure'.[157] The four representatives who witnessed and approved the documents sent to Vienna for delivery to St Petersburg by the Ottoman grand council were described as witnesses to the oath now taken by the Sultan 'in perpetuity'. All this was far from the bilateral pledge Menshikov had originally asked for, but very close to what he had finally declared his readiness to accept. If Russia genuinely wanted peace, here at least was a basis for it. Fortunately for the tsar, unfortunately for the cause of peace, Russia was not required to confront the Sultan's 'ultimatum'. Had it received the endorsement of the ambassadors of the great powers at Vienna, it is unlikely he would have risked refusing it, or that war would have followed.

Working against time, Stratford persuaded his colleagues to share the expense of a special courier, who set off post-haste on 23 July with the 'Turkish ultimatum', bound for the railhead at Belgrade. He carried also beseeching letters from Stratford to his colleagues in Vienna and St Petersburg. To the earl of Westmoreland at Vienna he wrote

> The present batch [of documents] is forwarded by an express . . . paid by 'the four'. We are anxious it should arrive [in St Petersburg] without a moment's delay. If you really wish for peace you must make the most of the present experiment. The Porte will hear of nothing else, and the war party is soon more likely to be in the ascendant than reduced to order. All the separate schemes have come to naught.

To Seymour at St Petersburg, Stratford hinted that the overall situation would be eased if the Russians left the Principalities and the Anglo-French squadrons quit the outer Straits simultaneously. 'An *ultimatum* and a condition may sound harsh to Russian ears, but I really do not see how the Porte can possibly, with justice to itself, take any other course after displaying so much unexpected moderation with respect to the Principalities, and being placed in so difficult a position with respect to its own subjects.'[158]

The weakness and incapacity of the European 'concert' as a consultative force in the affairs of the Continent was never more manifest than in the summer of 1853, confirming Brunnov's presentiment that 'too many chefs' were at work. Most serious was the slowness of diplomats to recognize the steps by which a Russo-Ottoman quarrel was reshaping into a potentially dangerous confrontation between Russia and Britain, and too many of them concentrated on the quarrel to the exclusion of the confrontation, hoping the solution of the former would remove the latter. To the extent that such things are measurable, Britain's failures were no less serious than Russia's. Had Palmerston been at the Foreign Office, or even Aberdeen more assertive, the government might have spoken with one authoritative voice, and curbed the 'drift to war'. Clarendon, dithering between the boldness of the first and the caution of the second, was never resolutely anything for long, as he now proceeded to show. To Stratford, he appeared more than supportive – he was positively rash. Besides sending the fleet, which the ambassador did not especially want to come too near, the foreign secretary got carried away intermittently by the excitements of the moment.[159] He recommended, during early July, that the Ottoman navy should go peeping into Russia's Black Sea harbours to assess the total naval strength disposed between them, advice Stratford wisely ignored. He also pressed the employment by the Ottomans of Colonel Outram who, 'for the management of Mahometans . . . is probably the best Christian in the world, he is a remarkable fellow'.[160] When the debate, which Palmerston and Russell were holding off, actually began, Clarendon wanted to be able to show some record of activity, and on 18 July he sent Stratford yet another manifestation of his concern. As Stratford seemed to be having difficulty getting a form of words out of the Ottomans, and there was 'little hope' of Vienna producing one, the foreign secretary had written his own. The French minister at London rather liked it, and Nesselrode had not actively disapproved of a preliminary version shown to him.[161] Would Stratford like to urge it on his hosts?

Clarendon's 'convention' reached Constantinople on 27 July, four days after the dispatch of the 'Turkish ultimatum' to Vienna. Stratford put it aside for three reasons: first, Clarendon said in a covering private letter that if any better solution were found his 'convention' could be retired to the embassy archives as 'a monument of good will'; second, he rounded off his letter by restating the principle that 'the Porte should surrender whatever Russia has a just claim to demand and nothing more'; and third, Clarendon's proposal, on scrutiny, seemed to Stratford little better in its wording than Bruck's failed plan, which the Porte had refused with London's approval.[162] So the Clarendon plan was soon 'on the way to that limbo where the separate nostrums of Austria and Prussia are happily reposing', though the explanation sent to the foreign secretary was more discreet than this: 'I did not hesitate to send your convention *privately*,' Redcliffe told his chief, '[and] it does not seem to have found favour in his [Reshid's] sight and he expressed himself with much vehemence against its adoption.'[163] So did other members of the council. So did the other European representatives.

It was also as well nothing was done to advance the foreign secretary's plan because, on 25 July, Clarendon officially cancelled it himself, though only in favour of one more controversial still, the document known to history as the 'Vienna Note', and of which he had so recently said he had 'little hope' of materialization or acceptance. The parentage of the Vienna Note is obscure, but it seems to have originated in talks in London between Clarendon and Walewski. According to Temperley, Napoleon III seized the chance to become the arbiter of the crisis, evolved his own form of words much as Clarendon did in his convention, and sent it off to St Petersburg.[164] The French ambassador 'took it to Nesselrode who read it attentively, and said he liked it very much'. The same day, the tsar examined the wording with great care, to declare himself 'non seulement satisfait, mais reconnaissant'. Accepting the document with an alacrity some were to find suspicious, Nicholas I said the crisis would be at an end if an Ottoman delegate brought him this exact form of words.[165] It seems that Clarendon was almost

The Preliminaries of the Crimean War 209

entirely converted to the Vienna Note on 25 July itself because, that morning, he was still telling Stratford, 'We have no predilection for this [Vienna] note or for our own project [i.e. his convention] but what we want is an arrangement that shall be perfectly safe for the Porte'. But later in the day he wrote again, saying 'the solution we have all been endeavouring to arrive at' had been found. In addition, he cabled Westmoreland at Vienna, endorsing the Vienna Note, with one or two small changes. Yet as late as the 28th, with his own convention formally cancelled, Clarendon ordered Westmoreland 'to inform Lord Stratford [by telegraph] that Her Majesty's government desire that [the Vienna] Note should be adopted by the Porte', but only if *'no other arrangement had already been made* [emphasis added]'.[166]

Now 'another arrangement' *had* been made: the 'Turkish ultimatum'. It reached Vienna on 29 July, and immediately raises the question of whether or not Westmoreland was justified in still telegraphing Stratford in the sense of Clarendon's instruction. That the Vienna Note should *not* have been pressed at Constantinople is arguable, and has been argued.[167] That the 'Turkish ultimatum' was suppressed by Buol on the orders of his monarch, Francis Joseph – why, he asked, should Russia 'accept as a defeat what she could have claimed as a victory' – has never been condemned enough. The 'ultimatum' was an Ottoman state document addressed by Reshid Pasha to the Russian government: the Austrians had no right to suppress it.[168] Worse, Baron Meyendorff, the Russian minister at Vienna, while refusing to assist the other ambassadors there in their deliberations, simply refused passports for any Ottoman messenger to proceed to the Russian capital. An Ottoman solution to the crisis had no interest, it seems, for the tsar, and on 7 August Westmoreland telegraphed Stratford to press the Ottomans to accept the Vienna Note, the tsar having accepted it five days previously.[169]

On 30 July, an abrupt instruction had already been sent out to Constantinople from the Foreign Office in the form of a dispatch: 'We rely with confidence upon you protecting the Turks against themselves, and using your utmost influence to cause them to accept the [Vienna] Note which I think you will agree with us differs in no essential particular from their own.' Not having seen the 'Turkish ultimatum' nor, indeed, the final version of the Vienna

Note itself, this was simply a pious hope, and Clarendon was too relieved to be ready to admit that peace might have been won at Ottoman expense. 'It would be unwise', his instruction went on, 'to *let any other scheme* run athwart the note *that we have approved as safe for Turkey* [emphasis added] and that Count Buol has reason to believe would be accepted by the tsar.'[170] Russell gratified and thoroughly surprised Clarendon with his whole-hearted agreement. He said the Vienna Note should be 'imposed' on the Ottomans, on pain of Britain abandoning them completely. Aberdeen and Brunnov shared, indeed originated, this view and Clarendon promised them all he would stress 'in strong terms privately to Stratford that the Vienna note *must* be accepted'.[171] Being Clarendon, he was far less emphatic in his private letters than he promised to be. Palmerston was unsure that the government should not see the final Vienna Note before endorsing it so emphatically, but, for the moment, did nothing. The tsar was transformed from villain to hero; it was the Sultan who was now on probation. The international crisis was virtually at an end. 'I think this settles the affair', Aberdeen said, and had reason to be pleased with himself.[172] Having been forced by the Cabinet activists in June to support France's naval policy, it was he and Clarendon who had followed up France's peace initiative in July, the Vienna Note, at Ottoman rather than Russian expense. In one week (18–25 July), Britain's official attitude, as expressed to Stratford de Redcliffe, had switched from concern for the Ottoman position to satisfaction with the Russian attitude. The government almost, but not quite, got away with its policy of appeasement or, as Stratford saw it, of betrayal.

On 9 August, Brunnov was at court, 'very smiling', to present the tsar's eldest daughter, the duchess of Leuchtenburg, to Queen Victoria.[173] Many public men and members of the diplomatic corps appeared in the highest spirits at the Spithead Review the same week. On the 11th, the *Morning Post* declared 'the Eastern Question is settled'.[174] On the 15th, *The Times* went one better, announcing that 'the Sultan has gratefully acceded to the terms recommended by the conference of Vienna and it is understood that the Principalities will be speedily evacuated'. The pacifist *Herald of Peace* was exultant. Even the belligerent papers were pleased, explaining how Anglo-French pressure had brought Russia to her senses. Palmerston, who had yet to realize that Clarendon was as confused as Aberdeen was timorous, 'rejoiced that the management of our foreign affairs was in such hands', and Gladstone, in one of those tortured sentences which caused Disraeli such pain, gave the highest credit to the prime minister for his 'combined calmness, solidity of judgement, knowledge of the question, and moderation of views (always exhibited) in a manner or degree (even independently of your personal and official authority) sufficient to have kept our course so nearly straight'.[175] Gladstone disliked the Ottomans as much as did his chief. But only someone paying slight attention to foreign affairs could have believed Britain's course 'so nearly straight'. For the moment, nevertheless, tension was released. The funds crept up again. The prince consort and the queen were very approving. It was Greville who noticed that Clarendon 'does not consider that we are *out of the wood*'.[176] What troubled Britain's foreign minister? Not the unappeasable hysteria of David Urquhart in the *Advertiser*, nor the silly letters of Walter Savage Landor in *The Examiner*. For the answer, one must look to Parliament, and the storm which broke there just before the end of the session.

The Aberdeen administration was much gratified with its domestic record, the prime minister telling Princess Lieven: 'We have carried many important and useful measures; our majorities were numerous, and although a coalition of many different materials, we have adhered well together.'[177] Its members were also 'in high spirits at the prospects of winding up their prosperous session with the settlement of the Eastern Question', and Clarendon was desperately anxious to gratify them by providing Parliament with a *fait accompli* before which all criticisms would fall silent.[178] Unfortunately for him, his fate lay with Stratford, for the parliamentary storm broke as the government awaited daily confirmation that the Vienna Note had been accepted by the Ottomans, and it is easy to see why, in his frustrations over the long wait, Clarendon should say 'he fully expected Stratford Canning to play some trick . . . and throw obstacles in the way of a settlement'.[179] His conduct of foreign policy was severely attacked, in both houses, for its supine, short-sighted, and even dishonourable character, and he became convinced Stratford was exacting revenge on him for adopting the Vienna Note. No one really had a good word for him. It was all a great humiliation.[180]

The marquis of Clanricarde, for instance, addressing Clarendon in the Lords, insisted that the government must make up its mind; the occupation of the Principalities was 'either war or piracy', executed while the British government was evading realities by 'sending notes' to and fro. He wanted a 'categorical demand' for evacuation, and confidently expected the foreign secretary to assure the House that the Anglo-French squadrons were already beyond the Dardanelles. Lords Fitzwilliam and Lyndhurst both required Clarendon to confirm that he had challenged Nesselrode's outrageous public statement, reported in all the papers, that Russian troops would only leave the Principalities 'when the British fleet shall remove [itself] from within sight of the city of Constantinople'. Lord Beaumont, taking his turn in the procession of critical peers, asked why the House should not think Russia was 'actually making war' already, the more so as the government would not say 'what is actually going on'. Lord Albemarle took up this last point. The House had been very patient 'notwithstanding deep anxiety in the country' and had been at pains not to say 'a word that can in the remotest degree tend to impede the success of the negotiations' alleged to be pending but never actually revealed. 'But, my Lords,' Albermarle went on, 'there is a point at which this patient conduct must cease. Parliament is to be prorogued, I believe, in about eight or ten days . . . when the country is on the very brink of war.'

In the face of all this criticism, Aberdeen remained almost totally silent, determined to sit out the storm and the session, leaving it to Clarendon to conceal, if he could, that Britain had loaned herself to an Austro-Russian collusion. His silence caused great irritation, though not as much as Clarendon's unwise confession that he too drew much of his knowledge of international developments from the press. 'Whether the [Austrian] mediation was asked for or not, or offered without being asked for, I don't know,' Clarendon said; 'I only know it was acted upon.' As to the note which had been devised in Vienna, the foreign secretary went on, it had gone to St Petersburg and Constantinople on the same day, a lie to which Beaumont would return months later. The tsar had accepted the Vienna Note, Clarendon added, 'if it met the views of the Sultan', a bigger lie still.[181] As the note contained 'nothing derogatory to the dignity or independence of the Porte' – it will be remembered that

Clarendon had not actually seen the form of words sent to the Ottomans – 'the ministry daily expected to hear the Sultan had accepted it'. Their lordships were very properly sceptical, and the earl of Hardwicke retorted that the foreign secretary 'had not given them one iota of information of which they were not in possession before'. This was a very serious responsibility for any government to take upon itself, for both Russia and the Ottoman Empire now seemed about to claim they had received British encouragement, the first for her aggressions, the second to capitulate.

Malmesbury would not let the debate in the Upper House terminate without pointing the finger at the taciturn prime minister as the major culprit, and on the last day, the 12th, he scornfully observed that Parliament contained

> a section of politicians – a small one, happily, who openly and without hesitation declare that the independence and integrity of Turkey are not worth a war – that it signifies little to whom Turkey belongs – and who do not scruple to say, when it is shown to them that unless the independence of Turkey be maintained, we could scarcely maintain our hold on India, that they do not see in such an event as that any great calamity.

Auditors could think, if they chose, that Malmesbury had Richard Cobden of the other chamber in mind, but Aberdeen, recognizing he was intended, forced himself to the briefest of replies in which he simply said Britain had no treaty obligations to the Ottoman Empire, which, besides being incorrect, was about the worst way to assist Clarendon.

The Commons debate reached its climax four days later, on 16 August, marked on the government side by Russell's 'tame, meagre, and unsatisfactory' performance and, on the other, by Layard's hard-hitting maiden speech and, more notably still, by a celebrated passage of arms between Cobden and Palmerston, 'a standing fight' as Graham called it 'between the champion of Russia and Christianity [and] the sworn ally of Turkey and Mahomedanism'.[182] Cobden wanted Britain to leave the Eastern duel between Russia and the Ottoman Empire to work itself out. Charges about Russian imperialism in the Middle East, he said, came rather improperly from a nation like Britain which had seized three times as much in India as Russia had wrenched from the

Ottoman Empire and Persia. Cobden then made the remark against which the House clamoured, but which Graham later said would eventually win the hearts of British people: 'If I were a rayah I should prefer a Russian . . . government rather than a Mohamedan one.' Palmerston counter-attacked with great vigour, saying the famous free-trading pacifist was a man more interested in profits than national honour, and into the bargain 'greatly misinformed as to the state of Turkey for the last thirty years'. He assured the House 'without fear of contradiction from anyone who knows anything about it that so far from having gone back, Turkey has made greater progress and improvement than any other country in the same period'. A modern writer has described Palmerston's rousing speech as 'based upon crass ignorance and falsified by history', but it was good enough for its 1853 audience and produced 'enchantment' among the Derbyites and the government's own back-benchers.[183] There is abundant evidence that Palmerston really believed what he said, though he had not always done so.[184] Aberdeen, of course, and to a lesser degree Clarendon were angered and humiliated that the most applauded speech on their behalf should be the achievement of their *most* Turcophile colleague. Palmerston had saved the day, without exonerating Clarendon's policy. He had also, by implication, championed all that Stratford stood for. Aberdeen was particularly disturbed. Many of the government's critics were potential recruits, men who, in some few cases, might already have been on the ministerial benches had the Peelites not seized far more than their fair share of the available posts at the start of the year. Their hostility was bound to test the stability of the coalition Cabinet itself.

★ ★ ★

After the prorogation on 20 August, most Cabinet members dispersed to the country, which Graham thought a good thing as those left in charge – meaning Clarendon and Aberdeen – 'shall now be able to act without interrogations administered in Parliament and without speeches calculated to mislead the Turk into false confidence'. Clarendon was also relieved as 'the Turks seem to be getting more stupid and obstinate every day'.[185] The first business was to discipline Stratford, who had still not written, except, as some people insisted on believing, mistakenly, to the more belligerent wing of the press. 'Stratford is hardening himself to resist the proposed Note of Vienna. . . . Notwithstanding the peremptory order to the contrary, he is quite capable of advising the Turks to be refractory.'[186] On 19 August, Aberdeen agreed the time had arrived to 'be plain with him, as well as his friend Reshid', and on the following day, encouraged by Prince Albert who was 'tempted to abandon the Turks to their fate', as by the queen who 'will not at all regret' the removal of a troublesome ambassador, he actually advised Clarendon to recall Stratford.[187] The parliamentary humiliation made Stratford's silence seem longer than it really was: when Aberdeen demanded his removal, the Vienna Note had only been nine days in his hands. The prime minister evidently expected Ottoman compliance by return of post. The foreign secretary was not prepared to be so hasty. Seymour, for instance, was at least as bad as Stratford, but it was a risky game to start remodelling the diplomatic service at such a juncture by removing two key men enjoying much prestige at home.

Then, on 26 August, a week after the parliamentary prorogation, Stratford's long-awaited dispatches arrived, reporting that the Ottoman government had accepted the Vienna Note, but with modifications. Aberdeen described the Ottoman behaviour as 'suicidal'. Clarendon was also very disturbed, saying he had 'all along felt Stratford would allow of no plan of settlement that did not originate with himself'.[188] In the letters exchanged at this time between Graham, Aberdeen, and Clarendon, there remains that common assumption that Stratford could at any time obtain any terms he wished. Hence, as the Ottomans had chosen to be refractory, it could only have been with his encouragement. Only once did Aberdeen concede, after hearing of the Ottoman response to the Vienna Note, that it might be worth waiting for Stratford's fuller reports to discover 'whether he has sanctioned [the Ottoman decision] or not'; to this, he added the revealing remark that 'Lord Stratford and the Turks must have known of the conditional acceptance of the note by the emperor'.[189] It was totally inconceivable to the prime minister that the Ottomans could have minds of their own, and he preferred to believe with Clarendon that two conspirators, one English, one Ottoman, were successfully tricking their respective governments and countries: 'Reshid Pasha thinks it is a good opportunity for settling matters with Russia having as he believes France and England to back him.'[190] Stratford, of course, knew that great blame would now fall upon him. 'I feel confident', he wrote, as he uncovered the full story of what his chief saw as his near-treasonable failure, 'you will give me credit for having done my official best in support of the Vienna Note. Reshid told me candidly no personal influence would have induced the Porte to give way.'[191] His detractors seized on that phrase, 'official best', and a malign legend was instantly in the making: Stratford de Redcliffe had sabotaged the Vienna Note.[192]

NOTES

1. Spencer Walpole, *The Life of Lord John Russell* (London, 1889), ii. 176; F.A. Simpson, *Louis Napoleon and the Recovery of France, 1848–1856* (London, 1923), pp. 179-81.
2. Third Earl Malmesbury, *Memoirs of an ex-Minister: An Autobiography* (London, 1884), ii. 308.
3. Brunnov to Nesselrode, 21 Feb. 1853, in A.M. Zaionchkovski, *Vostochnaya Voyna 1853–56q v Sviazi s Soureminnoi ei Politicheskoi Obstanovkoi (The Eastern War, 1853–56 and the Political Situation at the Time)* (St Petersburg, 1908–13), i. 367.
4. *The Cambridge History of British Foreign Policy, 1783–1919*, ed. A.W. Ward and G.P. Gooch (New York, 1922–3) [hereafter *CHBFP*], ii. 340 *et seq.*
5. See Gavin B. Henderson, 'The Seymour Conversations, 1853', in his *Crimean War Diplomacy and Other Historical Essays* (Glasgow, 1947), pp. 1-14.
6. *CHBFP*, ii. 344.
7. Seymour's reports of his conversations with Nicholas I are in Seymour to Russell, 11 and 22 Jan., 21 and 22 Feb. 1853, 'Correspondence Respecting the Rights and Privileges of the Latin and Greek Churches in Turkey', *British Sessional Papers*, lxxi (London, 1854) [hereafter *BSP*], part v, nos. 1, 2, 5, 6.
8. J.B. Conacher, *The Aberdeen Coalition, 1852–1855: A Study in Mid-Nineteenth-Century Party Politics* (Cambridge, 1968), p. 143; Aberdeen to Queen Victoria, 22 March 1853, *The Letters of Queen Victoria, 1837–61*, ed. A.C. Benson and Viscount Esher (1st series, London, 1907), ii. 442.
9. Seymour to Clarendon, 24 March 1853, *The Greville Memoirs*, ed. Henry Reeve (London, 1887), i. 55. Greville and Clarendon dined together every Sunday. On such occasions Clarendon showed many dispatches to Greville. Clarendon was also in the habit of showing confidential documents to Henry Reeve, *The Times'* influential leader writer.
10. Queen Victoria to King Leopold, 29 March 1853, *Letters of Queen Victoria*, ii. 444.
11. Brunnov to Nesselrode, 24 Jan. 1853, quoted in H.E. Howard, 'Brunnov's Reports on Aberdeen, 1853', *Cambridge Historical Journal*, iv (1932), 316.
12. Aberdeen to Queen Victoria, 8 Feb. 1853, *Letters of Queen Victoria*, ii. 531-2.

Palmerston believed that 'these private and verbal communications with Brunnov [were] not at all in accordance with the opinions of many of his colleagues and irreparable mischief was thereby occasioned'. See Palmerston to Clarendon, 22 Aug. 1854, in Temperley, *Crimea*, p. 300.
13. Walpole quotes Russell to Aberdeen, 19 Jan. 1853, 'The Whigs write to me imagining I have some influence in politics. . . . It is a mistake.' Walpole, *Russell*, ii. 165-6. Aberdeen wrote in reply, 21 Jan. 1853, 'To say the truth I thought I had done little else than comply with your wishes either at the formation of the government or ever since', ibid., ii. 165. Russell threatened to resign from the Foreign Office as soon as Parliament re-convened; Parliament met again on 10 February, and he duly resigned on the 22nd.
14. Russell to Seymour, 9 Feb. 1853, *BSP*, v, no. 4.
15. For Nicholas I's remarks on Russell to Seymour, 9 Feb. 1853, see Zaionchkovski, *Vostochnaya*, i. 359-62.
16. Brunnov to Nesselrode, 21 Feb. 1853, ibid.
17. Seymour to Russell, 22 Feb. 1853, *BSP*, v, no. 6.
18. Seymour to Russell, private, 9 Feb. 1853, in Temperley, *Crimea*, p. 275.
19. Russell to Aberdeen, 5 Feb. 1853, in Walpole, *Russell*, ii. 178-9.
20. For Aberdeen's preference for Layard over Rose see Aberdeen to Russell, 4 and 26 Jan. 1853, Add. MSS 43066.
21. Russell to Aberdeen, 2, 4, and 9 Jan., 3, 5, 9, 14, and 15 Feb. 1853; Aberdeen to Russell, 4 and 28 Jan., 15 Feb. 1853, Add. MSS 43066.
22. Memo by Stratford de Redcliffe, Feb. 1853, Clarendon MSS C/10.
23. Quoted in Sir Arthur Gordon (Lord Stanmore), *The Earl of Aberdeen* (New York, 1893), pp. 222-3.
24. Russell to Aberdeen, 14 Feb. 1853, Add. MSS 43066; Aberdeen to Russell, 15 Feb. 1853, Clarendon MSS C/4.
25. Stratford's instructions are in FO 195/396. See also Lane-Poole, *Life*, ii. 234-5.
26. Aberdeen to Clarendon, 15 Feb. 1853, Add. MSS 43066. The idea that Stratford had direct authority to summon the fleet is found, for example, in R.W. Seton-Watson, *Britain in Europe, 1789-1914* (New York, 1937), p. 309, where it is said he was 'empowered to summon the fleet from Malta'. As to Lane-Poole's statement (*Life*, ii. 235) that 'there is ample reason to believe that the wording [of the instructions regarding Stratford's calling up the fleet] is his own', there is in fact no evidence whatever.
27. Clarendon to Graham, 9 May 1853, quoted in Conacher, *Aberdeen Coalition*, p. 145.
28. Zaionchkovski, *Vostochnaya*, i. 371.
29. Reeve to Clarendon, 26 Feb. 1853, Stratford to Clarendon, 2 March 1853, Clarendon MSS C/10.
30. Parrish to Clarendon, 4 March 1853, Clarendon MSS, C/10.
31. Clarendon to Greville, 24 March 1853, Greville's *Memoirs*, i. 55.
32. Clarendon to Stratford, 5 April 1853, FO 352/36/1. Stratford marked this sentence in heavy pencil.
33. *The Times*, 18, 19, and 26 March 1853.
34. Brunnov to Aberdeen, 19 March 1853, Add. MSS 43144.
35. Walpole, *Russell*, ii. 181; Russell to Aberdeen, 29 April 1853, *The Later Correspondence of Lord John Russell, 1840-1878*, ed. G.P. Gooch (London, 1925), ii. 147.
36. Brunnov to Aberdeen, 24 March 1853, Add. MSS 43144.
37. Clarendon to Stratford, 23 March 1853, quoted in Lane-Poole, *Life*, ii. 240.

38. Clarendon to Stratford, n.d., FO 352/36/1.
39. Temperley, *Crimea*, p. 305. 'If you had been sent,' Seymour later said, 'all that has occurred would have been avoided', to which Orlov replied, 'I really believe you are right'. Seymour to Clarendon, 18 Oct. 1853, FO 65/431.
40. Carl Frederich Vitzthum von Eckstaedt, *St. Petersburgh and London. The Reminiscences of Count Charles Vitzthum*, ed. H. Reeve (London, 1887), pp. 3-12, 30-7; Clarendon to Stratford, 5 April 1853, FO 352/36/1.
41. The instructions given to Menshikov, and his own reports from Constantinople, are published in the extensive work by Zaionchkovski, *Vostochnaya*, i. 371-433. The instructions are dated 28 Jan. 1853, and so fall between the first two and the later two 'Seymour conversations'.
42. 'Project d'une Convention', Zaionchkovski, *Vostochnaya*, i. 382. For Nesselrode's dispatches to Menshikov, see pp. 371-81.
43. Temperley, *Crimea*, p. 308.
44. Rose to Malmesbury, 20 Nov. 1852, Add. MSS 42799.
45. Rose to Clarendon, 17 Feb. 1853, FO 78/929; Rose to Clarendon, 4, 5, 6, 8, 10, 14, 15, and 21 March 1853, FO 78/930. The assertion in the *CHBFP*, ii. 347, that the French government asked London why Rose had not kept in touch with Benedetti is meaningless.
46. Clarendon to Aberdeen, 17 and 18 March 1853; Aberdeen to Clarendon, 29 March 1853, Add. MSS 43188; Aberdeen to Brunnov, 23 March 1853, Brunnov to Aberdeen, 24 March 1853, Add. MSS 43144.
47. Cowley to Clarendon, 24 March 1853, FO 27/965; Clarendon to Cowley, 29 March 1853, FO 27/956. On hearing of the dispatch of the Toulon squadron, Cowley spoke to Drouyn, at the French foreign ministry, as follows: 'Conscientiously, I must say it was the fault of France and Austria, of France in raising without consideration the question of the Holy Places, which had given Russia a pretext for the present proceedings, of Austria in setting the example [over Montenegro] of menace and intimidation.' Cowley to Clarendon, 19 March 1853, FO 27/964. In reply Clarendon wrote, 'I am very glad you made Drouyn explain . . . dealing with the French is like having charge of wilful, ill-brought up children'. Clarendon to Cowley, 22 March 1853, FO 519/169.
48. Stratford to Clarendon, 10 March 1853, quoted in Lane-Poole, *Life*, ii. 236-9.
49. Ibid.
50. Stratford to Clarendon, 17 March 1853, Clarendon MSS C/10.
51. Stratford to his wife, 20 March 1853, quoted in Lane-Poole, *Life*, ii. 240.
52. Stratford to his wife, 28 March, 5 April 1853, quoted in ibid., ii. 244-5 (Lane-Poole dates the second letter 4 April).
53. Departing unhonoured and unsung, Rose was offered, but refused like Layard before him, the consul-generalship of Egypt. His argument was that acceptance would be a downward step, back into the consular service. As legation secretary and chargé d'affaires during Stratford's absence, the consul-general of Egypt had come under his authority. See Charles Murray to Russell, 2 March 1853; Rose to Clarendon, 22 June 1853; Stratford to Clarendon, 23 July 1853, Clarendon MSS C/10. Rose's career was saved by the coming of the Crimean War, and, even more, by the Indian Mutiny.
54. Stratford to his wife, [5 April] 1853, quoted in Lane-Poole, *Life*, ii. 246.
55. Rose to Clarendon, 15, 17, and 21 March 1853, Add. MSS 42799.
56. The full remarks in Nicholas I's handwriting in the margin of Menshikov's dispatch says 'Without a crisis of compulsion it would be difficult for the

The Preliminaries of the Crimean War 219

imperial legation to recapture the influence it formerly exercised over the divan', quoted in Zaionchkovski, *Vostochnaya*, i. 400.
57. Pisani to Stratford, 7 and 8 April 1853, quoted in Lane-Poole, *Life*, ii. 251-3. (Lane-Poole says Stephen Pisani, not Etienne.)
58. Stratford to Clarendon, 6 April 1853, *BSP*, v, no. 150.
59. Alexander W. Kinglake, *The Invasion of the Crimea: Its Origin and Account of Its Progress down to the Death of Lord Raglan* (London, 1863), i. 137.
60. Quoted in Lane-Poole, *Life*, ii. 250.
61. Stratford to Clarendon, 16 April 1853, *BSP*, v, no. 155.
62. Clarendon to Stratford, 18 and 26 April 1853, FO 352/36/1.
63. Menshikov to Nesselrode, 26 April 1853, Zaionchkovski, *Vostochnaya*, i. 405.
64. Memo by Stratford, quoted in Lane-Poole, *Life*, ii. 255-6; Stratford to his wife, 25 and 27 April 1853, ibid., ii. 260.
65. Quoted in Gordon Waterfield, *Layard of Nineveh* (London, 1963), p. 236.
66. Quoted in Lane-Poole, *Life*, ii. 256.
67. Clarendon to Stratford, 7 May 1853, FO 352/36/1.
68. Stratford to Rifaat, 23 April 1853, quoted in Lane-Poole, *Life*, ii. 258-9.
69. Stratford to Clarendon, 5, 6, and 9 May 1853, Clarendon MSS C/10.
70. Lane-Poole, *Life*, ii. 262; Temperley, *Crimea*, p. 319.
71. Menshikov to Nesselrode, 6 May 1853, Zaionchkovski, *Vostochnaya*, i. 414.
72. Stratford to Menshikov, 8 May 1853, *BSP*, v, no. 184; Stratford to Rifaat, 8 May 1853, in Stratford to Clarendon, 10 May 1853, FO 78/932; Rifaat to Menshikov, 10 May 1853; Menshikov to Nesselrode, May 1853, Zaionchkovski, *Vostochnaya*, i. 417-8, 423.
73. Encl. in Menshikov to Rifaat, 5 May 1853, ibid., i. 407-8.
74. 'Memorandum to the Porte', quoted in Lane-Poole, *Life*, ii. 264-5.
75. Stratford to Clarendon, 9 May 1853, Clarendon MSS C/10; Stratford to Clarendon, 10 May 1853, quoted in Lane-Poole, *Life*, ii. 266.
76. Menshikov to Nesselrode, 16 May 1853, Zaionchkovski, *Vostochnaya*, i. 423-7.
77. Stratford to Clarendon, 14 May 1853, *BSP*, i, no. 192.
78. For Reshid Pasha's reappointment see Temperley, *Crimea*, pp. 324-5; Sandwith to Layard, 9 June 1858, Add. MSS 38981; encl. by Wildenbruch in Stratford to Clarendon, 20 June 1853, Clarendon MSS C/10. In the latter it is stated that it was Menshikov who 'requested' Reshid Pasha's reappointment.
79. Stratford to Clarendon, 14, 15, and 19 May 1853, *BSP*, i, nos. 205-7.
80. Menshikov to Nesselrode, 16 May 1853, Zaionchkovski, *Vostochnaya*, i. 424-5.
81. Menshikov to Nesselrode, 16 May 1853, quoted in Temperley, *Crimea*, p. 326.
82. Menshikov to Nesselrode, 21 May 1853, Zaionchkovski, *Vostochnaya*, i. 428.
83. Stratford to Clarendon, 20 May 1853, *BSP*, i, no. 209. Temperley says that Menshikov's offer was 'quite illusionary', since his 'concession was not in the substance, only in the manner of presenting it'. Temperley, *Crimea*, p. 328.
84. Temperley, *Crimea*, p. 328. See also H.W.V. Temperley, 'Stratford de Redcliffe and the Origins of the Crimean War, Part I', *English Historical Review*, xlviii (1933), 611.
85. Stratford to Clarendon, 20 June 1853, Clarendon MSS C/10. From London Clarendon reported that 'Pr[ince] M[enshikov]'s story was that R[eshid] Pasha

distinctly declared to him that he desired and was prepared to sign the last project but that you would not allow him'. Clarendon to Stratford, 2 and 18 June 1853, FO 352/36/1. Interestingly, Menshikov does not blame Stratford in any way in his final report to Nesselrode. See Menshikov to Nesselrode, 21 May 1853, Zaionchkovski, *Vostochnaya*, i. 142.
86. Stratford to Reshid Pasha, 20 May 1853, quoted in Lane-Poole, *Life*, ii. 270-1.
87. Stratford to Clarendon, 22 May 1853, *BSP*, i, no. 234.
88. Stratford to Clarendon, 19 May 1853, quoted in Temperley, *Crimea*, p. 336; see also Stratford to his wife, 15, 19, 25, and 29 May 1853, quoted in Lane-Poole, *Life*, ii. 273-4.
89. Duke of Argyll, *Autobiography and Memoirs*, ed. duchess of Argyll (London, 1906), i. 445.
90. Quoted in Vernon J. Puryear, *England, Russia, and the Straits Question, 1844–1856* (Berkeley, 1931), p. 270; Kingsley Martin, *The Triumph of Lord Palmerston: A Study in Political Opinion in England Before the Crimean War* (London, 1924, rev. ed. 1963), p. 82.
91. Greville thought that this fact weighed heavily on Aberdeen. His information came from Henry Reeve who told him that Peel, Wellington, and Aberdeen

> drew up and signed a memorandum, the spirit and scope of which was to support Russia in her legitimate protection of the Greek religion and the holy shrines, and to do so without consulting France. . . . The existence of the memorandum was a profound secret known only to the Queen and to those ministers who held in succession the seals of the foreign department, each of whom transmitted it privately to his successor.

The Greville Diary, ed. Philip W. Wilson (London, 1927), i. 461.
92. Greville's *Memoirs*, i. 74 (12 July 1853).
93. Puryear, *Straits Question*, p. 275.
94. Vitzthum, *St. Petersburgh and London*, i. 57.
95. Graham to Clarendon, 9 May 1853, in Herbert E. Maxwell, *The Life and Letters of George William Frederick, Fourth Earl of Clarendon* (London, 1913), ii. 12.
96. Clarendon to Stratford, 26 May, 8 June 1853, FO 352/36/1.
97. 'Memorandum of a communication between Baron Brunnov and Her Majesty's Government drawn up by Baron Brunnov and communicated to the Earl of Clarendon', 26 May 1853, *BSP*, i, no. 191.
98. Brunnov to Aberdeen, 16 May 1853, Add. MSS 43144; Aberdeen to Clarendon, 17 May 1853, Clarendon MSS C/3.
99. Clarendon to Aberdeen, 18 May 1853, Add. MSS 43188. Cf. Conacher, *Aberdeen Coalition*, p. 147.
100. Russell to Clarendon, 28 May 1853, quoted in Temperley, *Crimea*, p. 335.
101. Clarendon to Aberdeen, 18 May 1853; Aberdeen to Clarendon, 30 May 1853, Clarendon MSS C/3.
102. Aberdeen to Clarendon, 30 May 1853, quoted in Temperley, *Crimea*, p. 335.
103. Seymour to Clarendon, 27 May 1853, *BSP*, i, no. 202. Clarendon's main concern as summarized in his own words, was that 'No sovereign having a proper regard for his own dignity and independence could admit proposals which conferred on another and more powerful sovereign a right of protection over his own subjects'. Clarendon to Stratford, 31 May 1853, Maxwell, *Clarendon*, ii. 9.

104. Nesselrode to Brunnov, 1 June 1853, *BSP*, i, no. 236.
105. Brunnov to Aberdeen, 6 June 1853, Add. MSS 43144.
106. Palmerston to Clarendon, 8 July 1853, Clarendon MSS C/3; Waterfield, *Layard*, pp. 237-8.
107. Greville's *Memoirs*, i. 74 (22 June 1853).
108. Seymour to Clarendon, 31 May 1853, *BSP*, i, no. 229.
109. Nesselrode to Reshid Pasha, 31 May 1853, in Nesselrode to Brunnov, 31 May 1853, ibid., no. 236.
110. Clarendon to Aberdeen, 5 May 1853, Add. MSS 43188; Brunnov to Aberdeen, 8 June 1853, Add. MSS 43144; *The Times*, 29 June 1853.
111. Palmerston to Graham, 29 and 30 May 1853, in same to Clarendon, 30 May 1853, Clarendon MSS C/3.
112. Stratford to Cowley, 5 June 1853, FO 519/293.
113. Russell to Clarendon, 22 May 1853, quoted in Temperley, *Crimea*, pp. 335-6.
114. Palmerston to Clarendon, 22 May 1853, quoted in Evelyn Ashley, *The Life of Henry John Temple, Viscount Palmerston* (London, 1876), ii. 25-6.
115. Palmerston to Clarendon, 22 May 1853, Clarendon MSS C/3; Palmerston to Graham, 29 May 1853, in same to Clarendon, 30 May 1853, ibid.
116. Russell to Clarendon, 29 and 31 May 1853, ibid.
117. Quoted in Martin, *Triumph of Lord Palmerston*, p. 106.
118. Aberdeen to Clarendon, 1 June 1853, Clarendon MSS C/3; Clarendon to Aberdeen, 29 May 1853, Add. MSS 43188.
119. Clarendon to Aberdeen, 1 June 1853, Add. MSS 43188; Clarendon to Stratford, 2 June 1853, FO 352/36/1; Palmerston to Clarendon, 2 June 1853, Clarendon MSS C/3.
120. Greville's *Memoirs*, i. 69 (13 June 1853).
121. Aberdeen to Clarendon, 1 June, 5 July 1853, Clarendon MSS C/4; Clarendon to Stratford, 1 June 1853, FO 352/36/1.
122. Clarendon, 'Circular Addressed to Her Majesty's Ministers Abroad', 13 June 1853, *BSP*, i, no. 251; Clarendon to Aberdeen, 6 June 1853, Add. MSS 43188; same to Stratford, 26 May 1853, FO 352/36/1.
123. Aberdeen to Clarendon, 7 June 1853, Add. MSS 43188; Clarendon to Stratford, 2 June 1853, FO 352/36/1; Greville's *Memoirs*, i. 67 (5 June 1853). Greville reports Clarendon as 'beset by different opinions and written suggestions and proposals, and all this worries him exceedingly'.
124. Aberdeen to Queen Victoria, 5 June 1853, quoted in Conacher, *Aberdeen Coalition*, p. 153; Clarendon to Stratford, 24 June 1853, FO 352/36/1.
125. Quoted in Donald Southgate, *The Most English Minister: The Policies and Politics of Palmerston* (London, 1966), p. 326.
126. Palmerston to Clarendon, 19 June 1853, quoted in Temperley, *Crimea*, p. 337.
127. Palmerston to Clarendon, 28 June 1853, Clarendon MSS C/3. On 7 July Palmerston wrote to Russell:

> I tried again to persuade the Cabinet to send the squadron up to the Bosporus, but failed. . . . I think our position, waiting timidly and submissively at the back door while Russia is violently, threateningly, and arrogantly forcing her way into the house, is unwise with a peaceful settlement, and derogatory to the character, and standing, and dignity of the two powers.

Palmerston to Russell, 7 July 1853, quoted in Ashley, *Palmerston*, ii. 30.
128. Palmerston to Ponsonby, 23 and 25 Oct. 1849, FO 78/780.
129. Aberdeen to Palmerston, 4 July 1853, Broadlands MSS; Palmerston to

Aberdeen, 12, 13, and 15 July 1853, Add. MSS 43069.
130. *The Times*, 28 Sept. 1853.
131. Stratford to Cowley, 6 Aug. 1853, FO 519/293; Lane-Poole's list of proposals is in Lane-Poole, *Life*, ii. 278-80; Charles Alison to Lady Stratford de Redcliffe, 25 Nov. 1853, quoted in ibid., p. 317.
132. Stratford to Clarendon, 11 May 1853, *BSP*, i, no. 206.
133. See Etienne Pisani to Stratford, n.d., FO 352/36/4.
134. Stratford to Dean Stanley, quoted in *The Letters of Dean Stanley*, ed. R.E. Prothero and E.G. Bailey (London, 1893), i. 463.
135. Adolphus Slade, *Record of Travels in Turkey, Greece, &c., and of a Cruise in the Black Sea with the Captain Pasha, in the years 1829, 1830 and 1831* (London, 1833), pp. 207-10.
136. Stratford to Clarendon, 22 May 1853, FO 78/932. See also Temperley, *Crimea*, p. 339.
137. Clarendon to Stratford, 26 May 1853, FO 352/36/1.
138. See Stratford to Stephen Pisani, 14 June 1853, FO 352/36/4.
139. Nesselrode's ultimatum, Zaionchkovski, *Vostochnaya*, i. 441-2. See also Nesselrode to Brunnov, 1 June 1853, *BSP*, i, no. 236.
140. Stratford to Clarendon, 16 June 1853, FO 78/933.
141. Clarendon to Stratford, 24 June 1853, FO 352/36/1.
142. Encl. in Seymour to Clarendon, 27 June 1853, *BSP*, i, no. 316, enclosure.
143. Stratford to Clarendon, 24 June 1853, FO 195/399.
144. On 1 June the Austrian chargé d'affaires (Baron Eduard von Lebzeltern) called on Nesselrode who told him that all Russia required was recognition of what was hers by the treaty of 1774. See Seymour to Clarendon, 4 June 1853, *BSP*, i, no. 246. Seymour, who saw Nesselrode the same day, was told that Russia would not accept the Ottoman Empire's refusal of the conditions, 'the acceptance of which was so warmly desired by the whole Greek population of Turkey'. Seymour to Clarendon, 31 May 1853, ibid., no. 229.
145. Clarendon to Stratford, 18 June 1853, FO 352/36/1.
146. Stratford to Clarendon, 25 June 1853, quoted in Lane-Poole, *Life*, ii. 281.
147. Clarendon to Stratford, 18 June 1853, FO 352/36/1.
148. Conacher, *Aberdeen Coalition*, p. 162; Seton-Watson, *Britain in Europe*, p. 311.
149. Clarendon's encouragement of Stratford was unknown to or misunderstood by Aberdeen, who was duly informed by Brunnov about it. 'What sort of proposal is this? Is it the French Note? The Bruck Note? This reminds me of what you said some time ago about [the] too many cooks.' Brunnov to Aberdeen, 29 July 1853, Add. MSS 43144; Stratford to Cowley, 23 July 1853, FO 519/293.
150. Stratford to his wife, 9 July 1853, quoted in Lane-Poole, *Life*, ii. 282.
151. *The Times*, 25 July, 8 and 22 Sept. 1853.
152. Stratford to Clarendon, 6 June 1853, FO 352/36/1.
153. Alison to Lady Stratford de Redcliffe, 20 Aug. 1853, quoted in Lane-Poole, *Life*, ii. 296.
154. Stratford to Clarendon, 9 July 1853, quoted in Lane-Poole, *Life*, ii. 283.
155. Stratford to Cowley, 6 Aug. 1853, FO 519/293.
156. Stephen Pisani to Stratford, 10 July 1853, quoted in Lane-Poole, *Life*, ii. 283-4.
157. Encl. no. 3 in Stratford to Clarendon, 20 July 1853, quoted in Temperley, *Crimea*, p. 342.
158. Stratford to Westmoreland, 23 July 1853; Stratford to Seymour, 23 July 1853, quoted in Lane-Poole, *Life*, ii. 286-7.

159. For greater detail on Cabinet discussions of war preparations see the voluminous exchange of letters in the Clarendon MSS C/3, particularly Palmerston to Clarendon, 16 June 1853, and Graham to Palmerston, 30 May 1853.
160. Clarendon to Stratford, 8 July 1853, FO 352/36/1.
161. Conacher quotes Greville as saying Nesselrode eventually preferred Clarendon's 'Convention' to all other solutions, Conacher, *Aberdeen Coalition*, p. 161, n. 7; Temperley similarly thought it a tragedy that Clarendon's plan was not adopted, without saying why he thought so. Temperley, 'Stratford de Redcliffe and the Origins of the Crimean War, Part II', *English Historical Review*, xlix (1934), 270-1. Clarendon's text of the Convention is in Clarendon to Stratford, 9 July 1853, *BSP*, i, no. 330, and Nesselrode's response is in Seymour to Clarendon, 26 July 1853, *BSP*, ii, no. 28.
162. Clarendon to Stratford, 18 July 1853, FO 352/36/1; Stratford to Clarendon, 23 July, 4 Aug. 1853, Clarendon MSS C/10.
163. Stratford to Clarendon, 23 July 1853, quoted in Lane-Poole, *Life*, ii. 288.
164. Temperley, *Crimea*, p. 344.
165. Edmond Papst believed Russia accepted so readily because experts at the Russian foreign office had seen in the 'Vienna Note' ambiguities that could be exploited in future negotiations with the Ottoman Empire; as it was inspired by France, it would also provide a convenient basis for a *rapprochement* between Nicholas I and Napoleon III. See Edmond Papst, *Les origines de la guerre Crimée: La France et la Russie de 1848 à 1854* (Paris, 1912), pp. 430-2. Louis Thouvenel even sees Nicholas I's cordial dealings with the French ambassador as a species of 'Seymour conversations', with a new partnership in view for the partition of the Ottoman Empire. See *Nicholas Ier et Napoléon III: les préliminaires de la guerre de Crimée (1852–1854) d'après les papiers inédites de M. Thouvenel*, ed. L. Thouvenel (Paris, 1891), pp. 182 *et seq*.
166. Clarendon to Stratford, 23 July 1853, FO 352/36/1. Clarendon's change of heart, and policy, did not prevent him sending Stratford his strong approval of his conduct; thus

> Her Majesty's government have entirely approved of the course pursued by Your Excellency in resisting the unjust claims of Russia and maintaining the principle of Turkish independence; and in the event of any further act of aggression by Russia, or of undue delay on her part in accepting the terms of any amicable settlement that may be proposed to her, Her Majesty's government, in conjunction with that of France, will be prepared to take more active measures for the protection of Turkey against a power of whose hostile designs there will then exist no reasonable doubt.

See Clarendon to Stratford, 28 July 1853, Clarendon MSS C/3; Clarendon to Westmoreland, 25 and 28 July 1853, *BSP*, ii, nos. 2, 5.
167. Lane-Poole, *Life*, ii. 290-1.
168. Buol to Apponyi, 21 June 1853, quoted in Temperley, *Crimea*, p. 342. *CHBFP*, ii. 351, says, quite wrongly, that the absence of a direct telegraph connection between Constantinople and Vienna was to blame for the next step in the crisis; the 'Vienna Note', it alleges, was sent on its way before the Turkish 'ultimatum' reached Vienna, implying that otherwise it might have been withheld. But the same work makes a better point when it states, 'How Lord Clarendon came to accept it, and to accept it without consulting Lord Stratford on the matter, is hard to understand'. Theodore Martin says the 'Vienna Note' was 'tainted to the core by the vagueness of language, the

danger of which, in the Convention proposed by Prince Menshikoff, had been strongly condemned' by all. See Theodore Martin, *The Life of His Royal Highness the Prince Consort* (London, 1875–80), ii. 512.
169. Clarendon to Stratford, 2 Aug. 1853, *BSP*, ii, no. 32.
170. Clarendon to Stratford, 30 July, 1 and 3 Aug. 1853, FO 352/36/1.
171. Russell to Clarendon, 20 and 27 July 1853, Clarendon MSS C/3; Clarendon to Aberdeen, 5 Aug. 1853, quoted in Conacher, *Aberdeen Coalition*, p. 163.
172. Quoted in *CHBFP*, ii. 367; Palmerston to Clarendon, 8 and 16 Aug. 1853, Clarendon MSS C/3.
173. Greville's *Memoirs*, i. 80 (9 Aug. 1853).
174. Nesselrode thought so too. Bapst, *Les origines de la guerre Crimée*, p. 432, n. 2.
175. Palmerston to Clarendon, 31 July 1853, Clarendon MSS C/3; Gladstone to Aberdeen, 12 Aug. 1853, quoted in Conacher, *Aberdeen Coalition*, p. 173.
176. Greville's *Memoirs*, i. 78–80 (8, 10, and 11 Aug. 1853).
177. Aberdeen to Princess Lieven, 8 Sept. 1853, quoted in *The Correspondence of Lord Aberdeen and Princess Lieven, 1832–54*, ed. E. Jones Parry (London, 1939), ii. 647.
178. Greville's *Memoirs*, i. 80 (9 Aug. 1853).
179. Ibid., i. 80 (11 Aug. 1853).
180. *Parl. Debs.*, 3rd series, cxxix, *Lords*, 12 and 18 July, 2, 8, and 12 Aug. 1853; *Commons*, 14, 21, and 22 July, 2, 8, and 16 Aug. 1853. A helpful discussion of the debates is in Conacher, *Aberdeen Coalition*, pp. 166–74.
181. Brunnov saw Clarendon on 12 August, bringing a letter from Nesselrode which said, 'we fully understand that we are not to have to examine or discuss fresh modifications and new drafts drawn up at Constantinople under the bellicose inspiration which at this moment seems to influence the Sultan'. Nesselrode to Brunnov, 6 Aug. 1853, *BSP*, ii, no. 56, enclosure.
182. Graham to Clarendon, 16 Aug. 1853, Clarendon MSS C/3.
183. *Parl. Debs.*, 3rd series, cxxviii, 16 Aug. 1853; Seton-Watson, *Britain in Europe*, p. 315.
184. In December 1850 Palmerston can be found saying 'If the Christian subjects of the Sultan are to be liable to become the victims of such abominable crimes, Christian Europe will come to the conclusion that the existence of the Ottoman Empire is an evil, and that its overthrow would be conducive to the general interests of the human race'. Quoted in Southgate, *Most English Minister*, p. 320.
185. Clarendon to Aberdeen, 26 Aug. 1853, quoted in Conacher, *Aberdeen Coalition*, p. 177.
186. Graham to Clarendon, 18 Aug. 1853, quoted in Charles Stuart Parker, *Life and Letters of Sir James Graham, Second Baronet, of Netherby, P.C., G.C.B., 1792–1861* (London, 1907), ii. 222. Kingsley Martin's explanation that Stratford could not be recalled because of his 'hold on the Press' is meaningless. He refused to see *The Times* correspondent, and gave some information indirectly to Hugh Alison, the local *Morning Chronicle* man. See Martin, *Triumph of Lord Palmerston*, p. 125.
187. Aberdeen to Clarendon, 19 Aug. 1853, Clarendon MSS C/4; Aberdeen to Clarendon, 20 Aug. 1853, Maxwell, *Clarendon*, ii. 17.
188. Aberdeen to Clarendon, 26 Aug. 1853, Clarendon MSS C/4; Clarendon to Russell, 25 Aug. 1853, quoted in Walpole, *Russell*, ii. 185.
189. Aberdeen to Clarendon, 20 Aug. 1853, Clarendon MSS C/4.
190. Aberdeen to Russell, 30 Aug. 1853, quoted in Russell, *Later Correspondence*,

ii. 152.
191. Stratford to Clarendon, 20 Aug. 1853, quoted in Lane-Poole, *Life*, ii. 295.
192. Greville's *Memoirs*, i. 82–3, 85 (28 Aug., 2 and 3 Sept. 1853); Clarendon 'suspects that Stratford has not bona fide striven to induce them to accept the proffered terms'; Clarendon is convinced that 'Lord Stratford was at the bottom of the difficulties raised by the divan'; Clarendon thinks Stratford

> might have persuaded the Turks to accept the terms if he had chosen to do so and set about it in a proper manner; but Clarendon says that he is himself no better than a Turk, and has lived there so long, and is animated with such personal hatred of the Emperor, that he is full of the Turkish spirit; and this and his temper together have made him take a part directly contrary to the wishes and instructions of his government.

CHAPTER VI

The Wrong Horse? Anglo-Ottoman Relations before the First World War

The first Ottoman parliament met on 19 March 1877. After 11 months of earnest rather than distinguished existence, it was dissolved by Sultan Abdulhamid II, and the deputies were sent home. A formal intimation that the legislative experiment was at an end was avoided, and the Sultan took the trouble to dismiss his grand vizier, Midhat Pasha, by its Article CXIII, and also to keep the parliament chamber itself in good decorative order as if it might be needed again at any moment. With two Sultans recently deposed, and critics of the dynasty on all sides, it was very difficult for patriots to believe that the era of the *Tanzimat* was really at an end, and none at first guessed that Abdulhamid II would try, far less that he would succeed, to institute a reign of personal despotism. Yet this, in fact, transpired, and the last important Ottoman Sultan proceeded to entrench himself behind the faceless walls of the Yildiz palace, to surround himself with a host of spies and bodyguards, and to accumulate the powers and prerogatives of the pre-*Tanzimat* sultanate. 'The initiative of reforming ministers', Abdulhamid II might have parodied, 'has increased, is increasing, and ought to be diminished.' In his progress, the Sultan revealed that he was shrewd as well as unscrupulous, capable of large views as well as small, and not without moments of courage in a career otherwise scourged by the fear of regicide. While no one would give an affirmative to Benjamin Disraeli's question, 'Will he be another Soliman the Magnificent?', it is also clear that the stream of progress, initiated by Reshid Pasha in the days of Mahmud II, and carried forward by Fuad and Ali Pashas, flowed on through the Hamidian era, and a recent opinion, resting upon an abundance of evidence, suggests that under Abdulhamid II 'the whole movement of the *Tanzimat* – of legal, administrative, and educational reform – reached its fruition and its climax'.[1]

British governments, however, took greater notice of the growth of arbitrary royal power and the Sultan's personal intransigence in his treatment of his Christian subjects. In his lifetime, Abdulhamid II seemed to British people to be an Oriental bigot of the worst sort, a sensuous buffoon in a fez whom one ambassador described in a public dispatch as a 'prince of Comedians'. Even had Ottoman progress in things like elementary education, vocational colleges, a modest railway system, rationalized civil and commercial codes, increased book production and newspaper circulation, been known commonly in Great Britain, they could never have counterbalanced the abrogation of parliamentary rights, the suppression of personal freedoms, or the lurid image of the royal spider trapping hapless opponents in a web of espionage and intrigue. It is also important to remember that Abdulhamid II did not have so unfortunate a reputation in those other European countries where liberal prejudices were weaker and constitutional forms less highly regarded. Certainly no public figure in Germany thundered against Ottoman barbarism in the way that Gladstone, Lecky, Carlyle, Darwin, Ruskin, Freeman, or Bryce did, and even less did anyone think of commemorating 'Abdul the Damned' in verse.[2]

The high tide of British Turcophilism passed with the Crimean War, the retirement of Lord Stratford de Redcliffe, and the death of Viscount Palmerston in 1865. Palmerston, the earl of Clarendon commented at the time, 'held a great bundle of sticks together: they are now unwound'; concern for the Ottoman Empire's surival and westernization was one of the biggest of those sticks. There was never again to be a Turcophile in Great Britain to compare in zeal and influence with David Urquhart, alongside whom Marmaduke Pickthall, with his Anglo-Ottoman Society and his enthusiastic belief that 'you will fall in love with the whole Turkish race if you come to know them', was to seem a puny figure in the early twentieth century. Significantly, Ernest Jackh's Turco-German Association, which was contemporary with Pickthall's organization, could raise in Germany an endowment fund to finance the further education of two thousand Ottoman students in Germany.[3] Fundamentally, British patience had been wearing thin even during the Crimean War, and the Ottoman Empire's poor military performance did not help, but from 1856 to 1908 active detestation of the Ottomans reached Burkeian heights. The failure to implement the grandiose promises of the *Hatt-i Humayun* of 1856 completed Foreign Office disillusionment, and both the famous *Hatt-i Sherif* of 1839 and the *Hatt-i Humayun* of 1856 came to be regarded as mere window-dressing, trumped-up programmes of reform and better government of Christians in the Ottoman Empire, whose sole purpose was to stave off British criticism. The treatment of the Christians was the acid test of Ottoman sincerity. The *Reports* laid before parliament in 1867[4] showed that, on this critical subject, the position was getting worse. Sultan Abdulaziz, visiting Great Britain that year, was civilly received, but there was no cordiality. The Crimean War lay on the nation like an old scar. In 1875, the year the insurrection in Bosnia began, the Ottoman Empire suspended payment of interest on the Ottoman debt; in the following year the Bulgarian massacres burst upon Europe. The German consul murdered at Salonika that May, it is sometimes forgotten, was an Englishman. Thus Abdulhamid II, coming to the Ottoman throne in mid-crisis, got off to a poor start.

Under these circumstances, it was inevitable that Midhat Pasha's constitution, produced as the Constantinople conference of great power delegates was assembling in December 1876, should seem yet one more shallow device to head off the active interference of outside powers in the internal affairs of the Ottoman Empire. Midhat, a genuine enough constitutionalist, was aware of this probable interpretation of his work, and was at pains to counter it in the pages of *Nineteenth Century* in 1878. He had previously disclosed his hopes to the British ambassador, Sir Henry Elliot, and much of Elliot's seeming partisanship for the Ottomans during the period of the Bulgarian massacres actually resulted from his desire to be fair to the constitutional experiment on the one hand and, on the other, to sift the mass of evidence from Bulgaria as honestly as he could. The famous telegram which Disraeli waved in the House of Commons, saying that in it the British ambassador had confirmed his own impressions of the exaggerated stories of repression, was not from Elliot at all, though Elliot was too loyal to say so.[5] The ambassador was transferred in 1877 to Vienna, Midhat fell, and his constitution soon followed him into oblivion. The new Sultan did not regard the final awards of the congress of Berlin as consistent with the Disraelian claim of 'peace with honour' since, by them, the Ottoman Empire actually lost more territory than she would have done by the treaty of San Stefano. Abdulhamid II was also aware that in Great Britain Disraeli may have won the majorities, but Gladstone had won the debates. Hardly anyone had taken Disraeli seriously when he called the Ottomans 'the gentlemen of the Orient', whereas the thunder of the 'bag and baggage' speech was to stand as the classic parliamentary exposition of British sentiment on the subject of the Ottomans for the rest of the Victorian period. But Abdulhamid II was unnecessarily pessimistic in his expectation that British policy must in the future align itself more faithfully alongside this hostile spirit.

Abdulhamid II disliked Great Britain and the British intensely throughout his reign, finding them the most censorious and interfering of his critics. The loss of Egypt, and the loss of Eastern Rumelia in 1886 which he also attributed to British machinations, helped to keep the fires of animosity well stoked, and on one occasion the Sultan discussed with Theodore Herzl, who was introduced to him by Arminius Vambéry, the possibility of colonizing Syria with Jews as a means of checking Christian infiltration.[6] The English *Levant Herald*, produced in Constantinople, was very critical of the regime, and published Ali Suavi's proclamation on the day prior to his unsuccessful *coup d'état* to remove the Sultan.[7] The British community in the capital was cautiously neutral in its opinions, but the succession of British ambassadors had a difficult time. Sir William White, called *Baba* (father) by Abdulhamid II, was probably the only Englishman except Sherlock Holmes to acquire a place in the royal affections: he had, the Sultan admitted, 'a sparing eye for our shortcomings . . . [I could like him more] if the policy of England would not contrast so much with the charms of his personality'. White died in 1891, and of all his successors only the first, Sir Clare Ford, came near to being liked at Yildiz. However, Ford stayed only a year and a half and was succeeded by Sir Philip Currie who, as a former under-secretary at the Foreign Office, had quite obviously been sent to intimidate Abdulhamid II over his treatment of the Armenians. Currie had a poor reception. Abdulhamid II kept him waiting about for hours in his thin ceremonial uniform on a bitterly cold day, and had the gratification to hear that the new ambassador had to take to his bed for a fortnight. Currie's problems over the Armenians nevertheless paled before those of his successor, Sir Nicholas O'Conor, who was enmeshed for a full decade in the tragic details of the Macedonian question.[8]

By that date far more Ottomans than Abdulhamid II alone were coming to resent the interference of foreigners, come to spy and criticize and write reports. A *muttesarif* of the remote Diarbekir region told a surprised British investigator that he would provide information on local conditions provided they were kept out of the Blue Books. Nearer the centre of affairs, the British community in Constantinople suffered quite heavily in the disorders of 1896, yet Abdulhamid II absolutely refused to pay the damages publicly, and the compensation was tacked quietly on to the price the Ottoman Empire paid for a British warship. By 1904 the Germans were more popular than the British, although they had only come into the country in appreciable numbers in the preceding decade. The military men were admired for their efficiency and impressed with their superb arrogance. The civilians took the trouble to learn Turkish and, coming from the land of obedience, did not pass political judgements. Even the Russians made some progress in the royal esteem, and Abdulhamid II recorded both his admiration of the tsar and his sympathy when Japan defeated Russia in the Far East.

The Sultan was stung that Turcophilism in Great Britain was dead, and bitter that he should be blamed almost exclusively for its demise. What he does not appear to have noticed was that Russophobia, the true foundation of Turcophilism, was still very much alive when he first came to the throne. He measured Great Britain's attitude too much by what she said, too little by what she did. He was not, of course, alone in his assumption that Ottoman integrity had been discarded unconditionally as an element in British foreign policy. Most British people thought such a principle ought to be discarded, and many thought it had been, not excluding the policy-makers themselves on occasion. As a major example of this change, many books invite us to see in the marquis of Salisbury a man shaking himself free from the tutelage of Disraeli, much as the earl of Derby had done before him, and going on, from the moment of his first enjoyment of the highest office, to re-educate his party and its followers to see that, for years past, they had been putting their money on 'the wrong horse'.

It seems salutary to bear in mind that the 'wrong horse' speech was not made until 1897, and that, in its correct context, it belongs to a speech in which Salisbury reaffirmed his adherence to the Disraeli tradition. The new Tory leader was no better than anyone else at finding a suitable alternative to the Ottomans at Constantinople (the earl of Aberdeen was the only foreign secretary who ever really tried), and he concentrated on ameliorating the lot of subject peoples within the Ottoman Empire as a task worthy in itself and easier to approach than the eternal conundrum of Ottoman sovereignty. The main point is that Salisbury did not drop the Disraelian shield, however privately embarrassing it was for a High Churchman to bear it. His sympathy for Balkan nationalities was, in any case, limited, and possibly jaundiced by his hostility to Irish Home Rule. The balance of his utterances suggests that he preferred amelioration under Ottoman rule – the old Palmerstonian optimism – to independence for Balkan peoples, which Disraeli had always thought an internal Ottoman affair, and which Salisbury himself regarded as a process which might get out of hand. In 1886 he favoured the union of Rumelia with Bulgaria merely as a personal union under Prince Alexander. When Serbia began to mutter about compensation, he recommended Austria-Hungary to keep her in check, by force if necessary. When Greece followed Serbia's example, she was blockaded. Even over the Armenian problem in 1894, where no question of territorial sovereignty was involved, Salisbury would not act alone, saying, in a phrase which echoes through all his pronouncements on the Eastern Question, that Great Britain did not have enough at stake.[9] He simply consigned Abdulhamid II to the devil, which is where Abdulhamid II supposed the British to have sent him years before. 'I do not see that we can take any other course except to exert what influence we may possess with the other powers of Europe to induce them to press on the Sultan such reforms as may be necessary not only to save his subjects from massacre, but to preserve his own empire from a ruin which, if he does not take requisite precautions in time, cannot be long delayed.' The Eastern Question, in its Balkan nationalistic aspect and its Armenian humanitarian aspect, was not worth the bones of a British grenadier.

William Ewart Gladstone is associated by many commentators, as he was by many of his contemporaries, with a keener moral sense, something closer to the austerity of the Victorian conscience. On examination, nevertheless, the 'bag and baggage' philippic is as misleading as 'the wrong horse' speech, and when some people actually did take it as a promise of stern action, it was Gladstone himself who put their ideas into perspective. A letter from him to *The Times* on 9 September 1876 explained that he did not intend that the Ottomans should be driven from the Balkans entirely, only from Bulgaria. On 10 September he corrected even this in a speech at Blackheath, explaining that only 'military and official Turks' should leave Bulgaria. Addressing Abdulhamid II *in absentia*, he said, 'you shall retain your titular sovereignty, you shall receive a reasonable tribute, your Empire shall not be invaded'. As one historian has written, could anything be closer to the actual arrangements made by the Tories at Berlin?[10]

Gladstone undoubtedly had to deal with greater misgivings in his party than the Tory leaders, but there were no great oscillations in Eastern policy as one party succeeded the other. Both parties favoured more humane conditions for Balkan subjects of the Ottoman Empire, and even the emergence of independent states if these were truly independent and not simply the playthings of great powers. Both drew a sharp distinction between the controlled reduction of Ottoman power in the Balkans and the inviolability of Ottoman Asia, where Foreign Office thinking rested upon the enduring articles of faith handed down since at least the Napoleonic period: concern for the routes to India, and the desire to keep energetic competitors out of the Persian Gulf, explain the conflict with Napoleon in Egypt, the opposition to Muhammad Ali in Syria, the wariness of Abdulhamid II's pan-Islamic notions in the 1880s, and the suspicions of Germany in the era of the Baghdad railway dispute. Palmerston would have approved the wide sweep of Lord Curzon's geopolitical views, and would, in all probability, have disliked Cecil Spring Rice. Both parties found it possible to ignore Ottoman sovereignty in Africa, even when the French and Italians infringed upon it. Both were ready to modify the rule of the Straits in the early 1890s by opening them equally to Russia and the other interested powers; both retreated from this view later on. In both parties the opinion began to harden that the Ottoman Empire was incorrigible except under outside pressure, yet neither found the time, the idealism, or the inclination to take a lead. Neither was

Relations before the First World War

pleased when Germany stepped into the picture with unfathomed intentions and an indulgent attitude to the delinquent ruler at Constantinople. Lastly, neither party dreamed that the Ottoman Empire would be revolutionized from within. The Ottoman Empire was a clock which had stopped, and Sir Edward Grey was one of the last British statesmen to glimpse the possibility of winding it up again. The difficulties in Macedonia, but above all the successful onslaught of the Balkan states on the Ottoman Empire in 1912, convinced even Grey that the mainspring had gone. But had it?

If there was truth in the Gladstonian argument that free Bulgarians were the surest obstacle to Russian advance through the Balkans, why not free Ottomans also, holding the Straits and the land routes to India in a firm and impartial grip? Great Britain, after all, retained substantial trading interests in the Levant and the Persian Gulf, and held one-third of the Ottoman debt. She built the Ottoman Empire's first railway, from Smyrna to Aydin, and introduced the telegraph and post office.[11] German economic penetration did not begin before 1898, the year of the Kaiser's second visit to the East, and even Wilhelm II put his travel arrangements in the hands of Thomas Cook. With numerous Young Turks in Great Britain, there was certainly time to win over some of them before they became pro-German. Were no clandestine approaches made by the refugee liberals to the mother of parliaments or to the Foreign Office, or vice versa? The answer seems to be in the negative, except for one isolated contact between British officialdom and what might be called the second wave of Young Turks.

As has been mentioned, English Turcophilism dwindled rapidly in the 1860s, and it was precisely then that the first wave of Young Turks – they would have called themselves Young Ottomans – were taking refuge in Vienna, Paris, and London. Exiled either for their political journalism, as in the case of Namik Kemal, or, like Sinasi and Ziya Pasha, by falling foul of the reactionary bureaucrats under whom they served in the Ottoman administration, these men sought sanctuary and opportunity for reading and reflection, rather than the chance to conspire. By the standards of western political radicalism, they were strongly conservative in their social and political thinking: by their own standards, they were patriotic Ottoman Muslims. Their weakness lay in their optimistic belief that the parliamentary mechanism would export easily, an error which the subsequent history of their country was to expose mercilessly. They read Rousseau, and the second wave of Young Turks read Demolin's *A quoi tient la supériorité des Anglo-Saxons?*, instead of Bagehot or the parliamentary debates. They read too much political theory and not enough history. In Paris, nevertheless, they acquired some degree of social recognition, and had contacts with the foreign ministry, but in London they were unknown to men of influence. Namik was zealous in his admiration – 'If London be called the model of the world, it would be no exaggeration' – and he described Parliament as 'the embodiment in stone of the indomitable power of public opinion against authority'. But the overall, external experience of the young patriots is seen in the internal circumstances of Ziya's famous political essay, *Rüya* (Dream): the dream begins when Ziya falls asleep on a bench on Hampstead Heath, and ends when the park-keeper wakes him.[12]

The second wave of young Ottoman refugees from the Hamidian despotism to take up residence in Europe was more widely spread, showed more practical initiative, and acquired a wider fame.[13] In Paris, Geneva, and London, the refugees quarrelled furiously in the columns of the newspapers and journals they founded. At times they made headlines in the European press too, as when Abdulhamid II sued the editors of *Mechveret* in Paris for defamation of his royal character, a case which only served to publicize the rude words his refugee subjects applied to him – cheat, hangman, bloody majesty – and he was snubbed before the world when the defendants were found guilty, but let off with a fine of sixteen francs.[14] It was this middle wave of Young Turks which coined the phrase Union and Progress, and while it passed on little else in a tangible way to the third wave, both waves had certain attitudes in common. Neither sympathized with the aspirations of subject nationalities in the Ottoman Balkans, and both regretted episodes like the Armenian massacres only for the unwelcome publicity they attracted. Their ideal was to deal with Abdulhamid II in their own way, to discipline rather than depose him, and to regenerate the Ottoman Empire in a way which would no longer allow Europe to presume upon its weakness.

The instinct for keeping the game in their own hands, and their fear of Abdulhamid II's spies, inhibited any idea of seeking practical help from the British government. This was perhaps as well, for the Foreign Office could be relied on to draw a sharp dividing line between supporting the Italians against the Austrians in Italy, or the Poles against the Russians in Poland, and intervention in the domestic squabbles of the Sultan and his legitimate subjects. The Young Turks had less chance of British recognition than, say, the Armenian refugees, with whom they fought like cat and dog. If the Young Turks had been able to pose as yet another oppressed minority, they might have got a readier hearing.

There was, nevertheless, one moment of official British interest in the middle wave of Young Turks which is worthy of notice. In his egotistical memoirs, Ismail Kemal, the later speaker of the Ottoman parliament, recounts one of the numerous episodes in which the overthrow of Abdulhamid II was the main aim.[15] This particular plot belongs to the year 1903, and was concocted in Paris by Sabaheddin, a refugee prince of the Ottoman royal family. It was intended that Rejep Pasha, the military commander in Tripolitania, should undertake an expedition to Salonika and thence to the Dardanelles. The great powers would sit up, and Abdulhamid II would abdicate in a fright. The plot was revealed to the British ambassador at Paris, Sir Edmund Monson, who would not commit himself as to British consent to the adventure. Nevertheless, Monson sent Ismail Kemal to London. As the foreign secretary, the marquis of Lansdowne, was escorting the Kaiser to Sandringham, Ismail Kemal was seen by the permanent under-secretary:

> The following day Lord Sanderson, Permanent Under-Secretary for Foreign Affairs, invited me to go and see him at his private house, and I gave him a detailed explanation of our proposed course of action, and of the nature of the protection which we asked for from the British Government, which was simply to protect us against any action which Russia might bring to bear to prevent the success of our patriotic action. Lord Sanderson promised to get into communication with his chief and let me know his decision. In less than two days I received a second invitation from the Under-Secretary to go to his house, and he then read me the letter Lord Lansdowne had written him on the subject. This gave a promise of support which was worthy of the traditional policy of Great Britain, though it was surrounded with a natural reserve dictated by the fact that our *coup* was not yet a *fait accompli*. I was greatly encouraged, and with the

consent of Lord Sanderson I took a copy of the Minister's letter, which was in French, to show my co-workers.

The circumstantial detail is convincing, and so is Sanderson's 'natural reserve'. There is no overpowering reason to reject the story. Anglo-German relations were at their worst over the naval rivalry and also the Baghdad railway project. The government of India was badgering Lansdowne to establish a protectorate over Kuwait, or at least curb German mischief by buying into the railway project. The earl of Cromer, at the height of his proconsular majesty, thought German hostility was an additional reason for rationalizing the British position in Egypt, and when he was challenged personally by Ismail Kemal on Great Britain's right to do any such thing, he grimly replied that there was no longer an Ottoman aspect of the question to be considered.[16] Lansdowne, on the threshold of discussions which were to lead to the Anglo-French entente, cannot have been averse to Ottoman patriots putting a spoke in the Kaiser's wheel. The French could probably persuade their Russian friends not to intervene. Altogether, the story of Lansdowne's letter of sympathy seems as genuine as the later Young Turks' gloss, that Lansdowne also offered British naval cover for the enterprise, seems improbable.[17] The plot, in any case, fell through because of faulty organization.

The third wave of Young Turks consisted of the men who actually carried out the revolution of 1908.[18] They came together as a conspiratorial knot of officers in the Ottoman Third Corps at Salonika, an important geographical circumstance which made for unanimity within the secret organization, and ignorance of its strength on the part of outsiders. The officers who joined the so-called Committee of Union and Progress (CUP) were politically aware, professionally well trained, and irritated by the prospect of teams of European soldiers and civilians administering Ottoman Macedonia in the furtherance of the 1903 Mürzsteg programme of reforms. They envied the European officers their status and their material conditions of service, but dearly wished to see the backs of all of them. As members of the CUP, they believed in the regeneration of the Ottoman Empire through the adoption of the parliamentary mechanism and the modernization of the army. Less doctrinaire than the earlier Young Turks, they were also considerably less liberal. On the day of freedom, the non-Muslims of the Empire would be decently treated, but they would also do as they were told.

The CUP wished, therefore, to make Ottoman history in its own way, and when the British embassy looked backwards over the events which so took it by surprise in 1908, it found a trigger-action for the revolution in the meeting of Edward VII and the tsar at Reval a few weeks before.[19] The CUP believed that the historic closing of the breach between Great Britain and Russia in 1907 by the agreements on Afghanistan, Persia, and Tibet was now being made complete by royal discussions on the final liquidation of the Ottoman Empire. They were wrong. The Russian foreign minister, Count Izvolsky, deliberately kept the Straits question in the background in 1907, for it was his intention that in 1908 Russia should do a deal with Austria-Hungary regarding them, rather than with Great Britain, who was unlikely to co-operate in the creation of zones of influence or conquest. It was only when the Austro-Hungarian foreign minister, Count Aehrenthal, outstripped Izvolsky by seizing Bosnia and Herzegovina that Izvolsky turned to Great Britain to extricate him from his humiliation by consenting to the opening of the Straits to Russia in particular. He was destined to be disappointed. The British interpretation of Ottoman integrity had dwindled pretty far, and the events of 1912 were to show that she would do nothing alone to conserve the tattered remnant of the Ottoman Empire in Europe. But Grey was not prepared to weaken the European concert further by following up the Austrian seizures with a concession to Russia at the Straits.

The British embassy was completely unprepared for the dramatic events of mid-1908, sharing the consternation of the general public in Constantinople. Although the mutiny of the Third Corps had been spreading throughout the spring and had reached Edirne, and although Semsi Pasha, sent to quell the trouble, had been assassinated on 7 July, there were no premonitions of a further deterioration of public order; and it was on 22 July, when most of the embassy staff was attending the Lawn Tennis Finals of the Ottoman Empire, that spectators coming out to Tarabya from the city brought the first rumours of ministerial changes.[20] On the 24th the revolution was disclosed, in the modest form of an insertion in the newspapers saying the Ottoman parliament was to be called again. It was only now, wrote Sir Telford Waugh, that the British chargé d'affaires (O'Conor was dead and Sir Gerard Lowther had not yet arrived as the new ambassador) 'inquired what was this C.U.P., of which people were beginning to talk'. A British reaction was soon forthcoming, nevertheless – *The Times* publishing an encouraging leader within a week, and Edward VII sending his congratulations to Kamil Pasha, the antique Anglophile whom Abdulhamid II called back hurriedly to his service. Kamil replied with the site for the English High School. The Pera Palace Hotel was presently overflowing with British members of parliament and journalists, come to witness the rebirth of the Ottoman parliament.[21] Turcophilism rallied bravely, and Sir Mark Sykes predicted that 'the Turk has something in his nature which may astound the world yet'. The Foreign Office, however experienced in disillusionment, could not fail to reason that a parliamentary Ottoman Empire must stand closer to Great Britain than to Germany. Sir Edward Grey called it all 'one of the most beneficent changes in history', and seems to have discerned in Kamil something of an oriental Mirabeau. No more than anyone else did Grey detect the men of Jacobinical determination standing in the wings, coercing the new assembly, which met on 17 December, without themselves appearing on the stage.

In the bitter struggle which followed with the so-called Liberal Union, the CUP at first went from strength to strength, controlling the royal choice of grand viziers, murdering Hasan Fehmi, the editor of the liberal *Serbesti*, crushing the counter-revolution of the First Corps in Constantinople, deposing Abdulhamid II without a flutter of protest from abroad, and keeping the capital city in a state of martial law for two years.[22] In Great Britain, it came to be assumed – wrongly – that the CUP must, after all, have the confidence of the Ottoman people, and Grey was challenged for giving countenance to the Liberal Union. He replied, with perfect truth, that Great Britain was neutral in Ottoman internal affairs, and would give warm support to any government which governed well. By this he meant any government which governed Christians well, for further Armenian atrocities had occurred in Adana in 1909, and the situation in Macedonia deteriorated sharply after the international commissioners and gendarmerie were withdrawn.

By 1911, Enver, Kemal, Talaat, and Mahmud Shevket seemed to

be securely established in power, though they were feared by many Muslims and hated by all Christians. 'To them', Sir Gerard Lowther wrote to Grey, ' "Ottoman" evidently means "Turk" and their present policy of "Ottomanization" is one of pounding the non-Turkish elements in a Turkish mortar.'[23] Certainly, CUP fanaticism damaged its reputation abroad. C.R. Buxton, chairman of the Balkan Committee and a great Turcophile in 1908, was a 'bag and baggage' man by 1912, and Sir Mark Sykes got a loud ovation for a strong 'bag and baggage' speech in 1913 on the Armenian question. Cromer and Edward Dicey had said all along that Grey was being impulsive with his congratulations. How could one encourage Young Turks without giving moral advantage to young Egyptians?

During the turmoil of these years the British embassy maintained a patient neutrality. It disliked the election-rigging, the political murders, and the intimidations, and there was a sigh of relief when the CUP sustained setbacks in 1912 amounting almost to political annihilation. The disapproval was of methods rather than of men, and certain key CUP men like Talaat and Kemal always commanded British respect. But the emergence of a military despotism could not be approved. The CUP rescued its fortunes at the height of the military disasters inflicted by Bulgaria in late 1912: on 23 January 1913 Enver forced his way into the cabinet which was supposed to be arranging the surrender of Edirne; Nazim Pasha, the minister of war, was shot, and Enver dictated the grand vizier's resignation. There was no hesitation in appealing for the intercession of Great Britain with the Ottoman Empire's Balkan foes at the London conference, which sat through the greater part of 1913 against a background of bloodshed, but Grey, whose eyes necessarily scanned wider horizons than the Balkans alone, was unwilling to act without the other great powers, and hoped vainly for a German lead. When this was not forthcoming, he told the Ottoman delegation 'it was not a question of words, but of facts'.[24] If the Young Turks could not maintain the Ottoman Empire in Europe, no great power had sufficient motive to attempt it for them. He was not deflected by an offer of the outright cession of Egypt within 24 hours. The CUP leaders were able only to salvage the Edirne *glacis* of the Ottoman Balkans from the wreckage of Macedonia. They did not believe this was the end of the story: they thought Bulgaria and Greece still harboured designs upon Ottoman territory and islands, and they were not without their own dreams of a war of recovery. What they also recognized, and with unprecedented clarity, was that the cry of 'Turkish integrity' could never again raise a fighting majority in Great Britain. The traditional protectress was gone: the traditional opponent remained.

In the 18 months before the outbreak of the First World War, Anglo-Ottoman relations contrived to enter upon a cordial phase. Grey had not gone beyond honest brokerage, but then neither had the Ottoman Empire's more vociferous friend, the Kaiser. The Young Turk grand vizier, Prince Said Halim, gave regular assurances of Ottoman goodwill to Sir Louis Mallet, an ambassador who tried hard to charm his hosts into trust and confidence. Great Britain and the United States put more hard cash into the relief of Macedonian refugees than all other donors put together, and 5,000 Muslims were fed daily in Constantinople by a British committee. The Ottomans did not hesitate to employ a British naval mission alongside the German military mission; Sir Richard Crawford overhauled the customs while Orme Clarke became inspector-general to the ministry of justice. Some very old difficulties were tackled with success: an Aden–Yemen boundary settlement was signed in March 1914, and a batch of long-resisted British claims going back to the days of Abdulaziz was referred to arbitration in July. When the British naval commander in the Mediterranean came to pay his respects that summer to the Sultan, he was permitted to sail through the Straits in the warship *Inflexible*, rather than in the customary yacht. As war grumbled nearer on the horizons of Europe, Sir Edwin Pears recollected that the attitude of the British embassy was 'one of quiet confidence in Turkish assurances' of neutrality. Talaat seemed anxious to have a Triple Entente guarantee of Ottoman integrity, and Kemal, the minister of marine, went on board a Messagerie steamer to toast French volunteers sailing to enlist in Paris. Yet, by October, the Ottoman Empire became involved in war with the two states which, as her statesmen had always known, could hurt her most.[25]

Enver Pasha, the Ottoman generalissimo, and former military attaché at Berlin, was conditioned by training and by his friendships to believe that the Triple Alliance must prevail over the Triple Entente. Most of his cabinet colleagues, without going this far, believed that Russia, having healed her differences with Great Britain, would keep the Straits open by force in any encounter with Germany, and that only Austria-Hungary and Germany could restrain the tsar. Nevertheless, Baron Wangenheim, the German ambassador to the Ottoman Empire, was indisposed to add such an enfeebled state to Germany's existing commitments, and was not impressed by Enver's hint that if his request for a defensive alliance against Russia were turned down, the Ottoman Empire would 'decide, with a heavy heart, in favour of a pact with the Triple Entente'. Only the Kaiser's personal intervention set treaty negotiations in train, and these were so secret that even Mahmud Muhtar Pasha, the Ottoman ambassador at Berlin, was kept out of the picture. So was most of the cabinet in Constantinople. As soon as the treaty of mutual defence was signed on 2 August, the German Admiral Suchon was ordered to sail his ships, the *Goeben* and *Breslau*, to the Straits, where he would probably take command of the Ottoman fleet. Enver and Field Marshal Liman von Sanders wanted to declare war on Russia immediately, now that Germany and Russia were at war. The British government, declaring war on Germany on 4 August, gave Enver powerful assistance by announcing that two Ottoman warships nearing completion in British yards, the *Sultan Osman* and the *Reshidie*, would be turned over to the Royal Navy. These vessels had been so eagerly awaited by the Ottomans as a means of reducing Ottoman vulnerability by sea (no Ottoman ship had been a match for the Greek *Averoff* in the Balkan Wars) that the government felt compelled to accuse Great Britain in an official communiqué of a breach of international law. That was on 7 August. On the 11th the *Goeben* and *Breslau* slipped into the Dardanelles, thus replacing the ships Great Britain withheld.[26]

Wilhelm II was astonished as well as gratified that the Ottoman Empire should, as he put it, 'offer herself' to Germany at a moment when hostilities between Russia and Germany had actually been announced. There could be no more valuable a recruit for his 'Balkan alliance' with which to stem the 'Slavic flood'. So surprised, indeed, was Berlin that Enver had managed so much so quickly that official opinion expected the Ottoman ministry to recoil from what had been agreed to, particularly after Great Britain's entry into the war. On 4 August the German foreign ministry cabled the ambassador at Constantinople: 'To prevent the Sublime Porte from deserting us at last moment under pressure of English action, a Turkish declaration of war on Russia this very day if possible appears to be of greatest importance'; on 15 August: 'Turkey must strike. His Majesty the Sultan must summon Mussulmans in Asia, India, Egypt and Africa to holy war for Caliphate.' As is well known, it required constant German pressure to obtain the closure of the Dardanelles on 27 September, and a further four weeks of plotting on the part of Enver and his German confederate, Hans Humann, to arrange the bombardment of Odessa by Ottoman–German naval forces.[27] Considering the immense issues at stake – securing the reciprocal flow of wheat and munitions through the Straits, and preventing the Young Turks offering Germany military opportunities in Ottoman Asia Napoleon had only dreamed of – the autumn of 1914 ought to have seen an intense diplomatic encounter between Great Britain and Germany for the soul of the Ottoman Empire. It was the kind of situation in which an independent autocrat like Stratford de Redcliffe would have fought like a dragon, and in all probability with success. This is not meant to throw blame on Mallet, although that was done at the time by the British press, but rather to suggest that, as late as 1914, Constantinople was the one major court where a diplomat of bold temperament might still determine the march of events by sheer perseverance and boldness. Enver proved that. Stratford would have defeated the local, pro-German conspiracy for sure. But would British policy in 1914 have permitted him to try?

'Policy' seems a dangerous word to use in connection with a state's appraisal of its foreign relations. It implies continuity of diplomatic action, the rational adaptation of the national attitude under the stress of changing interests and changing circumstances. As diplomacy deals with variables rather than constants, so there must actually be strict limits to its pretension to be 'scientific', and history shows that in diplomacy, as in the human mind, old ideas tend to coexist with new ones, rather than to be deposed by them. The impulsive encouragement given the Young Turks in 1908 was an echo of the old Turcophile optimism which had always predicted that the Ottoman Empire was capable of beneficent transformation. The Foreign Office, too, was conditioned by its own past achievements in the Victorian age to regard the Ottoman Empire as a country having a permanent, if undefined, position in the European state system even though, by 1913, it no longer held significant territories in Europe. But alongside this conservative and largely negative way of thinking, a contrary and more hostile attitude was emerging, and Lord Salisbury was only fencing it off when, in 1898, he said, 'we aim at no partition of territory, but only a partition of preponderance'. Even when persuading the Sultans to give up territory, Great Britain had always been able to argue, at least to her own satisfaction, that the Ottoman Empire's grip over her remaining territories had been strengthened; thus the case for 'the breasts of free men' had always been explained to the Ottomans in terms of the more acceptable metaphor that the Ottoman Empire would gain by cutting away 'diseased limbs'.

In 1914, with the empire in Europe expunged from the map, Great Britain needed to decide how much, if at all, she could countenance an Ottoman revival in the Balkans and, at the very least, how firmly she was prepared to uphold the Ottoman Empire in Asia and at the Straits. No ministry could hope to reverse the policy of liberating the small and Christian Balkan states, and this is not surprising. The 'free men' could not be put back in bondage. What is very striking is the unobtrusive way in which, sometime after the final retirement of Lord Salisbury – perhaps after the entente with France brought an accommodation with Russia into view? – Great Britain's earlier acceptance of the reduction of Ottoman power in the Balkans finally crossed the Bosporus. The arrangements made with Russia regarding the Middle East in 1907 provided a prototype for the settlement of Anglo-German rivalries in the Near East in 1914. Ottoman military incapacity, as exposed in the Balkan wars, made some such accommodation more desirable and urgent than ever before. It might still be one commensurate with Salisbury's dictum of 1898, but behind it there lurked unmistakably the ultimate possibility of political annexation.

In 1914 Great Britain, Germany, Austria-Hungary, France, and Italy were involved in discussions concerning the fate of Ottoman Asia, on the basis of economic spheres of interest. The discussions resulted in plans which were as detailed and specific as any spoliation invented by Catherine II. Mention of her serves to remind us that Russia was not a participant in the 1914 talks. Only shortly before the Ottoman–German treaty of 2 August was signed, Great Britain conceded Germany's right to exploit the economic potential of the Baghdad railway in its Anatolian and Cilician sectors, leaving the terminus region at the Gulf to Great Britain herself. By the time Suchon took charge of the Ottoman fleet, the old and new British attitudes were in a state of equipoise: one may put this more candidly and say there was no clear attitude at all. Mallet suffered accordingly.

On 4 August Grey sent advice from 'Turkey's oldest friend' warning the Ottoman Empire against 'the grave consequences' of a German alliance. Mallet, who glimpsed the need for a tougher line, was more to the point when he told the grand vizier that Great Britain regarded the Ottoman fleet 'as an annex of the German fleet and that if it went into the Aegean we should sink it'. London expected Ottoman self-interest to dictate a policy of neutrality, so the Ottoman Empire was neither trusted nor flattered. The greatest initiative from the side of the Entente came from Russia, who saw most clearly what loss of the Straits to German control implied.[28]

The enduring heart of the Eastern Question is the control of the Straits, a problem of great importance to Great Britain for as long as she opposed Russia in the Near East. In 1914 Ottoman ministers did not attempt to conceal that they were appalled by the feebleness of their country, afraid of their acquisitive neighbours, and unable to maintain their position at the Straits without the protection of a mighty patron. Thus Enver was not entirely insincere when he told Wangenheim that if Germany refused the Ottoman Empire an alliance, his pro-western colleagues would be enabled to make an arrangement with the Triple Entente. The Ottoman Empire needed protection and a period of recuperation rather than immediate opportunities of revenge. Now Russia understood this very well, and M.N. Giers, the ablest foreign representative at the Porte, firmly supported by his foreign minister, Count Sazonov, tried with a desperate energy to convince the Ottoman ministers that Russian fears and Ottoman fears could be removed most effectively if the two countries created an alliance of their own. Russia would provide the Ottoman Empire with the protection she required and guarantee her territories, the Ottoman Empire would shut the Straits to hostile powers, and the two countries would stand together in defensive alliance.

The proposals will be recognized as a return to the notions of 1833 and the treaty of Unkiar Skelessi. The Ottomans leaped at the offer, and Talaat visited Russia and proposed a formal alliance in May. In June, Kemal was in Paris, proposing actual alliance with the Entente powers, for a guarantee by three powers was clearly better than reliance on Russia alone. Three days after the Ottoman–German treaty was signed, Enver himself offered to sign an alliance with Russia. Sazonov was more than ready to share the burden of an Ottoman alliance, and put up proposals to Paris and London. When the war was won, the Ottoman Empire would receive all the German concessions in Asia and a guarantee of her frontiers. The deal could be clinched promptly if Greece could be got to surrender the island of Lemnos, off the Dardanelles, to the Ottoman Empire now, for the Ottoman ministers were very worried about Greek hostility in the islands. The French foreign minister, Théophile Delcassé, turned the idea down immediately: 'the *pourparlers* with Turkey could not lead to anything and he thought it more conforming with our purposes to guarantee, without delay, the restoration of the Balkan *bloc* in directing it against Turkey.' Grey's line was substantially the same. Why get involved for the Ottoman Empire's sake in the dangerous question of Balkan compensations for her, why turn her into an ally at all, when she had no alternative but to stay neutral, which was just as convenient to the Entente?[29] Grey agreed to a guarantee of Ottoman integrity in return for a declaration of neutrality, but there could be no alienation of Greece over Lemnos, nor discussion of an Ottoman return to Thrace. This would anger Bulgaria. The opportunity passed, the pro-Entente ministers in the Ottoman Empire lost ground, and in October the bombardment of Odessa took place. Even then, a majority in the Ottoman cabinet voted for peace, but the die was cast.

By 1914 a British government was no longer inclined by temperament to make any sort of major sacrifice to win over the Ottoman Empire. First, there was strong support for the purely military judgement that a Balkan alliance, suitably succoured, would best contain a German thrust to the Straits. Second, the opinion that the 'sick man of Europe' would recover his health as a result of his Balkan amputations was giving place to the sterner suspicion that he was nothing more than the 'sick man of Asia'. Third, Great Britain could not offer the Ottoman Empire anything to stay out of the war, partly because the imperial outlook made the surrender of places like Egypt or zones like the Persian Gulf unthinkable, but mainly because it was expected that Ottoman self-interest must dictate an attitude of neutrality. Still seeing herself as 'Turkey's oldest friend', she believed with a dangerous complacency that the withdrawal of her friendship must immobilize the Ottoman Empire. This was the more unfortunate as the Straits were infinitely more vital to Great Britain and Russia as allies than they had been to these powers in the great days of their rivalry. When the Straits were closed, Great Britain tried to force them open again by a combined operation. Her failure on the bronze headlands of Gallipoli placed a military burden on Russia which crushed the tsarist regime and led to an upheaval whose consequences for Europe and the world were to dwarf those of the French Revolution. The terrible dangers of the military situation in 1915 forced Great Britain to abandon completely the remaining vestiges of a policy which had been sustained, through many hesitations, for over a century. She offered Russia both Constantinople and the Straits, the lock and the key which Napoleon and Alexander I had been unable to divide. The Eastern Question had not disappeared: in Asia the old Palmerstonian structure of interests still prevailed, and the discovery of oil was to give it new strength. But it was no longer believed that, after the war, these interests would be promoted usefully through diplomatic effort in the Ottoman Empire.

★ ★ ★

Two great cemeteries overlook the blue waters of the Straits. They are separated by the sea of Marmara, one lying at the Dardanelles and the other on the Bosporus. They are separated in time, too, but only by half a century. The redcoats laid to rest at Üsküdar gave their lives to hold the Straits shut, and to save the Ottoman Empire. The men in khaki who sleep at Canakkale and the Dardanelles gave theirs to open the Straits despite the Ottoman Empire, that Russia might be saved.

Relations before the First World War 247

NOTES

1. B. Lewis, *The Emergence of Modern Turkey* (London, 1961), p. 174.
2. On Abdulhamid II, see Sir E. Pears, *Life of Abdul Hamid* (London, 1917); F. McCullagh, *The Fall of Abd-ul-Hamid* (London, 1910); P. Regla, *Les Secrets d'Yildiz* (Paris, 1897); Gilles Roy, *Abdul Hamid, Le Sultan Rouge* (Paris, 1936); A. Wittlin, *Abdul Hamid, The Shadow of God* (London, 1940). Pears's biography has a most abusive Introduction by Basil Williams who, as editor, seemed unhappy to have the Sultan in a series entitled *Makers of the Nineteenth Century*. W.E. Gladstone *et al.* were prominent in the national convention which denounced Disraelian indulgence of the Ottomans in 1876; Queen Victoria wished the attorney-general could be 'set at these men'. William Watson, creator of 'Abdul the Damned', later apologized to the Sultan, but only in the following way:
    For in a world where cruel deeds abound,
    The merely damned are legion; with such souls
    Is not each hollow and cranny of Tophet crammed?
    Thou with the brightest of Hell's aureoles
    Dost shine supreme, incomparably crowned,
    Immortally, beyond all mortals, damned.
3. E. Jäckh, *The Rising Crescent: Turkey Yesterday, Today and Tomorrow* (New York, 1944), p. 27.
4. See Sir H. Luke, *The Old Turkey and the New* (London, 1955), pp. 56–64.
5. Lewis, *Modern Turkey*, p. 163; Pears, *Forty Years in Constantinople* (London, 1916), p. 21; Sir H. Elliot, *Some Revolutions and Other Diplomatic Experiences* (London, 1922), pp. 254–95; 'The Death of Abdul Aziz and of Turkish Reform', *Nineteenth Century*, xxiii (1888), 276.
6. A. Vambéry, 'Personal Recollections of Abdul Hamid and His Court', *Nineteenth Century*, lxvi (1909), 69–88.
7. Lewis, *Modern Turkey*, p. 172.
8. Sir T. Waugh, *Turkey: Yesterday, Today and Tomorrow* (London, 1930), pp. 19–47; Sir Andrew Ryan, *The Last of the Dragomans* (London, 1951), pp. 28–51.
9. W.N. Medlicott, 'Lord Salisbury and the Turks', *History*, xii (1927), 244–7.
10. W.N. Medlicott, 'Gladstone and the Turks', *History*, xiii (1928), 136–7.
11. E.M. Earle, *Turkey, the Great Powers, and the Baghdad Railway* (New York, 1923); Lewis, *Modern Turkey*, p. 180; E.G. Mears, *Modern Turkey* (New York, 1924), ch. ix; D.C. Blaisdell, *European Financial Control in the Ottoman Empire* (New York, 1929).
12. A.H. Tanpinar, *XIX Asir Türk Edebiyati Tarihi* (Constantinople, 1956), is the standard general work on the philosophical and literary movements of the period. Lewis, *Modern Turkey*, pp. 132–42.
13. E.E. Ramsaur, *The Young Turks: Prelude to the Revolution of 1908* (Princeton, 1957).
14. Ibid., p. 36.
15. *Memoirs of Ismail Kemal Bey*, ed. S. Story (London, 1920), p. 310.
16. Ibid., p. 311.
17. Ramsaur. *Young Turks*, p. 79 and n.
18. Ibid., p. 94 *et seq*.
19. Ryan, *Dragomans*, p. 56 and n.
20. Waugh, *Turkey*, p. 110.
21. Ibid., p. 114; A. Vambéry, 'Europe and the Turkish Constitution', *Nineteenth*

Century, lxiv (1908), 224; E.S. Beesly, 'The Turkish Revolution', *The Positivist Review*, xvi (1908), 201; E.J. Dillon, 'The Unforeseen Happens as Usual', *Contemporary Review*, xciv (1908), 364. A characteristic hymn of praise is C.R. Buxton, *Turkey in Revolution* (London, 1909). It has been suggested that the origins of the Balkan Committee, of which Buxton was the chairman, 'are to be found in the widespread and uncomfortable feeling which existed at the turn of the century, that British policy was primarily responsible for the plight of Balkan Christians'. On this, see L.S. Stavrianos, 'The Balkan Committee', *Queen's Quarterly*, xlviii (1941), 258–67.
22. Lewis, *Modern Turkey*, pp. 209–22.
23. *BD*, IX. i. 207.
24. *BD*, IX. part II. 490, 495, 515, 529; E.C. Helmreich, *Diplomacy of the Balkan Wars* (Cambridge, Mass., 1938), p. 150.
25. Pears, *Forty Years*, pp. 337, 341, 347.
26. Jäckh, *Rising Crescent*, pp. 10–24, prints the exchange of telegrams between Wangenheim and Berlin during the creation of the alliance.
27. Ibid., pp. 22, 23, 116–18. Hans Humann's father had been director of the Oriental Museum in Berlin, and did extensive archaeological work in Asia Minor, notably at Pergamum.
28. Grey to O'Beirne, 23 Oct. 1911; *BD*, xi. 313; G. Young, *Corps de Driot Ottoman* (Oxford, 1905–6); H. Howard, *The Partition of Turkey* (Norman, 1931), pp. 91–6; Grand Admiral von Tirpitz, *My Memoirs* (New York, 1919), ii. 82.
29. Howard, *Partition of Turkey*, pp. 96–102; Grey of Falloden, *Twenty Five Years* (New York, 1925), p. 172, writes: 'In war, however, diplomacy is the handmaid of the necessities of the war office and the admiralty, and Mallet had to do his best to satisfy both. . . . Nothing was asked of her [Turkey] . . . no help, no facilities for the allies, open or covert, nothing except that she should remain neutral.' The Sazonov proposal is not mentioned, and Grey had already assumed that the Ottomans would join the German side from the moment the *Goeben* passed the Straits. He says so. It could be argued that a foreign secretary who allows his department to become 'the handmaid' of the military departments before peace has ended is already mentally at war.

Bibliography

I. DOCUMENTS AND CORRESPONDENCE

ABERDEEN, GEORGE GORDON, EARL OF, *The Correspondence of Lord Aberdeen and Princess Lieven, 1832–54*, ed. E. Jones Parry (London, 1939).
ADAIR, ROBERT, *A Reply to the Charges of Robert Adair Esq. against the Bishop of Winchester, in Consequence of a Passage Contained in His Lordship's Memoirs of the Right Hon. W. Pitt* (London, 1821).
—, *Negotiations for the Peace of the Dardanelles in 1808–09, with Despatches and Official Documents* (2 vols., London, 1845).
—, *Two Letters . . . to the Bishop of Winchester, in Answer to the Charge of a Treasonable Misdemeanour Brought by His Lordship against Mr. Fox and Himself in His Life of . . . William Pitt* (London, 1821).
AUCKLAND, WILLIAM EDEN, BARON, *The Journals and Correspondence of William, Lord Auckland*, ed. G. Hogge (4 vols., London, 1860–62).
British Documents on the Origins of the War, eds G.P. Gooch and H.W.V. Temperley (11 vols., London, 1927).
British Intelligence of Events in Greece, 1824–1827: A Documentary Collection, ed. David Dakin (Athens, 1959).
BURGES, JAMES BLAND, *Selections from the Letters and Correspondence of James Bland Burges*, ed. J. Hutton (London, 1885).
BURKE, EDMUND, *A Letter . . . to His Grace the Duke of Portland, on the Conduct of the Minority in Parliament Containing Fifty-Four Articles of Impeachment against the Rt. Hon. C.J. Fox. From the Original Copy, in the Possession of the Notable Duke* (London, 1797).
—, *Correspondence of Edmund Burke*, ed. T.W. Copeland *et al.* (10 vols., Cambridge and Chicago, 1958–78).
—, *Works of the Right Hon. Edmund Burke* (8 vols., London, 1854–89).
BYRON, GEORGE GORDON, BARON, *Byron: A Self Portrait. Letters and Diaries, 1798–1824*, ed. Peter Quennell (2 vols., London, 1950).
—, *Lord Byron: Selected Letters and Journals*, ed. Leslie A. Marchand (Cambridge, Mass., 1982).
—, *Lord Byron's Correspondence, Chiefly with Lady Melbourne, Mr. Hobhouse, the Hon. Douglas Kinnaird, and P.B. Shelley*, ed. John Murray (2 vols., London, 1922).

—, *The Works of Lord Byron: Letters and Journals*, ed. R.E. Prothero (6 vols., London, 1898–1901).
CANNING, GEORGE, *Some Official Correspondence of George Canning*, ed. E.J. Stapleton (2 vols., London, 1887).
—, *George Canning and His Friends*, ed. Josceline Bagot (2 vols., New York, 1909).
CASTLEREAGH, VISCOUNT, *Memoranda and Correspondence of Robert Stewart, Viscount Castlereagh*, ed. marquis of Londonderry (12 vols., London, 1848–54).
CHATHAM, WILLIAM PITT, EARL OF, *Correspondence of William Pitt, Earl of Chatham*, eds W.S. Taylor and J.H. Pringle (4 vols., London, 1838–40).
COLLINGWOOD, CUTHBERT, BARON, *The Private Correspondence of Admiral Lord Collingwood*, ed. E. Hughes (London, 1957).
Corps de Droit Ottoman, ed. G. Young (7 vols., Oxford, 1905–6).
Diplomacy in the Near and Middle East: A Documentary Record, ed. J.C. Hurewitz (2 vols., Princeton, 1956).
ELLENBOROUGH, EDWARD LAW, EARL OF, *A Political Diary, 1828–1830*, ed. Lord Colchester (2 vols., London, 1881).
European Diplomatic History, 1815–1914: Documents and Interpretations, ed. H.N. Weill (New York, 1972).
FOX, CHARLES JAMES, *Memorials and Correspondence of Charles James Fox*, ed. Lord John Russell (4 vols., London, 1853–57).
GENTZ, FRIEDRICH VON, *Briefe von und an F. von Gentz*, ed. C. Wittichen (3 vols., Berlin, 1909).
—, *Zur Geschichte der Orientalischen Frage, 1823–1829* (Vienna, 1877).
GEORGE III, *The Later Correspondence of George III*, ed. A. Aspinall (5 vols., Cambridge, 1963–70).
Geschichte des Abfalls der Greichen vom Turkischen Reiche, ed. Baron A.F. Prokesch von Osten (6 vols., Vienna, 1867).
GLADSTONE, WILLIAM EWART, *The Gladstone Diaries*, ed. M.R.D. Foot and H.C.C. Matthew (9 vols., Oxford, 1968–).
GRANVILLE, GRANVILLE LEVESON-GOWER, EARL, *Lord Granville Leveson-Gower: Private Correspondence, 1781–1821*, ed. Castalia, Countess Granville (2 vols., London, 1916).
GREVILLE, CHARLES, *The Charles Greville Diary*, ed. Philip W. Wilson (2 vols., London, 1927).
HISTORICAL MANUSCRIPTS COMMISSION: *Manuscripts of J.B. Fortescue Esq., Preserved at Dropmore* (10 vols., London, 1892–1927).
LEEDS, FRANCIS GODOLPHIN OSBORNE, DUKE OF, Royal Historical Society: *Political Memoirs of Francis, 5th Duke of Leeds* (London, 1884).
MALMESBURY, JAMES HARRIS, EARL OF, *Diaries and Correspondence of James Harris, First Earl of Malmesbury*, ed. earl of Malmesbury (4 vols., London, 1844).
MILES, WILLIAM AUGUSTUS, *Authentic Correspondence with M. Le Brun, the French Minister and Others, to Feb. 1793* (London, 1796).
MORRITT, JOHN B.S., *Letters of John B.S. Morritt of Rokeby, Descriptive of*

Bibliography 251

Journeys in Europe and Asia Minor in the Years 1794–1796, ed. C.E. Marindin (London, 1914).
MURRAY KEITH, SIR ROBERT, *Memoirs and Correspondence (Official and Familiar) of Sir Robert Murray Keith, K.B. Envoy Extraordinary and Minister Plenipotentiary at the Court of Dresden, Copenhagen and Vienna, From 1769 to 1792*, ed. Amelia Gillespie Smith (2 vols., London, 1849).
Parliamentary History of England from the Earliest Period, ed. W. Cobbett (36 vols., London, 1820).
Recueil d'actes internationaux de l'empire Ottoman, ed. Gabriel Noradounghian (4 vols., Paris, 1897–1903).
Recueil des Traités et Conventions conclus par la Russie avec les puissances étrangères, ed. Fedor F. de Martens (15 vols., St Petersburg, 1874–1909).
ROYAL HISTORICAL SOCIETY: *Despatches from Paris, 1784–1790*, ed. O. Browning (2 vols., London, 1909–10).
RUSSELL, LORD JOHN, *Early Correspondence of Lord John Russell, 1805–40* ed. Rollo Russell (2 vols., London, 1913).
—, *The Later Correspondence of Lord John Russell, 1840–1878*, ed. G.P. Gooch (2 vols., London, 1925).
SPENCER, GEORGE, EARL, Navy Records Society: *Private Papers of George, Second Earl Spencer, First Lord of the Admiralty 1794–1801*, eds J. Corbett and H.W. Richmond (4 vols., London, 1913–24).
STANHOPE, LEICESTER FITZGERALD CHARLES, EARL, *Greece in 1823 and 1824; Being a Series of Letters and Other Documents on the Greek Revolution, Written during a Visit to That Country. To Which Is Added the Life of Mustapha Ali* (London, 1824).
—, *Greece in 1823 and 1824 . . . A New Edition, Containing Numerous Supplementary Papers, Illustrative of the State of Greece in 1825 . . . To which Are Added Reminiscences of Lord Byron* (London, 1825).
STANLEY, EDWARD, DEAN, *The Letters of Dean Stanley*, eds R.E. Prothero and E.G. Bailey (2 vols., London, 1893).
SUTTON, ROBERT, *The Despatches of Robert Sutton*, ed. Adkes Nimet Kurat (London, 1957).
THOUVENEL, EDOUARD, BARON, *Nicholas Ier et Napoléon III: les préliminaires de la guerre de Crimée (1852–1854) d'àpres les papiers inédites de M. Thouvenel*, ed. Louis Thouvenel (Paris, 1891).
VICTORIA, *The Letters of Queen Victoria, 1837–61*, first series, eds A.C. Benson and Viscount Esher (3 vols., London, 1907).
Vostochnaya Voyna 1853–56 q v Sviazi s Souremennoi ei Poilticheskoi Obstanovkoi, ed. A.M. Zaionchkovski (2 vols., St Petersburg, 1908–13).
WELLESLEY, RICHARD, MARQUIS, *The Wellesley Papers*, ed. L.S. Benjamin (2 vols., London, 1914).
WELLINGTON, ARTHUR WELLESLEY, DUKE OF, *Despatches, Correspondence, and Memoranda of Field Marshal Arthur, Duke of Wellington*, ed. duke of Wellington (8 vols., London, 1867–78).
—, *Supplementary Despatches and Memoranda of Field-Marshal Arthur Duke of Wellington*, ed. duke of Wellington (15 vols., London, 1858–72).

WOOD, RICHARD, Royal Historical Society: *Early Correspondence of Richard Wood*, ed. Allan Cunningham (London, 1966).

II. MEMOIRS, TRAVELLERS' TALES, AND CONTEMPORARY WORKS

ARGYLL, GEORGE DOUGLAS, DUKE OF, *George Douglas, Eighth Duke of Argyll, Autobiography and Memoirs*, ed. duchess of Argyll (2 vols., London, 1906).
BALDWIN, GEORGE, *Political Recollections Relative to Egypt* (London, 1801).
BARKER, JOHN, *Syria and Egypt under the Last Five Sultans of Turkey: Being Experiences during Fifty Years of Mr. Consul-General Barker*, ed. E.B.B. Barker (London, 1876).
BEAUJOUR, LOUIS AUGUSTE FÉLIX DE, *A View of the Commerce of Greece, Formed after an Annual Average, from 1787–1797*, trans. Thomas Hartwell Horne (London, 1800).
BESSIÈRES, J., *Mémoire sur la vie et la puissance d'Ali Pacha* (Paris, 1820).
BLACKSTONE, SIR WILLIAM, *Commentaries on the Laws of England* (4 vols., London, 1783).
BLAQUIÈRE, EDWARD, *The Greek Revolution; Its Origin and Progess: together with Some Remarks on the Religion, National Character, &c. in Greece* (London, 1824).
BROUGHTON, JOHN CAM HOBHOUSE, FIRST BARON, *A Journey through Armenia and . . . Turkey in Europe and Asia to Constantinople during the Years 1809 and 1810* (2 vols., London, 1813).
—, *Recollections of a Long Life*, ed. Lady Dorchester (6 vols., London, 1909–11).
BULARD, ARSENE FRANÇOIS, *De la peste orientale d'après les matériaux recueillis à Alexandrie, au Cairo, à Smyrne et à Constantinople, pendant les années 1833, 1834, 1835, 1836, 1837 et 1838* (Paris, 1839).
BURNABY, FREDERICK GUSTAVUS, *On Horseback through Asia Minor* (2 vols., London, 1877).
BUSBECQ, AUGIERIUS GHISLAIN DE, *A.G. Busbequii . . . Legationis Turcicae Epistolae quatuor. Quarum priores duae . . . in lucem prodierunt sub nomine Itinerum Constantinopolitani et Amasiani. Adjectae sunt duae alterae. Ejusdem de re militari contra Turcam instituenda consilium* (Paris, 1589).
—, *Life and Letters of Ogier Ghislain de Busbecq*, eds. C.T. Forster and F.H. Blackburne Daniell (English trans., 2 vols., London, 1881).
CHALCONDYLAS, LAONICUS, *Laonici Chalcondylae . . . De Origine et rebus gestis Turcorum libri decem, nuper è Graeco in Latinum conuersi: Conrado Clausero . . . interprete . . . Adiecimus Theodori Gazae, & aliorum . . . eiusdem argumenti, de rebus Turcorum aduersus Christianos, & Christianorum contra illos . . . gestis di uersa opuscula, etc.* ed. J. Heroldt (Basel, 1556).
—, *L'Histoire de la décadence de l'Empire grec, et établissement de celuy des Turcs* (French trans., Paris, 1584).
CHATEAUBRIAND, FRANÇOIS RENÉ DE, VISCOUNT, *Travels in Greece,*

Bibliography 253

Palestine, Egypt, and Barbary, during the Years 1806 and 1807, trans. Frederic Shoberl (2 vols., London, 1811).
CHATFIELD, ROBERT, *An Appeal to the British Public, in the Cause of the Persecuted Greeks, etc.* (London, 1822).
—, *A Further Appeal to the British Public, in the Cause of the Persecuted Greeks* (London, 1823).
CHAUMETTE DES FOSSÉS, JEAN BAPTISTE GABRIEL AMEDÉE, *Voyage en Bosnie dans les années 1807 et 1808* (Berlin, 1812).
CLARKE, EDWARD DANIEL, *Travels in Various Countries of Europe, Asia, and Africa* (6 vols., London, 1810–1816).
COCKBURN, HENRY, *Memorials of His Time* (Edinburgh, 1856).
COLSON, FÉLIX, *De l'état présent et de l'avenir des principautés de Moldavie et de Valachie; suivi des traités de la Turquie avec les Puissances européennes, et d'une carte des Pays Roumains* (Paris, 1839).
CURZON, ROBERT, *Visits to Monasteries in the Levant* (5th ed., London, 1865).
DE KAY, JAMES ELLSWORTH, *Sketches of Turkey in 1831 and 1832* (New York, 1833).
DEMIAN, J.A., *Statistiche Beschreibung der Militär-Grenze* (Vienna, 1806).
DRAGASANU, I.C., *Peregrinual Transilvan* (Bucharest, 1842).
ELLIOT, SIR HENRY GEORGE, *Some Revolutions and Other Diplomatic Experiences* (London, 1922).
ERSKINE, THOMAS, LORD, *An Appeal to the People of Great Britain on the Subject of Confederated Greece* (London, 1824).
ETON, WILLIAM, *A Survey of the Turkish Empire* (London, 1799).
FRASER, JAMES BAILLIE, *A Winter's Journey from Constantinople to Teheran, with Travels through Various Parts of Persia* (2 vols., London, 1838).
GALT, JOHN, *Letters from the Levant* (London, 1813).
GARDANE, PAUL ANGE LOUIS DE, *Journal d'un voyage dans la Turquie d'Asie et la Perse, fait en 1807 et 1808* (Paris, 1809).
GREEN, P.J., *Sketches of the War in Greece* (London, 1826).
GREY, EDWARD, FIRST VISCOUNT GREY OF FALLODEN, *Twenty Five Years* (New York, 1925).
HAMMER-PURGSTALL, JOSEPH VON, BARON, *Geschichte des Osmanischen Reiches* (10 vols., Pest [Vienna], 1827–35).
HERTSLET, EDWARD, *Recollections of the Old Foreign Office* (London, 1901).
HOGARTH, DAVID GEORGE, *A Wandering Scholar in the Levant* (London, 1896).
HOLLAND, HENRY, *Travels in the Ionian Islands, Albania . . . during the years 1812 and 1813* (London, 1815).
HUGHES, THOMAS SMART, *An Address to the People of England in the Cause of the Greeks, Occasioned by the Late Inhuman Massacres in the Isle of Scio* (London, 1822).
—, *Considerations upon the Greek Revolution with a Vindication of the Author's 'Address to the People of England', from the Attacks of Mr. C.B. Sheridan* (London, 1823).

ISMAIL KEMAL BEY, *Memoirs of Ismail Kemal Bey*, ed. S. Story (London, 1920).
KENNEDY, JAMES, *Conversations on Religion, with Lord Byron and Others, Held in Cephalonia, a Short Time Previous to His Lordship's Death* (London, 1830).
KINGLAKE, ALEXANDER WILLIAM, *Eothen*, ed. H. Gorvett-Smith (London and Toronto, 1927).
KNOLLES, RICHARD, *The Generall Historie of the Turkes, from the First Beginning of That Nation to the Rising of the Otheman Familie . . . Together with the Lives and Conquests of the Otheman Kings and Emperours unto the Yeare 1610* (2nd ed., London, 1610); revised by Paul Rycaut (6th ed., 2 vols., London, 1687–1700).
LAYARD, AUSTEN HENRY, *Early Adventures in Persia, Susiana, and Babylonia, Including a Residence among the Bakhtiyari and Other Wild Tribes before the Discovery of Nineveh* (2 vols., London, 1887).
LEAKE, WILLIAM MARTIN, *Travels in the Morea* (3 vols., London, 1830).
LEYBLICK, BADIA Y, *Travels of Ali Bey* (London, 1816).
MACFARLANE, CHARLES, *Constantinople in 1828: A Residence of Sixteen Months in the Turkish Capital and Provinces, with an Account of the Present State of the Naval and Military Power, and of the Resources of the Ottoman Empire* (London, 1829).
—, *Turkey and Its Destiny: The Result of Journeys Made in 1847 and 1848 to Examine into the State of That Country* (2 vols., London, 1850).
MALMESBURY, JAMES HARRIS, EARL OF, *Memoirs of an ex-Minister: An Autobiography* (2 vols., London, 1884).
MCCULLOCH, JOHN RAMSAY, *A Dictionary, Practical, Theoretical and Historical of Commerce and Commercial Navigation* (London, 1832–39).
METTERNICH, CLEMENS WENZEL VON METTERNICH-WINNENBERG, PRINCE, *Memoirs of Prince Metternich, 1815–1829*, ed. Prince Richard Metternich, trans. Mrs. Alexander Napier (8 vols., London, 1881).
MILES, WILLIAM AUGUSTUS, *The Conduct of France towards Great Britain Examined* (London, 1793).
MILLINGEN, JULIUS, *Memoirs of the Affairs of Greece, . . . with . . . Anecdotes Relating to Lord Byron, and an Account of His Last Illness and Death* (London, 1831).
MONRO, V., *Summer Ramble in Syria, with a Tartar Trip from Aleppo to Stamboul* (2 vols., London, 1835).
MOURADJA D'OHSSON, IGNACE DE, *Tableau géneral de l'Empire Othoman, divisé en deux parties, dont l'une comprend la Législation Mohométane, l'autre l'histoire de l'Empire Othoman* (7 vols., Paris, 1788–1824).
OLIVIER, GUILLAUME ANTOINE, *Voyage dans l'empire Othomane, l'Egypt, et la Perse* (3 vols., Paris, 1801–7).
PARRY, WILLIAM, *The Last Days of Lord Byron; with His Lordship's Opinions on Various Subjects, Particularly on the State and Prospects of Greece* (London, 1825).
PEARS, SIR EDWIN, *Forty Years in Constantinople: The Recollections of Sir*

Edwin Pears, 1873–1915 (London, 1916).
PERTUSIER, CHARLES, *La Bosnie considérée dans ses rapports avec l'Empire Ottoman* (Paris, 1822).
PITTON DE TOURNEFORT, JOSEPH, *Rélation d'un Voyage du Levant . . . contenant l'histoire ancienne et moderne de plusieurs îsles de l'Archipel, de Constantinople, des côtes de la Mer Noire, de l'Arménie, de la Georgie, des frontières de Perse et de l'Asie mineure, etc.* (2 vols., Paris, 1717).
POUJADE, EUGENE, *Chrétiens et Turcs.: Scènes et Souvenirs de la vie politique, militaire et religieuse en Orient* (Paris, 1859).
POUQUEVILLE, FRANÇOIS CHARLES HUGHES LAURENT, *Voyage en Morée à Constantinople, en Albanie, et dans plusiers autres parties de l'Empire Othoman, pendant les années 1798–1801, enrichi d'un précis historique et géographique sur l'ancienne Empire, et de cartes dressées par M. Barbié de Bocage, etc.* (3 vols., Paris, 1805).
REDCLIFFE, STRATFORD CANNING, VISCOUNT STRATFORD DE, *The Eastern Question* (London, 1881).
RYCAUT, SIR PAUL, *The History of the Turkish Empire, from the Year 1623, to the Year 1677, Containing the Reigns of the Three Last Emperors . . .* (London, 1687).
SLADE, ADOLPHUS, *Records of Travels in Turkey, Greece &c., and of a Cruise in the Black Sea, with the Captain Pasha, in the Years 1829, 1830 and 1831* (2 vols., London, 1833).
STAPLETON, AUGUSTUS GRANVILLE, *The Political Life of the Right Honourable G. Canning . . . from Sept 1822, to His Death . . . Together with a Review of Foreign Affairs Subsequently to That Event* (3 vols., London, 1831).
THORNTON, THOMAS, *The Present State of Turkey* (2nd ed., 2 vols., London, 1809).
TIRPITZ, ALFRED PETER FRIEDRICH VON, *My Memoirs* (2 vols., London, 1919).
TOMLINE, G., *Memoirs of the Life of William Pitt* (2 vols., London, 1821).
TOTT, FRANÇOIS, BARON DE, *Mémoires sur les Turcs* (3 vols., Amsterdam, n.d.).
—, *Memoirs of Baron de Tott. Containing the State of the Turkish Empire and the Crimea, during the Late War with Russia. Trans. from the French* (London, 1785).
TOWNSHEND, ARTHUR FITZHENRY, *A Military Consul in Turkey: The Experiences and Impressions of a British Representative in Asia Minor* (London, 1910).
TRELAWNY, EDWARD JOHN, *Recollections of the Last Days of Shelley and Byron* (London, 1858).
UBICINI, ABDOLONYME, *Letters on Turkey*, trans. by Lady Easthope (2 vols., London, 1856).
URQUHART, DAVID, *The Spirit of the East, Illustrated in a Journal of Travels through Roumelia during an Eventful Period* (2 vols., London, 1838).
—, *Turkey and Its Resources* (London, 1833).

VILLÈLE, JEAN BAPTISTE, DE, COUNT, *Mémoires* (5 vols., Paris, 1880).
VITZTHUM VON ECKSTAEDT, CARL FRIEDRICH, *St. Petersburgh and London, the Reminiscences of Count Charles Vitzthum*, ed. Henry Reeves (London, 1887).
VOLNEY, CONSTANTIN FRANÇOIS DE, COUNT, *Travels through Syria and Egypt in 1783, 1784 and 1785* . . . Trans. from the French (2 vols., London, 1787).
WALSH, ROBERT, *A Residence at Constantinople, during . . . the Commencement, Progress, and Termination of the Greek and Turkish Revolutions* (2 vols., London, 1836).
WILKINSON, JOHN GARDNER, *Dalmatia and Montenegro: With a Journey to Mostar in Herzegovina, and Remarks on the Slavonic Nations: The History of Dalmatia and Ragusa, the Uscocs, etc.* (2 vols., London, 1848).
WILKINSON, WILLIAM, *An Account of the Principalities of Wallachia and Moldavia: with . . . Political Observations Relating to Them* (London, 1820).
WITTMAN, WILLIAM, *Travels in Turkey, Asia-Minor, Syria and . . . into Egypt during the Years 1799, 1800, and 1801* (London, 1803).
WRAXELL, SIR N.W., *The Historical and Posthumous Memoirs of Sir Nathaniel William Wraxall, 1772–1784*, ed. H.B. Wheatley (5 vols., London, 1884).

III. MONOGRAPHS AND GENERAL WORKS

ANDERSON, M.S., *Britain's Discovery of Russia, 1553–1815* (London, 1958).
—, *The Eastern Question, 1774–1923: A Study in International Relations* (London, 1966).
ANTLASMASI, EDIRNE, *Dilve Tarih-Cografiva Fakultesi Dergisi*: IX (Ankara, 1951).
ASHLEY, EVELYN, *The Life of Henry John Temple, Viscount Palmerston* (2 vols., London, 1876).
BALFOUR, LADY BETTY, *Life of George, Fourth Earl of Aberdeen* (London, 1922).
BEESLEY, E.S., 'The Turkish Revolution', *The Positivist Review*, xvi (1908).
BERKES, NIYAZI, *The Development of Secularism in Turkey* (Montreal, 1964).
BLAISDELL, D.C., *European Financial Control in the Ottoman Empire: A Study of the Establishment, Activities, and Significance of the Administration of the Ottoman Public Debt* (New York, 1929).
BOLSOVER, G.H., 'David Urquhart and the Eastern Question in 1833–1837', *Journal of Modern History*, viii (1936).
—, 'Lord Ponsonby and the Eastern Question (1833–1839)', *Slavonic Review*, xiii (1934–35).
BOPPE, A., *L'Albanie et Napoléon, 1797–1814* (Paris, 1914).
—, *La Mission de l'Adjutant-commandant Mériage à Vidin* (Paris, 1886).

BROWN, W.C., 'Byron and English Interest in the Near East', *Studies in Philology*, xxxiv (1937).
—, 'The Popularity of English Travel Books about the Near East, 1775–1828', *Philological Quarterly*, xv (1936); xvi (1937).
BUCKLE, HENRY THOMAS, *The History of Civilization in England* (2 vols., London, 1857).
BUXTON, CHARLES R., *Turkey in Revolution . . . With 33 illustrations and a Map* (London, 1909).
Cambridge History of British Foreign Policy, 1783–1919, The, eds A.W. Ward and G.P. Gooch (3 vols, New York, 1922–23).
Cambridge Modern History, The, eds A.W. Ward, G.W. Prothero, and Stanley Leathes (14 vols., London, 1902–12).
CIRCOURT, A., COUNT, *Histoire de l'Action commune de la France et de l'Amérique pour l'indépendance des Etats-Unis . . . traduit et annoté par le comte A. de Circourt* (3 vols., Paris, 1876).
CLARKE, EDWARD C., 'The Ottoman Industrial Revolution', *International Journal of Middle East Studies*, i (1974).
CLOGG, RICHARD, ed., *The Struggle for Greek Independence: Essays to Mark the 150th Anniversary of the Greek War of Independence* (London, 1973).
COCKBURN, HENRY, *Life of Lord Jeffrey* (2 vols., London, 1852).
CONAN, L., *From Granpa's Tea Chest* (London, 1951).
CRAWLEY, C.W., 'John Capodistrias and the Greeks before 1821', *Cambridge Historical Journal*, xiii (1957).
—, *The Question of Greek Independence: A Study of British Policy in the Near East, 1821–1833* (Cambridge, 1930).
CUNNINGHAM, ALLAN, 'The Levant Trade in 1912: The Journal of Christophe Aubin', *Archivum Ottomanicum*, viii (1988).
DAKIN, DOUGLAS, *British and American Philhellenes during the War of Greek Independence, 1821–1833* (Thessalonika, 1955).
—, *The Greek Struggle for Independence, 1821–1833* (London, 1973).
DANIEL, N., *Islam, Europe, and Empire* (Edinburgh, 1966).
DE BEER, E.S., AND WALTER SETON, 'Byroniana: The Archives of the London Greek Committee', *Nineteenth Century*, c (1926).
DILLON, E.J., 'The Unforeseen Happens as Usual', *Contemporary Review*, xciv (1908).
DOUIN, GEORGES, *Navarin* (Cairo, 1927).
EARLE, E.M., *Turkey, the Great Powers, and the Baghdad Railway: A Study in Imperialism* (London, 1923).
ELLIOT, HENRY GEORGE, 'The Death of Abdul Aziz and of Turkish Reform', *Nineteenth Century*, xxiii (1888).
EMBREE, A.T., *Charles Grant and British Rule in India* (New York, 1962).
EMIN, AHMED, *The Development of Modern Turkey as Measured by its Press* (New York, 1968).
FILITTI, J.C., 'Notice sur les Vogoridi', *Revue histoire du Sud-Est Europe*, vi (1927).
FINLAY, G., *A History of Greece from Its Conquest by the Romans to the Present*

Time, B.C. 146 to A.D. 1864, ed. H.R. Tozer (7 vols., Oxford, 1877–1971).
FONBLANQUE, E. BARRINGTON DE, *Lives of the Lords Strangford* (London, 1877).
GERCEK, S.N., *Turk Gazeteciligi, 1831–1931* (Istanbul, 1931).
GIBB, HAMILTON ALEXANDER AND HAROLD BOWEN, *Islamic Society and the West: A Study of the Impact of Western Civilization on Moslem Culture in the Near East* (London, 1950).
GOULD, A.G., 'Lords or Bandits? The Derebeys of Cilicia', *International Journal of Middle East Studies*, vi (1976).
HALPERN, JOEL MARTIN, *A Serbian Village* (New York, 1958).
HELMREICH, E.C., *The Diplomacy of the Balkan Wars, 1912–1913* (Cambridge, Mass., 1938).
HENDERSON, GAVIN B., *Crimean War Diplomacy and Other Historical Essays* (Glasgow, 1947).
HOBSBAWM, ERIC J., *Primitive Rebels: Studies in Archaic Forms of Social Movement in the 19th and 20th Centuries* (Manchester, 1959).
HORN, D.B., 'The Diplomatic Experience of the Secretaries of State, 1660–1852', *History*, xli (1956).
HOSKINS, H.L., *British Routes to India* (London, 1928).
HOWARD, H.E., *The Partition of Turkey: A Diplomatic History, 1913–1923* (Norman, 1931).
—, 'Brunnov's Reports on Aberdeen, 1842', *Cambridge Historical Journal*, iv (1932–34).
HUREWITZ, J.C., 'Ottoman Diplomacy and the European State System', *Middle East Journal*, xv (1961).
ISSAWI, CHARLES P., *Economic History of the Middle East, 1800–1914: A Book of Readings* (Chicago, 1966).
ITZKOWITZ, NORMAN, *Ottoman Empire and Islamic Tradition* (New York, 1972).
JÄCKH, E., *The Rising Crescent* (New York, 1944).
JONES-PARRY, E., 'Under-Secretaries of State for Foreign Affairs, 1782–1855', *English Historical Review*, xlix (1934).
KALDIS, WILLIAM P., *John Capodistrias and the Modern Greek State* (Madison, Wisc., 1963).
KARAL, ENVER ZIAYA, 'Ebu Bekir Ratib Efendi'nin "Nizam-i Cedit" Islahatinda Rolu', *Turk Tarih Kongresi, Ankara 12–17 Nisan 1956: Kongreye sunulan tebligler* (Ankara, 1960).
—, *Halet Efendinin Paris Büyük Elciligi* (Constantinople, 1940).
—, *Osmanli Interatorlugunda ilk nufus sayimi* (Ankara, 1943).
KARPAT, KEMAL, ed., *The Ottoman State and Its Place in World History* (Leiden, 1974).
KERNER, R.J., 'Russia's New Policy in the Near East after the Peace of Adrianople', *Cambridge History Journal*, v (1937).
KINGLAKE, ALEXANDER W., *The Invasion of the Crimea: Its Origin and Account of its Progress down to the Death of Lord Raglan* (8 vols., London,

1863).
KISSINGER, HENRY A., *A World Restored: Metternich, Castlereagh, and the Problems of Peace, 1812–1822* (Boston, 1957).
KNIGHT, GEORGE WILSON, *Lord Byron's Marriage: The Evidence of Asterisks* (London, 1957).
LAGARDE, L., 'Note sur les journaux français de Constantinople à l'époque révolutionnaire', *Journal Asiatique*, ccxxxvi (1948).
LANE-POOLE, STANLEY, *Life of the Right Honourable Stratford Canning, Viscount Stratford de Redcliffe* (2 vols., London, 1888).
LECKY, WILLIAM EDWARD HARTPOLE, *A History of England in the Eighteenth Century* (8 vols., London, 1878–90).
LEON, G.B., *Greek Merchant Marine* (Athens, 1972).
LEWIS, BERNARD, *The Emergence of Modern Turkey* (London, 1961).
—, 'The Impact of the French Revolution on Turkey', in *The New Asia: Readings in the History of Mankind*, eds G.S. Métraux and F. Crouzet (London, 1965).
LUKE, HARRY CHARLES, *The Making of Modern Turkey: The Old Turkey and the New: From Byzantium to Ankara* (London, 1955).
LYBYER, ALBERT HOWE, *The Government of the Ottoman Empire in the Time of Suleiman the Magnificent* (Cambridge, Mass., 1913).
MARCHAND, L.A., *Byron: A Biography* (London, 1957).
MARRIOTT, JOHN ARTHUR RANSOME, *The Eastern Question: An Historical Study in European Diplomacy* (4th ed., Oxford, 1940).
MARTIN, KINGSLEY, *The Triumph of Lord Palmerston: A Study in Political Opinion in England before the Crimean War* (London, 1924).
MARTIN, THEODORE, *The Life of His Royal Highness the Prince Consort* (5 vols., London, 1875–80).
MATHESON, CYRIL, *The Life of Henry Dundas, First Viscount Melville, 1742–1811* (London, 1933).
MAUROIS, ANDRÉ, *Byron* (2 vols., Paris, 1930).
MAXWELL, HERBERT E., *The Life and Letters of George William Frederick, Fourth Earl of Clarendon* (2 vols., London, 1913).
MCCULLAGH, FRANÇOIS, *The Fall of Abd-ul-Hamid* (London, 1910).
MEADE, WILLIAM EDWARD, *The Grand Tour in the Eighteenth Century* (New York, 1914).
MEARS, E.G., *Modern Turkey: A Politico-Economic Interpretation, 1908–1923* (New York, 1924).
MEDLICOTT, W.N., 'Gladstone and the Turks', *History*, xiii (1928).
—, 'Lord Salisbury and Turkey', *History*, xii (1927).
MERRIMAN, ROGER BIGELOW, *Suleiman the Magnificent, 1520–1566* (Cambridge, Mass., 1944).
MOORE, DORIS L., *The Late Lord Byron: Posthumous Dramas* (Philadelphia, 1961).
MOORE, W.E., *The Impact of Industry* (Englewood Cliffs, N.J., 1965).
NAFF, THOMAS, 'Ottoman Diplomatic Relations with Europe in the Eighteenth Century: Patterns and Trends', in *Studies in Eighteenth Cen-*

tury Islamic History, ed. Thomas Naff and Roger Owen (Carbondale, 1977).
—, 'Reform and the Conduct of Ottoman Diplomacy in the Reign of Selim III, 1789–1807', Journal of the American Oriental Society, lxxxiii (1963).
NAPIER, WILLIAM FRANCIS PATRICK, The Life and Opinions of General Sir J. Napier (4 vols., London, 1857).
NELSON, RICHARD R., 'A Theory of the Low Level Equilibrium Trap in Underdeveloped Economies', American Economic Review, xlvi (1956).
NICHOLS, IRBY C., JR. The European Pentarchy and the Congress of Verona, 1822 (The Hague, 1971).
NICOLSON, HAROLD, Byron: The Last Journey, April 1823–April 1824 (London, 1924).
NURI, MUSTAFA, Netaie ul-Vukuat (4 vols., Istanbul, 1877–79, 1909–18).
PAPST, EDMOND, Les Origines de la guerre de Crimée: La France et la Russie de 1848 à 1854 (Paris, 1912).
PARKER, CHARLES STUART, Life and Letters of Sir James Graham, second baronet, of Netherby, P.C., G.C.B., 1792–1861 (2 vols., London, 1907).
PATON, ANDREW ARCHIBALD, Researches on the Danube and the Adriatic; Or, Contributions to the Modern History of Hungary and Transylvania, Dalmatia and Croatia, Servia and Bulgaria (2 vols., Leipzig, 1861).
PEARS, SIR EDWIN, Life of Abdul Hamid (London, 1917).
PENN, VIRGINIA, 'Philhellenism in England, 1821–27', Slavonic Review, xiv (1936).
PENZER, NORMAN MOSLEY, The Harem: An Account of the Institution as It Existed in the Palace of the Turkish Sultans with a History of the Grand Seraglio from Its Foundation to the Present Time (London, 1936).
PHILLIPSON, COLEMAN AND NOEL BUXTON, The Question of the Bosphorus and Dardanelles (London, 1917).
PISANI, P., La Dalmatie de 1797 à 1815: Episode des conquêtes napoléoniennes (Paris, 1893).
PURYEAR, V.J., England, Russia and the Straits Question, 1844–1856 (Berkeley/Los Angeles, 1931).
—, France and the Levant (from the Bourbon Restoration to the Peace of Kutayah) (Berkeley/Los Angeles, 1941).
—, Napoleon and the Dardanelles (Berkeley/Los Angeles, 1951).
RAMSAUR, ERNEST EDMONDSON, The Young Turks: Prelude to the Revolution of 1908 (Princeton, 1957).
REGLA, PAUL, Les Secrets d'Yildiz (Paris, 1897).
RICE, W.G., 'Early English Travellers in Greece and the Levant', Essays and Studies in English and Comparative Literature (London, 1933).
ROBERTS, M., The Whig Party (London, 1939).
ROBINSON, GERTRUDE, David Urquhart: Some Chapters in the Life of a Victorian Knight-Errant of Justice and Liberty (Oxford, 1920).
RODKEY, F.S., 'Lord Palmerston and the Rejuvenation of Turkey, 1830–1841', Journal of Modern History, i (1929); ii (1920).

Bibliography 261

—, 'The Attempts of Briggs and Co. to Guide British Policy in the Levant in the Interest of Mahomet Ali', *Journal of Modern History*, v (1933).
ROLO, PAUL JACQUES VICTOR, *George Canning: Three Biographical Studies* (London, 1965).
ROSE, JOHN HOLLAND, *William Pitt and National Revival* (London, 1911).
ROSEN, G., *Geschichte der Türkei* (Leipzig, 1866).
ROSTOVSKY, ANDREI LOBANOV, *Russia and Europe, 1789–1925* (Durham, N.C., 1947).
ROY, GILLES, *Abdul Hamid, le sultan rouge* (Paris, 1936).
RYAN, ANDREW, *The Last of the Dragomans* (London, 1951).
SAINT DENYS, A. DE JUCHEREAU, *Révolutions de Constantinople en 1807 et 1808* (2 vols., Paris, 1918).
SCHIEMANN, THEODOR, *Geschichte Russlands unter Kaiser Nikolaus* (4 vols., Berlin, 1904–19).
SCHLECHTA-WSSEHRD, OTTOKAR M. VON, *Die Revolutionen in Constantinopel in den Jahren 1807 und 1808* (Vienna, 1882).
SCHROEDER, PAUL W., *Metternich's Diplomacy at Its Zenith, 1820–1823* (Austin, Tex., 1962).
SETON-WATSON, R.W., *Britain in Europe, 1789–1914: A Survey of Foreign Policy* (Cambridge, 1937).
SHAW, STANFORD J., *Between Old and New: The Ottoman Empire under Selim III, 1789–1807* (Cambridge, Mass., 1971).
—, 'The Nineteenth-Century Ottoman Tax Reforms and Revenue System', *International Journal of Middle East Studies*, vi (1975).
—, *History of the Ottoman Empire and Modern Turkey* (2 vols., Cambridge, Mass., 1976).
SIMPSON, F.A., *Louis Napoleon and the Recovery of France, 1848–1856* (London, 1923).
SKOK, P., 'Le mouvement illyrien et les Français', *Le Monde slave*, xii (1935).
SOLOVEYTCHIK, GEORGE, *Potemkin: A Picture of Catherine's Russia* (London, 1949).
SOREL, ALBERT, *The Eastern Question in the Eighteenth Century: The Partition of Poland and the Treaty of Kainardji* (London, 1898).
SOUTHGATE, DONALD, *The Most English Minister: The Policies and Politics of Palmerston* (London, 1966).
SOUTSOS, NICHOLAS, *Notions Statistiques sur la Moldavie* (Jassy, 1849).
SPENCER, TERENCE JOHN, *Fair Greece, Sad Relic: Literary Philhellenism from Shakespeare to Byron* (London, 1954).
SPENDER, EDWARD HAROLD, *Byron and Greece* (London, 1924).
ST CLAIR, WILLIAM, *That Greece Might Still Be Free: The Philhellenes in the War of Independence* (London, 1972).
STANMORE, SIR ARTHUR GORDON, LORD, *The Earl of Aberdeen* (New York, 1893).
STAPLETON, AUGUSTUS GRANVILLE, *George Canning and His Times* (London, 1859).

STAVRIANOS, L. S., *The Balkans since 1453* (New York, 1965).
—, 'The Balkan Committee', *Queen's Quarterly*, xlviii (1941).
STERN, BERNARD HERBERT, *The Rise of Romantic Hellenism in English Literature, 1732–1786* (Menasha, 1940).
STOIANOVICH, TRAIAN, 'The Conquering Balkan Orthodox Merchant', *Journal of Economic History*, xx (1960).
STOWE, HARRIET BEECHER, *Lady Byron Vindicated: A History of the Byron Controversy, from Its Beginning in 1816 to the Present Time* (Boston, 1870).
SVORONOS, N., *Le Commerce de Salonique au XVIIIe siècle* (Paris, 1956).
TANPINAR, A. H., *XIX Asir Türk Edebiyati Tarihi* (Constantinople, 1956).
TEMPERLEY, H. W. V., *England and the Near East: The Crimea* (London, 1936).
—, *The Foreign Policy of Canning, 1822–1827* (London, 1925).
—, 'Princess Lieven and the Protocol of 4 April 1826', *English Historical Review*, xxxix (1924).
—, 'Stratford de Redcliffe and the Origins of the Crimean War', Parts I and II, *English Historical Review*, xlviii, (1933); xlix (1934).
—, 'Joan Canning on Her Husband's Policy and Ideas', *English Historical Review*, xlv (1930).
—, AND LILLIAN M. PENSON, *The Foundations of British Foreign Policy from Pitt to Salisbury* (London, 1938).
THOMAS, M. A., *The Secretaries of State, 1681–1782* (Oxford, 1932).
TRICOUPI, SPIRIDION, *Histoire de la Révolution Grecque* (Paris, 1862).
UZUNÇARSILI, ISMAIL HAKKI, *Meshur Rumeli Ayanindan Tirsinikli Ismail, Yilik Oglu Süleyman Agalar ve Alemdar Mustafa Pasa [The Famous Rumelia Notables: Tirsinikli Ismail and Yilik Oglu Süleyman Agas and Alemdar Mustafa Pasa]* (Istanbul, 1942).
VALETAS, G., *Korais* (Athens, 1965).
VAMBÉRY, A., 'Europe and the Turkish Constitution: An Independent View', *Nineteenth Century*, lxiv (1908).
—, 'Personal Recollections of Abdul Hamid and His Court', *Nineteenth Century*, lxvi (1909).
VERETÉ, M., 'Palmerston and the Levant Crisis, 1832', *Journal of Modern History*, xxiv (1952).
VUCINICH, W., *The Ottoman Empire: Its Record and Legacy* (Princeton, 1965).
WALKER, FRANKLIN A., 'The Rejection of Stratford Canning by Nicholas I', *Bulletin of the Institute of Historical Research*, xl (1967).
WALPOLE, SPENCER, *The Life of Lord John Russell* (2 vols., London, 1889).
WARRINER, DOREEN, ed., *Contrasts in Emerging Societies: Readings in the Social and Economic History of South-Eastern Europe in the Nineteenth Century* (London, 1965).
WATERFIELD, GORDON, *Layard of Nineveh* (London, 1963).
WAUGH, T., *Turkey, Yesterday, Today and Tomorrow* (London, 1930).
WEBB, PAUL C., 'The Royal Navy in the Ochakov Affair of 1791', *International History Review*, ii (1980).

WEBER, SHIRLEY HOWARD, *Voyages and Travels Made in the Near East during the XIX century. Being part of a larger catalogue of works on geography, cartography, voyages and travels, in the Gennadius Library in Athens* (Princeton, N.J., 1952).
WEBSTER, CHARLES K., *The Foreign Policy of Castlereagh, 1815–1822* (2 vols., London, 1925–31).
—, *The Foreign Policy of Palmerston 1830–41* (2 vols., London, 1951).
—, 'Urquhart, Ponsonby and Palmerston', *English Historical Review*, lxii (1947).
WELCH, C.E., ed., *Political Modernization: A Reader in Comparative Political Change* (Belmont, Cal., 1967).
WITTLIN, ALMA STEPHANIE, *Abdul Hamid, the Shadow of God* (London, 1940).
WOOD, ALFRED C., *A History of the Levant Company* (London, 1935).
—, 'The English Embassy at Constantinople, 1660–1762', *English Historical Review*, xl (1925).
WOODHOUSE, C.M., *The Battle of Navarino* (London, 1965).
—, *Capodistria, the Founder of Greek Independence* (London, 1973).
—, *The Philhellenes* (London, 1969).
YASA, IBRAHIM, *Studies in Turkish Local Government* (Ankara, 1955).
ZALLONY, M.P., *Essai sur les Fanariotes; suivi de quelques reflexions sur l'état actuel de la Grèce* (Marseilles, 1924).
ZIMMERMAN, CARLE C. AND RICHARD E. DU WORS, eds, *Sociology of Underdevelopment* (Calgary, 1970).

Index

(Arrangement of material within entries is predominantly chronological though some material of a topical nature is alphabetically ordered.)

Note: Stratford Canning, 1st viscount Stratford de Redcliffe, is abbreviated to SC.

Abdulaziz, Sultan 228
Abdulhamid II, Sultan 41, 226–7, 228, 229–30, 232, 235–6, 238
Abdulmejid II, Sultan 74, 120, 198, 203; and Menshikov 150, 153, 171–3
Aberdeen, 4th earl of (George Hamilton Gordon): and Russian march on Adrianople 27–8, 188; and Greece 28; on Ottoman survival 75, 231; memorandum with tsar (1844) 125, 132–4, 183; and SC 111–12, 122, 125; and tsar's talks with Seymour 134, 135, 136; attitude to Ottomans 138, 181; and Brunnov 139, 146, 148, 149, 183–4, 184–5, 187; reappoints SC to Constantinople 141, 142, 144; policy to Austria 145; and naval support to Ottomans 145–6, 148, 173; and press 182, 188; and Menshikov's mission 148, 149, 183–4, 184–5, 186, 187; and dispatch of fleet 191, 192, 193, 194; domestic record 211; and parliamentary debate (Aug. 1853) 213, 214; and Vienna Note 210, 214–15
Acarnania 29, 30, 35, 47, 49
Acre 25, 42–3, 46, 90
Adair, Sir Robert 6, 7
Adana; massacre of Armenians 238
administration, Ottoman 114, 116
Adrianople: Russian attack on 25, 26–7; treaty of 29–30, 45, 112, 115, 188
Aehrenthal, Count Alouis 237
agriculture, Ottoman 78, 83–7
Ahmed Vefik 122
Ainslie, Sir Robert 3, 4
Akif (*reis effendi*) 118
Albania 32, 79, 82; troops in Ottoman army 33, 58, 204
Albemarle, 6th earl of (George Keppel) 212
Aleppo 82, 84, 91, 92, 93
Alexander, prince of Bulgaria 231
Alexandretta, gulf of 89–90
Alexandria 91; patriarchate 152

Ali Bey 81
Ali Pasha 109, 122, 125–6, 166, 199, 226
Ali Pasha of Janina 82, 89, 91
Alishan (dragoman) 19
Alison, Charles 14–15, 147, 197, 198, 204
Allom, Thomas 77, 91
Anastasi family of Cassandra peninsula 89
Anatolia: agriculture 85–7; commerce 92–3; demography 80–1, 83, 85, 86–7; Egyptian invasion 48, 58, 90; rebels 91, 115
Anglo-Ottoman Society 227
Arbuthnot, Charles 3
Argyll, 8th duke of (George Campbell) 182, 189
Argyropoulos (dragoman) 160, 168, 170
Armenians 93, 229, 231, 234, 235, 238
army, Ottoman: Albanian troops 33, 58, 204; decline 73, 82, 83, 243; manpower 82, 83, 87, 199; reforms 90, 91, 116, 236; and revolution of 1908 236, 237, 238
Athens 33, 35–6
attachés, oriental 11–15, 16–19
Aubin, Christophe 92–3, 95
Austria: and SC's mission (1831) 10, 65; Russian *rapprochement* 26; writers on Ottoman Empire 79, 94; and Montenegro 139, 141, 142, 154, 158; and SC's mission (1853) 142, 145, 158; and Russia 150; and Italian independence 235; and Straits question (1907/8) 237; and Ottoman Empire (1914) 243–4; *see also* Vienna
Aydin; railway to Smyrna 124, 233

Baghdad: commerce 91, 92, 93; railway 232, 236, 244
Bagot, Sir Charles 25
Balkan Wars 233, 243
banditry 82–3, 84
Bank, Ottoman 121, 122, 160
Barker, John 82, 89
Bathurst, 3rd earl (Henry Bathurst) 28
Beaujour, Félix de 77

Index

Beaumont, Lord 212
Beirut 92, 93
Belgium 26, 30, 31, 132, 133
Belgrade 91, 95
Benedetti, Count Vincent 142, 148, 155, 160
Berlin, congress of 228–9, 232
Bligh, John 55
Blue Books 196, 230
Borthwick, Peter 182
Bosnia 79, 81, 84, 228, 237
Bowring, John 89
Brant, R.W. 51
Briggs, Samuel 53–4
Britain *see individual events, institutions and personalities; for foreign relations, see under individual countries*
Bruck, Baron Karl von 142, 202, 204, 205
Brunnov, Baron Philip: and French threat 132–3, 137; and tsar's talks with Seymour 134, 135, 137; and Aberdeen 139, 146, 148, 149, 183–4, 184–5, 187; prevents SC visiting St Petersburg 146; and Menshikov's mission 147, 148, 149, 155, 183–4, 187, 189; on Clarendon 182; and dispatch of fleet to Turkey 190–1; and Vienna negotiations 207, 210
Bucharest 91; treaty of 29
Buckingham, James Silk 68
Bulgaria: Albanians move into 82; banditry 82–3; commerce 94; Russian plans for independence 141; massacres (1876) 228; union with Rumelia 231; Gladstone on 232; in Balkan Wars 239–40
Buol-Schauenstein, Count Carl Ferdinand von 131, 156, 158; and Vienna negotiations 196, 202, 204, 209, 210
Burnaby, Frederick 81
Bursa 91, 92, 93
Burton, Sir Richard 72
Busbecq, Augier de 76
Buxton, C.R. 239
Byron, Lord (George Gordon) 89

Calavro, George 4, 7, 14
Campbell, Colonel Patrick 13
Canak 92, 154
Canakkale 246
Canning, Stratford (1st viscount Stratford de Redcliffe): first mission to Constantinople 1, 113
second mission: and dragomans 9–10; and Greece 28, 54; recall 24–5; resumes parliamentary career 23–4; appointed to St Petersburg but tsar rejects 24–5, (special mission to east) (1831–32) 23–71; background 29–31; visits Greece 31–6;
arrives in Constantinople 36; embassy organization and staff 10–11, 36–8, 43, 49–50; relationships with Ottoman ministers 38–9, 113, 116, 117, 118, 122; and Egyptian invasion of Syria 42–3; on danger from Russia 45–6, 47; success in Greek frontier negotiations 47–8, 54; indiscretion in promising British aid 42, 47, 49, 118
appointed again to St Petersburg but refused by tsar 54–5; conversion to Turcophilism 25-6, 112; mission to Spain 55, 56; fails to obtain peerage 55, 56; memorandum on Eastern Question 56, 57–65, 117, 118; second marriage 118; moves to support Peel 23, 51; and Gülhane decree 118–20, 120–4, 124–7; presses for Ottoman alliance 125; viscountcy 130
final mission to Constantinople (1853) 141–216; background 141–7; visits Paris and Vienna 147, 156–8; and Holy Places 127–8, 130, 133, 141–2, 165; control of naval squadron 144, 145–6, 193–4; and dragomans 18–19; advises Ottomans on Menshikov's demands 161–2, 163, 166–7, 168–9, 170, 171, 172–3, 174, 175, 176–81; Russian complaints against 184, 186–7; decline in morale and authority 197–9; and Russian ultimatum 193–4, 199, 200–1; has Mustafa Pasha and Reshid Pasha reinstated 203; and 'Turkish ultimatum' 204–5, 206–7; and Vienna Note 211, 214–15; retirement 227; death 108
diplomatic style 38–9; and dragomans 1, 6–7, 9–10, 10–11, 16, 17, 18–19; moral probity 24; Turcophilism 25–6, 112, 227; vanity 50, 146, 160
and reforms 45–6, 52, 53–4, 108–9, 116, 117, 145, 164; British government's attitude to 111–12; and Gülhane decree 118–20, 120–4, 124–7, 138; on Islam as obstacle to 111, 118, 126; suggests as price of British support to Sultan 143–4, 145; superficial understanding 52–3; zeal for 18, 39–40, 43–4, 111–12, 124–7, 133
Cartwright, John 39, 40
Castlereagh, Viscount (Robert Stewart) 7, 8, 112
Chabert, Francis 6, 7, 9, 14, 17, 18; and fire of 1810 6, 8; unreliability 10–11, 12, 37
Chabert, Robert 9, 17, 18
Chalcocondylas, Laonicus 76
Charnaud, Francis and James 51
Chateaubriand, François-René, vicomte de 80, 81, 82

Chaumette des Fosses, Amadée 81
Chesney, Captain F.R. 41, 42, 54
Christians in Ottoman Empire: and army recruitment 82, 83, 199; Bulgarian church in Constantinople 50; European demands for better treatment 79, 114, 117, 228, 238; justice 124; missionaries 44; political loyalties 94, 95, 204; population 81, 82–3; Protestant millet recognized 124; reformers and 199, 237; Russian protection 139, 141, 147–8, 149, 164, 181, 186; taxation 116
Church, General Sir Richard 29, 33
Clanricarde, marquis of (Ulick de Burgh) 187, 212
Clarendon, 1st earl of (Edward Hyde) 76
Clarendon, 4th earl of (George Villiers): and tsar's talks with Seymour 136; becomes foreign secretary 138; and SC's mission to Constantinople 142, 145, 146, 147, 166, 169, 184; and Menshikov's mission 147, 148, 149, 150, 162–3, 180, 183, 184, 185–6; and dispatch of fleet 148, 155, 190, 192, 193, 194; and tsar's assurances 199; and Russian ultimatum 201; and Vienna conference 195, 202, 207–8, 208–9, 209–10, 211, 212–13, 214–15; and dragomans 18; indiscretion 136, 192; on Palmerston's death 227; and press and public opinion 182, 192, 212; sources of information 183, 212
Clarke, E.C. 77
Clarke, Orme 240
Cobden, Richard 213–14
Colloredo, Count Franz (Austrian diplomat) 142
Colson, Felix 83
Committee of Union and Progress (CUP) 236–40
communications 84, 85, 95, 233; diplomatic 181, 206; *see also* railways
Constantinople: siege (1802) 90; war fever (1853) 203–4; conference (1876) 228; disorders (1896) 230; Bulgarian church 50; European artists' views 77; medical school 52, 53, 114; plague 82; conservatism 115; newspapers 204, 229; patriarch 152; ship-building 92
Constantinople embassy, British: *cancellier* 4, 17; fires 6, 8, 36; Levant Company and 3–4; oriental attachés 11–15, 16–19; SC's organization and staff 36–8; shift to political emphasis 3, 4; Tarabya summer residence 11, 36, 82; *see also* dragomans
Cook, Thomas 233
Cowley, 1st earl of (Henry Charles Wellesley) 17, 131, 142, 148, 155
Crawford, Sir Richard 240
Crete 29, 30, 35, 47, 63
Crimean War, preliminaries to 130–55; reappointment of SC to Constantinople 141–7; SC in Paris and Vienna 156–8; Menshikov's mission 147–56; call for Anglo-French naval contingent 148, 155–6, 159; sened proposal 160–3; resolution of Holy Places dispute 164–5; sened discussed 166–72; Ottomans request British naval support 172–3; changes in Ottoman government 173–4; modified sened discussed 174–81; Menshikov leaves Constantinople 181; British reaction 182–8; Russia threatens Principalities 154–5, 158, 173, 187, 189; Britain sends fleet 189–94; Palmerston's views 194–5; Vienna conference 196–216; Russian ultimatum 10, 189, 194, 200–2; Russia invades Principalities 195, 201–2; 'Turkish ultimatum' 202–7, 209; Clarendon's 'convention' 207–8; Vienna Note 197, 208–11, 214–16; parliamentary debate on crisis 211–14; Ottoman acceptance of Vienna Note 214–16; British support for Ottomans 45, 112, (collapse after war) 74, 227–8; SC as catalyst 127–8, 216
Cromer, 1st earl of (Evelyn Baring) 36, 239
Currie, Sir Philip 229–30
Curzon, Marquis (George Curzon) 232

Dallaway, Revd 68
Damascus 84, 91, 92, 93
Dané, Anthony 4
Dardanelles: treaty of 6; fortifications 92; Straits Convention (1841) 132, 195; Russian naval preparations (1853) 154; Straits question (1890s) 232, (1907/8) 237; in First World War 242, 244, 246
Dawkins, Edward 30, 32, 34
Delane, John Thadeus 182, 188, 195
Delcassé, Théophile 245
Demian, Johann 79
Derby, 14th earl of (Edward Stanley) 23, 112, 133, 134, 230
derebeys, rebel 75, 78, 87–91, 114
dervishes, suppression of 52, 115
Diarbekir 92, 230
Dicey, Edward 239
Diebitsch-Zabalkanski, Count Hans 115
Disraeli, Benjamin (earl of Beconsfield) 188, 226, 228, 229, 230, 231
Djezzar Pasha 90
Dolgorouky (Russian minister) 184

Donizetti Pasha 52
Doria, William 18
Dragasanu, Ion 79
dragomans 1–22; anglicization policy 1, 11–15; in Crimean War 18–19; Foreign Office control 8; functions 1, 2–3, 4–5; *giovani di lingua* 4, 8, 9, 14, 17; and Holy Places dispute 18; and Levant Company 4–5, 8, 9; Palmerston and 1, 11–12, 13, 14, 15, 16, 18; political employment 4–5, 6, 8; salaries 5, 6, 8, 19
Drouyn de Lhys, Edouard 156
Dubucq, Aimée 113
Duckworth, Admiral Sir John Thomas 6
Ducos (French minister) 132
Dundas, Admiral Sir James 148, 155, 193
Durham, 1st earl of (John Lambton) 23

Edhem Pasha 173
Edirne 237, 239
Edward VII of Great Britain 237, 238
Egypt: Elgin in 9; dragomans 9, 12; invasion of Syria 25, 36–7, 42–3, 46, 157; advance into Anatolia 48, 58, 90; battle of Konya 56, 57, 117; British reaction 41, 42–3, 45–7, 49, 53–4, 56–60, 65–7, 232; SC's memorandum 56, 57–65; Russian intervention 66–7, 74, 117; British interest in 141, 157; and Crimean War preliminaries 201; British occupation 229, 236, 239, 246; *see also* Muhammad Ali
Elgin, 7th earl of 3, 4–5, 9, 36
Elhaj Said Effendi 48–9
Ellenborough, 1st earl of (Edward Law) 28
Ellice, Edward 23
Elliot, Sir Henry 228
Enver Pasha 238–9, 240–1, 242, 244
Eton, William 97

Fethi Ahmed Bey 174
Finlay, George 30
First World War 240–6
Fitzwilliam, 3rd earl (Charles Wentworth) 212
Ford, Sir Clare 229
Foreign Office, British: and Constantinople embassy 3, 8, 11–15; and Young Turks 235–6; *see also individual foreign secretaries and* Hammond, Edmund
Fox-Strangways, William (4th earl of Ilchester) 24
France: influence with Ottomans 5–6, 15, 39; Revolution 113; invasion of Egypt 232; British attitude to, 1831 26; and Belgium 26; and North Africa 26; and Greek frontier 30–1, 47–8; prospect of Franco-British aid to Ottomans 64–5; protests at Russian intervention in Turkey (1833) 66; writers on Ottoman Empire 78–9, 82; support for Muhammad Ali 118; accession of Napoleon III 130–3; and Holy Places 134, 143, 149, 157; tsar's fear of 136; Britain refuses alliance 145; Toulon squadron sent to Turkey 148, 155–6, 158, 201; SC's talks in 156–7; and Ottoman Empire, 1914 243–4, 245
Francis Joseph of Austria 209
Fraser, James Baillie 80, 81
Fuad Pasha 109, 110, 122, 159, 199, 226; and Menshikov's mission 152, 154, 148, 150, 153, 158, 166, 175

Galibert (artist) 91
George IV of Great Britain 28
Germany: on Abdulhamid II 227; murder of consul in Salonika 228; economic penetration 230, 233; and Baghdad railway 232, 236, 244; and Ottomans, 1913–14 240–2, 243–4, 245; bombardment of Odessa 242, 245
Giers, M.N. 244
giovani di lingua 4, 8, 9, 14, 17
Gladstone, William Ewart 138, 211, 227, 229, 231–2
Glarakis (Greek foreign minister) 35
Goderich, Viscount (John Robinson) 23
Goethe, Johann Wolfgang von 96
Gorchakov, Prince Alexander Mikhailovich 134
Gorchakov, General Mikhail 187
Gordon, Sir Robert 26, 29, 35, 49, 54
Graham, Sir James 31, 182, 183, 184; and dispatch of fleet 190, 191; on debate of Aug. 1853 213, 214
Grant, Charles 23
Granville, 2nd earl (Granville George Leveson-Gower) 190
Greece: Strangford pleads for Ottoman moderation 9; Ibrahim Pasha leaves 25; Poros conference 28, 29, 30; British policy on frontiers 28, 30–1; protocol (March 1829) 29; Leopold of Saxe-Coburg and throne 30–1; SC's mission 116, (background) 29–31, (visits Greece) 31–6; condition of 26, 31–2; Argos national assembly 32, 33, 34; John Kapodistrias assassinated 32–3; Agostino Kapodistrias as president 32, 33; Russian activity 32, 33–4; national assembly splits 35; new unified government 35; Otto I proclaimed 31, 35, 42; frontier settlement 41–2, 47, 48, 61, 116; succession question 133;

blockaded 231; Balkan War 241; Turkish fear of (1913/14) 240, 245 demography 82; cost of war to Ottomans 87, 116; navy 96, 241; traders 94, 96
Grenville, William (Baron Grenville) 5
Greville, Charles 136, 147, 192, 211
Grey, 2nd earl (Charles Grey): Cabinet 23; and SC 25, 54, 55, 56; and Ottoman–Egyptian war 57, 65–7
Grey of Fallodon, viscount (Edward Grey) 233, 237, 238, 239–40, 244, 245
Guilleminot, Count Armand Charles 34
Gülhane decree 118–20, 121–2, 173, 228

Haji Mustafa 95
Halil Rifat 116
Hamilton, Terrick 7, 8–9
Hammer-Purgstall, Baron Joseph von 67, 76, 79
Hammond, Edmund (1st Baron) 13–14, 15, 17, 19, 24, 138
Hanway, Jonas 68
Hardwicke, 4th earl of (Charles Philip Yorke) 213
Hasan Fehmi 238
Hatt-i Humayun 228
Hatt-i Sherif 118–20, 121–2, 228
Hawkesbury, 1st baron (Robert Banks Jenkinson) 9
Hay, Captain John 155
Herbert, Sidney 182
Herzl, Theodore 229
Heytesbury, 1st baron (William A'Court) 24
Hobhouse, John Cam (1st Baron Broughton) 68, 82, 89
Holland, 3rd baron (Henry Richard Fox) 23, 30, 57
Holland, Henry 96
Holy Places 18, 132, 134, 149; SC and 127–8, 130, 133, 141–2, 143, 157; Menshikov and 151; settlement 164–5
Howard, Mrs 131
Hughes, T.F. 18
Humann, Hans 242
Husrev Pasha 49, 118, 160, 175; and reforms 48, 52, 115, 116, 121
Hussein Pasha 58
Hydra 32, 33

Ibrahim Pasha: leaves Greece 25; invades Syria 25, 36–7, 42–3, 46; advance into Anatolia 48, 58, 90; battle of Konya 56, 57, 117; in SC's suggested settlement 63
India 57, 67, 157, 232, 236

Iraq 81, 83, 87
Islam: apostasy issue 123–4; commercial code and 121–2; and Muhammad Ali's reforms 118; as obstacle to progress 75, 98, 111, 118, 126
Ismail Kemal 235–6
Italy 2, 235, 243–4
Izvolsky, Count Alexander 237

Jackh, Ernest 227
janizaries 98, 112, 113; suppression 52, 61, 91, 95, 98, 113
Jones, Sir William 76
Juchereau de Saint-Denis, Antoine 77

Kamil Pasha 238
Kanun-i Ceraim 121, 122
Kapodistrias, Agostino 32, 33, 34, 35
Kapodistrias, John 30–1, 32–3
Kemal Ataturk 111, 238–9, 240, 245
Kinglake, Alexander 72–4, 80, 108, 165
Kingsley, Charles 195
Kisilev, Baron 155
Kléber, Jean Baptiste 73
Kletzl, Baron de 178, 202
Knight, Henry Gally 54
Knolles, Richard 76
Koehler, General Georg Friedrich 73
Kolettis, Ioannis 35
Kolokotronis, Theodoros 33, 35
Konya 84; battle of 56, 57, 117
Küçük Ali clan 89–90
Kutahiya, convention of 66
Kutchuk-Kainardji, treaty of 167, 175, 185–6

la Cour (French diplomat) 142, 156, 165, 204
Landor, Walter Savage 211
Lansdowne, 3rd marquis of (Henry Petty-Fitzmaurice) 23
Lansdowne, 5th marquis of (Henry Charles Petty-Fitzmaurice) 235, 236
Lavalette, Charles, marquis de 142
Layard, Austen Henry 81, 122, 138, 147, 159, 168–9; in Parliament 141, 187, 213
Leake, William 77
Lebanon 87, 92
Leiningen, Count Christoph 149, 154
Leopold I, king of the Belgians 30–1, 132
Leopold, Prince (duke of Albany) 199
Leuchtenburg, duchess of 210
Levant Company 3–4, 4–5, 8, 9, 82, 94
Lieven, Prince Christoph 25, 55, 56
Lieven, Princess Dorothea 23, 25, 55, 56
Liman von Sanders, Field Marshal Otto 241

Index

Liston, Sir Robert 3, 8
London: treaty of 30; conference on Greece 31, 35; Reshid Pasha's mission 118–19; Gordon Riots 204; Young Turks in 233; conference, 1913 239
Louis-Philippe of France 26
Lowther, Sir Gerard 238, 239
Lutzov, Count 9
Lyndhurst, 1st baron (John Singleton Copley) 212
Lyon, William 16

Macedonia 230, 233, 236, 238, 239, 240
Macfarlane, Charles 81, 86
MacGuffog, Dr Samuel 10, 37, 38, 43, 50, 117
Mahmud II, Sultan: accessibility 38, 39, 40–1; attitude to Britain 118; character 40–1; and Greek frontier question 41–2, 48, 61; and regional insubordination 91, 114; SC and 39, 41, 47, 49, 113; suppresses janizaries 52, 61, 91, 113; and ulema 114, 115; see also under reforms
Mahmud Muhtar Pasha 241
Mahmud Shevket 238–9
Mallet, Sir Louis 240, 242, 244
Malmesbury, 3rd earl of (James Howard Harris) 130, 133, 134, 149, 187–8, 213
Mandeville, John 36, 37
Matuszewic (Russian diplomat) 34
Maundrell, Henry 68
Mavrocordates, Alexandros 32–3, 35
Mavrojeni 46, 53, 56, 117
Mavromichalis, Petros see Petrobey
Mehemet Ali Pasha 163, 172, 173, 203; and Menshikov 153, 154, 158, 175
Mehmed Said Pertev 40, 116
Melbourne, 2nd viscount (William Lamb) 23
Menshikov, Prince Alexei 147–53; SC on mission 124, 133; tsar on mission 140–1, 150–2; and Abdulmejid II 150, 153, 171–2, 173; and Holy Places 151, 165; and Husrev Pasha 160; and secret alliance 151, 163, 164, 180; and sened 151–2, 164, 165, 166, 167–8, 170, 171–2; progressive reduction of demands 160–1, 164, 168, 170–1, 176–8, 180; suspends relations with Porte 174–5; leaves Constantinople 181, 182; see also under Crimean War
Mériage, Louis Auguste 77
Merriman-Lybyer, A.H. 98
Metternich, Prince Clemens von 119, 196
Meyendorff, Baron Peter von 209

Miaulis, Andreas 33
Midhat Pasha 228
millets 88, 110, 115, 124, 199, 201
Miltitz, Count 10
Mollerus, Baron 153
Monson, Sir Edward 235
Montenegro 79, 139, 141, 142, 143, 158
Montesquieu, baron de 77
Morier, James 68
Mount-Edgcumbe, earl of 137
Mouradja d'Ohsson, Ignace de 97
Muhammad Ali 48, 82, 89, 118; rebellion against Sultan see under Egypt
Muraviev, General Count N.N. 48, 66
Murray (Foreign Office clerk) 12–13
Mürzsteg Programme 236
Mustafa IV, Sultan 113
Mustafa Alemdar 113, 123
Mustafa Pasha 173–4, 203
Mustafa Reshid Effendi 116
Musurus, Constantine 142, 173

Namik Bey 171, 174
Namik Kemal 233, 234
Namik Pasha 57, 65, 117
Napier and Ettrick, 1st baron (Francis Napier) 17
Napoleon I of France 3, 232
Napoleon III of France 130–3, 136–7, 156–7, 208
Nazim Pasha 239
Nesselrode, Count Carl von: and rejection of SC as ambassador 24, 54, 55; and Greece 34; and French threat (1852) 132, 133–4; and tsar's talks with Seymour 135; on von Bruck 142; SC distrusts 146; and Menshikov's mission 140, 147, 148, 149, 150, 152, 181, 184, 186, 187; and ultimatum to Ottomans 189, 194, 200–2; and 'Turkish ultimatum' 206; on Anglo-French naval presence in Dardanelles 212
Newcastle, 5th duke of 182
newspapers: British 182-3, 188, 210–11, 212; in east 52, 204, 229; Turkish, in Paris 234
Nicholas I, tsar: rejects SC as ambassador 24, 25, 54, 55; talks with Aberdeen 125, 132-4, 183; and Napoleon III's accession 131; talks with Seymour 134–41, 149; counts on British support 146; and SC 146, 168; and Menshikov's mission 140, 181, 184, 186, 189; and dispatch of British fleet 195; and invasion of Principalities 199, 201, and Vienna Note 208, 209
Nicholas II, tsar 237
Niebuhr, Carsten 68
Nureddin Bey 173

O'Conor, Sir Nicholas 230
Odessa 154, 242, 245
Ottoman Empire: war with Russia (1711) 3; British and Russian severance of relations (1807) 5–6; French influence 5–6, 15; and Greece 9, 116; defeated by Diebitsch 115; Russian attack on Adrianople 25, 26–7; internal disorder (1829) 27; Russian fear of proceeding to demolish 27–8; treaty of Adrianople *see under* Adrianople; growth of Russian influence 45; SC's special mission, 1831–32 24, 25, 29–54; growing British sympathy 25–6; Egyptian invasion of Syria *see under* Egypt; Greek frontier settlement 41–2, 47, 48–9, 61, 116; and France 64–5, 118; Russian intervention 66–7, 74, 117; treaty of Unkiar Skelessi 11, 12, 47, 67, 118; growth of British Turcophilism 67–8; commercial treaty with Britain (1838) 12, 15–16; mission to London (1839) 118–19; Gülhane decree 118–19, 121–2, 228; British attitude (1847) 125; Holy Places dispute *see separate entry*; Russian mission and preliminaries to Crimean War *see under* Menshikov; Crimean War
  Anglo-Ottoman relations before First World War 226–48; reign of Abdulhamid II 226–38; Young Turks 110, 111, 233–8; revolution of 1908 237–8; internal political struggles 238–9; relations with Britain 239–40, 241, 242–4, 245–6; alliance with Germany 240–1, 241–2, 244, 245; in First World War 242, 245; *see also individual rulers and aspects*
Orlov, Prince Alexis 55, 149, 184
Ottenfels, Baron 10
Ottenfels, Baroness 39
Otto I of Greece 31, 35, 42
Outram, Colonel James 207
Ozerov 142, 152, 153, 154, 167, 170, 201

Palmerston, 3rd viscount (Henry John Temple): in Grey's Cabinet 23, 29; and SC's special mission 24, 25, 29, 30, 31, 34, 35, 54; and Ottoman–Egyptian war 42, 45–7, 51, 54, 56–7, 66, 67; out of office 132; and preliminaries to Crimean War 132, 138, 142, 187, 188, 194–5; and dispatch of fleet 148, 190–2; and Vienna negotiations 210, 211; in parliamentary debate 213–14; death 227
  and dragomans 1, 11–12, 13, 14, 15, 16, 18; and Ottoman reform 112, 119, 125, 138, 214; and press 182; and SC 112;

sources of information 183; Turcophilism 99
Paris 147, 156–7, 233, 234
parliament, British 74, 141, 234, 228, 229; and Crimean War 182, 184–9, 211–14; SC's career 23–4, 56
parliament, Ottoman 226, 227, 236, 237, 238
Parrish, Henry 147
patriarchs, Orthodox 151–2, 164, 168, 171, 180
Pears, Sir Edwin 240
Peel, Sir Robert 23, 51, 112, 183
Pellegrin (traveller) 81
Persian Gulf 232, 246
Pertev Effendi 43, 118
Petrobey 32; sons 33
philhellenism 32, 66
Pickthall, Marmaduke 227
Pisani family 2, 3
Pisani, Alexander (Count Pisani) 17, 147
Pisani, Antonio 7, 12, 14, 17, 18
Pisani, Bartholomew 3, 4, 6, 7, 8, 9
Pisani, Etienne 11, 14, 17, 19; and Crimean War 18, 159, 161–2, 178, 200
Pisani, Frederick 11, 14, 15–16, 17, 19; and SC 11, 18, 37, 41
Pisani, Stephen 158, 159
Planta, Joseph 55–6
Poland 26, 235
Polignac, Prince Auguste de 28
Ponsonby, viscount (John Ponsonby) 6, 11, 12, 15–16, 47, 118
Poros 33–4; conference 28, 30, 54
Porter, Sir James 3
Pouqueville, François 77, 81
Pozzo di Borgo, Count (Carlo Andrea) 31, 34
Principalities 29–30, 84, 141; Russian threat (1853) 158, 173, 184, 187, (ultimatum) 10, 189, 194, 200–2; Russian invasion 193–4, 195, 201, 203
Prussia 10, 142, 150, 196, 202

Raglan, 1st baron (Fitzroy Somerset) 132
railways 124; Baghdad 232, 236, 244; Smyrna–Aydin 124, 233
Rauf Pasha 120
rebellions, local 75, 78, 87–91, 114
Reeve, Henry 146–7
reforms, Ottoman: Selim III 90, 91; Mahmud II 39–41, 43–4, 52–3, 93, 113, 114, 115, 116, 121–2; Abdulmejid 74, 228; Abdulhamid II 226–7
  army 90, 91, 116, 236; Britain and 8–9; British assessment of implementation (1853) 138, 188, 214; and bureaucracy 114;

Index

Christian rights 198–9; and commerce 121–2; commission on (1851) 125–6; conservatives and 74, 111, 121–2; cost 116; council of justice directs 121; dress 115; external pressures as catalysts 127, 232; factions within reform movement 118; Gülhane decree 118–20, 121–2, 228; *Hatt-i Humayun* (1856) 228; and industry 93; justice 122, 124; Russian attitude to 150; secularism 109–10, 111, 115, 118, 124, 126; *Tanzimat* 108–29, 226–7; taxation 117, 119, 121, 122; Young Turks and 236; *see also under* Canning, Stratford
Rejep Pasha 235
Reshid Mehmed Pasha: Frenchmen on staff 15; and SC's mission (1832) 38, 48, 113, 116; has Akif disgraced 118; mission to London (1839) 118–19; and Gülhane decree 109, 118–20, 121; dismissal (1841) 120, 121–2; restoration (1846) 120; commission on reforms (1851) 125–6; political situation, 1853 159, 198, 199, 203; reappointed foreign minister 173, 174; and Menshikov 172, 174–6, 178–80, 187; and Russian ultimatum 189, 200–1; dismissed and reinstated 203; further negotiations 204, 205, 206, 215–16; Palmerston on 125; and reforms 109–10, 122, 226; SC's relationship with 122, 174, 176, 178–80, 200–1
Reval; Edward VII meets tsar 237
Revelaki (dragoman) 19
Rice, Cecil Spring 232
Ricord, Admiral 29, 33–4
Rifaat Pasha 153; and Menshikov 160, 161–2, 163, 166, 169, 170, 172, 173
Royal Navy: blockade of Crete 29; not deployed to Levant (early 1833) 56, 57, 59–60, 148, 154, 155, 158, 159; SC given discretionary control 144, 145–6, 172–3; dispatched to Levant (May 1853) 187, 188, 189–94, 201; mission in Turkey, 1913/14 240; keeps ships built for Turks, 1914 241
Roberts, David 77
Rose, Colonel Hugh 141, 147, 153, 190; and Menshikov's mission 152, 153–4, 155, 158, 159, 160
Rumelia 126, 229, 231
Russell, Lord John (1st Earl Russell): and tsar's approach (1853) 135, 137–41, 181; and Rose's request for Malta squadron 148; and SC's mission 141, 142, 144–5, 166, 185; and dispatch of fleet 190, 191, 192; and Vienna Note 210; in parliamentary debate 213; resignation 138; sources of information 183
Russell, Lord Odo 17
Russia: war against Ottomans (1711) 3; protocol of St Petersburg 9–10; severance of relations with Ottomans (1807) 5–6; blockade of Crete 29; advance to Adrianople 25, 26–7; suppresses Polish uprising 26; treaty of Adrianople 29–30, 45, 112, 115, 188; fear of proceeding against Ottomans 27–8; and Greece 32, 33–4, 47–8, 49; rejects SC as ambassador 24–5, 54–5; and Ottoman–Egyptian war 48, 65, 66–7, 117; treaty of Unkiar Skelessi 11, 12, 47, 67, 118; British fear of encroachment in Levant 59, 67, 76; Anglo-Russian memorandum of 1844 125, 132–4, 183; approach to Britain (1853) 134–41, 146, 150; Menshikov's mission, *see under* Menshikov; preparations for war 154–5, 158, 173, 187, 189; assurances to Britain 199; ultimatum to Sultan 10, 189, 194, 200–2; breaks off relations with Ottomans 201; invades Principalities 195, 201–2, 203; Abdulhamid II and 230; Japan defeats in Far East 230; British attitudes, 1870s 230; and Polish independence 235; and Straits question, 1907/8 237; arrangements with Britain on Middle East, 1907 243; and control of Dardanelles, 1914 244–5, 246; Ottoman–German bombardment of Odessa 242, 245

Sadik Rifat 120, 124
Safeti Pasha 120
Said Halim, Prince 240
St Petersburg, protocol of 9–10
Salisbury, 3rd marquis of (R.A.T.G. Cecil) 141, 230–1, 243
Salonika 82, 91, 115, 228, 236, 237
Samos 29, 35, 50–1
San Stefano, treaty of 229
Sanderson, Lord (T.H. Sanderson) 235–6
Sandison, Alfred (dragoman) 19
Sarell (dragoman) 19
Sarim (*reis effendi*) 120
Sazonov, Count Serge 244, 245
Sébastiani, General Horace 31, 39
secularism 109–10, 111, 115, 118, 124, 126
Selim III, Sultan 39, 90–1, 113
Semsi Pasha 237
Serbia 141, 231; social conditions 80, 82, 84, 87, 94
Seymour, Sir Hamilton 134–41, 149, 188–9, 215
Shaykh ul-Islam 52, 115, 175, 199
Shee, Sir George 24

Sheffield, earl of (John Holroyd) 147, 159
Simmons, Henry 9, 17, 19
Sinasi Pasha 233
Slade, Sir Adolphus 77, 174, 198, 199
Smith, Spencer 4–5
Smyrna 91, 92–3, 115, 124, 204, 233
Smythe, Percy Clinton (6th viscount Strangford) 8–9, 10
Smythe, Percy Ellen (8th viscount Strangford) 15, 17, 18
Sofia 82, 84, 95
Spetsia 32, 96
Stanley, Arthur Penrhyn, Dean 108, 198
Stanley, Edward *see* Derby, 14th earl of
Stanley of Alderley, Lord (Edward Stanley) 17
Stavrides (dragoman) 19
Straits Convention (1841) 132, 195
Strangford, viscounts *see under* Smythe
Suchon, Admiral 241, 244
Suleyman Necib Bey 36, 41, 49, 116
Sutton, Sir Robert 3
Sykes, Sir Mark 238, 239
Syria 81, 83, 229; *see also under* Egypt

Tahir Pasha 116
Talaat 238–9, 240, 245
Tanzimat see under reforms
taxation, Ottoman 84, 91, 93, 116; reforms 117, 119, 121, 122; tax-farming 87, 98, 121, 122
Tennyson, Alfred (1st baron Tennyson) 108
Thornton, Thomas 77, 97
Times, The 182–3, 232, 238; and Crimean War 137, 146–7, 147–8, 154, 188, 194, 196, 210
Tott, Baron François de 77
Tournefort, Joseph de 76
Townsend, A.F. 81
trade: Balkan 93–6; British Levantine 3, 4, 233; internal Ottoman 78, 84, 88, 91–3, 95, 121–2; and plague 82; proposed new code 121–2
Trebizond 84, 90, 92
Trikoupis, Spiridion 32–3, 35
Tunisia 132, 201
Turcophilism 67–8, 97, 99, 242; SC 25–6, 112; demise 227, 230

Ubicini, Abdolonyme 80–1, 83
ulema 114, 115, 118, 175

Unkiar Skelessi, treaty of 11, 12, 47, 67, 118
Urquhart, David 12, 89; and SC 10, 37, 38, 45, 48; and Crimean War 188, 195, 211, 227; and dragomans 1, 11, 12, 16; on reforms 44–5, 73
Üsküdar 92, 246

vakf 48–9, 52
Vambéry, Arminius 229
Veli Pasha 173
Verona, congress of 9
Victoria, Queen of Great Britain and Empress of India 130, 132, 136, 199, 210, 215
Vienna: SC visits (1853) 147, 158; conference (1853) 196–216; Young Turks in 233
Vienna Note 197, 208–11, 215–16
Vixen episode 56
Vogorides, Stefanaki 15, 16, 50–1; and SC 10, 37–8, 43, 49–50, 50–1
Volney, Count Constantin 77, 83, 84, 86, 98

Walewski, Count Alexander 182, 185, 208
Walker, Sir Baldwin 190
Wallachia 80, 83
Walsh, Robert 80
Wangenheim, Baron Karl von 241, 244
Waugh, Sir Telford 238
Wellesley, Henry *see* Cowley, Baron
Wellesley, Marquis (Richard Colley Wellesley) 7
Wellington, 1st duke of (Arthur Wellesley) 26–7, 28, 130, 183
Westmoreland, 11th earl of (John Fane) 206, 209
White, Sir William 229
Wilhelm II, Kaiser 233, 241
Wilkie, Sir David 77
Wilkinson, William 80
William IV of Great Britain 54
Wittman, William 73, 97–8
Wood, Almeric 18
Wood, George 9, 12
Wood, Richard 9, 11, 16, 17

Yeames, James 154
Young Ottomans 109–10, 111, 233
Young Turks 110, 111, 233–8

Ziya Pasha 233, 234
Zographos, Konstantine 32–3